the
Diabetes
Comfort
Food diet

the Diabetes Comfort Food diet

Laura Cipullo, RD, CDE
and the editors of **Prevention**

Robert ROSE

The Diabetes Comfort Food Diet
Text and photographs copyright © 2015 Rodale Inc.
Cover and text design copyright © 2015 Robert Rose Inc.
Prevention is a trademark of Rodale Inc.

This book was previously published as *The Diabetes Comfort Food Cookbook* in 2013 by Rodale Inc.
This edition has been updated with some changes.

For complete cataloguing information, see page 312.

Disclaimer
This book is a general guide only and should never be a substitute for the skill, knowledge and experience
of a qualified medical professional dealing with the facts, circumstances and symptoms of a particular case.

The nutritional, medical and health information presented in this book is based on the research,
training and professional experience of the authors, and is true and complete to the best of their
knowledge. However, this book is intended only as an informative guide for those wishing to know more
about health, nutrition, and medicine; it is not intended to replace or countermand the advice given by the
reader's personal physician. Because each person and situation is unique, the authors and the publisher
urge the reader to check with a qualified health-care professional before using any procedure where there
is a question as to its appropriateness. The authors and the publisher are not responsible for any adverse
effects or consequences resulting from the use of the information in this book. It is the responsibility of the
reader to consult a physician or other qualified health-care professional regarding his or her personal care.

This book contains references to products that may not be available everywhere. The intent of
the information provided is to be helpful; however, there is no guarantee of results associated with the
information provided. Use of brand names is for educational purposes only and does not imply
endorsement.

The recipes in this book have been carefully tested by our kitchen and our tasters. To the best of our
knowledge, they are safe and nutritious for ordinary use and users. For those people with food or other
allergies, or who have special food requirements or health issues, please read the suggested contents
of each recipe carefully and determine whether or not they may create a problem for you. All recipes
are used at the risk of the consumer. We cannot be responsible for any hazards, loss or damage that
may occur as a result of any recipe use. For those with special needs, allergies, requirements or health
problems, in the event of any doubt, please contact your medical adviser prior to the use of any recipe.

Design and production: Daniella Zanchetta/PageWave Graphics Inc.
Editor: Sue Sumeraj
Proofreader: Kelly Jones
Indexer: Gillian Watts
Photographs: Mitch Mandel/Rodale Images
Cover image: Roasted Vegetable Mac and Cheese (page 229)

The publisher gratefully acknowledges the financial support of our publishing program by the
Government of Canada through the Canada Book Fund.

Published by Robert Rose Inc.
120 Eglinton Avenue East, Suite 800, Toronto, Ontario, Canada M4P 1E2
Tel: (416) 322-6552 Fax: (416) 322-6936
www.robertrose.ca

Printed and bound in Canada

1 2 3 4 5 6 7 8 9 FP 23 22 21 20 19 18 17 16 15

To my family: Dennis, Gene, Richard, and Joan

Contents

Chapter 1: The Lowdown on Diabetes 8

Chapter 2: Change Your Recipes,
  Not Your Life 22

Chapter 3: The Plan to Defeat Diabetes 48

Chapter 4: Breakfast 67

Chapter 5: Soups, Salads & Sandwiches 88

Chapter 6: Appetizers & Snacks 119

Chapter 7: Meat 141

Chapter 8: Poultry 177

Chapter 9: Seafood 211

Chapter 10: Vegetarian 225

Chapter 11: Sides 243

Chapter 12: Desserts 261

Appendix A: Meal Plans 286

Appendix B: Calories, Carbs, and Fiber
  of Common Foods 294

References 310

Index 313

CHAPTER 1

The Lowdown on Diabetes

Like many people, you might think your life is over if you receive a diagnosis of prediabetes or type 2 diabetes. Suddenly, meals and lifestyle choices that you didn't think twice about before must come under scrutiny, and needing to make changes can be scary. You can't help but panic. Your mind just shuts down. You close your ears to the doctor's advice and explanations about blood sugar and insulin. It all sounds like a pronouncement that life's pleasures for you are over... forever. "Now I must be on a diet for the rest of my life" you may find yourself thinking. "Restaurants, favorite foods, holiday feasts, and all social events will become tainted and nearly impossible to enjoy." Well, think again. This does not have to be your reality. There's no need to plan your own pity party!

Diabetes is definitely not a doomsday diagnosis. You can still eat — and yes, even some of your favorite foods, like hot, crusty bread or sweet, silky ice cream, can stay on the menu! Research clearly supports the fact that there really are no off-limits foods for individuals with prediabetes or diabetes. You *can* have it all — you just need to be smart about how you do it.

That's where *The Diabetes Comfort Food Diet* comes in. This book is designed to give you the tools you need to manage or reverse insulin resistance while continuing to eat the foods you love. As a registered dietitian, I have directly witnessed this amazing nutrition plan in action with my clients. You'll read their stories over the next few chapters and be wowed by their results. Read on to learn how to transform your life, your diet, and your health. You can continue to love your food — and not fear what it will do to your blood sugar. Just implement the three simple steps to make over any meal so you can balance blood sugar, lose excess weight, and beat this disease. We'll talk about these three steps specifically in Chapter 2. First, though, let me help you understand a little more about diabetes and how to manage it.

While the advice in this cookbook is aimed at those who have the ability to prevent or reverse insulin resistance, the recipes themselves can also benefit individuals with type 1 diabetes and even people who want to eat healthier to lose weight, improve their heart health, or simply promote general good health and wellness.

What We Mean by "Diabetes"

When discussing prediabetes or type 2 diabetes in this book, we will refer to the diagnosis simply as "diabetes."

The Easy Eating Solution That Works for Life

Please keep this important reality in mind: The main goal of diabetes management is to learn how to best and most effectively balance your blood sugar levels through food and physical activity. *The Diabetes Comfort Food Diet* is about living your life to the fullest by learning to eat in ways that are beneficial to your body — and especially by understanding how different foods influence your blood sugar levels and endocrine system. Although this daily diet will likely result in weight loss, you must recognize that this is a lifetime methodology, not a fad plan.

You will see positive changes in just a few weeks, but you should not stop this diet when you feel you have reached your goals. Rather, it's a diet to learn thoroughly, implement totally, and follow diligently. You must make it your healthy nutrition habit for the rest of your life. The good news is that it is easy to learn and will help you look and feel great … and you'll still get to eat all the foods you enjoy! We'll show you how to make enjoyable foods work for you and ultimately help you beat diabetes.

Look up the definition of *diet* at Merriam-Webster.com, and you'll see the noun defined as "habitual nourishment." *The Diabetes Comfort Food Diet* focuses on this definition so that you, the reader, recognize this is a lifelong approach to nutrition and health. Stop thinking of a diet as restrictive and start thinking of it as providing the building blocks that nourish your body each day.

There's no reason to feel overwhelmed with despair when a doctor diagnoses you with prediabetes or diabetes! To immediately help dispel your fears, let's cover the basics of diabetes so that you better understand your body and why you need to fuel it in specific ways.

High Blood Sugar Symptoms

Hyperglycemia, or high blood sugar, can be identified by excessive thirst, frequent urination, and unexplained weight loss.

All About Blood Sugar

When we talk about blood sugar, what we really mean is blood glucose. This is a measure of the amount of sugar, also known as glucose, that is present in your blood at any given time. When you sit down to a meal, your body digests the food and breaks it down into three macronutrients known as carbohydrates, proteins, and fats. Carbohydrates, whether they are monosaccharides, disaccharides, or even some of the digestible polysaccharides, are further converted or broken down into the simple form of sugar known as glucose, which is then absorbed into your bloodstream. That glucose gets transported throughout your body for your muscles and organs to use as fuel. Most glucose is used immediately; however, excess glucose is converted to glycogen (which gets stored for use in your muscles and liver) or fatty acids (which are stored in your adipose tissue — a.k.a. your love handles and other visible body fat).

But how does the body know to use that glucose? The endocrine system is the body's active metabolic map that directs the "where, when, what, and how much" of hormones that help the body convert food into sugar and then energy. Insulin is one of the endocrine hormones produced by the pancreas. This organ releases insulin, which functions to open your cell doors and take up sugar from your blood. Sugar is mostly converted into energy when it enters the cells. This process helps you do everything from running a marathon to simply staying awake at your desk during that after-lunch slump. If this sugar gets locked out of your cells due to a malfunction with insulin, you are likely to feel shaky, sweaty, mentally foggy, and anxious. This means your blood sugar is likely very high. When this starts to happen, you probably have developed insulin resistance.

Insulin resistance is a condition in which the body does not use insulin properly. The muscle, fat, and liver cells do not respond appropriately to insulin; thus, the body thinks it needs more insulin to lower its blood sugar. The pancreas consequently goes into overdrive, pumping out more insulin. After years of being in overdrive, the pancreas can begin to burn out, resulting in prediabetes and diabetes. Insulin resistance is evident by both elevated blood sugar and elevated insulin levels.

Brain Food

Our brains use only the form of sugar known as glucose.

Prediabetes

As defined by the American Diabetes Association (ADA), prediabetes is diagnosed when a person's blood glucose levels are higher than normal (an A1C of 5.7% to 6.4%) but not high enough to qualify as type 2 diabetes (an A1C of 6.5% or higher). People who have prediabetes are more likely to develop type 2 diabetes in the future and may already have some problems stemming from the disease.

The good news is that you can take steps right now to reverse insulin resistance and prevent diabetes. Research shows that you can lower your risk of type 2 diabetes by 58%. The trick is to focus on one magic number: 7. By losing 7% of your current body weight, you can balance your blood sugars and get back to feeling great again. *The Diabetes Comfort Food Diet* can help — by eating healthy (we'll show you how!)

and by exercising just 90 to 150 minutes per week, you will achieve these goals and consequently bring your blood sugar back to the normal range.

A Healthy Lifestyle

If you don't need to lose weight, well, don't worry. Our easy eating plan is flexible enough to decrease your blood sugar and help you live a healthier lifestyle.

Type 2 Diabetes

If your doctor diagnoses you with type 2 diabetes, this indicates that your body has difficulty with insulin. Either your pancreas is not able to produce enough insulin or, for some unknown reason, your body's cells are ignoring the hormone. If your body is unable to obtain sugar from your bloodstream and move it into your cells, your blood sugar levels rise and can cause complications such as heart disease, nerve damage, and kidney disease. As mentioned earlier, this diagnosis is made when your A1C is equal to or greater than 6.5% or your blood sugar measures greater than 126 mg/dl on a fasting plasma glucose test.

Calculate Your Risk

If you are worried about diabetes but haven't yet been tested for it, use the list at right to determine your risk. The American Diabetes Association recommends you get tested for prediabetes and type 2 diabetes — even if you have no symptoms — if you are overweight or obese and have one or more additional risk factors. For people without these risk factors, testing should begin at age 45 and be repeated a minimum of every 3 years if tests are normal.

Risk factors for prediabetes and diabetes — in addition to being overweight or obese or being age 45 or older — include the following:

The Lowdown on Common Carbohydrates

Carbohydrates include many different sugars. Below are common carbs you may read about or see on a food label. Your body digests the simplest form of sugar, known as monosaccharides, the fastest and takes the longest to digest the most complex sugars, known as polysaccharides. Be aware that the body may not digest or may only partially digest some carbs falling under the category of polysaccharides, including cellulose and inulin. Use caution when eating these carbs or increasing your consumption of them, as they are healthy but can cause gas!

Three Common Monosaccharides
- **Fructose:** found in honey and fruits such as apples, peaches, and watermelon
- **Galactose:** found in dairy products such as milk, yogurt, and ice cream
- **Glucose (also known as dextrose):** found in a wide range of foods, such as fruits, sweet corn, and honey

Three Common Disaccharides
- **Sucrose** (table sugar, from sugarcane) = glucose + fructose
- **Lactose** (sugar found in milk) = glucose + galactose
- **Maltose** (malt sugar found in germinating grains) = glucose + glucose

Three Common Polysaccharides
- **The indigestible:** cellulose (found in broccoli, celery), pectin (apples, pears), and algal substances like seaweed. These polysaccharides are bulking agents that slow digestion.
- **The partially digestible:** inulin (wheat, onions, and artichokes), raffinose (beans, cabbage, Brussels sprouts), and stachyose (beans and legumes). These polysaccharides are likely culprits of gas and bloating.
- **The digestible:** starch and dextrin (grains and starchy vegetables) and glycogen (meat products and seafood — it's stored in muscle)

- Being physically inactive
- Having a parent or sibling with diabetes
- Having a family background that is African, Native North American, Asian, Hispanic/Latino, or Pacific Islander
- Having given birth to a baby weighing more than 9 pounds (4 kg) or being diagnosed with gestational diabetes (diabetes during pregnancy)
- Having high blood pressure — 140/90 mmHg or above — or being treated for high blood pressure
- Having polycystic ovary syndrome (PCOS)
- Having HDL ("good" cholesterol) below 35 mg/dl or a triglyceride level above 250 mg/dl
- Having impaired fasting glucose (IFG) or impaired glucose tolerance (IGT) on previous testing
- Having other conditions associated with insulin resistance, such as severe obesity or a condition called acanthosis nigricans, which is characterized by a dark, velvety rash around the neck or armpits
- Having a personal history of cardio-vascular disease

Know Your Blood Tests

- **Hemoglobin A1C (A1C):** Hemoglobin A is another name for red blood cells. This test specifically measures how much glucose is attached to hemoglobin in your blood over the life of the cell — a 3- to 4-month period. This test is now used alone or in conjunction with a fasting plasma glucose test to diagnose prediabetes or diabetes. An A1C value of 5.7% to 6.4% is consistent with a diagnosis of prediabetes. If this value is 6.5% or greater, it is consistent with a diagnosis of diabetes.

- **Fasting plasma glucose (FPG):** Commonly used to diagnose prediabetes, this blood test measures your blood sugar after you have fasted for about 12 hours. If your blood sugar falls in the range of 100 to 125 mg/dl, you are considered to have an impaired fasting glucose and are diagnosed with prediabetes. If your FPG is 126 mg/dl or higher, your results indicate diabetes.

- **Oral glucose tolerance test (OGTT):** This test is also used to diagnose diabetes. You are given a beverage with 75 grams of a sugar solution to drink after fasting for 12 hours. Your blood glucose is then measured every hour, and a plasma glucose of 140 to 199 mg/dl on the second hour is considered an impaired glucose tolerance and diagnosed as prediabetes. If it is higher than 200 mg/dl at 2 hours post-consumption, you are diagnosed with diabetes.

So You've Been Diagnosed... Now What?

When I first became a certified diabetes educator, I learned two profoundly valuable take-home messages that still lead the way for diabetes self-management and self–blood glucose monitoring. The first message: A carbohydrate is a carbohydrate is a carbohydrate. The second: Meet you, the client, where you are in terms of food and fitness — then empower you to make the lifestyle changes you need. *The Diabetes Comfort Food Diet* is an extension of these messages.

In October 2012, the most recent standards for professionals — the National Standards for Diabetes Self-Management Education and Support — were published in the journal *Diabetes Educator*. These standards are designed for both individuals with prediabetes and those with diabetes and are intended to help encourage daily healthy behavior changes, both physically and mentally. *The Diabetes Comfort Food Diet* will use these standards to help you not only determine your starting point and progress through the next several weeks but also keep your eye on the prize — maintaining lifelong changes.

Remember, this will be your diet routine for the rest of your life. As the educator, it is my job to help provide nutrition education and support so that you can successfully attain and sustain these self-care behaviors. Many dietitians, as do I, use a model called the Stages of Change to help clients identify where they are in terms of readiness to make nutrition changes. *The Diabetes Comfort Food Diet* has adapted these stages into a unique program, just for you! This plan is called START. First identify where you are using the chart at right. Then begin

START

Read the descriptions of each stage to identify your current level of readiness.

Stage	Description
Shock	You have just been diagnosed with prediabetes or diabetes. You may be in shock or denial. This is the time to raise your level of personal awareness. Perhaps you notice how awful you feel when you have high blood sugar. Think about your nutrition choices. Do you think you need to make any dietary changes? Identify education resources like this book as well as a support system to help you understand what prediabetes or diabetes means to you and your daily life. List pros and cons for making dietary and fitness changes.
Tiptoeing	You dabble with a few new choices but continue to have resistance and skepticism. You recognize the need to change your lifestyle for the purpose of preventing or beating diabetes. You read this book and are even willing to try new foods such as whole wheat bread and salmon or to take a walk for just 5 minutes to start decreasing your blood sugar. You focus on decreasing your list of cons from the previous phase by reducing these barriers. You are thinking about the need for lifestyle change. Temptations like eating out seem overwhelming and may prevent you from advancing to the next phase.
Achieving	You are starting to do what you need to do. You reduce temptations and triggers such as eating out or ordering in by grocery shopping weekly, prepping meals in advance on weekends, or planning a healthy-themed dinner party. You get as much support as possible from family members, your personal dietitian, or this book. You are ready to start a fitness program and begin curbing your carbs. Notice how your sleep, mood, and energy level improve as you continue to make changes.
Repeating	You are now a doer. You are implementing your new behaviors with the emphasis on the three tips to make over any meal (see Chapter 2). You are action-oriented. This is one of the busiest stages as you incorporate the new behaviors encouraged in these chapters, such as food shopping, prepping, cooking, and the best part: eating! You are learning to curb carbs, increase fiber, and choose healthy fats. This is where you start to see results. The process doesn't seem like such a process anymore, because the pounds seem to be falling off you.
Time	You have new, healthy self-care habits promoting balanced blood sugar. After 6 months, your nutrition changes are part of your daily routine, and you can foresee a bright, manageable future. Curbing carbs is a way of life, but so is going out to dinner every Friday night. Focus is on eating all foods in moderation so you can stick with these healthy behaviors. You know how to eat a piece of cake without risking a binge or high blood sugar. Life is literally sweet again.

moving through each stage at your own pace to ensure that this new way of eating will be most effective at helping you turn your health — and your life — around. Carefully read each stage's description and see which one you relate to most. For more information on START and specific advice for each stage of the program, flip to Chapter 3.

Not everyone will need to start at the Shock phase. It's okay to start this process at whatever stage represents your level of readiness. Your nutrition goals must be written specifically for your present stage. We'll talk more about START and how to write nutrition goals in Chapter 3, but for now, just keep in mind that no matter where you start, you need to proceed in order through all remaining stages. For example, if you fit the description consistent with Tiptoeing, do not expect to skip to Repeating right away. Pace yourself!

Reading this book may help you get from Tiptoeing to Achieving by realizing you can manage diabetes while still enjoying a serving of potatoes (truly — check out our recipe for Creamy Mashed Potatoes on page 250). The Achieving phase may consist of food shopping for one recipe from this book or reading nutrition labels for grams of carbohydrates. This is the time to plan for any possible triggers that may cause old behaviors (such as eating two large bowls of pasta). Repeating could be regularly preparing recipes from

The START Process

Once you know where you fall on the START chart, start thinking about how to get to the next stage. Remember, you cannot skip a stage. Just know that you really can use this process — and the recipes and other tools in this cookbook — to achieve better blood glucose control and lose weight.

this cookbook and finally seeing results (such as pants fitting loosely around your smaller waist).

How Do We Know This Works?

By using the recipes and other tools in *The Diabetes Comfort Food Diet*, you really will achieve better blood sugar control and lose weight. We have the evidence right here!

In 2002, the results of a major research study called the Diabetes Prevention Program (DPP) were published in the *New England Journal of Medicine*. The goal of this study was to determine if a small amount of weight loss through dietary changes and increased physical activity could prevent or delay the onset of type 2 diabetes. The research found that by eating properly, exercising regularly, and changing daily behaviors, study participants reduced their risk of developing diabetes by 58%. Even better, participants older than 60 reduced their risk by 71%. This reinforces the message that diet and physical activity together are the most effective ways to prevent uncontrolled blood sugar — and it's never too late to get started!

The DPP focused on decreasing calories, cutting saturated fat, and exercising for 150 minutes a week (that's 30 minutes, 5 days a week), along with learning new behaviors such as keeping a food log. *The Diabetes Comfort Food Diet* takes these steps — particularly the nutrition guidelines — and goes further, so you don't have to sacrifice the comfort foods you love to get back on the path to health. You will learn how to make any meal healthier by addressing not only carbohydrates but also fiber and fat content.

Food Basics: Understanding Your Choices

You now know how diabetes works — and that prevention or reversal is absolutely possible. So let's talk about the food that will get you there. Prepare to learn everything you need to know about eating in ways that will either prevent or manage diabetes.

As shown earlier, there are three basic macronutrients — carbohydrates, proteins, and fats. When you digest these macronutrients, your body responds with hormones that help get the macronutrients where they need to be. Whenever you eat carbohydrates of any kind — whether table sugar, agave, an apple, or a slice of bread — insulin opens the cell doors that transport the sugar from the bloodstream into the cells.

When you eat any form of carbohydrate, your blood sugar rises to a certain degree. However, when you eat carbohydrates with protein or fat, this does not happen. That's because it takes the body longer to break down proteins and fats, which are much more complex. If you eat a modest amount of carbohydrate with either protein or fat — or both — your blood sugar levels will not rise as high, because the sugar enters the bloodstream more slowly so there is less sugar available at any one point.

Therefore, if you moderate how many carbohydrates you consume at each meal and spread your intake throughout the day, your pancreas will not be overwhelmed by overproducing insulin. This will prevent further aggravation of insulin resistance. At the same time, by limiting carbs, you decrease your overall caloric intake.

A Carb Is a Carb Is a Carb

Research in the *Journal of the American Dietetic Association* reports that the primary determinant affecting your after-meal blood sugar levels is the total amount of carbohydrates consumed at meals, regardless of whether the source is sucrose or starch. This tells you that sucrose, otherwise known as table sugar, can stay on your table. You can actually consume up to 35% of your total daily intake in the form of sucrose without adversely affecting your blood sugar control. If you follow a daily diet of 60 grams of carbohydrates per meal, you could potentially eat a piece of cake or a scone without triggering a negative glycemic response. However, I don't suggest you do that often — while the cake may not budge your blood sugar, it doesn't have as many nutrients as a starchy vegetable or a healthier source of carbs. I simply mention cake as an example to set your mind at ease that you can safely indulge your occasional cravings — or even enjoy a small sweet snack every day.

And don't think you'll be relegated to artificial sweeteners. In fact, it may be better to have the real stuff. Research has suggested that noncaloric sweeteners — Splenda, Sweet'N Low, Equal, and others — may affect appetite and energy intake, further disrupting your feelings of hunger and fullness. Plus, overly sweet foods make you crave more sweet foods. Furthermore, the Third National Health and Nutrition Examination Survey found that individuals who drank diet soda — soda with noncaloric sweeteners — had poorer glycemic control overall.

When all is said and done, you need to learn how to manage your sugar intake, and eating the real deal is less likely to cause brain and body confusion. This isn't permission to start adding sugar at every meal, however. The goal of the Diabetes Comfort Food Diet is to show you how you can enjoy all foods in moderation. Eating real, natural, wholesome meals as often as possible is ideal. This is a lifelong approach

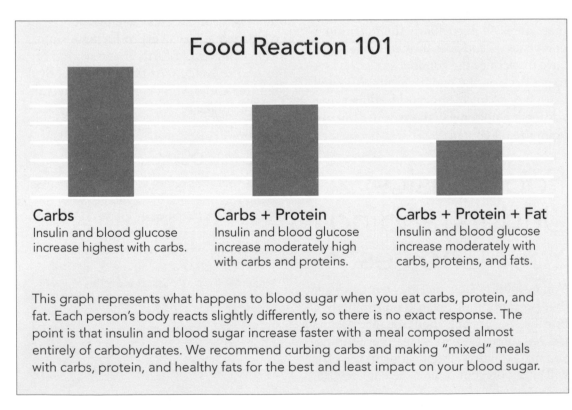

Food Reaction 101

Carbs
Insulin and blood glucose increase highest with carbs.

Carbs + Protein
Insulin and blood glucose increase moderately high with carbs and proteins.

Carbs + Protein + Fat
Insulin and blood glucose increase moderately with carbs, proteins, and fats.

This graph represents what happens to blood sugar when you eat carbs, protein, and fat. Each person's body reacts slightly differently, so there is no exact response. The point is that insulin and blood sugar increase faster with a meal composed almost entirely of carbohydrates. We recommend curbing carbs and making "mixed" meals with carbs, protein, and healthy fats for the best and least impact on your blood sugar.

to beating diabetes, and there is a way to eat all foods — you just need to know when and how much.

Determining Just When to Eat — And How Much!

If you have prediabetes or diabetes, food is one of the best medicines you can give yourself. The trick is to determine what to eat the majority of the time and how to finesse your favorite foods into your meal plan. The ADA makes many recommendations on how to do this successfully, and *The Diabetes Comfort Food Diet* builds them into the plan that will help you lose weight and get your blood sugar back on track.

If you have prediabetes or diabetes, our recommendations are as follows:

- Aim to lose 7% of your body weight if you are overweight or obese. Our plan will show you how!

- Follow an eating plan that is lower in carbohydrates, saturated fat, and calories and higher in healthy fats.

- Consume about 22 grams of dietary fiber per day (based on a 1,600-calorie diet) if you are at risk of diabetes.

- Limit intake of sugar-sweetened beverages if you are at risk of diabetes.

- Work up to getting 90 to 150 minutes of physical activity per week. (Read more about the importance of daily movement on page 18.)

If you already have diabetes:

- Eat mixed meals — include carbohydrates, proteins, and fats at each meal.

- Monitor carbohydrate intake via carbohydrate counting or experience-based estimation. (We'll talk more about this in Chapter 2.)

- Limit saturated fat and minimize trans fats while increasing intake of healthy fats, such as omega-3 fatty acids.

- If you choose to drink alcohol, drink moderately — one serving per day for women and two or less per day for men — and with a meal.

- Follow individualized meal planning.

- Spread exercise over at least 3 days a week and do not skip more than 2 consecutive days.

- Perform strength training 2 days per week, if approved by your doctor.

- Self-monitor blood glucose in addition to making the fitness and nutrition changes above.

The Diabetes Comfort Food Diet incorporates the above nutrition recommendations in all 200 recipes. The most important thing to remember is to curb carbs. "Curbing carbs" is basically a fun way of saying "consistent carbohydrate counting." This is the most effective way to control blood glucose, especially after meals.

Addressing Your Unique Needs

Every individual differs in nutrition and movement needs, degree of medical risks, and, of course, willingness to change. Eating to beat diabetes is about addressing these needs while maintaining the pleasure and joy of eating.

Just Imagine … Weight Loss, Too!

Your effort to curb carbs and calories isn't just about your blood sugar — it's also a means to lose weight. Many weight-loss programs use body mass index (BMI) as an across-the-board way to determine whether you need to lose weight. However, it is extremely important to recognize that BMI is not considered a perfect measure of your overall health. Having a BMI greater than 25, defined as overweight and/or obese, does not necessarily mean you need to lose weight. Consider this: Most gymnasts and other athletes would be considered overweight or obese according to their BMIs. Higher weight can be a result of muscle mass, not just fat mass.

The diabetes community recognizes this flaw and encourages a different assessment. All you need is a tape measure. A waist circumference greater than 35 inches (88 cm) for women or greater than 40 inches (100 cm) for men is a more definitive measurement that takes into account excess abdominal fat. This excess fat, also called adipose tissue, increases your risk of complications such as cardiovascular disease. But even this measurement is not "one size fits all."

If you do need to lose weight, your focus should be on changing your behaviors and letting weight loss happen secondarily to your new, consistent daily habits. Diabetes can be prevented with just a 7% weight loss, and you are more likely to fend it off for the long haul if you then maintain a 5% loss for 3 years. For example, if you weigh 180 pounds (82 kg) today and lose about 12 pounds (5.5 kg), and then keep off at least 9 of those pounds (4 kg), you will be successful! As evidence proves, this is attainable. You can do this!

Losing weight is a great strategy for reversing insulin sensitivity, but it's no secret that it is also highly challenging. If dropping a lot of weight is important to you, be very realistic when setting your goals. We choose to think slow and steady, because this is about a healthy lifestyle, not a fad diet. Start with the nutrition changes, as they will most dramatically affect your blood sugar, and add in exercise as soon as you are ready.

Don't let slow weight loss frustrate or discourage you. Instead, focus on making the positive behavior changes we mention in Chapters 2 and 3, such as food shopping and meal planning. Simply making healthier food choices is effective at staving off diabetes. By incorporating a Mediterranean-style diet, you can decrease your risk of diabetes by 52%. Yes, diet — one that focuses on fruits, vegetables, whole grains, legumes, and healthy fats such as olives and nuts — is effective enough. This is fantastic news, because we all know how extremely hard it is to lose weight once we have gained it, despite the fact that we may be eating less and even exercising more. That's why *The Diabetes Comfort Food Diet* gives you so many helpful tools, such as recipes that incorporate the beneficial Mediterranean fats, to make healthy changes easy, enjoyable, and livable.

Benefits of Exercise

Exercise benefits extend beyond weight loss. Aerobic exercise lowers low-density lipoprotein (LDL), or "bad," cholesterol by about 5%. Blood glucose remains lower for 2 to 72 hours after mild- and moderate-intensity exercise. Both aerobic exercise and weight training are recommended to aid in blood sugar control.

Complementing Your Daily Diet with Movement

As mentioned previously, regular physical activity is a critical component for both weight loss and diabetes management. Reliable evidence suggests that to achieve significant weight loss, you must move for 60 minutes daily, but if you aren't already that active, it's important to build up slowly. It's valuable to move daily because, in addition to burning calories, research shows that physical activity actually improves blood glucose control, regardless of weight loss! Physical activity also reduces cardiovascular risk and enhances overall well-being. If you have type 2 diabetes, working up to meeting a weekly activity goal of 90 to 150 minutes is ideal. Whether you walk for 30 minutes, 5 days a week, or take a Spinning class 2 days and do Zumba for 3, try to meet your movement goals. Most commonly, people choose walking for their physical activity, but your surest path to success is to find a form of movement you love. This will ensure you stick with it.

What exactly do we mean by "physical activity," "movement," and "exercise"? We're not just talking about running on a treadmill or lifting weights. There are all kinds of ways to get out of your seat and get moving. Many types of movement benefit blood sugar balance, heart health, and weight management.

The key to long-term blood sugar control is to make sure that no more than 2 days pass without physical activity. So if you exercise on Monday, be sure to get back to moving by Thursday. If reading all of the material presented here seems overwhelming, please don't fret. Just begin by assessing your level of readiness using START, and we'll help you put together an action plan in Chapter 3.

Hyperinsulinemia

More reasons to move: Hyperinsulinemia (high levels of insulin in the blood) is associated with high blood pressure, heart disease and heart failure, obesity (particularly abdominal obesity), osteoporosis (thinning bones), and certain types of cancer, such as colon, breast, and prostate. In contrast, having low circulating insulin levels is associated with greater longevity; most centenarians without diabetes have low circulating insulin levels.

Meeting Your Minutes

Getting cleared for exercise by your doctor is the first step to meeting the recommended 90 to 150 minutes of movement per week. Then simply begin to walk or move. If you feel ready to take action, consider walking for 5 minutes a day, 2 days a week, and continue building on this. If you can take a 5-minute walk every evening after dinner, that's even better. Then you can work your way to increasing your walk to 20 and then 30 minutes to obtain the most benefits. Not only does walking or light exercise help lower your blood glucose and, consequently, your insulin levels, but physical activity also makes your body more sensitive to insulin. So if your body was not responding to insulin before, the addition of physical activity means less insulin is needed to open up your cells to receive sugar. Physical activity without weight loss is also associated with improved cholesterol — specifically, as waist circumference decreases, so does total cholesterol.

This is just more evidence that making nutrition and exercise changes can only improve your health and overall lifestyle. There will always be benefits from making these changes.

There you have it. A sweet life *is* possible when preventing diabetes or managing the disease. Eating real food (including real sugar) and losing just a small amount of weight is your new diet-and-lifestyle prescription. Let it sink in. Restaurant meals, holiday feasts, and even birthday celebrations will be a part of your future to enjoy — not just observe. The magic starts with curbing carbs, increasing fiber, and focusing on healthy fats. Check out Chapter 2 to learn how these three steps will help you make changes that are realistic and delicious!

❉ DIABETES SUCCESS STORY

REBECCA WEISS FOUND her way to my New York City private nutrition practice in January of 2012. At age 40, this communications and marketing director at a New York City auction house and mother of two felt physically awful. She was fatigued, sluggish, and had difficulty sleeping. She felt depressed and soothed herself with emotional eating. To top it off, Rebecca was often sick and had terrible gastric reflux. She was living on Maalox. Every morning she had swollen ankles, diarrhea, and a puffy body.

"I'd wake up each morning feeling like I had a hangover — with nausea, a headache, and a stomachache from eating sweets before bedtime," Rebecca says. This smart and savvy woman was losing herself to food and was on the path to diabetes.

One major risk factor working against Rebecca was that she had been diagnosed with gestational diabetes during both of her pregnancies. After delivering her second child, she was told she had a 50/50 chance of developing diabetes. Her weight had climbed to 235 pounds (107 kg) and rather than help her come up with a plan to avert diabetes, her doctors shamed her, telling her she was too fat and that she needed to lose 50 to 100 pounds (23 to 46 kg) — but not how to achieve this goal.

When her A1C hit 5.6, on the border of prediabetes, Rebecca decided to get support from a registered dietitian so that she could get her health on track and be a positive role model for her young children. When she learned how to count carbohydrates — with the manageable goal of losing 7% of her weight — she felt capable and ready. "I felt empowered, realizing I could eat all foods, but that I had to make choices about when and how much. I would have done this long ago if someone had just told me to look at my behaviors and start small."

Together we looked at her lifestyle and how food was woven through it. The easiest change for Rebecca was to stop eating at the most problematic part of her day: She was consuming one-third of her entire day's calories at night, between 9 and 11 p.m. Rebecca began journaling and realized she needed to take that time for herself in a new way. She was binge eating for 2 hours to numb her painful emotions rather than learning to face those emotions. For food to be comforting, she realized it should make her feel good — not sick. Soon, her self-care routine changed from soothing with food to de-stressing each night by riding her recumbent bike and reading fun, non-mommy magazines like US Weekly and People. Rebecca is shocked by her new love of physical activity. She feared sweating and was always told no one liked to exercise. "No one could be more surprised than me! I love that bike," she says.

Rebecca easily gave up fake sugar and diet foods such as diet drinks (except for one diet soda a day), diet ice creams, and sugar-free pudding. Through journaling and using the IRS hunger/fullness scale (see page 45), Rebecca gained a new level of awareness. This mindfulness helped her to realize she actually preferred savory foods to the sweets she had been eating. And she didn't feel restricted by her new carbohydrate guidelines — she learned how to eat enough of the right foods during meals and snacks throughout the day to prevent blood sugar spikes and combat cravings and nighttime eating.

Buying lunch at the local salad cafés became one of Rebecca's favorite discoveries. She loves trying the different dressings and varying her high-fiber salad toppings, such as sun-dried tomatoes and chickpeas. When it comes to high-carb sources like pasta, she can't discern a difference in taste between whole wheat pasta and white pasta, but she knows which makes her body feel better — the whole wheat! Rebecca also knows she cannot just eat half a bagel for breakfast (one half bagel has 30 grams of carbs), so instead she opts for bagel chips, which are just 15 grams, with a side of hummus at snack time to keep her carbs curbed and her appetite for bagels satiated. Rebecca feels empowered knowing she is her own nutrition gatekeeper.

Her new outlook on food and diabetes prevention has paid off! When Rebecca first came to my office, she weighed 222 pounds (101 kg). In 6 months she lost 10% of her original body weight (that's 22 pounds/10 kg) and dropped from a size 16 to a size 14. Rebecca can cross her legs again and shop at any store for clothes, no longer relegated to the plus-size section. Her husband constantly reminds her how great she looks. Rebecca's blood pressure remains high, but she no longer needs medication to manage it. She has prevented prediabetes, and her doctor said her liver and gallbladder readings have normalized.

She no longer takes antacids, nor does she even buy them. The nausea, the stomach pain, the diarrhea, and the nighttime eating have been replaced with exercise, energy, and renewed self-esteem. Rebecca has become protective of her bike, and her husband now knows it is neither his laundry basket nor his closet. It is Rebecca's bike: providing 35 minutes of freedom, sweat, and self-fulfillment almost daily.

Now she spends 2 hours a day on herself, doing the things she loves. "A fog has lifted. I'm awake and ready for the day. I now love my walk to and from Penn Station. I used to resent that walk, and now this mile and a half round-trip is my favorite part of the day." She's more productive at work and has started a regular date night with her husband — and they enjoy a renewed sex life, too.

"Basically, when I was told to focus on behaviors, small changes, and small weight loss, I learned I actually loved foods that were lower in carbs, like hummus and vegetables. These foods work with my body rather than against me."

Another plus: When Rebecca stopped eating dessert, so did her children. They typically don't even ask for it anymore, she says. If they do, Rebecca is happy to give it to them. She is ecstatic that everyone in her family has benefited from her nutrition changes. Now she looks forward to getting weighed at her doctor's office. It will be the first time in 10 years she weighs less than 200 pounds (91 kg). And now she can finally sleep through the night, free from the fear of diabetes.

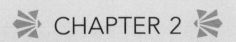

CHAPTER 2

Change Your Recipes, Not Your Life

Why call it "comfort food" when it actually makes you feel uncomfortable? These rich, traditionally carb-laden dishes make a person with insulin resistance feel lethargic, shaky, emotional, and perhaps even guilty. Well, forget that! It's time to learn how to make comfort food what it should be: energizing, balancing, and stabilizing. You can take almost any meal you love — mac 'n' cheese, mashed potatoes, or fried chicken — and transform it into a recipe that works *with* your body, not *against* it. Ideally, your meals should fuel your body without raising your blood sugar to a harmful level. This new, harmonious way of eating will allow you to reverse insulin resistance, lose weight, and lower your risk for disease. All you need to remember are these three steps to make any dish defeat diabetes. They are:

- **Step 1: Curb carbs.** The average woman should consume about 45 grams of carbs at each meal, while the average man should consume about 60 grams. The trick to managing diabetes is to hit that magic number consistently during each meal throughout the day. This is one of the easiest ways to improve blood sugar, lose weight, and be free from deprivation.

- **Step 2: Fill up on fiber.** For every 6 grams of fiber you add to a meal, you can cut 6 grams of carbs off your total! That means opting for whole grains, leafy greens, and other fibrous foods that are a cinch to incorporate into classic dishes.

- **Step 3: Favor healthy fats.** When it comes to fats, make sure you're getting the right kind. You want to decrease your intake of harmful saturated fats and increase the diabetes-friendly fats — monounsaturated fatty acids (MUFAs) and omega-3 fatty acids.

Step 1: Curb Carbs

Your recipe for success lies in "curbing your carbs." This means women should consume up to 45 grams of carbohydrates at breakfast, lunch, and dinner, or no more than 135 grams over all three meals. In addition, each woman has the option of adding one to three snacks throughout the day, at an average of 15 to 30 grams of carbohydrates per snack. Men should consume up to 60 grams of carbs at breakfast, lunch, and dinner (no more than 180 grams over all mealtimes), plus one to three 30-gram snacks.

Curbing carbs is a solution that can work for anyone, in part because it's easy to customize. By including snacks, you can tailor your daily diet to meet your individual needs. If three meals a day sounds limiting to you, don't worry. Just start by consuming three meals and three snacks. On the other hand, if three meals and three snacks sounds like too much food (especially for someone who has been inactive or is older than 60), you can start with three meals and slowly add in snacks as your metabolism increases with the addition of physical activity. Most importantly, be sure to meet at least 45 grams of carbohydrates per meal (or a minimum of 130 grams of digestible carbs per day) to ensure your body is properly fueled.

All the recipes in this book have been uniquely designed to help prevent you from exceeding the 45- or 60-gram carbohydrate allotment. As long as you are not taking medication for diabetes, don't fret if your carb intake falls below the 45 or 60 grams for some of your meals. Just be sure you achieve the minimum of 130 grams of total carbs per day.

When making over a dish or a meal, be sure you know what carbohydrates are and where to find them on a food label. Did you know vegetables are carbohydrates? Yes, broccoli and lettuce are carbs — and so are beans! Some foods are even considered

Whole Wheat Pasta

Did you know whole wheat pasta is better for you than brown rice pasta? That's right: whole wheat pasta contains more natural fiber per serving. Cook whole wheat pasta al dente for better blood sugar management. Long cooking times can break down starches, allowing carbohydrates to be absorbed into your blood faster.

American Table

Nutrition Facts

Serving Size 1 cup (228 g)

Amount Per Serving

Calories 250	**Calories** from Fat 110

	% Daily Value
Total Fat 12 g	**18%**
Saturated Fat 3 g	**15%**
Trans Fat 3 g	
Cholesterol 30 mg	**10%**
Sodium 470 mg	**20%**
Total Carbohydrate 31 g	**10%**
Dietary Fiber 0 g	**0%**
Sugars 5 g	
Protein 5 g	

Vitamin A 4%	●	Calcium 20%
Vitamin C 2%	●	Iron 4%

* Percent Daily Values are based on a 2,000 calorie diet. Your Daily Values may be higher or lower depending on your calorie needs.

	Calories	2,000	2,500
Total Fat	Less than	65 g	80 g
Sat Fat	Less than	20 g	25 g
Cholesterol	Less than	300 mg	300 mg
Sodium	Less than	2,400 mg	2,400 mg
Total Carbohydrate		300 g	375 g
Dietary Fiber		25 g	30 g

Canadian Table

Nutrition Facts

Per 250 mL (228 g)

Amount	% Daily Value
Calories 250	
Fat 12 g	18%
Saturated 3 g + Trans 3 g	15%
Cholesterol 30 mg	
Sodium 470 mg	20%
Carbohydrate 31 g	10%
Fibre 0 g	0%
Sugars 5 g	
Protein 5 g	

Vitamin A	4%	Vitamin C	20%
Calcium	2%	Iron	4%

both carbs and proteins. But don't worry about the nitty-gritty details; we'll take care of that for you. Let's get familiar with the foods in the carbohydrate category: grains, beans, low-fat dairy, fruits, vegetables, and, of course, sugar. For any carbohydrate, the ideal form is the least processed and most wholesome.

The Go-To Grains

When it comes to grains, aim for whole-grain options whenever possible. When making muffins and other baked goods, substitute oat bran or whole wheat flour for refined white flour. If you are cooking pasta, always choose the whole wheat or sprouted grain varieties. When shopping, aim for the least processed foods. You can find them by reading the ingredients. Choose products that have short ingredient lists and that include sugar as the third ingredient or beyond. Compare Nutrition Facts labels and choose the food higher in total natural fiber.

What is natural fiber? There is no legal definition, but we consider it to be foods that have not been stripped of the bran and the germ or are in the least-modified state, so they are less processed and much healthier. Breads, cereals, cookies, and other foods with "added fiber," such as the partially digestible polysaccharide inulin or foods marketed as low-carbohydrate products, are typically not high in fiber until fiber is added through food processing. We do not encourage you to eat these foods in large quantities. Rather, seek out products, like sprouted wheat bread or cereal with millet and flax, that have not been refined or altered to meet fiber recommendations for marketing purposes.

A 2003 study of thousands of men and women showed that including more fiber-rich whole grains in your diet can prevent diabetes. At the beginning of the study, the participants were ages 40 to 69, and none had been diagnosed with diabetes. After 10 years of follow-up, the researchers found that those who ate the most fiber-rich whole grains had a 35% lower risk of developing diabetes than those who ate the least. And even more shocking, participants who ate the most fiber from cereals had an amazing 61% lower risk of developing diabetes. That's a greater reduction of risk than was seen in a study that involved diet, exercise, and significant weight loss (see page 14).

Ironically, many diets tell you to avoid cereal products, such as wheat, rye, corn, and rice. These wholesome foods, enjoyed in whole-grain form, are abundant in our diet, making them the best way of all to stay healthy. Just make sure to stick with unprocessed foods. Be cautious: Those who consume processed foods often report bloating and gas.

Besides wheat products, there is an entire world of delicious whole grains to choose from: amaranth, barley, buckwheat, bulgur, millet, oats, and quinoa are all great choices. Barley is delicious as a side in place of rice. Quinoa can be used when stuffing peppers or even for a hot morning cereal. The options are endless. Check out Good Morning "Grits" (page 72) or Vegetable Sauté with Quinoa (page 227) to try quinoa.

From this point forward, trade white flour for whole-grain wheat flour, oat flour, spelt flour, or sprouted wheat flour — or any naturally high-fiber grain. Not only can these whole grains help you manage your blood sugar, but they really taste great.

Clues for Curbing Carbs and Increasing Fiber

- **Cereal:** Opt for 30 grams of carbs or fewer and 5 grams of fiber or more per serving.
- **Bread:** Opt for 15 to 20 grams of carbs and about 3 grams of fiber per slice.
- **Pasta:** Opt for 45 grams of carbs or fewer and about 5 grams of fiber per 2-ounce (60 g) serving.

Breakdown of Breads

Beware of breads that are too high in fiber (we recommend no more than 5 grams) or too low in carbs (we recommend no less than 15 grams). Below are examples of different types of breads, with sample ingredient lists and amounts of fiber and carbs. Minimize or avoid breads with harder-to-digest added fiber, such as inulin or cellulose.

Bread	Serving Size	Ingredients	Fiber (g)	Carbs (g)
100% whole wheat NO ADDED FIBER	1 slice (43 g)	Whole wheat flour, water, sugar, wheat gluten, yeast, raisin juice concentrate, wheat bran, molasses, soybean oil, salt, monoglycerides, calcium propionate (preservative), calcium sulfate, DATEM, grain vinegar, citric acid, soy lecithin, whey, nonfat milk	3	20
Organic 100% whole wheat NO ADDED FIBER	1 slice (43 g)	Organic whole wheat flour, water, organic cracked wheat, organic brown sugar, organic wheat gluten, organic wheat bran, yeast, organic high oleic sunflower and/or safflower oil, sea salt, organic vinegar, organic oat flour, organic molasses, cultured organic wheat starch, organic barley malt, ascorbic acid, natural enzymes	3	18
Organic sprouted whole-grain NO ADDED FIBER	1 slice (34 g)	Organic sprouted wheat, organic sprouted barley, organic sprouted millet, organic malted barley, organic sprouted lentils, organic sprouted soybeans, organic sprouted spelt, filtered water, fresh yeast, organic wheat gluten, sea salt	3	15
7-grain with flax NO ADDED FIBER	1 slice (40 g)	Water, organic whole wheat flour, organic evaporated cane juice, organic wheat gluten, organic quinoa flour, organic oat fiber, organic sesame seeds, organic millet, organic Kamut flour, organic whole spelt flour, yeast, organic sunflower seeds, sea salt, organic high oleic sunflower/safflower oil, organic potato flour, organic flaxseed, organic rolled oats, organic oat bran, organic vinegar, organic molasses, organic wheat starch, ascorbic acid, natural enzymes	3	15

continued, next page…

Bread	Serving Size	Ingredients	Fiber (g)	Carbs (g)
Organic soft multigrain NO ADDED FIBER	1 slice (40 g)	Organic wheat flour, water, organic whole wheat flour, organic grain and seed blend (organic cracked rye, organic cracked yellow corn, organic cracked wheat, organic cracked barley, organic steel-cut oats, organic flaxseed, organic hulled millet), organic cane sugar, contains less than 2% of each of the following: organic soybean oil, organic wheat gluten, yeast, organic molasses, salt, organic oat flour, organic potato flour, enzymes, organic cultured wheat starch, citric acid, organic reduced-fat soy flour, ascorbic acid, organic soy lecithin	3	21
100% whole wheat ADDED FIBER	2 slices (41 g)	Whole wheat flour, water, wheat gluten, cellulose fiber, polydextrose, sugar, contains 2% or less of the following: yeast, oat fiber, molasses, salt, calcium, sulfate, vinegar, soybean and/or canola oil, soy protein isolate, dough conditioners (one or more of the following: DATEM, mono- and diglycerides, ethoxylated mono- and diglycerides, ammonium sulfate, sodium stearoyl lactylate, potassium iodate), calcium propionate (preservative), wheat flour*, guar gum, ferrous fumarate, folic acid, citric acid * trivial amount of wheat flour	6	16
Double-fiber ADDED FIBER	1 slice (43 g)	Whole wheat flour, water, sugar, inulin (chicory root fiber), wheat gluten, wheat fiber, yeast, soybean oil, cellulose fiber, polydextrose, wheat bran, molasses, salt, DATEM, calcium propionate (preservative), monoglycerides, grain vinegar, calcium sulfate, citric acid, soy lecithin, calcium carbonate, whey, nonfat milk	6	21
Double-fiber ADDED FIBER	1 slice (38 g)	Whole wheat flour, water, sugar, inulin (chicory root fiber), wheat gluten, wheat fiber, yeast, cellulose fiber, polydextrose, soybean and/or canola oil, salt, wheat bran, molasses, enrichment (calcium sulfate, vitamin E acetate, vitamin A palmitate, vitamin D_3), mono- and diglycerides, calcium propionate (preservative), DATEM, soy lecithin, citric acid, grain vinegar, sodium stearoyl lactylate, ethoxylated mono- and diglycerides, azodicarbonamide	5	19

Balance with Beans

Beans are a superfood. These little powerhouses have both carbohydrates and protein. They are packed with vitamins, high in soluble fiber, and noted for their ability to lower cholesterol. Basically, you are getting two for one when eating beans: this nutritious carb is not only diabetes-friendly but also heart-healthy!

When choosing beans, it's okay to either purchase dry and soak overnight or buy the canned version, which can be much more convenient. Remember, the goal is to make over your meals, not have the ingredients sit in your cabinets. When you purchase any canned item, whether it is beans, vegetables, or soup, make sure the label says "no added salt" and read the ingredient list to make sure there are no added sugars or fats.

Low-Fat and Fat-Free Dairy and Dairy Alternatives Are Carbs

Low-fat and even fat-free dairy options, such as fat-free (skim) milk, contain carbohydrates as well as proteins and must be counted when curbing your carbs. Typically, low-fat versions of milk, yogurt, and even frozen yogurt contain 12 grams of carbohydrates per cup (250 mL) or more. Only a few low-fat or fat-free dairy or dairy alternative options are low enough in carbs (less than 10 grams per cup/250 mL) that they can be counted as proteins: low-fat (1%) or fat-free (0%) Greek yogurt, unsweetened soy milk, unsweetened almond milk, and low-fat (1%) cottage cheese.

Watch Words

Beware of fake sugars, added sugars, and added fats in the ingredient list.

Fake Foes: Avoid the Artificial

- Acesulfame K
- Equal, NutraSweet (aspartame)
- Nectresse
- Sweet'N Low, Sugar Twin (saccharin)
- Splenda (sucralose)
- Truvia and PureVia (stevia and erythritol)

Sugar Fraud: Steer Clear

- High-fructose corn syrup

Fat Foes: Beware of These Heartbreakers

- Cocoa butter
- Vegetable shortening, also called shortening (e.g., Crisco)
- Lard
- Olestra (fake fat replacer)
- Monoglycerides and diglycerides (fat-based fat replacer)
- Partially hydrogenated oil
- Palm kernel oil

Carbs Climb with Fat-Free Foods

Taking the fat out of a food leaves two macronutrients, carbohydrates and proteins. Typically one of these nutrients increases in quantity, and more often it is the carbohydrates. Think about fat-free dressing or fat-free cookies. They may be sans fat, but they have plenty of sugars. Read this as a blood-sugar bomb and stay away from these products. As you will read later in this chapter, fats such as olive oil for dressing and avocado for sandwiches offer heart-protective benefits. You can't say that about artificial ingredients. Your new motto is "Low fat, not no fat."

The one exception to this rule is dairy that is low enough in carbs to be considered proteins, such as fat-free Greek yogurt. Instead of being mostly carbohydrate-based, like other yogurts, this fat-free option contains 14 to 21 grams of protein and between 7 and 22 grams of carbohydrates, depending on whether it is fruit-flavored. Across the board, low-fat and fat-free Greek yogurts are winners and go-to options for beating diabetes.

Aside from these lower-carb, higher-protein dairy options, we recommend choosing low-fat dairy options rather than fat-free or full-fat. Choose 1% milk (not fat-free/skim), low-fat yogurt, and low-fat ice cream (or possibly the real thing — good old full-fat ice cream). Low-fat dairy options have a small amount of fat to help satiate you, regulate your blood sugar, and keep the product wholesome. Minimizing the amount of saturated fat you eat is heart-protective; therefore, lower-fat options are typically the better choice for dairy. But when it comes to cheese or a sweet food, like ice cream, that contains protein, vitamins, and minerals, opt for full-fat but keep the quantity small. While curbing carbs is our focus, portion control will also automatically and advantageously curb your calories.

Although most grocery aisles are a maze, you will soon have them mapped out for your own success! So when turning down the milk aisle, for example, choose from these options to make sure your blood sugar stays balanced:

- Choose 1% milk only if using cow's milk.
- Opt for soy, almond, and sunflower milks that are unsweetened and fortified with

calcium and vitamin D. If using regular almond milk, make sure it is enriched with protein (typically 5 grams of protein or more per serving).

- Try hemp milk — it's a great source of omega-3 fatty acids. Make sure it is fortified with calcium and vitamin D.

Flavor with Fruit

Nothing in life is free, and this includes fruit. Fruits fall into the carbohydrate category. Many times, clients have told me about all of the nutrition changes they are making, yet they can't seem to get their blood sugar under control. That's when we review their food log to read about breakfast with a glass of orange juice to take their medications or vitamins, an extra-large fruit smoothie before hitting the treadmill, and lunch meals of only fruit. And let's not forget the entire bunch of grapes while watching TV at night. Bingo. Fruit is absolutely good for us, but like anything, it must be eaten in moderation and preferably as part of a mixed meal, with a protein or a fat like cottage cheese or almonds. Go for two servings of fruit daily.

One piece of fruit, such as a big apple, can contain 30 grams of carbohydrates. As fruit ripens, the complex sugars known as starch are broken down into simple forms and can raise your blood sugar more quickly. Therefore, small pieces of less-ripe fruit are best to work into your daily intake. These less-mature fruits remain in their complex forms, taking longer to break down.

If you love juice, you can find a way to work it into your intake. Just recognize that it should be 100% juice and it will count toward your carbohydrate allotment for that particular meal.

Choose Less-Ripe Fruit

Ripe fruit is more likely to raise your blood sugar; opt for the harder, less-ripe pieces.

Five Common Fruits for 15 Grams of Carbs

- 1 small apple (4 oz/125 g)
- 1 small banana (4 oz/125 g)
- ¾ cup (175 mL) blueberries
- 17 small grapes (3 oz/90 g)
- 1 small orange (6.5 oz/195 g)

Very Veggie

As astonishing as it may seem, veggies are considered carbohydrates. There are two categories of vegetables: starchy and non-starchy. Starchy vegetables are typically the root of the plant and include beets, potatoes, sweet potatoes, turnips, jicama, and radishes. Other starchy vegetables include pumpkin, butternut squash, peas, corn, and zucchini. The non-starchy vegetables include, but are not limited to, the cruciferous veggies such as broccoli and cauliflower as well as dark leafy greens like kale, spinach, collards, and Swiss chard.

These roots, leaves, and stems afford you the luxury of quantity! You need to consume many vegetables daily to affect your blood sugar. Three cups (750 mL) of raw non-starchy veggies (or 1½ cups/375 mL of cooked non-starchy vegetables) equals 15 grams of carbohydrates. So including many veggies at meals gives you the opportunity to get quantity and variety.

When making over your meals, double or even triple your vegetable quantity to help fill you up, plus meet your daily needs of veggies, while keeping the carb level curbed. Most North Americans do not eat enough veggies, and many recipes fall short in the quantity of veggies they use. Eat at least three servings of veggies per day. Go ahead and make your meal colorful!

Having Your Cake And Eating It Too

If you eat 1½ cups (375 mL) of cooked vegetables as your only carb source for dinner, you will have 30 to 45 grams of carbohydrates left over to enjoy another form of carbohydrate at that same meal. The other form of carbohydrate is your choice, whether it is a fresh bowl of fruit or a refined carb such as a cookie or even a piece of cake. That's right, dessert. This is how you can easily manage eating a sweet dessert at a dinner party or a restaurant. Eat protein, such as a piece of grilled chicken or salmon, paired with non-starchy vegetables so that your carbohydrate allotment is not used up for that meal. Then when the waiter offers dessert, you can look on the menu for an option that will serve up less than 45 grams of carbohydrates. If you are at home, you can easily use one of the recipes in this cookbook to find a sweet dinner complement. If you are reading the menu and feel stumped, a safe bet would be to eat half of a smaller dessert. You *can* enjoy any food, when you do it smartly.

Opt for Organic

Grocery stores, fruit stands, and farmers' markets now offer organic and conventional options. Organic farms adhere to earth-friendly practices that rely on biological controls rather than chemical interventions and use methods that build soil fertility, such as crop diversity and crop rotation, to minimize pests and maximize produce output. Conventional produce, on the other hand, may come from a farm that uses synthetic pesticides.

Organic fruits and vegetables aren't necessarily more nutritious than nonorganic produce, but it is recommended that individuals (especially pregnant women, children under the age of 5, and immune-compromised individuals) minimize their exposure to pesticides. Though more research in this area is needed, studies have found links between exposure to certain pesticides and impaired liver function, blood sugar control, and obesity. Eating organic produce is the surest way to reduce your pesticide exposure. However, the best way to protect your health — and your wallet — is to focus on limiting the foods that are most likely to come into contact with these chemicals.

The Real Scoop on Real Sugar

There are sticky forms of sugar, such as honey, agave, and maple syrup. There are the powdered varieties of raw sugar, brown sugar, white (granulated) sugar, and natural cane sugar. Last but not least, there is the controversial high-fructose corn syrup. When it comes to using these sweeteners, the trick is to choose the form that is the least processed and most sweet — that way, you can use less of it to satisfy your sweet tooth.

Use the sweetness meter below to help you decide which sugars to favor. Though agave has been touted as a lower-glycemic sugar, there is no conclusive beneficial evidence. The research also has mixed reviews on high-fructose corn syrup, but because it is highly processed, it's best to avoid it. The Diabetes Comfort Food Diet recommends you use as little added sugar as possible in a form that is the least modified and that minimally affects your blood sugar.

Avoid Artificial Sweeteners

Unfortunately, sugar has gained a bad reputation over the years, and many people try to avoid real sugar at all costs. Thinking they can cut calories and "cheat" the effects of real sugar, many turn to artificial sweeteners, also known as non-nutritive sweeteners: aspartame (Equal,

The Dirty Dozen and the Clean 15

Every year, a nonprofit organization called the Environmental Working Group compiles two lists to help American consumers identify produce containing higher and lower levels of pesticides. Use this list to help you save time and money when deciding which organic produce items are worth the extra dollars. To lessen your exposure to pesticides, stay up-to-date and educate yourself on the most recent lists each year at ewg.org/foodnews/summary.php. Here's the 2015 version:

The Dirty Dozen (Plus Two)

In the United States, this produce is most likely to come into contact with pesticides. Choose organic and sustainable vendors whenever possible.

1. Apples
2. Peaches
3. Nectarines
4. Strawberries
5. Grapes
6. Celery
7. Spinach
8. Bell peppers
9. Cucumbers
10. Cherry tomatoes
11. Snap peas (imported)
12. Potatoes
   + Hot peppers
   + Kale/collard greens

The Clean 15

It's okay to buy these fruits and veggies from a conventional farm.

1. Avocados
2. Sweet corn
3. Pineapples
4. Cabbage
5. Sweet peas (frozen)
6. Onions
7. Asparagus
8. Mangos
9. Papayas
10. Kiwi
11. Eggplant
12. Grapefruit
13. Cantaloupe
14. Cauliflower
15. Sweet potatoes

NutraSweet), saccharin (Sweet'N Low, SugarTwin), acesulfame K, neotame, and sucralose (Splenda). When substituting artificial sweeteners for the real deal, it's important to consider the pros and cons. While these little packs of white sweetness seem harmless, no matter how they may taste or look, artificial sweeteners are chemicals. Although they have no effect on glycemic response, one study found that people who drank one or more diet sodas (sweetened with aspartame) had a higher A1C than people who drank none. Also, it is possible that eating these sweeteners makes you crave more sweet foods high in real or added sugars — and lots of calories.

Finally, consuming these "fake friends" can actually lead to long-term weight gain.

Remember that sugar-free doesn't mean calorie-free when it comes to food. The little packets may be without calories, but the foods they are used in certainly contain calories. With artificial sweeteners, we may trick ourselves into thinking we consumed less — when we actually end up consuming more. Artificial sweeteners often distort our perception of calories by satisfying our current cravings but causing our bodies to crave those sweet calories later in the day.

With these factors in mind, we think eating real sugar is worth the calories and carbs when defeating diabetes.

Sweet Stevia

Stevia is a form of natural sugar found in the leaves of the stevia plant. This natural sugar is about 200 times sweeter than regular table sugar and does not affect blood sugar. Pure stevia is a real sugar alternative. Read the labels of packaged stevia to ensure it is 100% pure. Beware — some brands may add the sugar alcohol erythritol.

What About Wine?

We can't forget about wine and other beverages. You should know that the easiest way to curb your carbs when talking drinks is to switch from diet drinks and caloric beverages like juice and soda to water or seltzer. Water and seltzer are refreshing, hydrating, filling, and don't add any extra calories or carbs (or other nutrients). You can slice oranges, lemons, or limes and toss them in for some zesty flavoring. Plus, increasing your water consumption will improve your digestion as you increase your fiber intake. Hydrating will help to prevent the fiber from binding to cause constipation.

But what about wine, beer, and liquor? Well, like everything else on the Diabetes Comfort Food Diet, you can have them, but in moderation. This means one serving

of alcohol per day for women and two for men — but you must drink alcoholic beverages with meals from now on. There are two reasons: first, because alcohol is dehydrating; and second, because it can cause hypoglycemia (low blood sugar). Even though it lowers blood sugar, you must still count that beer toward your total carb count at that meal. Decide whether it's worth it. If you don't already drink, don't start drinking now.

Alcohol: Counting Carbs

12-oz (341 mL) beer = 13 grams (regular) or 5 grams (light beer)
4-oz (125 mL) glass of red wine = 3 grams
4-oz (125 mL) glass of white wine = 1 gram
1½-oz (45 mL) shot of liquor = 0 grams in gin, rum, or vodka

Step 2: Fill Up on Fiber
Magic Carbs

As you curb carbs, we have a little more magic for your toolbox: fiber. A carbohydrate contains fiber, and there are two types: soluble and insoluble. It doesn't matter which form of fiber you eat, but if your meal boasts 6 or more grams of fiber per serving, part of your carbohydrate intake "disappears"! For instance, if your entrée tallies up to 56 grams of carbohydrates but has 12 grams of fiber, you can subtract the 12 grams of fiber from the total carbohydrates. This means 56 grams of carbs, minus 12 grams of fiber, equals 44 total carbohydrate grams. These magic carbs help prevent you from exceeding 45 or 60 grams of carbohydrates per meal.

Fiber also allows you to choose foods with higher total carbohydrates. For instance, let's say you choose a cereal that has 42 grams of total carbohydrates per cup (250 mL). You may initially think, "Not only is this cereal too high in carbohydrates, but I won't have enough carbs left for my milk choice!" But let's say you then look below this number on the Nutrition Facts label and see that the cereal also has 12 grams of dietary fiber per cup (250 mL). This means your cereal choice is really equivalent to 30 grams of carbs. Thus, the cereal is a great high-fiber, moderate-carbohydrate breakfast choice.

1 cup (250 mL) cereal

  42 grams of carbs
− 12 grams dietary fiber
= 30 grams of carbs

½ cup (125 mL) 1% milk

+ 6 grams carbs
= 36 grams of carbs for breakfast

Not Net Carbs

Don't confuse the popular concept of net carbs with our magic carbs. Most people subtract total fiber from total carbs and call this net carbs. For the best results, you must go a step further than net carbs. Subtract fiber from your carb count only if the fiber quantity is greater than 6 grams per serving.

Why Fiber?

Numerous research studies support the benefits of fiber specifically in relation to blood sugar management. Dietary fiber, especially soluble fiber, decreases insulin resistance and prevents prediabetes and diabetes. Furthermore, the American Diabetes Association recommends that *all individuals* consume on average at least 22 grams of fiber per 1,600 calories per day, and studies show that a diet with 44 to 50 grams of fiber daily improves blood sugar management. In fact, in a study published in the *New England Journal of Medicine*, researchers reported that when patients with type 2 diabetes ate more fiber, they experienced dramatic health improvements. Their blood sugar levels went down an average of 13 points, and their blood fats (cholesterol and triglycerides) also went down steeply. The fiber used in this study came from ordinary, natural foods, not supplements. This is the same source of fiber you'll find in this book.

So what else can fiber do for your diabetes? Research shows that fiber can actually reduce the need for medication in those with diabetes. In a study of men with diabetes who had high blood sugar levels, adding fiber to their diets produced truly stunning results: The men who were taking oral diabetes medications all had their medication discontinued! And those

More Wholesome Foods = Higher Fiber

Compare the fiber content of foods in a more wholesome form versus a less wholesome form.

More Wholesome Food	Fiber (g)	Less Wholesome Food	Fiber (g)
1 small apple	3.0	½ cup (125 mL) applesauce	1.8
1 cup (250 mL) bran flakes	5.0	1 cup (250 mL) frosted flakes	1.0
1 cup (250 mL) steamed kale	4.0	1 cup (250 mL) boiled kale	3.0
Raw fruit and nut bar (100 g)	5.0	Chewy granola bar (100 g)	1.0
1 large slice sprouted whole-grain bread (41 g)	3.0	1 large slice white bread (30 g)	0.8

Curb Carbs with Cereal

When curbing carbs and filling up on fiber, find cereals with nutrition facts similar to our favorites in the left column. First read the Nutrition Facts label and then check ingredients to make sure the grains are wholesome options such as stone-ground whole wheat, and look for the "watch words" (see page 27). Choose the better option and enjoy.

	Kashi GOLEAN	Kashi GOLEAN Crunch!
Serving size	1 cup (250 mL)	1 cup (250 mL)
Calories	140	190
Total fat	1 g	3 g
Saturated fat	0 g	0 g
Total carbs	30 g	39 g
Total fiber	10 g	8 g
Protein	13 g	9 g
	Kellogg's All-Bran Complete Wheat Flakes	Kellogg's Raisin Bran
Serving size	1 cup (250 mL)	1 cup (250 mL)
Calories	113	190
Total fat	0.6 g	1 g
Saturated fat	0 g	0 g
Total carbs	31 g	46 g
Total fiber	6 g	7 g
Protein	4 g	5 g
	Bob's Red Mill Granola, Natural	Bear Naked Granola Heavenly Chocolate
Serving size	½ cup (125 mL)	½ cup (125 mL)
Calories	170	260
Total fat	2 g	7 g
Saturated fat	0 g	2 g
Total carbs	33 g	42 g
Total fiber	3 g	4 g
Protein	5 g	6 g

taking insulin in doses of less than 30 units a day were able to discontinue their injections. The message is clear: The more fiber you consume, the less likely it is that the carbs you eat will negatively affect your blood sugar.

Filling up on fiber is easy when you use the recipes in this book. Whole grains, beans, fruits, and vegetables are all naturally high in fiber. Be sure to use these foods in whole form. For example, a whole apple with the skin on has more fiber than a mini cup of applesauce.

Step 3: Favor Healthy Fats

Now you know to spread your fiber-filled carbohydrates evenly throughout the day. What goes on the rest of your plate? For starters, lean proteins like beans, eggs, tofu, chicken, and fish should accompany your grains, veggies, and fruits. Most important is the word *lean* — meaning low in saturated fat. When curbing carbs, filling up with fiber, and decreasing saturated fat in your proteins, you automatically cut calories, which can help you lose weight. It's also important to eat plenty of healthy unsaturated fats. That's why step 3 of the Diabetes Comfort Food Diet is to favor healthy fats! This essential step to making over your meals will keep you full, enhance your whole-body health, and further protect against diabetes.

A Small Waistline

Obtaining — and maintaining — a small waistline is crucial when preventing and/or managing blood sugar. A larger waistline for women and men is associated with diabetes and metabolic syndrome, so we must keep this in mind for prevention and treatment.

Eat More MUFAs

In Chapter 1, we mentioned the benefits of a Mediterranean-style diet, which is high in monounsaturated fats, or MUFAs (found in olive oil, olives, and avocados), and omega-3 fatty acids (especially found in fish). Coupled with a healthy lifestyle (daily physical activity and no smoking), a Mediterranean-style diet is significantly associated with less weight gain and a smaller waistline. Furthermore, this dietary pattern, characterized by a higher consumption of plant foods, a higher intake of olive oil as the main source of fat, and a moderate intake of fish, correlates with preventing the cognitive decline associated with diabetes. The diet is also beneficial for reducing complications of diabetes, such as a fatty liver.

MUFAs are known to be heart-protective and do not cause inflammation the way other dietary components do. The evidence supports a diet rich in MUFAs as your primary source of fats. Simply put, eat more MUFAs.

What Oils to Choose

- Olive oil is best used when cooking with low to medium heat.
- Canola oil is best used when cooking with medium to high heat.
- Coconut oil is not yet proven to be protective; limit use, if any.
- Peanut oil, specifically gourmet peanut oil, is okay, especially if cooking with high heat.
- Cold-pressed canola, peanut, and olive oils are great options.
- Avoid vegetable oil or blends, as they are not specific to type or ratio of oils.

Oh, Oh, Omega-3 Fatty Acids

The other fat to favor is the polyunsaturated fat called omega-3 fatty acid. There are two forms of polyunsaturated fatty acids: omega-3s and omega-6s. The North American diet is already high in omega-6 fatty acids, so you need to make a specific effort to increase the omega-3 fatty acids in your daily diet. This essential fatty acid is an anti-inflammatory agent, protects your heart, and helps to prevent diabetes. The latest research reveals that diets high in total omega-3 fatty acids are directly related to a lower risk of developing diabetes.

Omega-3 fatty acids come in three forms: Docosahexaenoic acid (DHA) and eicosapentaenoic acid (EPA) are both found in fish, while alpha-linolenic acid (ALA) is found in plants. The vegetarian sources of ALA should be eaten daily. Get your daily dose from canola oil, walnuts, Brazil nuts, hemp seeds, sesame seeds, pumpkin seeds, chia seeds, and flaxseeds. DHA surrounds your nerves and helps with nerve transmission, brain development, and even depression. Our bodies cannot make this essential fatty acid, so to get enough EPA and DHA, you must eat direct sources found in marine life. Aim to include these foods two or more times a week: salmon, trout, bass, bluefish, sardines, tuna, catfish, cod, and/or halibut. If choosing canned tuna, check the label and buy only "chunk light in water, no added salt." Chunk light tuna is lower in mercury than canned albacore (white) tuna.

Avoiding Chemicals

To alleviate worries about chemicals such as polychlorinated biphenyls (PCBs) and mercury in your fish, eat different types of wild fish from different sources of water each week. To stay current on fish advisories, check the Environmental Protection Agency's website.

Go Fish

When it comes to selecting the most healthful sources of fish, go wild or sustainably farmed. Wild and sustainably farmed fish have higher levels of omega-3 fatty acids and lower levels of undesirable fats. They are more environmentally friendly and have not been exposed to growth hormones, antibiotics, or dyes — common practices when it comes to imported farmed fish. Some grocery chains are making finding wild fish or sustainably farmed fish easy. All of their fish are labeled to indicate where the fish was sourced. Fish raised in a sustainable farm have lived in a natural body of water free of chemicals unless warranted for therapeutic use.

There are now certifications and seals of approval to help make finding sustainable fish and/or wild fish simple no matter where you shop. Look for labels such as "Friend of the Sea" and the Marine Stewardship Council's "Fish Forever." To educate yourself, visit FriendoftheSea.org, FishWatch.gov, seafoodsource.com, seachoice.org or www.nmfs.noaa.gov/aquaculture.

If you do buy regular farmed fish, try to make sure it comes from the United States or Canada. Aim to get fish from a variety of water sources, in case one water source is contaminated with mercury or environmental toxins. But remember, in the end, it's still better to eat farmed fish twice a week than no fish at all!

The Lean Protein and Favored Fat Cheat Sheet

Use this cheat sheet as your new guide for grocery shopping, recipe modifications, and meal planning. It will make following the Diabetes Comfort Food Diet simple! It is ideal for recipes to contain sources of both or at least one favored fat: MUFAs and omega-3 fatty acids.

Lean Proteins

- Fish and seafood (monkfish, tilapia, shrimp)
- White meat (skinless chicken, turkey)
- Lean grass-fed beef (sirloin, round, and tenderloin/filet mignon)
- Vegetable protein (tofu, lentils, and dried beans, such as lima beans, black beans, pinto beans, or split peas)

Healthy Fats
Omega-3 Fatty Acids
ALA: Eat daily

- Canola oil
- Chia seeds
- Ground flaxseeds
- Hemp seeds
- Pumpkin seeds
- Walnuts

EPA and DHA: Eat twice weekly

- Bass
- Bluefish
- Cod
- Mackerel
- Salmon
- Sardines
- Trout
- Tuna (chunk light canned in water, no added salt)

MUFAs: Eat Daily

- Olives
- Avocados
- Nuts (such as peanuts, almonds, cashews, and pecans)
- Hummus (when possible, choose hummus without tahini)
- Oils (such as olive oil, canola oil, and peanut oil)

Saturated Fat

- Limit or eliminate saturated fat.
- Choose foods with labels showing 2 grams or less of saturated fat per serving.
- If butter is used, there should be no added salt; preferably, choose olive oil instead.
- Avoid trans fat (partially hydrogenated oils).
- Remove all visible fat.
- Choose lean proteins that are low in saturated fat.
- Limit whole (homogenized) and reduced-fat (2%) milk.
- Choose low-fat dairy and yogurt (with the exception of cheese).
- Choose harder cheeses and use small quantities.

Steer Away from Saturated Fats

Consuming foods high in saturated fats — such as sausage, buttery biscuits, or highly processed foods — can increase your level of "bad" cholesterol known as low-density lipoprotein (LDL). LDL cholesterol deposits into tissues, causing fatty streaks, plaque buildup, and damage to your blood vessels. Higher levels of LDL are associated with increased inflammation and risk of cardiovascular disease. In fact, lowering your dietary intake of saturated fat can be more beneficial in lowering LDL levels than just decreasing dietary cholesterol. Decreasing dietary cholesterol to less than 200 milligrams per day lowers your cholesterol by about 3% to 5%, whereas getting less than 7% of your daily calories from saturated fat has been shown to lower cholesterol by 8% to 10%. Therefore, focus on eating foods lower in saturated fat and higher in monounsaturated fats, such as almonds.

There is one exception: cheese. Though high in calories and saturated fat, cheese is a great source of protein and calcium and thus can help to manage blood sugar levels and provide a hard-to-get mineral for bone density.

Continue to limit added sugars and eat fruits, vegetables, low-fat dairy products, and whole grains to help decrease your cholesterol and your risk for cardiovascular disease, which is associated with diabetes.

Combat Diabetes with Calcium

You've probably heard it time and time again: "Calcium helps build strong bones and teeth." And it's true! Calcium is an essential mineral, and vitamin D helps the body absorb it. Consuming adequate calcium and vitamin D is crucial, especially if you have prediabetes or diabetes, because high levels of insulin are associated with weakening of the bones (known as osteopenia) and loss of bone (known as osteoporosis). Your goal should be to consume enough calcium and vitamin D to prevent these bone diseases. Aside from low-fat dairy products, good sources of calcium include green leafy vegetables, the stems of broccoli, and fortified milk alternatives such as almond milk. Opt for four servings of low-fat dairy per day. Weight-bearing exercise can also help build bone mass — add it to your list of pros for building up your exercise routine!

Give Salt the Shake

One thing we haven't talked about yet is salt. Table salt — sodium chloride — is 40% sodium and 60% chloride. Sodium is a natural mineral also known as an electrolyte and is necessary for fluid balance in your body. However, excessive dietary salt intake is known to raise blood pressure. Be sure to check all nutrition labels for sodium content. The general recommendation for Americans and Canadians is to limit salt intake to 2,300 milligrams of sodium daily — or, if you already have diabetes and are therefore at risk for high blood pressure, no more than 1,500 milligrams of sodium per day.

That may seem like a lot, but it's surprising how much hidden sodium lurks in the foods you eat every day. To help you keep your sodium under control, our rule of thumb is that entrées should have no more than 600 milligrams of sodium. Snacks and small meals should have no more than 400 milligrams. If you are eating three meals and three snacks, you need to reduce this even more, to about 400 milligrams per meal or snack. If you are eating three meals and three snacks and already have diabetes, use 250 milligrams as your rule of thumb.

Most importantly, do not use a salt shaker and, if you are eating processed foods, check the nutrition label. First, identify how many servings are in the package. Processed foods such as a can of soup often have 800 milligrams of sodium per serving but pack two servings per can. This means if you ate all the soup in the can, you would be taking in 1,600 milligrams of salt! That is an entire day's worth of sodium for someone with diabetes. See "Satisfy Your Salt Buds" (opposite) for three strategies to get a salty flavor without damaging your health.

Satisfy Your Salt Buds

Season with Mushrooms

A good way to skip the salt shaker is to cook with mushrooms. Button mushrooms contain glutamic acid, which is an almost-sodium-free version of MSG (monosodium glutamate, the flavor enhancer found in many processed foods). Instead of salting your food, season with mushrooms for a dose of potassium, added texture, and, of course, a salty flavor.

Substitute Spice

Another option to sidestep salt is to give your meal a kick of flavor. Chop up a variety of chile peppers to add hot spice and extra nutrition — the antioxidant vitamins A and C.

Learn to Love Bitter Greens

Swiss chard and other dark, bitter greens like beet greens naturally contain sodium, with as much as 300 milligrams per cup (250 mL). Of course, these flavorful leaves are nutritious, containing exceedingly high levels of vitamin A and even calcium. Bitter greens are not likely the culprit for your high blood pressure. Be sure to keep greens in your diet and instead focus on eating fewer processed and fast foods.

Planning, Prepping, and Plating

The recipes in this cookbook are all designed to satisfy you as only your favorite comfort foods can — and to be absolutely healthy. But for real success, planning ahead for a week's worth of meals and snacks is highly recommended. This means choosing one day a week to write up a meal plan and grocery shop. When planning, think about how much time it will take to prep a recipe. Perhaps cutting the veggies the night before or buying precut vegetables will make your new lifestyle easier and your goals attainable. Think about the little things, as they add up to big change, such as weight loss.

Planning

Stock your pantry with healthy essentials like olive oil, canola oil, low-fat and low-salt chicken broth, olives canned in water, chunk light tuna with no added sodium, canned beans with no added salt, and whole grains like whole wheat pasta. Keep spray cans of canola oil and olive oil on hand at all times. White wine and lemon juice are other great staples for cooking and eating healthy with flavor. Olive oil, canola oil, chicken broth, wine, and lemon juice can all be great mediums for sautéing and stir-frying.

When it comes to stocking your fridge, always keep a dozen eggs on hand. Use real eggs rather than egg substitutes with food colorings and other artificial ingredients. You can use egg whites, but recognize that your blood sugar will increase more than if you had just kept the fat, specifically the yolk. The yolk does contain saturated fat, but it is also a great source of nutrition,

Stock Up: Smart Choices for Your Pantry and Fridge

Keep these regular items in your kitchen at all times so you can whip up diabetes-reversing dishes at a moment's notice.

Pantry Powerhouses

Grains

- Buckwheat
- Bulgur
- Cereals with 30 grams of carbs or less per serving and 5 grams of fiber or more per serving
- Quinoa
- Spelt
- Stone-ground oats
- Wheat berries
- Whole wheat flour
- Whole wheat pancake mix

Beans (Dry or Canned with No Added Salt)

- Black beans
- Chickpeas
- Kidney beans
- Lentils

Canned Goods (With No Added Salt or Sugar)

- Artichokes in water
- Hearts of palm in water
- Mandarin oranges
- Olives in water
- Salmon, low-sodium
- Tomatoes, chopped
- Tuna, chunk light in water, low-sodium

Nuts and Seeds (Roasted or Raw, Unsalted)

- Almonds
- Chia seeds
- Flaxseeds, ground
- Natural nut butters, such as peanut or almond butter
- Peanuts
- Pecans
- Walnuts
- Wheat germ

Herbs and Spices (No Added Salt)

- Basil
- Black pepper
- Chili powder
- Cinnamon
- Cumin
- Dillweed
- Garlic powder
- Onion powder
- Oregano
- Paprika
- Rosemary
- Sage
- Tarragon

Condiments

- Balsamic vinegar
- Chicken or vegetable broth, reduced-sodium or no-added-salt, low-fat
- Cold-pressed canola oil
- Cold-pressed olive oil
- Mustard
- Natural canola oil spray
- Natural olive oil spray

Refrigerator Regulars

Fruits

- Apples
- Avocados
- Lemons
- Limes
- Oranges

Vegetables

- Broccoli
- Carrot sticks or baby carrots
- Cauliflower
- Garlic
- Onion
- Spaghetti squash

Dairy

- 1% milk
- Hard cheeses, such as Parmesan and Romano
- Low-fat (1%) or fat-free (0%) Greek yogurt

Protein

- Fresh eggs
- Tofu (optional)

Other

- Seltzer (soda water)

especially vitamin A, and helps to regulate your blood sugar, making it worthy of eating some of the time. If you choose to use just egg whites, incorporate a healthy fat, such as avocado, into that meal to attain a mixed meal.

Keep grated Parmesan and other hard cheeses in the refrigerator. Harder cheeses are naturally lower in saturated fat and great for flavor, with the added benefits of calcium. When reading nutrition labels, you will notice that provolone is usually lower in saturated fat and calories than other cheeses, especially soft cheeses. Always read nutrition labels, even if you think you know the product. Ingredients and nutrition facts are constantly changing and are different for every brand.

Check out the chart on the facing page for a complete list of staples to keep in your pantry, fridge, and freezer.

Mix Up Your Meals

Your plate needs to have a balance of carbohydrates (especially foods high in fiber), lean proteins, and healthy fats such as canola oil, nut butters, salmon, walnuts, and ground flaxseeds. You want to eat these foods together. Because fat and protein slow the absorption of sugar into the bloodstream, eating mixed meals containing carbohydrates, proteins, and fats is the ideal way to manage blood sugar, insulin resistance, and diabetes.

Prepping

Now that you have chosen your recipes and stocked your pantry, think about cooking methods. Olive oil and canola oil are healthy oils to cook with. Use canola oil when cooking over high heat and olive oil when making dressings or using low heat. Canola oil is best for baking, as olive oil's strong flavors may overwhelm a quick bread or cookie.

The best methods for cooking vegetables are steaming or sautéing in a broth with a little bit of olive or canola oil and lots of garlic. If you sauté in broth (or white wine or lemon juice), incorporate that broth into the dish to get the full dose of vitamins. Many foods contain water-soluble vitamins that are lost in the liquid cooking method. So use this nutritious broth. You can drizzle it over the meal, serve the vegetables in it, or moisten grains with it.

If you are cooking lean proteins, baking is the best option. You can also roast, broil, or barbecue. If roasting, use a roasting rack. Also, drain off fat. Remove poultry skin and visible fat before roasting or cooking. The skin and fat add flavor but are very high in saturated fat. When broiling or barbecuing, be sure to use a lower heat/flame with some form of moisture, such as a broth, lemon juice, or marinade to prevent burning (also known as charring). The black char you see on a steak or grilled piece of chicken is carcinogenic, meaning it has cancer-causing properties. You will be able to avoid charring with the use of moisture and a lower heat.

Canola: The High-Heat Oil

Use canola oil when stir-frying or sautéing over high heat. It has a higher smoke point and will not smoke as quickly as olive oil. This means it will not become carcinogenic, since it is not burning.

Plating

Did you know something as simple as the color of your plate or the size of your glass can affect how much you consume? Dr. Brian Wansink of the Cornell Food Lab studies food psychology. The research suggests that creating color contrast on your plate helps to decrease the amount of

The Diabetes Comfort Food Diet Meal Planning Chart

Make your life easy with this weekly meal planner. Use this chart as a guide to plan out your meals for the week. You can put Xs in the box when you are planning to dine out.

		Sunday	Monday	Tuesday	Wednesday
Meals (include 45–60 g Carbs, Lean Protein, and Healthy Fat)	**Breakfast**				
	Lunch				
	Dinner				
Snacks (include 15–30 g Carbs, Lean Protein, and/or Healthy Fat)	**Snack #1 (optional)**				
	Snack #2 (optional)				
	Snack #3 (optional)				
DAILY TOTALS: Tally your servings of these four food groups for each day	**Fish Servings (2x/week)**	○	○	○	○
	Low-Fat Dairy Servings (4x/day)	○○○○	○○○○	○○○○	○○○○
	Vegetable Servings (3x/day)	○○○	○○○	○○○	○○○
	Fruit Servings (2x/day)	○○	○○	○○	○○

Thursday	Friday	Saturday	New Recipes to Try This Week (Pick 1 or 2)
			Pantry Refills
			Refrigerator Refills
◯	◯	◯	Freezer Refills
◯◯◯◯	◯◯◯◯	◯◯◯◯	
◯◯◯	◯◯◯	◯◯◯	
◯◯	◯◯	◯◯	

food you eat. This means you should use a white plate for brightly colored foods like steak with mashed sweet potatoes and green bean casserole. These foods will contrast with the white plate, and you will likely serve yourself less food and feel just as full. Using a colored plate for starchy and neutral-colored foods, like pasta and white potatoes, will create a stark contrast, helping you to decrease your intake of these of hard-to-portion foods. The reverse is true for veggies. If you want to increase your intake of vegetables, serve a salad in a green bowl so there is less contrast and you will be more likely to eat more of those leafy greens.

Dr. Wansink's research also finds that tall, thin glasses can decrease your fluid intake. For caloric beverages like wine, juice, and smoothies, this is the way to go! Conversely, use a short, wide glass for water. Most people don't get enough water, so drinking water from a short, wide glass can be a great way to help you drink more.

Plate size is another easy way to keep portions and calories under control. Dr. Wansink's study found that eating off a 10-inch (25 cm) plate helped participants eat less than those who dined off a standard 12-inch (30 cm) dinner plate. Plus, even though they ate less overall, the small-plate group didn't feel deprived.

Your Own IRS — Internal Regulation System

Another helpful hint for managing meal portions without feeling overly restricted is to use a hunger/fullness scale. This scale weighs the internal thoughts and feelings guiding your portion choices. The Diabetes Comfort Food Diet automatically curbs the grams of carbohydrates per meal. However, the lean protein and the healthy fat quantities are less specific. You can individualize your grams of protein and

fat based on your personal physical needs (whether you are male or female, how active you are, and how much weight you want to lose all play a role), allowing this to be a long-term nutrition plan.

Using your hunger level to identify the physical need for food versus emotional and behavioral eating gives you options. Eating for physical reasons, paying attention to your hunger and fullness cues, and using smart diabetes-friendly recipes from this book will leave you feeling balanced, empowered, and free. This is your path to weight loss. If you realize you are eating for emotional reasons, such as stress or even happiness, or for behavioral reasons, such as social eating or mindless eating while watching TV, you can address the "why" and choose whether to continue eating or stop until your body is physically hungry for more food.

Free Yourself

Use your IRS to prevent the deprivation and binge cycle associated with dieting and food restriction. Take this opportunity to free yourself from externally focused diets and learn to eat for fuel, and some pleasure, without causing harm to your blood sugar.

The Hunger/Fullness Scale

Truly understanding your unique levels of hunger and fullness is a very important element in developing a balanced and intuitive eating lifestyle. A person who is accustomed to eating mindfully understands the body's cues that indicate hunger and fullness or the levels in between. When adults are allowed to make choices regarding their food portions without overt restriction and guilt, they can access their internal hunger/fullness feelings for the purpose of portion control. This is called internal self-regulation. Use this scale in conjunction with the Diabetes

Internal Regulation System

This scale is subjective and may vary for each individual.

0 **You're probably feeling unsteady and woozy and possibly faint.** You are starving, sweating, and shaking. You may have skipped one or even two meals, or waited longer than 7 hours in between meals. You are now hypoglycemic, which means your blood sugar is too low.

1 **You're past hungry** — not to mention irritable, shaky, and light-headed.

2 **You're very hungry** — just short of actually feeling "starved." You needed to eat an hour ago.

3 **You really want to eat.** Your brain and stomach are telling you it is time to eat. Your last meal was 3 to 4 hours ago.

4 **You're a little bit hungry,** and your body is trying to tell you it's time for a meal. You feel your blood sugar start to drop.

5 **You feel content.** You are satisfied, physically fueled. You are not hungry but also not feeling full. You will probably need to eat in the next $1\frac{1}{2}$ hours. Your blood sugar is hopefully back in normal range or about there.

6 **You feel almost full.** One or two more bites would equal fullness. Wait 10 minutes to check in and see if you need a few more bites.

7 **You're feeling energized and sated.** Now is a good time to push your plate away or stand up from the table and recognize that your body has fueled itself. You probably won't need to eat for another 3 to 4 hours.

8 **You've passed a comfortable fullness.** You took one or two more bites. You feel a little pressure in your belly/abdomen area.

9 **You feel uncomfortable.** You're overfull and on the verge of being stuffed.

10 **You're super-uncomfortable,** with belly pain and pressure, and it feels like your stomach is stretching — think of how you usually feel after Thanksgiving dinner. You need to rest in order to digest. Your blood sugar has gone through the roof. Your vision may be blurry, you feel agitated from hyperglycemia (high blood sugar), and you are sweating.

Comfort Food Diet as a tool to empower choice and mindfulness.

The zero-to-10 IRS scale above (zero is "starving, sweating, and shaking" and 10 is "sugar shock" or "stuffed like a turkey") provides a useful guide for learning your body's signals. Although you shouldn't wait longer than 3 to 4 hours between meals, and about 2 to 3 hours for snacks, a rating of 3 or 4 on this scale will tell you for certain that it's time to eat. Stop before you feel too full, however — somewhere between 6 and 7.

Use this scale to help you determine when to eat and how food makes you feel at each meal. If you find yourself starting to eat at a 5 or 6, assess whether you may be eating for boredom or emotional reasons.

If you are always starting at a 1, notice if you finish at a 9. Use this tool to gain mindfulness and identify what foods keep you full for about 3 hours on average.

The IRS will be easier to implement when used in conjunction with the three steps for a meal makeover to beat diabetes. Ideally your color-contrasted 10-inch (25 cm) plate will have 45 to 60 grams of fiber-rich, filling carbohydrates, some lean proteins, and favored fats. Your hunger fullness scale is an additional tool to help you eat mindfully while eliminating emotional and behavioral eating. Now that you have your lunch box filled with tools and food, you can start your nutritious journey to prevent or reverse diabetes in Chapter 3.

❉ DIABETES SUCCESS STORY

KORI SMITH, 36, could never lose weight and keep it off, no matter what she tried — whether it was Body for Life, Weight Watchers, or the South Beach Diet. "I wasn't able to transfer those ways of eating into real life," Kori says. But by curbing her carbs, increasing her fiber, and favoring healthy fats, she discovered a realistic lifestyle diet that was easy to maintain.

Kori, an assistant principal at a public elementary school, was frustrated and confused when she received her diagnosis of insulin resistance. She thought her mostly vegetarian food choices were healthy: pastas, beans, tofu, and low-fat dairy. She always chose fat-free dressings for her salads, while eating lots of beans and rice for adequate vegetarian protein.

Not only was Kori following a lower-fat diet, but she had exercised consistently since high school, through college, and now as a career woman. She cheered competitively, danced, and ran one marathon, one half-marathon, and multiple 10-Ks. She continues to work out at the local gym three or four times a week, alternating between Spinning and Zumba classes. "I knew I worked really hard, but my body wasn't a physical representation of that. It was all in my stomach. I always looked bloated. I was so frustrated."

Kori's diagnosis of insulin resistance came last year, quite by surprise. She and her husband had decided to start a family, and because she was over 35, her pregnancy would be considered high risk. Her doctor, therefore, ran a battery of tests. Before she was even able to try to conceive, Kori was diagnosed with insulin resistance. Subsequently, her doctor stressed the risks of gestational diabetes and type 2 diabetes. Kori quickly cut her carbs, but she was scared and felt deprived. She thought diabetes was a sure thing for her. "Once I was told I needed to change my diet, I was more scared than anything. I really did not know what the new rules were."

After consulting with me and trying the Diabetes Comfort Food Diet recommendations, Kori turned an important corner. She learned this was not a diet of deprivation, but rather one of choices. She learned she could still go out to dinner with her husband. What really hit home for Kori was the fact that she was losing weight for the first time in her life! "After those sessions, I felt I had a road map and tools in my belt. It was more empowering than anything. Seeing the weight come off was exciting, and realizing the impact certain foods had on how I felt was eye-opening."

Many foods that Kori had thought were healthy were actually driving her carbohydrate intake way up. "I didn't realize that my favorite foods, such as fat-free dressings and even fruit, were high in carbs!" Kori had grown up eating tortillas, rice, and beans. Her grandfather was Mexican, and these carbohydrates were part of the family's culture. Even though she had given up red meat long ago, she had replaced it with low-fiber pastas and breads. Now Kori incorporates carbs that are naturally high in fiber, such as spouted whole-grain breads, whole wheat pasta, barley, and quinoa. "I just make different choices. Like when we eat out at a Mexican restaurant, I don't eat the chips on the table and I skip the rice. I still have beans, and some sort of grilled chicken or tofu. I love guacamole! At other restaurants, I choose bread or wine, and I order fish or poultry and a vegetable."

Kori was finally able to connect the dots and recognize that her body was not able to handle large loads of carbohydrates at each meal. Now, equipped with reliable nutrition knowledge and a positive outlook, she is making active steps toward preventing diabetes and losing weight. And she feels so much better. "I didn't know that changing my food would have such a dramatic effect on how I felt overall, especially my energy. There was no more after-meal bloating or stomach pain."

Not only did Kori feel suddenly energized, but she also dropped 22 pounds (10 kg) between May and July. Her clothing size shrank from a 12 to an 8. The belly bloating and belly fat were gone. And most surprising for Kori, she could breathe easier — she had never realized she had difficulty breathing until then. When she returned to her elementary school position in August, her fellow educators were as surprised as she had been. Her colleagues had not seen her during the summer break, and the changes in Kori's appearance and energy levels were quite obvious.

Using the three steps to make over any meal allowed Kori to tackle her insulin resistance easily. But the best part was yet to come — Kori became pregnant! Regulating her weight and hormones helped her to start a family and has helped prevent her from getting gestational diabetes. As of her 17-week appointment, her doctor had found no indicators of diabetes.

She is grateful for her supportive family and friends, who refrain from making any comments about her opting to skip the pre-meal bread in exchange for a grain with dinner. Because she knows she must choose between the bread basket and dessert, Kori makes her meal choices before she even walks into a restaurant. She knows her decision to reverse her insulin resistance and prevent diabetes and gestational diabetes is a very worthy choice — one that has helped her to feel better than ever, to be in the best shape of her adult life, and to finally start her family.

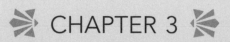

CHAPTER 3

The Plan To Defeat Diabetes

Now you understand how blood sugar control works and you know the three essential steps to make over any meal — as well as the secrets to prepping, planning, and plating. Let's approach the action plan together so that you may implement your tools for dietary change to manage blood sugar, lose weight, and achieve long-term health. In Chapter 1, we introduced START. This five-stage plan is designed to help you make the lifestyle changes needed to avert diabetes and the risks associated with long-term insulin resistance.

Flip back to page 13, reread the descriptions, and figure out where you are on your journey, whether it is Shock, Tiptoeing, Achieving, Repeating, or Time. Remember that your nutrition goals will be tailored to your present stage. To make this system as easy to follow as possible, we have designed a five-step plan that is uniquely formulated to help you balance your blood sugar, wherever you are. Recognize that some steps will naturally take longer than others; you may be beyond Shock and perhaps at the Tiptoeing stage, which may take just a few days. But if moving from one stage to the next takes 6 months, that's normal, too. Just focus on the action plans and move to the next step when you are ready.

Many readers will find they are ready to follow steps 2, 3, or even 4. The easiest way to figure out where you should start your action plan is to begin at "Step 1: Shock" and begin checking off every item on the action plan that you have accomplished. If you are missing three or more items, you must complete those exercises before moving on to the next step. Since everyone moves at his or her own rate, keep in mind that a step may take you 2 weeks or longer as you become accustomed to new routines and dietary changes. Remember: Don't rush to the next stage until you are ready. Moving too fast or skipping steps will backfire on you and make change seem harder than it really is! The goal is to achieve success through consistent behaviors that ultimately become habits.

Relapse

If you try to skip a stage, or start the next step before you have completed the previous stage, you run the risk of a "relapse" — returning to old thought patterns and behaviors that stand in the way of creating your diabetes success story.

Step 1: Shock

You are likely to identify with this stage if you have just learned you are at risk for prediabetes or have prediabetes or type 2 diabetes. Before you can start reversing your symptoms, you need time to absorb your new reality and truly consider the pros and cons of making lifestyle changes. You may find yourself looking for solutions that sound easier, like turning to medication, or wonder if you can get away with taking no action at all. Give yourself permission to feel the anger, fear, and worry that you might be trying to push to the back of your mind. Don't turn to food now. Instead, grab a journal or write your answers below to release your emotions on paper. Here are some questions to ask yourself:

1. What were my first thoughts when the doctor told me I had prediabetes or diabetes? How did I feel and how do I feel now (possibly angry, mad, sad, or scared)? Why do I feel this? How can I cope with these feelings?

_____

_____

_____

_____

_____

_____

_____

_____

2. Did I exhibit signs of high blood sugar? (Check off the signs you felt.)

- ☐ Very thirsty
- ☐ Sweaty after meals
- ☐ Blurry vision
- ☐ Sleepless
- ☐ Irritable
- ☐ Lethargic
- ☐ Other

Do I understand why I wasn't feeling well?

☐ Yes   ☐ No

If Yes, write why.
If No, refer to www.diabetes.org.

_____

_____

_____

_____

_____

_____

_____

_____

3. What was I eating before that made me feel the symptoms I checked off?

- ☐ Large portions (eating appetizers, entrées, and desserts when dining out)
- ☐ Sugary drinks (soda, smoothies)
- ☐ Fast food (hamburgers, fries)
- ☐ Restricting meals (during the day) and bingeing (during the evening)
- ☐ Skipping meals (brunch on weekends with no breakfast or lunch)
- ☐ High-carb meals without protein or fat
- ☐ Other

4. Am I ready to accept this diagnosis and make changes within the next week to the next 6 months? If yes, what changes seem possible?

_____

_____

_____

_____

_____

_____

_____

_____

5. Who will help me through this? (Identify who your support team may be. We will refer to this person as your "diabetes support person."

- ☐ Spouse
- ☐ Partner
- ☐ Parent
- ☐ Sibling
- ☐ Friend
- ☐ Other

6. What am I at risk for? (See "Calculate Your Risk" on page 10.)

_____
_____
_____
_____
_____
_____
_____
_____
_____
_____
_____

7. Identify education sources like the American Diabetes Association and magazines and books about diabetes.

_____
_____
_____
_____
_____
_____
_____
_____
_____
_____
_____

8. What are three things I can easily change to be proactive without much effort? Scheduling my next doctor's appointment? Reading this book from cover to cover? Can I ask my partner for help with the nutrition changes?

_____
_____
_____
_____
_____
_____
_____

This is the time to talk and think. There is no expectation to make immediate behavioral change. Your action plan is focused on getting in touch with your feelings, gathering education materials, starting to educate yourself, and getting inspired to make a change.

Shock Action Plan

- Identify what you are feeling and journal about these feelings to help address them. Is it denial, shock, anger, or sadness? Are you scared?

- In your journal, make a list of pros and cons about making nutrition and exercise changes. To get started, have a look at the sample list on the facing page.

- Find a support group at a local hospital or house of worship for individuals with diabetes. Consider whether a mental health counselor may be useful in your acceptance of your new diagnosis of prediabetes or diabetes. Use this as an opportunity to understand and even embrace a diagnosis that you can prevent and reverse. Self-efficacy will favorably enable you to meet your soon-to-be lifestyle goals (nutrition and physical activity behaviors).

Pros and Cons

Use this sample list to start generating your own pros and cons about committing to lifestyle changes that will prevent, reverse, or manage your diabetes.

Pros

- Managing blood sugar
- Preventing loss of vision, nerve, and kidney function
- Living longer
- Improving quality of life
- Seeing the grandkids graduate
- Improving sex life
- Increasing energy and endurance
- Positively affecting cardiovascular health
- Reducing waist size
- Buying clothes more easily
- Being free from acid reflux
- Eating all food: Recipes in this book look comforting and delicious

Cons

- Planning meals in advance
- Drinking alcohol only with meals
- Finding time to move
- Reading nutrition labels
- Eating out sounds like a disaster
- Telling friends
- Feeling overwhelmed
- Needing medicine

- Identify your support system and share with at least one person that you have diabetes.

- Observe how different foods make you feel (shaky, sweaty, energetic, tired, moody, content).

- Start to educate yourself about diabetes and the long list of complications that can arise, such as losing the ability to feel in your hands or feet. Visit www.diabetes.org for more information.

- Talk with your spouse and/or family about your diagnosis. Ask one person to attend doctor visits and diabetes education with you.

- Read Chapters 1 through 3 of this cookbook thoroughly, if you have yet to do so.

- Flip through the recipes in this cookbook. Make a mental note of a few you might like to try. Check out the sidebars to see how simple tweaking these foods for health can be!

- Think about what type of physical activity may be fun and not intimidating. Do you prefer to exercise alone or with others? Do you want to try a class at the local gym or do you prefer to be outside and move at your own pace?

- Read the stories of Rebecca (page 20), Kori (page 46), and Michael (page 64), who have successfully prevented diabetes and even lost weight. You can join them!

Step 2: Tiptoeing

After making your list of pros and cons, you have come to the conclusion that you must make changes for the better. "I need to change if I want to see my children or grandchildren graduate," you may be thinking. Or perhaps learning you may lose sensation in your extremities was convincing enough. No matter what your driving motivation, you have accepted that you will need to make dietary changes. You are feeling ready to start now, but not necessarily 100% committed to the process. You aren't even 100% sure of what your process will look like.

You are willing to try the new high-fiber cereal your spouse purchased for you. You try it with an open mind. It tastes good, and you observe yourself feeling better after eating it: no lethargy, and you stay full until lunchtime. However, the next day, the pancakes at the diner call louder than the high-fiber cereal. Or maybe you consider going to the gym for the second time since becoming a member 6 months ago. Your sore muscles prevented you from going back last time. This time, you plan to walk for 5 minutes on the treadmill and then hit the steam room for 10 minutes. By planning for a gradual start to your nutrition and fitness routine, you understand you'll be more likely to achieve your goals and continue with them.

Start Small

Small, consistent change is better than no change or one big change that is so unrealistic you cannot commit.

Tiptoeing Action Plan

- Look back at your list of cons from Step 1. Create a mini action plan that will help you turn those negatives into positives! See page 54 for some examples.

- Attend a support group if you are feeling overwhelmed or alone. If a support group doesn't feel sufficient, you may want to consider counseling. Reread individuals' success stories for beating diabetes. Think about how realistic this is for you.

- Decide which activity you will pursue and plan for one lifestyle modification, such as taking the stairs or parking your car farther from the mall. Choose a physical activity that is realistic to pursue and decide when you can start it. We suggest starting with small movement goals and working up to regular activity. (Example: Walk for 5 minutes after dinner three nights this week, and move up to 10 minutes next week.) Decide if you prefer to be active alone or would rather identify exercise buddies.

- Draw up a food log in your journal or create one on your computer. Use it twice a week. If you have a glucometer (a device to measure your blood sugar), you can add a section to log your blood sugar in mg/dl before and after meals. See pages 56–57 for a sample food log you can copy.

- Reread Chapter 2 of this book. Highlight the things you can easily do. You do not need to do all of them now, but use this as a time to recognize what changes you can easily make. Choose two or three small goals for this step — perhaps to eat whole wheat pasta and use only olive oil–based salad dressing. The three main changes you can get ready to make are based on our three meal makeover guidelines. If you feel able, choose one of these three to start pursuing (see box, opposite).

Three Meal Makeover Guidelines

1. **Curb carbs** at 45 grams per meal (if you are a woman) or 60 grams per meal (if you are a man) and determine whether you need zero, one, two, or three snacks a day (equal to 15 or 30 grams of carbs per snack depending on if you are a woman or a man). Reading food labels and identifying total grams of carbohydrates per serving in the foods you usually eat can help you to easily achieve this. Don't forget to make sure you identify how many servings you are really consuming. Food labels always provide information for one serving, but many foods have multiple servings per package.

2. **Fill up on fiber** and aim for 22 to 40 grams of total dietary fiber per day. You can achieve this goal the same way you count carbs — by reading food labels. But instead of looking at the carbohydrates, add up the dietary fiber. Remember: If your meal contains 6 or more grams of dietary fiber, you can subtract this amount of fiber from the total carbs of that meal.

3. **Favor healthy fats** such as MUFAs and omega-3 fatty acids. You can find MUFAs in olive oil, canola oil, avocados, natural peanut butter, and many varieties of nuts and seeds. Vegetarian sources of omega-3 fatty acids include chia seeds, pumpkin seeds, and walnuts. Marine sources include salmon, trout, canned chunk light tuna, and bluefish.

- Begin developing mindfulness. Become aware of why you eat, whether due to physical hunger, emotional hunger, or behavioral hunger. Discerning why you eat will help you curb your overall intake of calories and help you learn to eat only when you are truly hungry. You can make notes about your motivation for eating on your food log as well.

- Check your pantry to see what foods you have and identify which items you should remove or begin to replace. Simple ways to start include replacing white bread with whole grains and replacing vegetable oil with olive and canola oils. Also note how many grams of carbohydrates and fiber are in your cereals. Aim for brands with fewer than 30 grams of carbs but 5 or more grams of dietary fiber.

- Go food shopping with your spouse or diabetes support person. Stroll the aisles to see if there are new-to-you naturally high-fiber products like stone-ground wheat bread or cocoa-powdered almonds that you may want to try. Buy two or three new products to try.

- If you don't already have them at home, buy new dinner plates and glassware. Six 10-inch (25 cm) white plates and six 10-inch (25 cm) colored plates will be enough, plus a set of tall, thin glasses (for caloric beverages) and short, wide glasses (for water).

- Identify foods that might raise your blood sugar. Are you willing to modify certain ingredients, cooking techniques, or portion sizes to lessen the impact?

New Tools

Some new kitchen utensils or cooking tools might help inspire you as you commit to making dietary changes. Here are some of our favorite kitchen essentials:

- Chef's knife
- Cutting board
- Can opener
- Garlic press
- Nonstick skillet
- Spatula
- Vegetable peeler
- Vegetable scrubber
- Whisk

Convert Your Cons into Pros

Con #1: *Planning Meals in Advance —> Pro:*

- This is an excuse to try new recipes.
- You get to enjoy comfort food without the guilt — or the blood sugar spikes.
- You always know what you're eating.

Take Action: Spend 1 hour on Sunday planning meals with your diabetes support person; choose two recipes from this book to try.

Con #2: *Drinking Alcohol Only with Meals —> Pro:*

- You can still enjoy a glass of beer or wine.
- When socializing, you don't have to feel like a stick-in-the-mud.

Take Action: Schedule "Sunday football beers" after a 10-minute walk at lunchtime; perhaps walk to the local bar in town, eat lunch, and enjoy a beer while watching football with friends.

Con #3: *Finding Time to Move —> Pro:*

- You will start to feel energized.
- You may increase your muscle mass and will likely whittle your waistline.
- You get built-in time for yourself.
- You'll help your heart.
- You'll become a positive role model for your family.

Take Action: Start with 5-minute walks twice a week wearing your day clothes. Take the stairs at work. Research the cost of a gym membership or a personal trainer. Buy walking sneakers and consider a heart rate monitor.

Con #4: Reading Nutrition Labels —> Pro:

- You'll become nutrition-savvy.
- Soon you'll know what products are not only healthy but taste good. You can use the cheat sheets from this book!
- Even if you buy the wrong product, with the help of this book you know all foods fit, so you can still work them into your diet.

Take Action: Start by comparing the labels of pasta at the grocery store and choose the pasta with the most fiber. Make a note to compare carbs, fiber, and saturated fat on labels in the future.

Con #5: Eating Out Sounds like a Disaster —> Pro:

- You can still dine out — many restaurants have diabetes-friendly options or can tailor menu items to your order.
- You can still have dessert and alcohol and enjoy your favorite foods in moderation.

Take Action: Go online to read the nutrition facts of your favorite meals at local restaurants (most chains make this available). Figure out how to make your meal fall into the range of 45 to 60 grams of carbohydrates.

Con #6: Telling Friends —> Pro:

- You can tell others in your own time. Since you can still eat all foods, you won't automatically "out" yourself when dining with friends.
- You don't need to tell everyone, but we encourage you to confide in at least one person.
- If you decide to share with more people, you may find others who are also managing diabetes and you may have a greater support network.

Take Action: Expand your support network by sharing your diagnosis with your good friends with whom you dine out. Decrease triggers by requesting that bread not be served at the table so you can save your carbs for later, or order wine by the glass rather than the bottle.

Con #7: Feeling Overwhelmed —> Pro:

- Using START and the many tools in this cookbook will make managing blood sugar easy — one step at a time.
- You will feel and look better.
- You can reverse prediabetes and prevent insulin resistance from progressing.

Take Action: Photocopy "The Lean Protein and Favored Fat Cheat Sheet" (page 37) and take it to the grocery store with you. Spend time talking with your support person.

The Diabetes Comfort Food Diet Log

Use this sample as a guide in logging your food and exercise. You can customize it with the number of snacks you eat and columns to track your blood glucose numbers if you have a glucometer. Be sure to note the time and location of your meals, how hungry you felt before and after eating, and your motivation for eating (was it physical hunger [P], emotional eating [E], or a behavioral response [B]?). There are also columns to note what you ate, how many grams of carbs and fiber those meals included, and whether there were healthy fats such as MUFAs

Today's date	Time and Location	Hunger Scale Rating (0–10) (page 45) BEFORE / AFTER		Why Are You Eating? (P, E, B)	Foods/Calories Eaten
Breakfast					
Snack #1 (optional)					
Lunch					
Snack #2 (optional)					
Dinner					
Snack #3 (optional)					
DAILY TOTALS:	Calories_____ Carbs_____g Fiber_____g				
DAILY EXERCISE:					

and omega-3 fatty acids in your meals. Near the bottom, there is a place to tally up your daily total calories, carbs, fiber, protein, fat, and sodium intake. For blood sugar control, you'll absolutely want to track calories, carbs, and fiber — but the rest is optional and may be helpful if you are also tracking a weight-loss goal. Finally, at the bottom, you'll see a place to note your daily movement. Whether it is a 5-minute walk or a Pilates class, be sure to note the time and location, since you may see a correlation between your activity and your blood glucose numbers.

Carbs (g)	Fiber (g)	Did You Include Healthy Fats (g)?	Pre-Meal Blood Glucose (optional)	2-Hour Post-Meal Blood Glucose (optional)

Protein_____g   Fat_____g   Sodium_____mg

Step 3: Achieving

You are committing yourself to change. You accept your diagnosis of prediabetes or type 2 diabetes. You feel empowered and know the new foods and recipes you've tried were not only edible, but also delicious. You realize that walking two times a week for 5 minutes is not only doable, but you want to move even more. You are taking advantage of your support system and you are ready to start curbing carbs when dining out. You are getting used to drinking water, seltzer (soda water) and natural beverage options. It's easier to replace the salt shaker with your own herbal mix to flavor your food (consider mixing oregano, basil, garlic, and lemon peel). Health, longevity, and a higher quality of life now seem attainable.

Achieving Action Plan

- Talk to your doctor and consider getting a glucometer to see how food and exercise affect your blood sugar. This can be a turning point for some people. The glucometer measures your blood sugar in mg/dl. When you are ready, take your blood sugar immediately before eating and 2 hours after. Notice how each food and the combination of foods, especially mixed meals, affect your blood sugar and your mood.

- Curb carbs at 45 or 60 grams per meal. If you require one or more snacks per day, prepare some snacks with either 15 or 30 grams of carbs and carry them with you. See page 60 for "20 Grab-and-Go Snacks."

Combat Mindless Eating

During this step, you should focus on becoming more aware of the habits that undermine your dieting success. Through journaling over the past two steps, you are becoming more mindful of your old, counterproductive habits and able to recognize when you eat for emotional and behavioral reasons instead of physical hunger. Design an action plan to combat mindless eating or even binge eating. This list of alternatives will protect you from sabotaging your healthy efforts and can even help to improve social bonds or channel your energy to be productive. Below is a sample action plan to guide you in creating your own.

1. Journal your feelings.
2. Get out of the house and walk to decrease anxiety.
3. Distract yourself by engaging in a hobby, such as playing games, listening to music, or going for a run.
4. Call a friend.
5. Tap into a creative outlet such as painting, drawing, knitting, or woodworking.

- Fill up on fiber and aim for 22 to 40 grams of total dietary fiber per day. Remember: If your meal contains 6 or more grams of dietary fiber, you can subtract this amount of fiber from the total carbs of that meal. Increase your fiber consumption slowly, as too much fiber too quickly can cause constipation and gas. Increase your water consumption when increasing fiber to prevent constipation. Add one glass more per day than usual.

- Favor healthy fats such as MUFAs and omega-3 fatty acids. Cut down on your saturated fat intake by eating lean protein and low-fat dairy and limiting fried foods. Use your IRS (internal regulation system) to aid in portion control of proteins and fats. Include fish two times a week.

- Replace soda, energy drinks, and other high-calorie beverages with seltzer (soda water) and water.

- Rehab your pantry and refrigerator. Toss out or donate the rest of the tempting carb- and sugar-laden foods like cookies, crackers, and chips that are hard to portion. Stock up on eggs, hard cheeses, and fat-free (0%) Greek yogurt (plain or fruit-flavored). Fill your cupboard and fridge with the suggestions on page 40.

- Plan a full week's worth of meals and snacks at the start of each week (see our sample meal plans in Appendix A on page 286). Follow it up with food shopping and any other prepping that will make cooking during the week quicker and easier. Refill any needed pantry essentials, such as cinnamon, canola oil spray, and canned tuna.

- Plan to eat breakfast at home. You can dine out for lunch one or two times a week and pack your lunch the rest of the week. Prepare dinners 5 days a week and dine out a maximum of two times a week.

- Keep a food log for 3 to 7 days per week. Include your food, feelings, hunger/fullness ratings before and after meals, and your blood sugar, if you have a glucometer.

- Walk or move for 10 minutes per day, three times per week. Increase by 5 minutes per workout every week until you achieve 30 minutes of walking or physical activity per day. Each week, add 1 additional day of movement until you have achieved 90 to 150 minutes of movement a day.

- Schedule a doctor's visit 3 months from the day you started making nutrition changes to check your A1C.

- Plan a healthy potluck party and invite your guests.

- If you decide to weigh yourself, weigh one time a week or less and monitor for a trend. The goal is 7% weight loss. Be sure to weigh yourself at the same time every time: in the morning, after going to the bathroom and before breakfast. We recommend weighing every Wednesday.

- If mindless munching is a problem you struggle with, carry an action plan in your wallet to prevent yourself from eating for nonphysical reasons. See the sample on the facing page.

- Use your new dishes and glasses regularly. Eat colorful foods from the white plates and eat white and beige foods from the colorful plates. Drink water from short, wide glasses and drink caloric beverages from tall, narrow glasses.

20 Grab-and-Go Snacks

These snacks are great to pack if you're going to be away from home. Make a copy of this list and keep it close by for a quick and easy reference.

For Women (~15 Grams of Carbohydrates)

- 6 oz (175 g) Greek yogurt, fat-free (0%), fruit-flavored
- 6 oz (175 g) Greek yogurt, fat-free (0%), plain, topped with one small cookie
- One mini cheese round and 1 cup (250 mL) berries
- One 1-oz (30 g) part-skim cheese stick and 1 small apple
- One higher-fiber, lower-carb, higher-protein bar (~5 grams fiber, 15 grams carbs, 7 to 14 grams protein)
- 10 to 23 almonds and ½ large orange
- 2 tsp (10 mL) natural nut butter and 1 small banana
- 4 oz (125 g) low-sodium, low-fat (1%) cottage cheese and ¾ cup (175 mL) chopped fresh pineapple
- 10 to 15 olives and 5 high-fiber crackers (size of a Wheat Thin, 1 oz/30 g total)
- 2 tbsp (30 mL) guacamole and half of a 6-inch (15 cm) toasted whole wheat pita

For Men (~30 Grams of Carbohydrates)

- 6 oz (175 g) Greek yogurt, fat-free (0%), fruit-flavored, mixed with ½ cup (125 mL) berries and 1 tbsp (15 mL) wheat germ
- 6 oz (175 g) Greek yogurt, fat free (0%), plain, with 1 small apple and ½ cup (125 mL) berries
- 1 to 2 oz (30 to 60 g) hard cheese, 15 grapes, and 1 slice sprouted whole wheat toast
- 8 oz (250 mL) unsweetened soy or sunflower milk with a 1½-oz (45 g) mini cupcake (sometimes)
- 15 to 25 almonds with 1 large orange
- 2 tsp (10 mL) natural nut butter and 1 large banana
- ¼ cup (60 mL) hummus, 1 cup (250 mL) carrot sticks, and one 6-inch (15 cm) toasted whole wheat or spelt pita
- ¼ cup (60 mL) hummus and 20 to 25 whole-grain pretzels (1½ oz/45 g total)
- One granola bar (6 grams fiber, 25 to 28 grams carbs, 10 to 14 grams protein or healthy fats)
- ¼ cup (60 mL) guacamole with 10 to 15 low-sodium baked tortilla chips (1½ oz/45 g total) and 1 cup (250 mL) carrot sticks for dipping

Step 4: Repeating

You are now a "doer." You are implementing your new behaviors. You are action-oriented. This is one of the busiest stages, when you are incorporating the new behaviors encouraged in these chapters, such as food shopping, prepping, cooking, and eating. You are curbing carbs, increasing fiber, and choosing healthy fats. This is where you start to see results. The process starts to feel effortless and automatic.

By now, you are probably feeling pretty good! You likely have more energy, have even moods throughout the day, and are opening up your palate to a world of exciting new foods. You have learned that eating out is manageable — and that there's room for dessert! The Diabetes Comfort Food Diet is now a lifestyle. This is your present and your future. You may or may not have lost weight. Even if you have not lost weight, your after-meal blood sugars are decreasing! There are no ups and downs or constant highs when you test your blood sugar. If you don't test, don't worry. You can feel the difference in your blood sugar as evidenced by better moods, sleeping through the night, increased energy and productivity at work, and lessening of other symptoms that bothered you before you got your blood sugar under control. By your next blood test, don't be surprised if your A1C has decreased to less than 5.7 — meaning you no longer have prediabetes. If you already have diabetes, your A1C has probably decreased since your last appointment and you are likely managing your blood sugar to less than 140 to 160 mg/dl 2 hours after meals or even better.

New Habits

Curbing carbs, filling up on fiber, and favoring healthy fats is your prescription for inner and outer well-being. The foods you eat, the portions you choose, and your new body awareness are all habits now. These habits are relatively new and still need to be reinforced by continuing to reduce temptations and triggers.

Repeating Action Plan

- Plan a full week's worth of meals and snacks at the start of each week (if you need inspiration, see our sample meal plans on page 286). Follow it up with food shopping and any other prepping that will make cooking during the week quicker and easier. Refill any needed pantry essentials, such as cinnamon, canola oil spray, and canned tuna.

- Keep a food log for 3 to 5 days per week. Include your food, feelings, hunger/fullness ratings before and after meals, and your blood sugar, if you have a glucometer.

- If you are keeping track of your weight, weigh in weekly. Remember to weigh yourself at the same time every day, in the morning, after going to the bathroom and before breakfast.

- If mindless munching is a problem you struggle with, carry an action plan in your wallet to prevent yourself from eating for nonphysical reasons.

- Prepare some snacks designed to have either 15 or 30 grams of carbs and carry them along with you.

- Use your IRS (internal regulation system) to aid in portion control of proteins and fats.

- Gather friends and host healthy potluck parties. Host the first one this Saturday night to set the tone. Impress your guests with the recipes from this book.

20 Ways to Reinforce the Diabetes Comfort Food Diet

1. Meet friends for exercise, not food.

2. Host a healthy dinner party weekly or monthly.

3. Make your carbohydrate choice *before* going to restaurants.

4. Eat 45 to 60 grams of carbohydrates at each meal, three times a day.

5. Continue to use the magic carb solution. If your meal totals more than 6 grams of fiber, subtract the total grams of fiber from total grams of carbohydrates to get your magic number at each meal.

6. Do not skip meals.

7. Recognize if you need snacks and plan accordingly.

8. Food shop at markets that offer wholesome foods, such as a farmers' market or local health food store.

9. Include healthy fats (such as avocado and olive oil) daily.

10. Eat fish two or more times a week. Select a different type of fish each week to minimize exposure to mercury and PCBs.

11. Purchase food items with less than 2 grams of saturated fat and 0 grams of trans fat per serving.

12. Use coping skills rather than emotional eating.

13. Plan ahead when you want to include sweets or refined carbohydrates. There is no cheating on the Diabetes Comfort Food Diet — all you have to do is make trade-offs and be careful about your timing.

14. If you have been tracking your blood sugar with a glucometer, continue using it to gauge your response to various foods and activities as needed.

15. Remember, small changes are better than no changes, and small steps are better than no steps. If you can't get to the food store or the gym, look at this as an opportunity rather than a failure. You can choose a takeout food that meets your grams of carbohydrates, and you can break your 30 minutes of physical activity into three 10-minute increments — or just exercise on a different day.

16. Try at least one new recipe from *The Diabetes Comfort Food Diet* per week for variety and adequate nutrition.

17. Continue eating all breakfasts at home, and dine out one or two times a week each for lunch and dinner.

18. Continue moving for 90 to 150 minutes a week, doing activities you love.

19. Continue to use "The Lean Protein and Favored Fat Cheat Sheet" (page 37) when grocery shopping.

20. Stay in touch with how you are feeling. If you've been maintaining a food log and feel that your new behaviors are now habits, you can choose to log less often.

Step 5: Time

This is your maintenance phase. You have made your lifestyle changes, and they are now healthy habits. You can declare maintenance after you have implemented your new behaviors for more than 6 months or up to 1 year. Following the Diabetes Comfort Food Diet has become your way of life. You love the foods you choose and feel proud knowing you have defeated diabetes by curbing carbs, filling up on fiber, and favoring the right fats to ultimately manage your blood sugar. Money is spent on food and fitness (and maybe new clothes in smaller sizes!) rather than over-the-counter gastrointestinal medicines, prescriptions, and junk food.

The "20 Ways to Reinforce the Diabetes Comfort Food Diet" (opposite) have become second nature. Choosing to eat 45 grams of cake for dessert and forgoing a carbohydrate with the main meal is easy and enjoyable for you. You realize this diet is about making choices, not about deprivation. You feel empowered, successful, and beautiful. Diabetes no longer scares you. Going forward, you have this book for support and a constant reminder of what you can do rather than what you can't do.

Seven Guidelines for Maintaining the Diabetes Comfort Food Diet

1. Curb carbs at 45 grams per meal three times a day for women or 60 grams for men. Enjoy up to three snacks of 15 grams of carbs per day for women or 30 grams for men.

2. Fill up on fiber by choosing whole grains, legumes, vegetables, fruits, and even whole nuts and seeds.

3. Favor healthy fats found in nuts, seeds, oils, deep-sea fish, and other sources.

4. Continue to increase physical activity until you are moving for 30 minutes per day, 5 days per week.

5. If you have met a goal of losing 7% of your weight, your new goal is to keep off 5%. (If you haven't lost weight, don't worry as long as your blood glucose is normalized.)

6. Continue to use your IRS (internal regulation system) to aid in portion control of proteins and fats.

7. Continue regular doctor visits to monitor your A1C, fasting plasma glucose, and other markers for diabetes.

✳ DIABETES SUCCESS STORY

AT AGE 59, Michael Sears* was shocked to learn he had prediabetes. In fact, with a fasting glucose of 124 mg/dl and an A1C of 6.4, he was bordering on a clinical diagnosis of diabetes.

"I knew I had a genetic predisposition to diabetes, but I did not think I would be facing diabetes or even prediabetes in my late fifties," he says. "My father has type 2 diabetes, but he is eighty-nine years old."

When Michael first visited my office in May of 2012, I, too, was quite shocked by his diagnosis. He was a rather tall and thin man, though he did hold extra weight in his midsection, well disguised by his dress shirt, and had very little muscle, as he had started exercising only recently.

Michael's troubles started about 7 years ago, when he was diagnosed with high cholesterol. As an engineer, he would often work long hours under consistently high levels of stress. Finding time for exercise was hard enough, but eating regularly was even harder. He was skipping breakfast and eating lunch at his desk — if he was even lucky enough to find the time to eat lunch. When he wasn't traveling for work, Michael would eat dinner with his wife and teenage daughters, but dinner was usually late, around 8 p.m., and consisted of starchy dishes like pasta with sauce or chicken with white rice and vegetables.

Once he received his cholesterol diagnosis, Michael made diet changes, including decreasing red meat and butter. He was also put on cholesterol medication. While being treated for high cholesterol, he was also diagnosed with high blood pressure. In addition to putting him on blood pressure medication, Michael's doctor advised him to lose weight and to exercise. In "type A" fashion, Michael did as his doctor recommended. He joined a gym next to his office and hired a personal trainer for two weekly sessions of weight training. He was seeing his doctor every 4 months to keep an eye on his blood pressure, when the doctor gave him more bad news — a diagnosis of prediabetes.

Michael was surprised and saddened, having thought he was doing everything right. He had been exercising twice a week for the past year and had even lost 11 pounds (5 kg). However, he realized he still didn't feel "normal" — having mental fogginess, sleeping poorly, and making frequent trips to the bathroom at night. Plus, he experienced daily fatigue.

It was at this point that Michael came to see me. During his first nutrition session, he realized he was doing all the wrong things with his carbs. Rather than curbing carbs, he had mistakenly been increasing them by drinking fat-free smoothies and bingeing on fruit for nighttime snacks. With the tenets of the Diabetes Comfort Food Diet in hand, Michael left the nutrition session feeling ready to reverse prediabetes — and he has been quite successful! Over the course of about 6 months, he lost 5 more pounds (2.3 kg) and his blood sugar has really improved. His A1C gradually dropped from 6.4 in May 2012 to 6.0 in December of 2012. He is finally sleeping through the night, feels more energized during the day, and eats breakfast every morning.

The easiest part of his new lifestyle was learning to incorporate three meals and three snacks daily. He has maintained this routine since his first day of dietary changes. He says this is especially easy at the office, where he keeps granola bars in his desk drawer for daily snacks. A typical day's meals may include a fat-free Greek yogurt with a piece of fruit for breakfast, a granola bar for a morning snack, a turkey sandwich on whole wheat bread and another piece of fruit for lunch, nuts or another bar for the afternoon snack, and then wild rice, veggies, and a lean protein such as fish or chicken for dinner. And he still enjoys a cookie every day as part of his carbohydrate intake.

Michael's greatest challenge has been curbing carbs on evenings and weekends, which often involve dining at restaurants and socializing with family and friends. The lack of structure throws his meal pattern off. Plus, since he and his family get home late, Michael is hungry and usually eats his dinner carbohydrates before dinner is even served. Many nights he just eats pasta for dinner, as it is easy and fast. Another challenge is adding in more exercise. He already does weight training twice a week and has added in one weekly run. Though this already meets the 150-minute exercise recommendation, he needs to increase his cardio routine — especially if he wants to lose more weight.

During Michael's most recent nutrition appointment, he set new goals to overcome some of his daily challenges.

1. **Vary afternoon snacks and incorporate a protein and a fat.** For example: ¼ cup (60 mL) hummus with 5 stone-ground whole wheat crackers (1 oz/30 g) and 1 cup (250 mL) carrots or 1 to 2 tablespoons (15 to 30 mL) natural, salt-free peanut butter on 2 pieces of sprouted grain bread.

2. **Eat mixed meals, especially at dinner.** Make grilled chicken breasts ahead of time on Sunday to add to dinners later in the week that are typically just carbs, such as pasta.

3. **Increase fiber.** Include carrots in the afternoon snack and change to whole wheat pasta or sprouted wheat pasta.

4. **Increase cardio to twice a week.** Change gym memberships to allow exercise near home on the weekends and add one Spinning class per weekend in addition to one weekly run.

5. **Skip the entrée carbohydrate when dining at restaurants on weekends.** By avoiding the baked potato with his steak, he'll leave the 60 grams of carbohydrate for a dessert choice after his meal.

Michael has made many changes and continues to make many more. He is happy to share that not only has his overall blood sugar improved, but his clothes fit better and he has dropped a pants size from 38 to 36. His wife notices his more muscular physique, and his whole family says that he just looks better.

"I am feeling better," he says. "I have a better mood, greater stamina, and I am less tired."

* A pseudonym has been used at the request of the client.

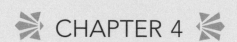

CHAPTER 4

Breakfast

Grilled Steak and Eggs 68

Salmon Breakfast Burrito 69

Cheesy Scrambled Eggs and Ham 70

Apple, Sausage, and Potato Casserole 71

Good Morning "Grits" 72

Country-Style Hash Browns 73

Zucchini and Sweet Potato Latkes 74

Tex-Mex Breakfast Pizza 75

Homemade Breakfast Sausage 76

PB&J Stuffed French Toast 77

Chocolate-Banana-Stuffed French Toast 78

Spiced Apple Pancakes 79

Belgian Waffles 80

Raspberry-Lemon Muffins 81

Lox-Cheddar Scones 82

Sunrise Oatmeal 83

Hearty Fruit and Nut Granola 84

Peach-Blueberry Yogurt Parfait 85

Sundae Breakfast Smoothie 86

Chocolate Cake Smoothie 87

Grilled Steak and Eggs

 Makes 4 servings

Prep time: 5 minutes • Total time: 25 minutes

Curb carbs: This dish is naturally low in carbs, so be sure to add some black beans and rice or a whole-grain tortilla with 20 to 25 grams of carbs.

Fill up on fiber: The fiber in this recipe must come from your black beans or your whole-grain wrap. You can get fiber only from carbohydrates, so put aside guilt and meet your 45 to 60 grams of carbs per meal.

Favor fats: Canola oil is a great source of both healthy fats, omega-3s, and MUFAs. You can add 2 tablespoons (30 mL) of avocado to each serving for even more MUFA power.

- Grill pan

2 tbsp	Worcestershire sauce	30 mL
½ tsp	paprika	2 mL
¼ tsp	salt-free onion powder	1 mL
¼ tsp	ground black pepper	1 mL
8 oz	boneless beef sirloin steak	250 g
2 tbsp + 2 tsp	canola oil, divided	40 mL
16 cups	fresh spinach (about 1 lb/500 g)	4 L
4	large eggs	4

1. In a small bowl, combine the Worcestershire sauce, paprika, onion powder, and pepper. Rub the mixture onto the steak.

2. In grill pan, heat 1 tsp (5 mL) oil over medium-high heat. Grill the steak for 6 minutes, turning once, or until a thermometer inserted in the center registers 145°F (63°C) for medium-rare. Let the steak rest for 10 minutes before slicing.

3. In a large skillet, heat 2 tbsp (30 mL) oil over low heat. Add spinach and cook, stirring, for 1 minute, or until it begins to wilt. Divide the spinach among 4 plates.

4. Heat the remaining oil in the skillet over medium-low heat. Crack the eggs into the skillet. Cook for 3 minutes, or until the egg whites are set. Serve with soft yolks, or cover and cook for 2 minutes, or until the yolks are cooked through.

5. Place the egg on top of the spinach and serve with the sliced steak.

Makeover Magic

Before		After
318	Calories	226
20 g	Fat	16 g
7 g	Sat Fat	3 g
3 g	Carbs	5 g
1 g	Fiber	2 g
31 g	Protein	17 g
596 mg	Sodium	232 mg

Salmon Breakfast Burrito

 Makes 4 servings

Curb carbs: Choosing 8-inch (20 cm) whole wheat tortillas instead of a standard 10-inch (25 cm) white flour equivalent helps to curb carbs and balance your blood sugar.

Fill up on fiber: The whole wheat tortilla and spinach add fiber to keep you full.

Favor healthy fats: Salmon is one of the best sources of DHA, the marine form of omega-3 fatty acids.

Say Cheese

Cheese is a great source of protein, calcium, and vitamin D. The fat in cheese also helps to slow the breakdown of your breakfast meal and therefore aids in blood sugar balance.

4	large eggs	4
1/3 cup	1% milk	75 mL
1 cup	spinach leaves, chopped	250 mL
4	green onions, sliced	4
	Nonstick cooking spray	
4	8-inch (20 cm) fat-free whole wheat tortillas	4
8 oz	skinless wild salmon fillet, cooked and flaked into pieces	250 g
1/4 cup	crumbled feta cheese	60 mL
1 tsp	chopped fresh dill (or 1/3 tsp/1.5 mL dried)	5 mL

1. In a large bowl, whisk together the eggs, milk, spinach, and green onions.

2. Coat a nonstick skillet with cooking spray and heat over medium heat. Cook the egg mixture, stirring, for 2 minutes, or until scrambled and set.

3. Fill the tortillas with the eggs and salmon, dividing equally. Sprinkle with the cheese and dill. Fold the outer edges in and roll up.

Makeover Magic		
Before		**After**
840	Calories	322
39 g	Fat	12 g
13 g	Sat Fat	4 g
63 g	Carbs	29 g
5 g	Fiber	4 g
59 g	Protein	24 g
1,205 mg	Sodium	574 mg

Cheesy Scrambled Eggs and Ham

 Makes 4 servings

Curb carbs: This breakfast is naturally low in carbohydrates, so go ahead and add a naturally wholesome slice or two of sprouted wheat bread.

Fill up on fiber: Green peppers and tomatoes are a great source of vitamin C and do add a bit of fiber. For the real fiber fill-up, be sure to accompany this yummy breakfast with your toast — ideally 3 grams of fiber per slice.

Favor healthy fats: The canola oil in this recipe is a great source of monounsaturated fat, but since there is only a small amount, you can add 1 to 2 tablespoons (15 to 30 mL) of avocado to each serving to maximize MUFAs.

4	large eggs	4
8	large egg whites	8
1 tsp	canola oil	5 mL
4	slices (4 oz/125 g) low-sodium nitrate-free deli-style ham, cubed	4
1	green bell pepper, finely chopped	1
½ cup	cherry tomatoes, chopped	125 mL
¼ cup	shredded Cheddar cheese	60 mL
½ tsp	ground black pepper (optional)	2 mL

1. In a large bowl, whisk together the eggs and egg whites.

2. In a large nonstick skillet, heat the oil over medium heat. Cook the ham, bell pepper, and tomatoes, stirring, for 2 minutes, or until the pepper pieces soften.

3. Add the eggs. Cook, stirring, for 2 minutes, or until the eggs are almost set. Stir in the cheese and black pepper (if using) and heat until set.

Makeover Magic		
Before		**After**
383	Calories	178
33 g	Fat	9 g
17 g	Sat Fat	3 g
3 g	Carbs	4 g
1 g	Fiber	1 g
20 g	Protein	20 g
594 mg	Sodium	447 mg

Apple, Sausage, and Potato Casserole

 Makes 6 servings

Curb carbs: Substituting potatoes for the more typical biscuits in this dish reduces the carbs by 4 grams.

Fill up on fiber: The apples, onion, and potato skins all add fiber to this dish.

Favor healthy fats: By combining whole eggs with egg whites, we can reduce the amount of saturated fat in this recipe.

Makeover Magic		
Before		**After**
340	Calories	283
19 g	Fat	8 g
8 g	Sat Fat	3 g
39 g	Carbs	35 g
1 g	Fiber	5 g
15 g	Protein	21 g
590 mg	Sodium	203 mg

Prep time: 15 minutes • Total time: 1 hour, 15 minutes + cooling time

* Preheat oven to 375°F (190°C)
* 8-cup (2 L) glass baking dish, sprayed with nonstick cooking spray

4	apples, coarsely chopped	4
	Nonstick cooking spray	
6	Homemade Breakfast Sausage patties (page 76), crumbled	6
2	red-skinned potatoes, cubed and steamed	2
1	onion, chopped	1
6 tbsp	shredded reduced-fat mild Cheddar cheese	90 mL
2 cups	1% milk	500 mL
4	large eggs	4
4	large egg whites	4
½ tsp	dry mustard	2 mL
¼ tsp	ground black pepper	1 mL

1. Place the apples in a microwaveable bowl and cover. Microwave on High for 3 minutes. Uncover to cool.

2. In a medium nonstick skillet coated with cooking spray over medium-low heat, cook the sausage, stirring, for 2 minutes, or until browned and cooked through.

3. Scatter the apples, sausage, potatoes, onion, and cheese in the bottom of the prepared baking dish.

4. In a large bowl, whisk together the milk, eggs, egg whites, mustard, and pepper. Pour over the apple mixture in the baking dish.

5. Bake in preheated oven for 50 minutes, or until a knife inserted in the center comes out clean. Let stand for 15 minutes and serve hot or warm.

Smart Start

Add salmon to this recipe for a source of omega-3 fatty acids.

Good Morning "Grits"

 Makes 1 serving

Curb carbs: Fresh fruit adds bulk and flavor to these "grits" without the added quantity of sugar that dried fruit, such as raisins, usually provides.

Fill up on fiber: While quinoa is higher in carbs than traditional grits, it's also higher in fiber and protein!

Favor healthy fats: For a boost of omega-3s, sprinkle in some walnuts!

3 tbsp	quinoa, rinsed	45 mL
¾ cup	water	175 mL
¼ cup	blackberries	60 mL
¼ tsp	ground cinnamon	1 mL

1. Combine the quinoa and water in a medium microwaveable bowl. Cover with vented plastic wrap or a loose lid and microwave on High for 3 minutes, stirring halfway through cooking. Microwave on Medium (50%) power for 4 minutes, or until the quinoa grains are tender.

2. Sprinkle with the berries and cinnamon.

Makeover Magic		
Before		**After**
370	Calories	134
22 g	Fat	2 g
13 g	Sat Fat	0 g
33 g	Carbs	24 g
1 g	Fiber	4 g
11 g	Protein	5 g
580 mg	Sodium	588 mg

Country-Style Hash Browns

Prep time: 10 minutes • Total time: 45 minutes

Curb carbs: We added onions and peppers to our potatoes, creating a carbohydrate-friendly, portion-perfect side dish for Cheesy Scrambled Eggs and Ham (page 70) or another breakfast dish.

Fill up on fiber: The key to upping fiber in this recipe is to leave the vitamin-packed skins on the potatoes. Add extra bell peppers and onions for even more fiber and vitamins.

Favor healthy fats: Olive oil and ground flaxseeds provide diabetes- and heart-friendly fat, while removing sausage and cheese cuts down on saturated fat.

1 lb	Yukon gold potatoes, cut into ¾-inch (2 cm) cubes	500 g
	Nonstick cooking spray	
1	small onion, finely chopped	1
1	green bell pepper, finely chopped	1
2 tsp	olive oil	10 mL
2 tsp	chopped fresh rosemary (or ⅔ tsp/3 mL dried)	10 mL
⅛ tsp	ground black pepper	0.5 mL
⅛ tsp	cayenne pepper	0.5 mL
4 tsp	ground flaxseeds (optional)	20 mL

1. Place the potatoes in a large saucepan. Cover with cold water and bring to a boil over high heat. Reduce the heat to medium and simmer for 15 minutes, or until just tender when tested with a sharp knife. Drain.

2. Coat a large nonstick skillet with cooking spray and place over medium heat. Cook the onion and bell pepper, stirring occasionally, for 5 minutes, or until softened.

3. Add the oil, rosemary, black pepper, cayenne, flaxseeds (if using), and the cooked potatoes. Mix well, cover, and cook for 8 minutes, or until the underside is crispy and golden brown. Using a wide spatula, turn the potatoes over. Cover and cook for another 8 minutes, or until the potatoes are golden brown. (For extra-crispy hash browns, cook for an additional 5 to 10 minutes, turning the potatoes occasionally.)

Makeover Magic		
Before		**After**
347	Calories	121
39 g	Fat	3 g
13 g	Sat Fat	0.5 g
28 g	Carbs	23 g
1 g	Fiber	3 g
19 g	Protein	3 g
1,257 mg	Sodium	9 mg

Zucchini and Sweet Potato Latkes

 Makes 6 servings

Prep time: 10 minutes • Total time: 25 minutes

Curb carbs: Sweet potatoes are nutrient-packed carbs that you want to include in your diet. Accompany your pancakes with a filling side of Greek yogurt rather than sour cream and applesauce. This really keeps carbs curbed and you happily full.

Fill up on fiber: The skins on the sweet potatoes are great forms of fiber.

Favor healthy fats: Eliminating butter lowers saturated fat and calories for weight reduction. Favoring canola oil and walnuts gives you a dose of the omega-3 fatty acid ALA.

1	small zucchini, shredded	1
1	small onion, finely chopped	1
2	medium sweet potatoes, shredded	1
2 tbsp	whole wheat pastry flour	30 mL
2	large eggs, lightly beaten	2
1½ tbsp	canola oil, divided	22 mL
1 tsp	ground cinnamon	5 mL
	Vanilla or plain nonfat (0%) Greek yogurt	
2 tbsp	chopped walnuts	30 mL

1. In a large bowl, toss the zucchini, onion, potatoes, and flour to combine. Add the eggs to the mixture and stir gently until combined.

2. In a large skillet, heat 1 tsp (5 mL) oil over medium-high heat. Working in batches, spoon ¼ cup (60 mL) of the mixture to shape into 3-inch (7.5 cm) diameter latkes.

3. Place a few latkes in the skillet and cook for 6 minutes, turning once, or until golden brown on the bottom. Repeat this process for additional batches, adding the remaining oil to the skillet and adjusting heat between batches as needed. You should have about 12 latkes. Sprinkle with cinnamon.

4. Serve with the yogurt and walnuts.

Go Greek

Whether nonfat or low-fat, Greek yogurt is typically low in carbohydrates, containing only 7 to 14 grams of carbs per 6-ounce (175 g) serving. Look for Greek yogurt with 20% to 50% of your daily value of calcium to help keep your bones strong.

Makeover Magic		
Before		**After**
250	Calories	126
16 g	Fat	5 g
5 g	Sat Fat	1 g
22 g	Carbs	16 g
2 g	Fiber	3 g
5 g	Protein	4 g
40 mg	Sodium	60 mg

Tex-Mex Breakfast Pizza

 Makes 4 servings

Prep time: 10 minutes • Total time: 25 minutes

Note: This recipe is higher in sodium, so be sure to choose lower-sodium meals later in the day to ensure you don't go over the recommended daily allowance.

Curb carbs: A whole wheat tortilla is an easy way to control portion size rather than taking slices from a pizza.

Fill up on fiber: The whole wheat tortilla, onion, and pepper are packed with fiber and nutrients.

Favor healthy fats: Egg yolks contain saturated fat, but they can be beneficial for their large dose of vitamin A. Choosing a harder cheese, such as provolone or Parmesan, helps to decrease saturated fat and calories.

- Preheat oven to 400°F (200°C)

4	6-inch (15 cm) low-carb whole wheat flour tortillas	4
2 tbsp	olive oil	30 mL
1	small onion, thinly sliced	1
1	red bell pepper, cut into thin strips	1
½	jalapeño pepper, finely chopped	½
4	large eggs	4
8	large egg whites	8
2 tsp	water	10 mL
½ cup	shredded reduced-fat provolone cheese	125 mL
¼ cup	salsa	60 mL
¼ cup	chopped fresh cilantro	60 mL

1. Coat both sides of each tortilla with cooking spray and place on a baking sheet. Bake in preheated oven for 6 minutes, or until golden and crisp.

2. Meanwhile, heat the oil in a large nonstick skillet over medium heat. Cook the onion, bell pepper, and jalapeño pepper, stirring, for 5 minutes, or until tender. Transfer to a plate.

3. In a mixing bowl, beat the eggs, egg whites, and water. Pour the eggs into the same skillet and cook over medium heat, stirring to scramble, for 2 minutes, or until almost set, sprinkling the cheese onto the eggs halfway through cooking. Sprinkle two-thirds of the onion mixture onto the tortillas, dividing equally. Top with the cooked eggs, remaining onion mixture and salsa, dividing equally. Sprinkle cilantro onto each pizza.

Smart Start
Add our favorite diabetes-friendly fat, avocado.

Makeover Magic		
Before		**After**
420	Calories	306
22 g	Fat	16 g
9 g	Sat Fat	4 g
37 g	Carbs	18 g
1 g	Fiber	9 g
19 g	Protein	20 g
790 mg	Sodium	667 mg

Homemade Breakfast Sausage

 Makes 8 servings (2 patties each)

Prep time: 5 minutes • Total time: 20 minutes

Curb carbs: Maple syrup is naturally sweet, so you need only a small amount. This recipe is low in carbs and calories, so you can pair it with a higher-carb recipe like Zucchini and Sweet Potato Latkes (page 74) for a full breakfast.

Fill up on fiber: Be sure to serve a fiber-filled carbohydrate like fruit, veggies, or grains with these sausage patties.

Favor healthy fats: The ground walnuts are a fantastic source of diabetes-friendly omega-3 fatty acids.

2 tbsp	pure maple syrup	30 mL
2 tbsp	ground flaxseeds	30 mL
2 tbsp	ground walnuts	30 mL
1½ tsp	ground black pepper	7 mL
1½ tsp	ground sage	7 mL
½ tsp	onion powder	2 mL
¼ tsp	salt	1 mL
12 oz	extra-lean ground turkey	375 g
8 oz	extra-lean ground pork	250 g
2 tsp	canola oil, divided	10 mL

1. In a large bowl, combine the syrup, flaxseeds, walnuts, pepper, sage, onion powder, and salt and mix with a fork until smooth. Add the turkey and pork and mix gently until the seasonings are evenly distributed. Divide the mixture into 16 small balls, approximately 1 inch (2.5 cm) in diameter each.

2. Heat 1 tsp (5 mL) oil in a skillet over medium-high heat. Place half of the balls in the skillet and flatten with a spatula. Cook for 6 minutes, turning once, or until no longer pink. Add the remaining oil and repeat with the remaining patties.

Makeover Magic		
Before		**After**
200	Calories	124
15 g	Fat	5 g
0 g	Sat Fat	0.5 g
36 g	Carbs	5 g
0 g	Fiber	1 g
10 g	Protein	17 g
324 mg	Sodium	44 mg

PB&J Stuffed French Toast

 Makes 4 servings

Curb carbs: Using slices of sprouted whole-grain or oat bran bread makes each serving of stuffed French toast both bite-size and easy on your blood sugar! Look for bread that has 15 grams of carbs and 3 to 5 grams of fiber per slice. Decreasing jam and using real fruit also keeps carbs curbed.

Fill up on fiber: Fiber is found in fresh strawberries, especially the tiny seeds, and of course in the naturally higher-fiber bread.

Favor healthy fats: Natural peanut butter is low-sodium, low-carb, and high in MUFAs.

4 tbsp	natural creamy peanut butter, divided	60 mL
2 tbsp	all-fruit (no added sugar) strawberry jam, divided	30 mL
8	thin slices sprouted whole-grain bread	8
1 cup	sliced strawberries, divided	250 mL
2	large eggs	2
½ cup	unsweetened almond milk	125 mL
1 tsp	vanilla extract	5 mL
1 tsp	ground cinnamon	5 mL
	Nonstick cooking spray	

1. Spread 1 tbsp (15 mL) peanut butter and ½ tbsp (7 mL) jam on 4 slices of the bread. Top each slice with 2 tbsp (30 mL) strawberries, evenly spread. Top with a second bread slice and press lightly to form a sandwich.

2. In a medium bowl, whisk together eggs, milk, vanilla extract, and cinnamon. Working one sandwich at a time, dip both sides of each sandwich in the egg mixture and set on a plate.

3. Coat a large nonstick skillet with cooking spray and heat over medium heat. In batches as necessary, cook the sandwiches for 8 minutes, turning once, until golden and cooked through. Serve hot, topped with the remaining strawberries.

Smart Start
Adding 1 teaspoon (5 mL) of cinnamon to this recipe aids in optimal glycemic control.

Makeover Magic		
Before		**After**
390	Calories	331
19 g	Fat	12 g
5 g	Sat Fat	2 g
43 g	Carbs	41 g
5 g	Fiber	9 g
15 g	Protein	15 g
519 mg	Sodium	209 mg

Chocolate-Banana-Stuffed French Toast

 Makes 4 servings

Prep time: 5 minutes • Total time: 20 minutes

Curb carbs: Out with the white and in with the wholesome grains, seeds, and nuts. This not only increases the firmness of the bread, but adds flavor and keeps carbs curbed.

Fill up on fiber: Both whole-grain bread and banana slices boost the fiber in this old-time favorite. Using sprouted whole-grain bread gives you the advantage of magic carbs.

Favor healthy fats: Using cooking spray instead of butter to grease the pan decreases the saturated fat. Using almond butter and even hazelnut butter provides you with MUFAs.

Filling

1	unripe banana, thinly sliced	1
2 tbsp	almond butter	30 mL
2 tbsp	chocolate hazelnut spread	30 mL
4 tsp	dark chocolate chips	20 mL
1/8 tsp	ground nutmeg	0.5 mL
1/8 tsp	ground cinnamon	0.5 mL

French Toast

8	slices sprouted whole-grain bread	8
1/2 cup	unsweetened soy or almond milk	125 mL
2	large eggs	2
1/2 tsp	vanilla extract	2 mL
1 tsp	ground cinnamon	5 mL
	Nonstick cooking spray	
	Confectioners' (icing) sugar (optional)	

1. *To make the filling:* Mash about one-quarter of the banana slices in a small bowl with the back of a spoon. (You should have about 2 tbsp/30 mL mashed.) Stir in the almond butter, chocolate hazelnut spread, chocolate chips, nutmeg, and cinnamon until smooth.

2. *To make the French toast:* Spread 4 slices of the bread with the banana filling, dividing evenly. Top with the remaining banana slices and bread slices to make 4 sandwiches.

3. In a shallow dish or pie plate, whisk together the milk, eggs, vanilla, and cinnamon until blended. Dip the sandwiches into the egg mixture, turning them over with a spatula to coat both sides, and set on a plate.

4. Heat a large nonstick skillet or griddle over medium-low heat and coat with cooking spray. In batches as necessary, cook the sandwiches for 8 minutes, turning once, until golden and cooked through. Dust with confectioners' sugar (if using).

Makeover Magic		
Before		**After**
660	Calories	367
34 g	Fat	13 g
24 g	Sat Fat	4 g
79 g	Carbs	50 g
4 g	Fiber	8 g
10 g	Protein	15 g
460 mg	Sodium	223 mg

Spiced Apple Pancakes

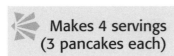

**Makes 4 servings
(3 pancakes each)**

Curb carbs: Using a measuring cup helps you portion pancakes and serve yourself more so you feel psychologically satisfied while keeping carbs minimized and calories in check. Using unsweetened milk keeps your carbs in range.

Fill up on fiber: The fresh unpeeled apples, whole-grain pastry flour, and wheat germ really make everyone's favorite flapjacks a great source of fiber for breakfast!

Favor healthy fats:
Using cooking spray instead of butter to coat the pan decreases the saturated fat. Walnuts and chia seeds provide a vegetarian source of omega-3 fatty acids.

Prep time: 5 minutes • Total time: 15 minutes

	Nonstick cooking spray	
1	medium apple (unpeeled), thinly sliced	1
2 tsp	ground cinnamon, divided	10 mL
1½ cups	whole-grain pastry flour	375 mL
1½ tsp	baking powder	7 mL
3 tbsp	wheat germ	45 mL
½ tsp	apple pie spice	2 mL
1	large egg, lightly beaten	1
1 tsp	vanilla extract	5 mL
1½ cups	unsweetened soy, sunflower, or almond milk	375 mL
3 tbsp	unsweetened applesauce	45 mL
¼ cup	chopped walnuts	60 mL
2 tbsp	chia seeds	30 mL

1. Heat a small skillet over medium heat. Lightly coat the pan with cooking spray and add the apple. Sprinkle 1 tsp (5 mL) cinnamon over the apple. Cover the pan and cook for 5 to 10 minutes, or until tender. Set aside.

2. Meanwhile, in a large bowl, whisk together the flour, baking powder, wheat germ, remaining cinnamon, and apple pie spice. Add the egg, vanilla, milk, and applesauce. Mix well to combine.

3. Heat a large nonstick skillet or griddle pan coated with cooking spray over medium heat. Working in batches as necessary, scoop ¼-cup (60 mL) measures of batter onto the skillet or griddle. Sprinkle with the chopped walnuts and chia seeds. Cook for 2 minutes, or until bubbles appear on the edges of the pancakes. Flip with a spatula and cook for 2 minutes, or until cooked through. Top the pancakes with the cooked apple slices.

Makeover Magic		
Before		**After**
350	Calories	313
9 g	Fat	11 g
5 g	Sat Fat	1 g
60 g	Carbs	42 g
1 g	Fiber	10 g
5 g	Protein	13 g
450 mg	Sodium	26 mg

Belgian Waffles

**Makes 5 servings
(1 waffle each)**

Curb carbs: Since whole grains make you feel fuller faster, you'll feel satisfied with just one of these decadent waffles. Add a side of protein and a calcium source, such as Greek yogurt or low-fat cottage cheese, for even better blood sugar control.

Fill up on fiber: Fiber up your morning with whole-grain pastry flour, fresh fruit, nuts, and seeds.

Favor healthy fats: Canola oil, chia seeds, and wheat germ pack MUFAs and omega-3 fatty acids in this recipe.

- Waffle iron, preheated

1⅔ cups	whole-grain pastry flour	400 mL
1 tbsp	wheat germ	15 mL
1 tbsp	baking powder	15 mL
¼ tsp	salt	1 mL
2	large eggs	2
1⅔ cups	1% milk	400 mL
1 tbsp	pure maple syrup	15 mL
2 tbsp	canola oil	30 mL
¾ cup	blueberries, sliced	175 mL
	Nonstick cooking spray	
1 cup	strawberries, sliced	250 mL
5 tbsp	slivered almonds	75 mL
5 tsp	chia seeds	25 mL

1. In a large bowl, whisk together the flour, wheat germ, baking powder, and salt.

2. In another bowl, whisk together the eggs, milk, maple syrup, and canola oil.

3. Add the wet ingredients into the dry ingredients and stir until combined. Mix in the blueberries.

4. Coat the waffle iron with cooking spray. For each waffle, use a full ½ cup (125 mL) of batter and cook according to manufacturer's directions.

5. In a bowl, combine the strawberries, almonds, and chia seeds.

6. Serve the waffles immediately, topped with the strawberry mixture.

Makeover Magic		
Before		**After**
696	Calories	324
41 g	Fat	14 g
25 g	Sat Fat	2 g
72 g	Carbs	40 g
1 g	Fiber	7 g
10 g	Protein	12 g
712 mg	Sodium	182 mg

Raspberry-Lemon Muffins

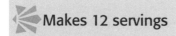 **Makes 12 servings**

Prep time: 5 minutes • Total time: 30 minutes

Curb carbs: Using honey or agave instead of white sugar keeps this recipe lower in carbs.

Fill up on fiber: The flours, fresh raspberries, and chia seeds in these muffins add over 2 grams of fiber per serving.

Favor healthy fats: The olive oil is a healthy fat that provides for a moist muffin. Chia seeds add omega-3s, and you can add even more beneficial fats by spreading natural nut butter on half of the muffin.

- Preheat oven to 400°F (200°C)
- Muffin pan, lined with paper liners or sprayed with nonstick cooking spray

1½ cups	whole-grain oat flour	375 mL
1½ cups	whole wheat flour	375 mL
1 tbsp	baking powder	15 mL
1 tsp	ground cinnamon	5 mL
2	large eggs	2
1¼ cups	1% milk	300 mL
3 tbsp	light olive oil	45 mL
3 tbsp	liquid honey (or 1½ tbsp/22 mL agave syrup)	45 mL
1 tbsp	grated lemon zest	15 mL
1 tsp	freshly squeezed lemon juice	5 mL
1 cup	raspberries	250 mL
¼ cup	chia seeds	60 mL

1. In a large bowl, combine the oat flour, whole wheat flour, baking powder, and cinnamon.

2. In a small bowl, whisk together the eggs, milk, oil, honey, lemon zest, and lemon juice. Stir into the flour mixture just until blended. Gently stir in the raspberries and chia seeds.

3. Fill prepared muffin cups two-thirds full with the mixture. Bake in preheated oven for 20 minutes, or until a tester inserted in the center comes out clean. Remove to a rack to cool.

Makeover Magic		
Before		**After**
272	Calories	195
12 g	Fat	8 g
3 g	Sat Fat	2 g
37 g	Carbs	28 g
1 g	Fiber	6 g
4 g	Protein	6 g
258 mg	Sodium	25 mg

Lox-Cheddar Scones

 Makes 8 servings

Prep time: 10 minutes • Total time: 35 minutes

Curb carbs: Keep carbs in check by filling up on higher-fiber grains like whole wheat flour and whole-grain cornmeal.

Fill up on fiber: Whole wheat flour and whole-grain cornmeal give these scones a huge kick of fiber to get you "moving" in the morning.

Favor healthy fats: Opt for reduced-fat cheese when using butter to keep saturated fat at a minimum. Lox provides the omega-3 fatty acids you want to be including regularly.

- Preheat oven to 425°F (220°C)
- Baking sheet, lined with parchment paper

	Nonstick cooking spray	
3	green onions, sliced	3
2 oz	smoked salmon (lox), chopped	60 g
1½ cups	whole wheat flour	375 mL
½ cup	yellow cornmeal	125 mL
1 tbsp	baking powder	15 mL
¼ cup	cold unsalted butter, cut into small cubes	60 mL
½ cup	reduced-fat shredded Cheddar cheese	125 mL
1½ tsp	agave syrup	7 mL
1 cup	low-fat (1%) buttermilk	250 mL

1. Heat a large nonstick skillet coated with cooking spray over medium heat. Cook the green onions and salmon, stirring, for 3 minutes, or until the green onions are softened.

2. In a large bowl, combine the flour, cornmeal, and baking powder. Cut in the butter with a pastry blender or fork until the mixture resembles small crumbles. Stir in the green onion mixture and Cheddar.

3. In a small bowl, combine the agave and buttermilk. Pour this mixture into the large bowl with the flour mixture and stir until just combined and the dough comes together.

4. Pat the dough into an 8-inch (20 cm) circle, about ¾ inch (2 cm) thick. Transfer the disk to the prepared baking sheet, cut into 8 wedges, and separate the wedges on the pan.

5. Bake in preheated oven for 20 minutes, or until golden. Cool in the pan on a rack for 5 minutes. Remove from the rack and cool completely.

Makeover Magic		
Before		**After**
510	Calories	204
27 g	Fat	9 g
16 g	Sat Fat	5 g
50 g	Carbs	25 g
2 g	Fiber	3 g
17 g	Protein	8 g
2,680 mg	Sodium	158 mg

Sunrise Oatmeal

 Makes 4 servings

Curb carbs: Freshly cooked steel-cut oats provide a healthy unrefined carbohydrate option just like your grandmother used to make! Using fat-free Greek yogurt keeps fat and carbs in range.

Fill up on fiber: Steel-cut oats are higher in fiber than instant or quick-cooking oatmeal.

Favor healthy fats: Flaxseeds, wheat germ, and pecans add not only fiber but also essential fatty acids and a dose of vitamins B and E. Say goodbye to saturated fat when using naturally creamy steel-cut oats — there's no need for cream or even butter.

4 cups	water	1 L
1 cup	steel-cut oats	250 mL
1 tbsp	flaxseeds	15 mL
1 tbsp	wheat germ	15 mL
2 tbsp	chopped pecans	30 mL
½ tsp	ground cinnamon	2 mL
½ cup	vanilla nonfat (0%) Greek yogurt	125 mL
1 cup	blueberries	250 mL

1. In a medium saucepan, bring the water to a boil over high heat. Add the oats and stir until they begin to thicken. Reduce the heat and simmer, stirring occasionally, for 30 minutes, or until the oatmeal is thick and creamy. Add the flaxseeds, wheat germ, and pecans and mix evenly.

2. Spoon the oatmeal into 4 bowls and sprinkle with the cinnamon. Top each with equal portions of the Greek yogurt and blueberries. Serve hot.

Makeover Magic		
Before		**After**
340	Calories	214
10 g	Fat	5 g
6 g	Sat Fat	1 g
51 g	Carbs	36 g
5 g	Fiber	6 g
13 g	Protein	10 g
380 mg	Sodium	21 mg

Hearty Fruit and Nut Granola

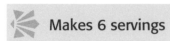 **Makes 6 servings**

Prep time: 5 minutes • Total time: 35 minutes + cooling time

Curb carbs: Adding nuts and seeds to an oatmeal-based granola can curb carbohydrates while still providing energy!

Fill up on fiber: The combination of oats, millet, and almonds makes an unstoppable fiber trio.

Favor healthy fats: The nuts and seeds are jam-packed with beneficial fats.

- Preheat oven to 350°F (180°C)
- Large rimmed baking sheet, sprayed with nonstick cooking spray

1½ cups	old-fashioned (large-flake) rolled oats	375 mL
¼ cup	millet	60 mL
¼ cup	unsweetened dried cranberries	60 mL
¼ cup	ground flaxseeds	60 mL
2 tbsp	unsalted sunflower seeds	30 mL
¼ cup	slivered almonds	60 mL
3 tbsp	pure maple syrup	45 mL
1 tsp	ground cinnamon	5 mL
½ tsp	ground cardamom	2 mL

1. In a large bowl, combine oats, millet, cranberries, flaxseeds, sunflower seeds, almonds, maple syrup, cinnamon, and cardamom. Stir well to combine.

2. Spread evenly on prepared baking sheet. Bake in preheated oven for 35 minutes, or until golden brown, stirring carefully once or twice. Remove from the oven and break up any large pieces of granola while it is still warm.

3. Cool completely before storing in an airtight container at room temperature for up to 1 week.

Makeover Magic		
Before		**After**
308	Calories	194
15 g	Fat	7 g
2 g	Sat Fat	0.5 g
41 g	Carbs	27 g
4 g	Fiber	6 g
7 g	Protein	7 g
70 mg	Sodium	10 mg

Peach-Blueberry Yogurt Parfait

 Makes 4 servings

Curb carbs: Adding a protein source like Greek yogurt means we can reduce carbs at breakfast. The carbs in this recipe come from granola and fresh fruit.

Fill up on fiber: Flaxseeds and sunflower seeds are an excellent source of fiber in this recipe.

Favor healthy fats: Almonds are a delicious source of MUFAs.

- Parfait glasses

2 cups	plain fat-free (0%) Greek yogurt	500 mL
2 tsp	lemon juice	10 mL
2	peaches, chopped	2
1 cup	blueberries	250 mL
⅔ cup	Hearty Fruit and Nut Granola (page 84)	150 mL
2 tbsp	ground flaxseeds	30 mL

1. In a small bowl, stir together the yogurt and lemon juice.

2. In 4 parfait glasses, layer the yogurt, peaches, blueberries, granola, and flaxseeds.

Makeover Magic		
Before		**After**
330	Calories	218
10 g	Fat	5 g
2 g	Sat Fat	0.5 g
51 g	Carbs	29 g
3 g	Fiber	5 g
12 g	Protein	15 g
170 mg	Sodium	48 mg

Sundae Breakfast Smoothie

 Makes 4 servings

Prep time: 5 minutes • Total time: 5 minutes

Curb carbs: Greek yogurt helps curb carbs in this smoothie.

Fill up on fiber: Bananas, cherries, and flaxseeds provide fiber in this delicious drink that won't make your blood sugar blast off.

Favor healthy fats: Hemp or chia seeds give a morning dose of omegas, while nonfat Greek yogurt gives you a little bit of protein to help keep your blood sugar from peaking too fast.

• Blender

2	bananas, frozen	2
1 cup	vanilla nonfat (0%) Greek yogurt	250 mL
½ cup	freshly squeezed orange juice	125 mL
1 cup	frozen cherries	250 mL
1	scoop vanilla whey protein powder	1
2 tbsp	ground flaxseeds	30 mL
2 tbsp	hemp or chia seeds	30 mL

1. In a blender, combine the bananas, yogurt, orange juice, cherries, protein powder, flaxseeds, and hemp seeds. Blend until smooth and creamy.

Makeover Magic		
Before		**After**
190	Calories	205
3 g	Fat	4 g
2 g	Sat Fat	0.5 g
36 g	Carbs	29 g
1 g	Fiber	3 g
6 g	Protein	14 g
95 mg	Sodium	36 mg

Chocolate Cake Smoothie

 Makes 2 servings

Prep time: 5 minutes • Total time: 10 minutes

Curb carbs: Unsweetened almond milk and chocolate-flavored protein powder give you a sweet kickoff to your morning while keeping carbs naturally low.

Fill up on fiber: The hazelnuts create texture and provide fiber while enhancing the chocolate flavor.

Favor healthy fats: This recipe may look high in fat, but that's because it's full of the good kind! The nuts and almond butter in this recipe are packed full of MUFAs.

• Blender

½ cup	part-skim ricotta cheese	125 mL
1½ cups	unsweetened almond milk	375 mL
1	scoop chocolate whey protein powder	1
2 tbsp	almond butter	30 mL
¼ cup	hazelnuts, chopped	60 mL
2 tbsp	ground espresso (decaf or regular)	30 mL
2 tsp	vanilla extract	10 mL
½ tsp	ground cinnamon	2 mL
8	ice cubes	8

1. In a blender, combine the ricotta, almond milk, protein powder, almond butter, hazelnuts, espresso, vanilla, cinnamon, and ice cubes. Blend until smooth and creamy.

Smart Start

Increase to 1 tsp (5 mL) cinnamon per smoothie to reduce your after-breakfast blood sugar.

Makeover Magic		
Before		**After**
570	Calories	389
17 g	Fat	27 g
11 g	Sat Fat	5 g
91 g	Carbs	13 g
1 g	Fiber	3 g
12 g	Protein	24 g
240 mg	Sodium	313 mg

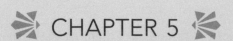

CHAPTER 5

Soups, Salads & Sandwiches

Soups

Fiesta Turkey Soup 90

Minestrone 91

Beef Barley Soup 92

Creamy Potato, Lentil, and Ham Chowder 93

Cheesy Vegetable Chowder 94

Manhattan Clam Chowder 95

South-of-the-Border Shrimp Soup 96

Kicked-Up Tomato Soup 97

Lentil–Broccoli Rabe Soup 98

Apple–Sweet Potato Soup 99

Salads

Apple and Blue Cheese Salad 100

Spinach-Cranberry Salad 101

Warm Zucchini Salad 102

Citrus–Grilled Shrimp Salad 103

Tricolor Slaw and Potato Salad 104

Warm German Potato Salad. 105

Corn, Black Bean, and Edamame Salad 106

Couscous and Chickpea Salad. 107

Chilled Cilantro–Soba Noodle Salad. 108

Creamy Pasta Salad. 109

Sandwiches

Philly Cheese Steaks 110

Sausage and Pepper Wraps 111

Monte Cristos. 112

Open-Faced Asian Chicken Sandwiches. 113

Sweet Turkey Paninis 114

Buffalo Grilled Cheese Sandwiches. 115

Bacon and Apple Grilled Cheese. 116

Tuna Salad Wraps 117

Roast Beef Rolls. 117

Barbecue Shrimp Wraps 118

Fiesta Turkey Soup

 Makes 6 servings

Curb carbs: There's no need for tortillas with this filling, veggie-packed soup. Save the carbs for the sandwich served on the side.

Fill up on fiber: Zucchini, corn, and the superstar beans are the major sources of fiber in this recipe.

Favor healthy fats: The avocado topping adds healthy MUFAs.

Prep time: 10 minutes • Total time: 50 minutes

1 tbsp	canola oil	15 mL
1	onion, chopped	1
1	small jalapeño pepper, seeded and finely chopped	1
1	zucchini, chopped	1
2 tsp	ground cumin	10 mL
1/2 tsp	ancho chile powder	2 mL
1 lb	extra-lean (99% fat-free) ground turkey	500 g
4 cups	low-sodium ready-to-use chicken broth	1 L
1	can (14 to 15 oz/398 to 425 mL) no-salt-added diced tomatoes, with juice	1
1	can (15 oz/425 mL) no-salt-added black beans, drained and rinsed	1
1 cup	frozen corn kernels	250 mL
1/2 cup	chopped fresh cilantro	125 mL
1/2	avocado, chopped	1/2
6 tbsp	shredded Cheddar cheese	90 mL

1. In a large saucepan, heat the oil over medium-high heat. Cook the onion and jalapeño pepper, stirring occasionally, for 5 minutes, or until lightly browned. Stir in the zucchini, cumin, and chile powder. Cook, stirring, for 10 minutes, or until the zucchini is lightly browned. Add the turkey and cook, stirring to break up with a spoon, for 5 minutes, or until no longer pink.

2. Stir in the broth, tomatoes, beans, and corn. Bring to a boil over high heat. Reduce the heat to low and simmer for 20 minutes, or until the liquid has reduced by one-quarter. Remove from the heat.

3. Stir in the cilantro. Divide among 6 bowls. Sprinkle each serving with a spoonful of avocado and 1 tbsp (15 mL) shredded cheese.

Makeover Magic		
Before		**After**
400	Calories	244
26 g	Fat	8 g
9 g	sat Fat	2 g
26 g	Carbs	19 g
3 g	Fiber	5 g
20 g	Protein	26 g
1,450 mg	Sodium	152 mg

Minestrone

Prep time: 10 minutes • Total time: 45 minutes

Curb carbs: Instead of the traditional pasta in minestrone soup, we used wild rice, which is naturally lower in carbs.

Fill up on fiber: Cabbage, chickpeas, and wild rice are the key to a high fiber count.

Favor healthy fats: Be sure to accompany this soup with a salad featuring sources of healthy fats, such as olive oil and sunflower seeds.

2¼ cups	water	550 mL
¾ cup	wild rice	175 mL
1 tbsp	canola oil	15 mL
4 oz	Italian chicken or turkey sausage, thinly sliced	125 g
5 cups	shredded green cabbage	1.25 L
1	medium zucchini, thinly sliced	1
2	cloves garlic, minced	2
1	stalk celery, diced	1
1	can (14 to 15 oz/398 to 425 mL) no-salt-added diced tomatoes, with juice	1
1	can (15 oz/425 mL) no-salt-added chickpeas, drained and rinsed	1
8 cups	low-sodium ready-to-use chicken broth	2 L
2	sprigs parsley, finely chopped	2

1. In a microwaveable glass bowl, combine the water and the rice and cook on High in a microwave oven for 5 minutes. Set aside.

2. In a large soup pot, heat the oil over medium-high heat. Cook the sausage, stirring, for 4 minutes, or until no longer pink. Add the cabbage, zucchini, garlic, and celery and cook, stirring, for 4 minutes, or until just tender.

3. Add the tomatoes, chickpeas, and broth. Bring to a boil over high heat, reduce the heat to medium, and simmer for 10 minutes. Stir in the rice and parsley, reduce the heat to low, and simmer for 10 minutes to blend the flavors.

Makeover Magic		
Before		**After**
588	Calories	229
19 g	Fat	5 g
9 g	Sat Fat	0.5 g
64 g	Carbs	33 g
6 g	Fiber	6 g
36 g	Protein	14 g
2,164 mg	Sodium	243 mg

Beef Barley Soup

 Makes 6 servings

Prep time: 15 minutes • Total time: 2 hours

Curb carbs: We used just a small amount of pearl barley, which cut the carbs but also added body to this hearty soup.

Fill up on fiber: Barley itself is full of fiber, but we've also added luscious, fiber-filled veggies.

Favor healthy fats: We used a lean cut of beef for this soup to reduce saturated fat. Pair this soup with a salad or sandwich high in healthy fats.

1 tbsp	olive oil	15 mL
1 lb	well-trimmed lean boneless beef top sirloin, cut into ¾-inch (2 cm) cubes	500 g
2	onions, halved and thinly sliced	2
3	cloves garlic, minced	3
½ tsp	dried thyme, crumbled	2 mL
8 oz	cremini mushrooms, sliced	250 g
2	stalks celery, thinly sliced	2
3	carrots, sliced	3
1	parsnip, halved lengthwise and sliced	1
¼ cup	no-salt-added tomato purée	60 mL
3 cups	water	750 mL
3½ cups	low-sodium ready-to-use beef broth	875 mL
1	bay leaf	1
½ cup	pearl barley	125 mL

1. In a Dutch oven or a large, heavy saucepan, heat the oil over medium heat. Lightly brown the beef for 3 minutes, or until the liquid evaporates.

2. Add the onions and garlic and cook, stirring, for 3 minutes, or until the onions soften. Add the thyme and cook for 1 minute. Add the mushrooms and cook, stirring, for 3 minutes, or until the mushrooms begin to soften. Add the celery, carrots, and parsnip and stir for 2 minutes.

3. Reduce the heat to medium-low. Add the purée, water, broth, and bay leaf and simmer for 45 minutes.

4. Stir in the barley and simmer for 45 minutes, or until the barley is soft. Discard the bay leaf before serving.

Makeover Magic		
Before		**After**
332	Calories	229
11 g	Fat	5 g
5 g	Sat Fat	2 g
35 g	Carbs	28 g
6 g	Fiber	6 g
25 g	Protein	18 g
1,681 mg	Sodium	125 mg

Creamy Potato, Lentil, and Ham Chowder

 Makes 8 servings

Prep time: 10 minutes • Total time: 45 minutes

Curb carbs: We cut the potatoes in this traditional soup by adding lentils, which are higher in fiber and protein.

Fill up on fiber: Lentils are an added fiber source that sets this apart from the average potato soup!

Favor healthy fats: Loaded baked potato soups are usually full of bacon, cheese, and heavy cream. We substituted 1% milk and ham to reduce saturated fat. For a dose of healthy fats, be sure to pair with a salad drizzled with olive oil and sliced olives.

- Blender or food processor

1 tbsp	olive oil	15 mL
2	onions, chopped	2
2 tbsp	whole wheat flour	30 mL
3 cups	low-sodium chicken broth	750 mL
2 cups	water	500 mL
4	red potatoes, cut into ¾-inch (2 cm) pieces	4
1	stalk celery, chopped	1
½ cup	dried green lentils, rinsed	125 mL
1 tsp	dry mustard	5 mL
1⅔ cups	1% milk	400 mL
8 oz	fully cooked lean low-sodium ham, cut into ¾-inch (2 cm) pieces	250 g

1. In a large saucepan, heat the oil over medium-high heat. Cook the onions, stirring occasionally, for 5 minutes, or until translucent. Stir in the flour and cook, stirring, for 1 minute. Gradually stir in the broth until well blended.

2. Add the water, potatoes, celery, lentils, and mustard. Bring to a boil. Reduce the heat to low, cover, and simmer for 20 minutes, or until the potatoes are tender.

3. Working in batches, transfer the vegetables to a blender and process until puréed. Return to the saucepan. Stir in the milk and ham. Gently simmer, stirring occasionally, for 5 minutes.

Makeover Magic		
Before		**After**
369	Calories	227
14 g	Fat	5 g
7 g	Sat Fat	2 g
47 g	Carbs	33 g
4 g	Fiber	5 g
11 g	Protein	15 g
638 mg	Sodium	337 mg

Cheesy Vegetable Chowder

 Makes 6 servings

Prep time: 10 minutes • Total time: 45 minutes

Curb carbs: This soup cuts carbs by replacing gravy mix and other prepackaged ingredients with fresh whole foods such as whole wheat flour and apple juice.

Fill up on fiber: White whole wheat flour, potatoes (with the skin!), broccoli, and corn all add extra fiber compared to the traditional cheese chowder.

Favor healthy fats: Instead of heavy cream and too much cheese, we used 1% milk and a minimal amount of cheese. Sneak a dose of healthy fats into this soup by adding ground flaxseeds.

• Blender or food processor

1	small red or green bell pepper, minced	1
1	small onion, minced	1
¼ cup	unsweetened apple juice	60 mL
1	clove garlic, minced	1
¼ cup	white whole wheat flour	60 mL
2 cups	low-sodium ready-to-use chicken broth, divided	500 mL
2	potatoes, diced	2
1¼ cups	1% milk	300 mL
1 cup	frozen chopped broccoli, thawed	250 mL
½ cup	frozen corn kernels, thawed	125 mL
¾ cup	shredded Cheddar cheese	175 mL
¼ cup	shredded Monterey Jack cheese	60 mL

1. In a Dutch oven, combine the pepper, onion, apple juice, and garlic. Cook, stirring, over medium-high heat for 5 minutes. Add the flour and ½ cup (125 mL) broth. Cook, stirring, for 2 minutes. Add the potatoes and the remaining broth. Bring to a boil. Reduce the heat to medium. Cover and cook for 20 minutes, or until the potatoes are tender. Check by inserting the tip of a sharp knife into 1 piece.

2. Transfer 1 cup (250 mL) of the soup to a blender and process until smooth. Return to the pot. Add the milk, broccoli, corn, and cheeses. Stir to combine. Cook, stirring, for 3 minutes, or until the cheeses melt and the vegetables are heated through.

Makeover Magic		
Before		**After**
270	Calories	198
7 g	Fat	7 g
2 g	Sat Fat	4 g
32 g	Carbs	25 g
2 g	Fiber	4 g
11 g	Protein	10 g
1,490 mg	Sodium	178 mg

Manhattan Clam Chowder

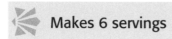 **Makes 6 servings**

Note: If you cannot find 6½-ounce (195 g) cans of chopped clams, use four 85-gram cans.

Curb carbs: The majority of the carbohydrates in this soup are from the potatoes. We cut the carbohydrates compared to our "before" chowder, because we added additional vegetables to add flavor and nutrients.

Fill up on fiber: All of the added vegetables boost the fiber compared to the original recipe.

Favor healthy fats: We used turkey bacon as opposed to regular bacon, and we did not add any extra oil. This soup is almost fat free, so be sure to eat it with healthy fats.

2	slices turkey bacon	2
2	stalks celery, thinly sliced	2
1	onion, finely chopped	1
1	green bell pepper, chopped	1
1	clove garlic, minced	1
2	cans (each 6½ oz/195 g) chopped clams	2
¾ cup	bottled clam juice	175 mL
2	large potatoes, cubed	2
2	carrots, chopped	2
1	fresh thyme sprig	1
1	bay leaf	1
1	can (14 to 15 oz/398 to 425 mL) no-salt-added diced tomatoes, with juice	1
⅛ tsp	cayenne pepper	0.5 mL

1. In a large saucepan over medium heat, cook the bacon until crisp. Transfer to a plate lined with paper towels. Crumble into a small bowl. Set aside.

2. Add the celery, onion, bell pepper, and garlic to the bacon drippings in the saucepan. Cook, stirring occasionally, for 5 minutes, or until the onion and celery are tender. Drain the juice from the clams into a small bowl. Set the clams aside.

3. Add the juice to the onion mixture. Stir in the bottled clam juice, potatoes, carrots, thyme, and bay leaf. Bring to a boil. Reduce the heat to low. Cover and simmer for 20 minutes. Stir in the tomatoes. Bring to a boil over high heat. Reduce the heat to low. Add the reserved clams. Cover and simmer for 8 minutes. Discard the bay leaf and thyme stem. Stir in the bacon and cayenne.

Smart Start

Serve with 1 slice toasted low-sodium whole wheat bread, covered with 1 to 2 tablespoons (15 to 30 mL) of low-sodium olive tapenade.

Makeover Magic		
Before		**After**
310	Calories	164
11 g	Fat	1 g
2 g	Sat Fat	0 g
46 g	Carbs	30 g
3 g	Fiber	4 g
10 g	Protein	10 g
1,150 mg	Sodium	574 mg

South-of-the-Border Shrimp Soup

 Makes 6 servings

Prep time: 10 minutes • Total time: 1 hour 15 minutes

Curb carbs: The carbs in this zesty soup come from the fresh vegetables, like peppers and corn, leaving plenty of room for a slice of crusty bread or a half sandwich on the side.

Fill up on fiber: All of the vegetables in this soup provide 3 grams of fiber per serving. To boost the fiber even more, add whole-grain pasta to the soup or a dinner roll and make it a meal.

Favor healthy fats: Be sure to add a side high in healthy fats, like guacamole, to this dish. Check out single packs of guacamole, if you can find them.

- Preheat oven to 350°F (180°C)

1	bulb garlic	1
1 tbsp	olive oil	15 mL
3	stalks celery, chopped	3
1	red bell pepper, chopped	1
1	green bell pepper, chopped	1
1	small leek, split, washed, and thinly sliced	1
1	serrano chile pepper, seeded and finely chopped	1
2	cans (14 to 15 oz/398 to 425 mL each) no-salt-added diced tomatoes, with juice	2
3 cups	low-sodium ready-to-use chicken broth	750 mL
1 tbsp	Cajun seasoning mix	15 mL
1 cup	frozen corn kernels, thawed	250 mL
1 lb	medium shrimp, peeled and deveined	500 g

1. Place the garlic bulb on a piece of foil, moisten it with water, and wrap it to seal. Bake in preheated oven for 45 minutes. When cool enough to handle, squeeze the garlic from the bulb.

2. Heat the oil in a large pot over medium-high heat. Cook the garlic, celery, bell peppers, leek, and serrano pepper, stirring, for 10 minutes, or until soft. Add the tomatoes, broth, and seasoning mix and bring just to a boil. Add the corn and shrimp and cook for 5 minutes, or until the shrimp are opaque.

Smart Start
Get creative and fun: Savor this soup with a few blue corn chips and guacamole.

Makeover Magic		
Before		After
317	Calories	185
13 g	Fat	4 g
4 g	Sat Fat	0.5 g
23 g	Carbs	18 g
2 g	Fiber	3 g
26 g	Protein	19 g
689 mg	Sodium	454 mg

Grilled Steak and Eggs (page 68)

Chocolate-Banana-Stuffed
French Toast (page 78)

Raspberry-Lemon Muffins (page 81)

Fiesta Turkey Soup (page 90)

Apple–Sweet Potato Soup (page 99)

Couscous and Chickpea Salad (page 107)

Philly Cheese Steaks (page 110)

Tuna Salad Wraps (page 117)

Kicked-Up Tomato Soup

 Makes 6 servings

Prep time: 15 minutes • Total time: 50 minutes

Curb carbs: Instead of using flour and processed tomato purée, as in a typical tomato soup, we thickened ours up with fresh vegetables, leaving plenty of room to add tortilla strips.

Fill up on fiber: This chunky tomato soup is full of high-fiber veggies and black beans, for a belly-filling meal!

Favor healthy fats: Swap out heavy cream for a dollop of Greek yogurt to reduce saturated fat and pump up nutrition. To add healthy fat, try tossing in some kalamata olives or a bit of avocado.

2¼ cups	water, divided	560 mL
3	carrots, chopped	3
3	stalks celery, chopped	3
1	red bell pepper, chopped	1
1 tbsp	olive oil	15 mL
1	small onion, chopped	1
1	jalapeño chile pepper, seeded and finely chopped	1
1	can (28 oz/796 mL) no-salt-added diced tomatoes, with juice	1
1	can (15 oz/425 mL) no-salt-added black beans, drained and rinsed	1
½ cup	chopped fresh cilantro	125 mL
2 tbsp	lime juice	30 mL
2	6-inch (15 cm) corn tortillas, cut into ¼-inch (0.5 cm) strips	2
6 tbsp	plain nonfat (0%) Greek yogurt	90 mL

1. In a large saucepan, heat ¼ cup (60 mL) cup of water over medium heat. Add the carrots, celery, and bell pepper and cook, stirring, for 5 minutes, or until the vegetables are softened.

2. Add the oil to the saucepan and heat. Add the onion and jalapeño pepper. Cook, stirring occasionally, for 5 minutes, or until the vegetables are softened and golden.

3. Add the tomatoes and the remaining water. Add the beans and cilantro and stir to blend. Bring to a simmer. Reduce the heat to low and cook for 25 minutes.

4. Add the lime juice. Ladle into 6 bowls and top with tortilla strips and a dollop of yogurt.

Makeover Magic		
Before		**After**
305	Calories	136
23 g	Fat	3 g
14 g	Sat Fat	0.5 g
22 g	Carbs	22 g
4 g	Fiber	5 g
5 g	Protein	6 g
1,131 mg	Sodium	70 mg

Lentil–Broccoli Rabe Soup

 Makes 6 servings

Prep time: 10 minutes • Total time: 40 minutes

2 tsp	olive oil	10 mL
2	carrots, chopped	2
1	onion, chopped	1
2	cloves garlic, minced	2
1 cup	dried red lentils	250 mL
4 cups	low-sodium ready-to-use vegetable broth or water	1 L
2 tbsp	no-salt-added tomato paste	30 mL
1 tsp	ground cumin	5 mL
8 oz	broccoli rabe, trimmed and chopped	250 g
1 tbsp	finely chopped fresh oregano (or 1 tsp/5 mL dried)	15 mL
2 tbsp	grated Parmesan cheese	30 mL

Curb carbs: Lentils are a major carb source, so instead of using a full pound (500 g) of lentils for 6 servings, as many lentil soups do, we replaced some with broccoli rabe and other lower-carb veggies.

Fill up on fiber: Lentils do provide a lot of fiber, which is why our recipe has half as much as the comparison. To make up for lost fiber, add some crusty bread or a half sandwich to make a complete meal.

Favor healthy fats: Olive oil is a source of healthy fats in this recipe, and using just a little grated Parmesan cheese gives the soup melty goodness without too much fat.

1. In a large saucepan, heat the oil over medium heat. Cook the carrots, onion, and garlic, stirring, for 5 minutes, or until the vegetables start to soften. Stir in the lentils, broth, tomato paste, and cumin. Cover and bring to a brisk simmer.

2. Reduce the heat to low and simmer for 20 minutes. Stir in the broccoli rabe. Cover and simmer for 5 minutes, or until the lentils and broccoli rabe are tender. Add more water, if necessary, to thin the soup to the desired consistency. Serve garnished with the oregano and cheese.

Makeover Magic		
Before		**After**
372	Calories	179
8 g	Fat	3 g
1 g	Sat Fat	0.5 g
55 g	Carbs	28 g
13 g	Fiber	7 g
24 g	Protein	11 g
762 mg	Sodium	154 mg

Apple–Sweet Potato Soup

 Makes 8 servings

Curb carbs: This dish uses fewer sweet potatoes than typical sweet potato soups and just enough apples to add a depth of flavor without piling on too many carbs.

Fill up on fiber: The fiber in this dish comes from the main ingredients — don't forget the apple skins!

Favor healthy fats: This soup is still creamy even without added fat from butter, oils, and creams! Be sure to have a source of healthy fats on the side, or try sprinkling the soup with ground flaxseeds.

- Minimum 4-quart slow cooker
- Blender

4 to 5	sweet potatoes (2 lbs/1 kg), peeled and cut into chunks	4 to 5
2	Granny Smith apples, quartered	2
1	onion, finely chopped	1
3	cans (each 14.5 oz/410 mL) low-sodium chicken broth	3
1 tsp	chopped fresh thyme (or ⅓ tsp/1.5 mL dried)	5 mL

1. Place the sweet potatoes, apples, onion, broth, and thyme in a slow cooker and stir to combine. Cover and cook on low for 8 hours, or until the sweet potatoes are tender.

2. Let cool slightly, about 10 minutes. Purée the soup in a blender until smooth.

> **Smart Start**
> *Serve with 1 slice sprouted whole-grain bread topped with 1 tablespoon (15 mL) natural almond butter, or serve with fish and a green veggie for dinner.*

Makeover Magic		
Before		**After**
390	Calories	99
20 g	Fat	0.5 g
11 g	Sat Fat	0 g
44 g	Carbs	23 g
4 g	Fiber	4 g
11 g	Protein	2 g
930 mg	Sodium	385 mg

Apple and Blue Cheese Salad

 Makes 6 servings

Prep time: 5 minutes • Total time: 10 minutes

Curb carbs: Many salads like this use added sweeteners, such as maple syrup or brown sugar, but with ripe apples, this dish doesn't need them!

Fill up on fiber: The apples are the major source of fiber in this dish.

Favor healthy fats: Flaxseeds and walnuts are our source of ALA omega-3 fatty acids, while olive oil provides additional MUFAs. To cut saturated fat, we made a light mustard vinaigrette in place of a sweet, creamy dressing.

2 tbsp	extra virgin olive oil	30 mL
3 tbsp	white vinegar	45 mL
2 tbsp	Dijon mustard	30 mL
1 tsp	lemon juice	5 mL
10 oz	baby lettuce mix	300 g
	Salt and ground black pepper (optional)	
3	firm-ripe Granny Smith apples, sliced	3
3 oz	reduced-fat blue cheese, crumbled	90 g
⅓ cup	walnut halves, chopped	75 mL
1 tbsp	ground flaxseeds	15 mL

1. In a small bowl, whisk together the oil, vinegar, mustard, and lemon juice.

2. Add the lettuce and toss gently to coat. Season with salt and pepper to taste, if using.

3. Divide the lettuce among 6 salad plates. Top each with apple slices, blue cheese, and walnuts and sprinkle with flaxseeds.

Makeover Magic		
Before		**After**
330	Calories	170
24 g	Fat	11 g
5 g	Sat Fat	3 g
27 g	Carbs	14 g
4 g	Fiber	4 g
5 g	Protein	5 g
630 mg	Sodium	319 mg

Spinach-Cranberry Salad

 Makes 6 servings

Prep time: 5 minutes • Total time: 10 minutes

Curb carbs: Salads like this one are naturally low in carbs, meaning we have plenty of room to add a little carb-heavy dried fruit.

Fill up on fiber: Using spinach as a base and not spring greens makes the fiber and other nutrients shoot way up. Keep in mind that the fresh fruit is blended into the vinaigrette, so it does not pack as much fiber as the whole berries would.

Favor healthy fats: Olive oil packs MUFAs, and walnuts pack the vegetarian source of omega-3 fatty acids known as ALA. And the goat cheese gives a creamy lift to this salad without going overboard on fat.

• Food processor

Vinaigrette

¼ cup	raspberries	60 mL
¼ cup	cranberries	60 mL
2 tbsp	extra virgin olive oil	30 mL
1 tbsp	white vinegar	15 mL
1 tsp	Dijon mustard	5 mL

Salad

12 oz	baby spinach	375 g
1	small red onion, thinly sliced	1
2 tbsp	unsweetened dried cranberries	30 mL
2 oz	goat cheese, softened	60 g
¼ cup	walnut halves	60 mL

1. *To make the vinaigrette:* In a food processor, combine the raspberries, cranberries, oil, vinegar, and mustard and blend until smooth. Transfer to a small serving bowl.

2. *To make the salad:* In a large serving bowl, combine the spinach, onion, and cranberries. Drizzle the vinaigrette over the greens and toss to coat. Top with the goat cheese and walnuts.

Makeover Magic		
Before		**After**
500	Calories	140
45 g	Fat	10 g
16 g	Sat Fat	3 g
10 g	Carbs	10 g
1 g	Fiber	4 g
15 g	Protein	4 g
230 mg	Sodium	160 mg

Warm Zucchini Salad

 Makes 4 servings

3	zucchini	3
2 tsp	canola oil	10 mL
1	small red onion, thinly sliced	1
3	plum (Roma) tomatoes, chopped	3
1 tbsp	lemon juice	15 mL
¼ cup	thinly sliced fresh basil	60 mL
2 tbsp	grated Parmesan cheese	30 mL

1. Using a vegetable peeler or mandoline, thinly slice the zucchini lengthwise, about $\frac{1}{16}$-inch (2 mm) thick.

2. Heat the oil in a large nonstick skillet over medium-high heat. Cook the onion, stirring, for 3 minutes, or until soft. Add the tomatoes and zucchini and cook, stirring, for 5 minutes, or until tender.

3. Transfer the mixture to a serving bowl. Add the lemon juice and toss to coat. Sprinkle with the basil and cheese.

Curb carbs: We swapped out corn for fresh tomatoes, which curbed the carbohydrates slightly. The thing we love about this salad is that the carbohydrates come from the vegetables, so it's all healthy! Plus, there's plenty of room to add more carbs to this meal.

Fill up on fiber: With just a few ingredients, this side salad serves up 2 grams of fiber, which makes a great addition to a main-course dish.

Favor healthy fats: We think sometimes less really is more. In this case, smothering a salad in dressing is not going to help the freshness or flavor of the vegetables. We opted for a light drizzle of lemon juice and fresh herbs, which cut the fat back — the canola adds healthy fats, and a little Parmesan goes a long way to give this dish something special.

Makeover Magic		
Before		**After**
150	Calories	73
10 g	Fat	4 g
5 g	Sat Fat	1 g
10 g	Carbs	8 g
1 g	Fiber	2 g
6 g	Protein	3 g
200 mg	Sodium	53 mg

Citrus–Grilled Shrimp Salad

 Makes 4 servings

Prep time: 5 minutes • Total time: 45 minutes

Curb carbs: Many shrimp salads include noodles or rice, but this veggie version cuts carbs and adds crunch and flavor.

Fill up on fiber: Be sure to pair this salad with a half sandwich, a whole-grain pita, or another good source of fiber.

Favor healthy fats: Olive oil and flaxseeds in one recipe is a perfect way to boost MUFAs and omega-3s!

- Barbecue grill
- Vegetable grill basket (optional)

3 tbsp	orange juice, divided	45 mL
2 tbsp	lime juice, divided	30 mL
½ tsp	cayenne pepper, divided	2 mL
½ tsp	ground cumin, divided	2 mL
10 oz	medium shrimp, peeled and deveined	300 g
1	red onion, cut into thick rounds	1
2	red bell peppers, thickly sliced lengthwise	2
1	green bell pepper, thickly sliced lengthwise	1
2 tbsp	ground flaxseeds	30 mL
1	large tomato, cut into 8 wedges	1
1 tbsp	olive oil	15 mL

1. In a medium bowl, combine 2 tbsp (30 mL) orange juice, 1 tbsp (15 mL) lime juice, ¼ tsp (1 mL) cayenne, and ¼ tsp (1 mL) cumin. Add the shrimp and onion, turning to coat. Set aside to marinate for 30 minutes at room temperature.

2. Preheat barbecue grill to medium. Oil a grill grate (and grill basket, if using).

3. Place the onion and bell peppers, skin side down, on the grill. Cover and grill, turning occasionally, for 7 minutes, or until the peppers are charred and the onion is crisp-tender. Transfer to a serving bowl.

4. In a small bowl, toss the shrimp with the flaxseeds until coated. Discard the remaining marinade. Place the shrimp on the grill, cover, and grill for 4 minutes, turning once, or until pink and opaque.

5. In the serving bowl, toss together the bell peppers, onion, shrimp, tomato wedges, and oil. Add in the remaining orange juice, lime juice, cayenne, and cumin. Toss to coat.

Makeover Magic		
Before		**After**
280	Calories	175
23 g	Fat	7 g
3 g	Sat Fat	1 g
16 g	Carbs	12 g
6 g	Fiber	4 g
7 g	Protein	17 g
1,990 mg	Sodium	114 mg

Tricolor Slaw and Potato Salad

 Makes 6 servings

Curb carbs: By replacing a portion of the potatoes in a traditional potato salad with peppers, cabbage, and corn, we curbed carbs while creating a salad that was both filling and delicious.

Fill up on fiber: This veggie-fied version has enough grams of fiber to take the "magic carbs" effect into account — this salad has just 26 grams of carbs once you do the math!

Favor healthy fats: Mayonnaise is an obvious base for this type of salad, but by using vinegar we allow the ingredients to shine while cutting fat. Olive oil, meanwhile, provides healthy fats.

- Vegetable steamer

1½ lbs	red potatoes, cut into ½-inch (1 cm) chunks	750 g
2	large red bell peppers, slivered	2
1½ cups	frozen corn kernels, thawed	375 mL
¼ cup	white vinegar	60 mL
2 tbsp	olive oil	30 mL
1 tsp	paprika	5 mL
½ tsp	ground cumin	2 mL
6 cups	shredded cabbage	1.5 L

1. In vegetable steamer, cook the potatoes for 8 minutes, or until firm-tender. Add the bell peppers for the last 2 minutes.

2. Transfer to a large bowl, along with the corn.

3. In a small bowl, whisk together the vinegar, oil, paprika, and cumin. Drizzle over the potatoes and peppers. Add the cabbage and toss to combine.

Makeover Magic		
Before		**After**
320	Calories	185
17 g	Fat	5 g
3 g	Sat Fat	1 g
38 g	Carbs	32 g
4 g	Fiber	6 g
5 g	Protein	5 g
1,200 mg	Sodium	23 mg

Warm German Potato Salad

 Makes 6 servings

Prep time: 5 minutes • Total time: 35 minutes

Curb carbs: We used just enough potatoes to make the perfect serving size.

Fill up on fiber: Between the potatoes, celery, and flaxseeds this salad is a fibrous side dish!

Favor healthy fats: Instead of a heavy dressing of bacon and gorgonzola, we went with a vinegar-based dressing and added ground flaxseeds, which contribute healthy fats known as omega-3 fatty acids.

- Vegetable steamer

2 lbs	red potatoes, unpeeled, cut into large chunks	1 kg
3 oz	Canadian bacon (lean smoked back bacon), chopped	90 g
6	green onions, thinly sliced	6
5	stalks celery, sliced	5
3 tbsp	ground flaxseeds	45 mL
3 tbsp	cider vinegar	45 mL
3 tbsp	unsweetened apple juice	45 mL
2 tbsp	stone-ground mustard	30 mL
3	sprigs parsley, finely chopped	3

1. Set a vegetable steamer in a medium saucepan. Fill with water to just below the steamer.

2. Place the potatoes on the steamer. Cover and bring to a boil over high heat. Reduce the heat to medium high. Cook for 15 minutes, or until tender. Transfer to a large bowl and allow to cool for 10 minutes.

3. In a medium nonstick skillet set over medium heat, cook the bacon for 3 minutes. Add the green onions and celery. Cook, stirring, for 3 minutes, or until the onion is soft and the bacon is browned. Reduce the heat to low. Add the flaxseeds and toss to coat. Add the vinegar, apple juice, mustard, and parsley. Cook for 2 minutes, or until heated through. Pour over the potatoes. Toss to evenly coat.

Makeover Magic		
Before		**After**
566	Calories	165
36 g	Fat	3 g
12 g	Sat Fat	0.5 g
43 g	Carbs	29 g
4 g	Fiber	5 g
16 g	Protein	7 g
1,226 mg	Sodium	232 mg

Corn, Black Bean, and Edamame Salad

 Makes 6 servings

Curb carbs: The carbohydrates in this dish come from the various veggies and beans, leaving plenty of room for a half sandwich or another lunchtime treat.

Fill up on fiber: By adding a greater variety of fiber-packed ingredients to our corn salad, we not only double the fiber, but the flavor as well!

Favor healthy fats: Instead of dousing the salad in mayo, we used a light coating of olive oil (our healthy fat!) and lime juice for a zesty, fresh flavor.

Prep time: 5 minutes • Total time: 10 minutes

2 cups	frozen shelled edamame	500 mL
1½ cups	cooked fresh corn kernels (from 2 large ears or thawed frozen)	375 mL
1½ cups	canned black beans, drained and rinsed	375 mL
3	plum (Roma) tomatoes, chopped	3
1	small red onion, chopped	1
¼ cup	chopped fresh cilantro	60 mL
1 tbsp	extra virgin olive oil	15 mL
3 tbsp	freshly squeezed lime juice	45 mL
½ tsp	cayenne pepper	2 mL

1. Prepare the edamame according to package directions. Drain and rinse under cold water. Transfer to a large bowl.

2. Stir in the corn, beans, tomatoes, onion, cilantro, oil, lime juice, and pepper. Toss well.

> **Smart Start**
>
> *Check out our meal plans in Appendix A (page 286) to see what you can pair this salad with.*

Makeover Magic		
Before		**After**
190	Calories	164
6 g	Fat	5 g
1 g	Sat Fat	0.5 g
33 g	Carbs	20 g
4 g	Fiber	6 g
5 g	Protein	10 g
50 mg	Sodium	141 mg

Couscous and Chickpea Salad

 Makes 6 servings

Curb carbs: Adding chickpeas to this couscous salad reduces the carbs while adding some fiber.

Fill up on fiber: In addition to the whole wheat couscous, chickpeas, peppers, tomatoes, and olives all boost the fiber.

Favor healthy fats: Olives and olive oil both contribute to the fat in this dish, and best of all, they contribute healthy MUFAs.

Prep time: 10 minutes • Total time: 50 minutes

1½ cups	water	375 mL
1 tbsp + 1 tsp	olive oil, divided	20 mL
1 cup	whole wheat couscous	250 mL
1	can (15 oz/425 mL) chickpeas, drained and rinsed	1
1	plum (Roma) tomato, chopped	1
1	red or yellow bell pepper, chopped	1
1 oz	pitted kalamata olives, sliced	30 g
1½ tbsp	pine nuts	22 mL
1½ tbsp	lemon juice	22 mL
⅓ cup	crumbled feta cheese	75 mL

1. In a medium saucepan over high heat, bring the water and 1 tsp (5 mL) oil to a boil. Stir in the couscous. Remove from the heat and cover. Let stand for 5 minutes, or until the liquid is absorbed. Fluff with a fork.

2. Transfer the couscous to a large bowl. Add the chickpeas, tomato, pepper, olives, and nuts. Toss gently until mixed.

3. In a small bowl, whisk together the lemon juice and remaining oil. Mix and pour over the salad. Toss to mix well. Cover and refrigerate for 30 minutes to blend the flavors. Top the salad with feta cheese.

Makeover Magic		
Before		**After**
304	Calories	185
17 g	Fat	8 g
3 g	Sat Fat	2 g
31 g	Carbs	24 g
2 g	Fiber	4 g
8 g	Protein	6 g
619 mg	Sodium	235 mg

Chilled Cilantro– Soba Noodle Salad

 Makes 6 servings

Prep time: 5 minutes • Total time: 45 minutes

Curb carbs: A cup (250 mL) of soba noodles has nearly half as many carbs as a cup of spaghetti, making it a great alternative in pasta dishes.

Fill up on fiber: Both soba noodles and the beans in this salad provide fiber.

Favor healthy fats: This salad is full of flavor, and much of it comes from the sesame oil, a great source of polyunsaturated fats!

8 oz	soba noodles	250 g
2 cups	frozen shelled edamame	500 mL
1	red bell pepper, thinly sliced	1
1	green bell pepper, thinly sliced	1
3	green onions, thinly sliced	3
1/4 cup	thinly sliced fresh cilantro	60 mL
3 tbsp	sesame oil	45 mL
2 tbsp	low-sodium soy sauce	30 mL
1 tsp	grated orange zest	5 mL
2 tbsp	freshly squeezed orange juice	30 mL
1/2 tsp	hot pepper flakes	2 mL

1. In a large pot of boiling water, cook the noodles and edamame for 6 minutes. Empty into a colander and rinse well with cold water. Drain and place in a serving bowl.

2. Stir in the bell peppers, green onions, and cilantro. Toss gently.

3. In a small bowl, whisk together the oil, soy sauce, orange zest, orange juice, and hot pepper flakes. Pour the dressing over the noodle mixture. Toss gently and refrigerate for 30 minutes to allow the flavors to blend. Serve cold or at room temperature.

Makeover Magic		
Before		**After**
330	Calories	273
12 g	Fat	10 g
2 g	Sat Fat	1 g
48 g	Carbs	37 g
4 g	Fiber	4 g
9 g	Protein	13 g
550 mg	Sodium	436 mg

Creamy Pasta Salad

 Makes 4 servings

Curb carbs: We cut the amount of penne in this pasta salad with peppers, tomatoes, and romaine hearts that add body without adding many carbs.

Fill up on fiber: Using whole-grain pasta boosts the fiber.

Favor healthy fats: To cut saturated fat, we used a lighter dressing made from Greek yogurt, vinegar, and seasonings instead of mayonnaise. Be sure to pair this dish with a healthy fat source.

6 oz	whole-grain penne	175 g
1/2 cup	plain nonfat (0%) Greek yogurt	125 mL
2 tbsp	grated Parmesan cheese	30 mL
1/4 cup	finely chopped fresh basil	60 mL
1 tbsp	red wine vinegar	15 mL
1/2 tsp	dry mustard	2 mL
1	clove garlic, minced	1
1	green bell pepper, chopped	1
2	romaine hearts, chopped	2
1 cup	cherry tomatoes, halved	250 mL

1. Cook the pasta according to package directions, omitting the salt. Rinse under cold water and drain.

2. In a large bowl, stir together the yogurt, cheese, basil, vinegar, mustard, and garlic. Add the red pepper, romaine, tomatoes, and pasta. Toss to coat well.

Smart Start
Add two 6-ounce (170 g) cans of tuna for a dose of DHA.

Makeover Magic		
Before		**After**
282	Calories	210
6 g	Fat	2 g
2 g	Sat Fat	0.5 g
46 g	Carbs	39 g
3 g	Fiber	7 g
11 g	Protein	11 g
200 mg	Sodium	58 mg

Philly Cheese Steaks

 Makes 4 servings

Curb carbs: This version has 6 grams of fiber, which can be subtracted from the carbs for a total of 34 grams of carbs — 11 grams fewer than the traditional version.

Fill up on fiber: By using whole wheat rolls and topping the steak with more vegetables than usual, you can really boost the fiber in this sandwich!

Favor healthy fats: We used thin-sliced deli roast beef instead of chipped steak to cut down the saturated fat. For a dose of healthy fats, consider adding more olive oil, or a few sliced kalamata olives on top.

1½ tsp	olive oil	7 mL
1	onion, sliced	1
1	red bell pepper, sliced	1
1	green bell pepper, sliced	1
12 oz	thinly sliced low-sodium deli-style roast beef	375 g
¼ cup	shredded Cheddar cheese	60 mL
4	whole-grain hoagie rolls, split	4
2	low-sodium dill pickle spears, halved	2

1. In a large nonstick skillet, heat the oil over medium-high heat. Cook the onion and bell peppers, stirring, for 5 minutes, or until tender. Transfer to a bowl.

2. Reduce the heat to medium. Cook the roast beef slices in the skillet, stirring, for 1 minute, or until heated through. Top with the cheese and cook for 1 minute, or until the cheese is melted.

3. Divide the beef mixture among the 4 rolls and top with the onion and peppers. Serve each sandwich with half a pickle.

Makeover Magic		
Before		**After**
540	Calories	367
24 g	Fat	11 g
9 g	Sat Fat	4 g
45 g	Carbs	40 g
4 g	Fiber	6 g
35 g	Protein	26 g
1,000 mg	Sodium	424 mg

Sausage and Pepper Wraps

 Makes 4 servings

Prep time: 5 minutes • Total time: 20 minutes

Curb carbs: We turned the traditional sausage sandwich into a wrap, replacing the doughy bun with a tortilla to curb carbs.

Fill up on fiber: Use a whole wheat tortilla and pair the sausage with fiber-packed veggies. This dish has 9 grams of fiber, meaning with the magic carbs, you get just 13 grams!

Favor healthy fats: To reduce saturated fat, opt for turkey sausage instead of pork. Be sure to pair this sandwich with a source of healthy fat, such as sliced olives.

- Preheat broiler
- Baking sheet, lined with foil

8 oz	sweet Italian turkey sausages, sliced	250 g
1	small onion, thinly sliced	1
1	green bell pepper, thinly sliced	1
2 cups	low-sodium tomato-basil pasta sauce	500 mL
4	6-inch (15 cm) whole wheat tortillas	4
2 tbsp	grated Parmesan cheese	30 mL

1. In a large nonstick skillet, cook the sausage over medium-high heat, stirring, for 5 minutes, or until no longer pink. Add the onion and pepper and cook for 3 minutes, or until slightly browned. Stir in the sauce and cook for 5 minutes, or until heated through and the flavors blend.

2. Stuff the tortillas with the sausage mixture and sprinkle 1½ tsp (7 mL) cheese on each tortilla. Put on the prepared baking sheet and broil for 1 minute, or until the cheese is melted and golden.

Makeover Magic		
Before		**After**
470	Calories	197
31 g	Fat	8 g
11 g	Sat Fat	2 g
26 g	Carbs	22 g
2 g	Fiber	9 g
18 g	Protein	17 g
1,100 mg	Sodium	408 mg

Monte Cristos

 Makes 2 servings

Prep time: 5 minutes • Total time: 10 minutes

Curb carbs: Instead of using 3 slices of bread to make a club-style layered sandwich, we stuck with 2 slices and piled the filling high.

Fill up on fiber: Whole-grain bread is versatile and works perfectly for this sandwich, providing 4 grams of fiber!

Favor healthy fats: We cut the fat by not frying the sandwich in butter, and we used 1% milk and only egg whites, instead of 3 large eggs. Add healthy fats to this dish by substituting canola oil for cooking spray or adding olives or avocado slices into the sandwich.

- Cast-iron skillet

4	slices whole-grain bread, toasted	4
¾ oz	low-sodium deli ham (about 2 slices)	23 g
¾ oz	low-sodium deli turkey (about 2 slices)	23 g
1	slice Gruyère cheese, halved	1
2 tsp	Dijon mustard	10 mL
2	large egg whites	2
2 tbsp	1% milk	30 mL
	Nonstick cooking spray	

1. On 2 slices of toast, layer the ham, turkey, and cheese.

2. Spread the mustard on the remaining 2 slices of toast and top the sandwiches.

3. Heat cast-iron skillet over medium heat for 2 minutes.

4. In a shallow bowl, whisk together the egg whites and milk. Dip 1 side of a sandwich into the egg mixture and let the excess drip off. Repeat on the other side. Repeat with the other sandwich.

5. Coat the skillet with cooking spray. Cook the sandwiches for 6 minutes, turning once, until the meat is warmed through, the cheese is melting, and the egg is cooked.

Makeover Magic		
Before		**After**
890	Calories	244
59 g	Fat	7 g
17 g	Sat Fat	3 g
65 g	Carbs	25 g
3 g	Fiber	4 g
26 g	Protein	19 g
970 mg	Sodium	598 mg

Open-Faced Asian Chicken Sandwiches

 Makes 4 servings

Prep time: 15 minutes • Total time: 25 minutes

Curb carbs: It's easy to curb the carbs on this sandwich by making it an open-faced version that uses just 1 slice of bread.

Fill up on fiber: Thanks to using whole-grain bread, our open-faced sandwich has as much fiber as a regular banh mi sandwich that uses 2 slices.

Favor healthy fats: Ground flaxseeds add healthy fats.

- Preheat barbecue grill, coated with nonstick cooking spray, or broiler
- Broiler pan, coated with nonstick cooking spray (if using broiler)

4	chicken breast cutlets (3 oz/90 g each)	4
1 tbsp + 2 tsp	low-sodium soy sauce, divided	25 mL
2 tbsp	seasoned rice vinegar	30 mL
1	clove garlic, minced	1
¼ tsp	red chile paste	1 mL
1 tbsp	liquid honey, divided	15 mL
1	small cucumber, thinly sliced	1
1 cup	shredded cabbage	250 mL
¼ cup	chopped fresh cilantro, divided	60 mL
2 tbsp	ground flaxseeds	30 mL
4	slices whole-grain bread	4
½ cup	plain nonfat (0%) Greek yogurt	125 mL

1. Brush each chicken cutlet with 1 tsp (5 mL) soy sauce. Place on prepared broiler pan (if using). Grill or broil the cutlets, turning once, for 10 minutes, or until no longer pink and the juices run clear.

2. In a small bowl, whisk together the vinegar, garlic, chile paste, and 2 tsp (10 mL) honey. In a medium bowl, toss together the cucumber, cabbage, half of the cilantro, and the flaxseeds. Toss with half of the vinegar mixture. Set aside.

3. Add the remaining soy sauce and 1 tsp (5 mL) honey to the remaining vinegar mixture. Place 1 bread slice on each of 4 plates. Top each with a chicken cutlet and one-quarter of the cabbage mixture. Drizzle with 2 tbsp (30 mL) of the soy mixture. Top each with 2 tbsp (30 mL) yogurt and sprinkle with the remaining cilantro.

Smart Start
Go ahead and use 2 slices of sprouted whole-grain bread if you want a traditional sandwich.

Makeover Magic		
Before		**After**
740	Calories	234
34 g	Fat	5 g
9 g	Sat Fat	1 g
66 g	Carbs	22 g
4 g	Fiber	4 g
41 g	Protein	25 g
3,470 mg	Sodium	594 mg

Sweet Turkey Paninis

 Makes 2 servings

Curb carbs: Swap in a whole wheat tortilla for a white roll for instant carb control.

Fill up on fiber: At 9 grams of fiber, we can use magic carbs to bring the total carbs of this meal down to just 10 grams — plenty of room for a side of chips or pasta salad!

Favor healthy fats: We used a lean cut of turkey and a small amount of olive oil–based mayo and cheese instead of tons of cheese, fatty spreads, and meat. For more healthy fats, add in some ground flaxseeds or drizzle each sandwich with a tablespoon (15 mL) of olive oil.

1 tbsp + 1 tsp	olive oil mayonnaise	20 mL
2 tsp	Dijon mustard	10 mL
4	6-inch (15 cm) whole wheat tortillas	4
1	pear, thinly sliced	1
8 oz	deli-sliced no-salt turkey breast	250 g
½ cup	fresh arugula	125 mL
2 oz	Asiago cheese, shredded	60 g

1. In a small bowl, whisk together the mayonnaise and mustard.

2. Lay the tortillas on a clean work surface. Divide the pear slices, turkey, arugula, and cheese among the top halves of the tortillas. Drizzle with the mayonnaise mixture. Fold over the other half of each tortilla.

3. Heat a nonstick skillet over medium heat. Add the sandwiches and place a second skillet on top, pressing down slightly. Cook for 6 minutes, turning once, until slightly flattened and toasted.

Smart Start
Add 1 tbsp (15 mL) pine nuts or walnuts for diabetes-friendly fats and more fiber.

Makeover Magic		
Before		**After**
450	Calories	212
51 g	Fat	9 g
19 g	Sat Fat	3 g
41 g	Carbs	19 g
4 g	Fiber	9 g
25 g	Protein	22 g
1,610 mg	Sodium	293 mg

Buffalo Grilled Cheese Sandwiches

 Makes 4 servings

Prep time: 5 minutes • Total time: 10 minutes

Curb carbs: Grilled cheese doesn't have to be a blood sugar shocker when you use whole-grain bread.

Fill up on fiber: Adding celery and red onion gives this sandwich crunch as well as fiber.

Favor healthy fats: Olive oil–based mayo adds MUFAs and gives this Buffalo-flavored sandwich the desired creaminess.

- Grill pan or skillet

1 tbsp	olive oil mayonnaise	15 mL
1 tbsp	hot pepper sauce	15 mL
8	slices whole-grain bread	8
4	thin slices red onion	4
2	stalks celery, sliced	2
4	slices Cheddar cheese	4
4 tbsp	crumbled reduced-fat blue cheese	60 mL
	Nonstick cooking spray	

1. In a small bowl, stir together the mayonnaise and hot pepper sauce.

2. Place 4 bread slices on a work surface. Spread the mayonnaise on the bread slices. Layer with the onion, celery, Cheddar cheese, and blue cheese and top with the remaining bread slices. Coat the top bread slice of each sandwich with cooking spray.

3. Place the sandwiches coated side down on a grill pan. Coat the remaining bread slice of each sandwich with cooking spray. Place a heavy pan over the top of the sandwiches. Cook for 4 minutes, turning once, until lightly browned.

Makeover Magic		
Before		**After**
445	Calories	278
27 g	Fat	14 g
10 g	Sat Fat	7 g
32 g	Carbs	24 g
2 g	Fiber	4 g
20 g	Protein	14 g
759 mg	Sodium	659 mg

Bacon and Apple Grilled Cheese

 Makes 4 servings

Prep time: 5 minutes • Total time: 20 minutes

Curb carbs: Ditch the white bread and replace it with whole-grain slices, which are lower in carbs thanks to magic carbs.

Fill up on fiber: The whole-grain bread is also an excellent source of fiber.

Favor healthy fats: We used turkey bacon instead of pork and a light mustard spread instead of a high-fat creamy dressing to moderate saturated fat. Add healthy fat to this meal by enjoying a handful of almonds on the side.

	Nonstick cooking spray	
4	strips turkey bacon, cut into small pieces	4
8	slices whole-grain bread	8
1 tbsp	Dijon mustard	15 mL
4	slices sharp (old) Cheddar cheese	4
1	Granny Smith apple, peeled and sliced	1

1. Coat a large nonstick skillet with cooking spray. Cook the bacon over medium-low heat, stirring, for 2 minutes, or until golden brown. Transfer bacon to a plate lined with paper towels. Reduce the heat to low.

2. Spread 4 slices of bread with the mustard and divide the cheese, apple, and bacon among them. Top with the other bread slices and add to the hot pan. Cook for 12 minutes, turning once, until each side is deep brown and crunchy.

Makeover Magic Bacon and Apple Grilled Cheese		
Before		After
820	Calories	283
42 g	Fat	12 g
22 g	Sat Fat	6 g
75 g	Carbs	28 g
3 g	Fiber	5 g
37 g	Protein	18 g
1,500 mg	Sodium	658 mg

Makeover Magic Tuna Salad Wraps		
Before		After
330	Calories	150
19 g	Fat	7 g
9 g	Sat Fat	0.5 g
25 g	Carbs	15 g
1 g	Fiber	8 g
15 g	Protein	14 g
490 mg	Sodium	21 mg

Makeover Magic Roast Beef Rolls		
Before		After
810	Calories	288
74 g	Fat	4 g
12 g	Sat Fat	2 g
19 g	Carbs	40 g
1 g	Fiber	8 g
18 g	Protein	24 g
590 mg	Sodium	508 mg

Tuna Salad Wraps

Makes 4 servings

Prep time: 10 minutes • Total time: 10 minutes

Curb carbs: Using 6-inch (15 cm) tortillas instead of the usual 10-inch (25 cm) or larger varieties is an easy way to cut carbs while getting more filling in every bite.

Fill up on fiber: These whole wheat tortillas are packed with fiber!

Favor healthy fats: The walnuts in this wrap are a yummy source of ALA omega-3 fatty acids — plus the tuna packs DHA!

2 tbsp	plain nonfat (0%) Greek yogurt	30 mL
1 tsp	lemon juice	5 mL
1	can (6 oz/170 g) white tuna packed in water, drained	1
½ cup	red grapes, halved	125 mL
1	stalk celery, chopped	1
¼ cup	walnut halves, chopped	60 mL
2	slices red onion, chopped	2
4	6-inch (15 cm) whole wheat tortillas	4
2 cups	arugula	500 mL

1. In a bowl, stir together the yogurt and lemon juice. Add the tuna, grapes, celery, walnuts, and onion.

2. Lay the tortillas on a flat surface, top with the arugula and tuna mixture, and roll.

Roast Beef Rolls

Makes 2 servings

Prep time: 5 minutes • Total time: 5 minutes

Curb carbs: Quinoa is a carb that is higher in protein, so it's the perfect choice for someone eating to beat diabetes. Using roast beef as the roll instead of a wrap further curbs carbs.

Fill up on fiber: You can find fiber in grains like quinoa, chopped fresh fruits like the pear, and in the pine nuts.

Favor healthy fats: By excluding cheese and adding nuts, you can decrease saturated fat and increase our favorite fats.

1 cup	cooked quinoa, chilled	250 mL
1	pear, finely chopped	1
1 tbsp	lemon juice	15 mL
2 tbsp	chopped pine nuts	30 mL
¼	small red onion, finely chopped	¼
1 cup	shredded romaine lettuce	250 mL
8	slices low-sodium, lean deli roast beef (¾ oz/23 g each)	8

1. In a medium bowl, combine the quinoa, pear, lemon juice, pine nuts, onion, and romaine. Stir to mix.

2. Fill the center of each roast beef slice with the mixture and roll up. Use a tester to hold the roll together. Serve.

> **Smart Start**
> *If eating this dish as an appetizer, serve 2 rolls per person. If eating this dish as an entrée, serve 4 rolls per person, with a side.*

Barbecue Shrimp Wraps

 Makes 2 servings

Curb carbs: Substituting a whole wheat tortilla for 2 slices of bread is a surefire way to reduce the carbs. Look for tortillas with 20 grams of carbohydrates.

Fill up on fiber: Not only does the whole wheat tortilla have fiber, but lettuce and celery contribute an additional gram.

Favor healthy fats: Thick, creamy dressings are usually filled with fat, so we opted for shrimp cooked in a small amount of oil, and a barbecue sauce to top! In this dish, cashews are our source of blood sugar–friendly MUFAs.

2 tsp	canola oil	10 mL
2	cloves garlic, minced	2
4 oz	medium shrimp, peeled and deveined	125 g
2	6-inch (15 cm) whole wheat tortillas	2
2	stalks celery, chopped	2
2 tbsp	raw cashews	30 mL
2 tbsp	barbecue sauce	30 mL
1 cup	shredded romaine lettuce	250 mL

1. In a nonstick skillet, heat the oil over medium-high heat. Cook the garlic, stirring, for 1 minute, or until fragrant. Add the shrimp and cook, stirring, for 2 minutes, or until the shrimp are opaque.

2. Lay the tortillas on a clean work surface. Divide the shrimp mixture among the 2 tortillas. Add the celery and cashews. Drizzle 1 tbsp (15 mL) barbecue sauce on each tortilla. Top with the lettuce and roll up.

Makeover Magic		
Before		**After**
440	Calories	230
16 g	Fat	11 g
3 g	Sat Fat	1 g
39 g	Carbs	21 g
3 g	Fiber	8 g
34 g	Protein	19 g
1,850 mg	Sodium	269 mg

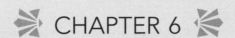

CHAPTER 6

Appetizers & Snacks

Papaya-Tomato Bruschetta. 120

Hawaiian Chicken Skewers 121

Mediterranean Chicken Pinwheels. 122

Kickin' Chicken "Wings" 123

Greek Meatballs. 124

"Pigs" in a Blanket. 125

Vegetable-Tofu Wontons 126

Salmon Slider Bites 128

Sweet-'n'-Spicy Grilled Shrimp. 129

Crab Cakes with Lemon-Dijon Sauce 130

Buffalo Chicken Quesadillas. 132

Mango-Tuna Spring Rolls 133

Stuffed Potato Skins 134

Spiced Sweet Potato Chips 135

Salt-'n'-Vinegar Potato Chips 136

Grand Slam Nachos. 137

Fresh Guacamole with Vegetables. 138

Mexican Dip. 139

Guilt-Free Spinach-Artichoke Dip 140

Papaya-Tomato Bruschetta

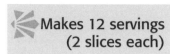 **Makes 12 servings (2 slices each)**

Curb carbs: Swap a typical refined white bread for high-fiber, wholesome grains like this whole wheat baguette. Fresh fruit like papaya adds sweetness and antioxidants at the same time, but keep in mind that one serving has 21 grams of carbs, so you may need to choose a lower-carb entrée to complement the appetizer.

Fill up on fiber: Choosing whole wheat adds fiber to help make you feel full. If you can find a sprouted wheat baguette, choose that one for even more fiber.

Favor healthy fats: Olive oil is chock-full of monounsaturated fats, making it the best oil for your bruschetta.

Prep time: 10 minutes • Total time: 20 minutes

- Preheat oven to 450°F (230°C)

1	whole wheat baguette, cut into 24 slices (each ½-inch/1 cm thick)	1
2 tbsp	olive oil, divided	30 mL
1	clove garlic, halved	1
1	papaya, peeled, seeded and chopped	1
4	plum (Roma) tomatoes, finely chopped	4
½	small red onion, finely chopped	½
½ cup	chopped fresh cilantro	125 mL
1 tsp	liquid honey	5 mL
½ tsp	grated lemon zest	2 mL

1. Brush the bread on both sides with 1 tbsp (15 mL) oil. Place on a baking sheet and bake in preheated oven for 7 minutes, or until golden brown and crisp. Rub the toasted bread very lightly with the cut garlic clove.

2. In a medium bowl, combine the papaya, tomatoes, onion, cilantro, honey, lemon zest, and remaining oil. Spoon on top of the toasted garlic bread.

Makeover Magic		
Before		**After**
230	Calories	112
13 g	Fat	2 g
3 g	Sat Fat	0.5 g
25 g	Carbs	21 g
2 g	Fiber	2 g
6 g	Protein	3 g
450 mg	Sodium	338 mg

Hawaiian Chicken Skewers

 Makes 6 servings

Prep time: 10 minutes • Total time: 1 hour, 25 minutes

Curb carbs: This appetizer is surely friendly when curbing carbs!

Fill up on fiber: Low-carb apps are typically lower in fiber as well, since fiber comes from plant sources. Simply enjoy this healthy appetizer and choose a high-fiber entrée to accompany it.

Favor healthy fats: Our marinade beats out bottled sauces that are high in saturated fat and processed ingredients. Serve with Hawaiian cashews for a dose of healthy fats.

- Barbecue grill
- 6 metal skewers

2	cloves garlic, minced	2
1 tbsp	grated fresh gingerroot (or 1 tsp/5 mL ground ginger)	15 mL
1	jalapeño pepper, seeded and finely chopped	1
2 tbsp	low-sodium soy sauce	30 mL
2 tbsp	honey	30 mL
2 tbsp	freshly squeezed lime juice	30 mL
½	pineapple, cored, sliced, cut into 1-inch (2.5 cm) cubes	½
2	boneless skinless chicken breasts, cut into 1-inch (2.5 cm) cubes	2
1	small red onion, cut into 8 wedges	1
1 tbsp	chopped fresh cilantro	15 mL

1. In a small saucepan, combine the garlic, ginger, jalapeño, soy sauce, honey, and lime juice. Slowly bring to a boil over medium heat. Set aside and cool.

2. Toss the pineapple and chicken into the marinade and refrigerate. Let marinate for 1 to 2 hours.

3. Preheat the barbecue grill to medium-high.

4. Thread the pineapple, chicken, and onion onto skewers, dividing equally. Grill for 10 minutes, turning once, until the chicken is browned and cooked through. Transfer to a serving platter and sprinkle with chopped cilantro.

Makeover Magic		
Before		**After**
240	Calories	112
10 g	Fat	2 g
4 g	Sat Fat	0.5 g
20 g	Carbs	12 g
<1 g	Fiber	1 g
17 g	Protein	13 g
630 mg	Sodium	121 mg

Mediterranean Chicken Pinwheels

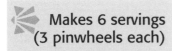 **Makes 6 servings (3 pinwheels each)**

Curb carbs: Unlike many pinwheel recipes, which use store-bought crescent roll dough, we opted to use a thin chicken breast as our wrap.

Fill up on fiber: We snuck spinach into this recipe, which adds great flavor but also packs in many nutrients.

Favor healthy fats: Pitted black olives serve up a dose of MUFAs.

Makeover Magic		
Before		**After**
400	Calories	98
20 g	Fat	4 g
6 g	Sat Fat	1 g
34 g	Carbs	3 g
1 g	Fiber	1 g
20 g	Protein	12 g
1,230 mg	Sodium	260 mg

Prep time: 5 minutes • Total time: 55 minutes

- Preheat oven to 375°F (190°C)
- Kitchen string
- Baking sheet, sprayed with nonstick canola oil cooking spray

2 cups	packed baby spinach leaves	500 mL
1	large boneless skinless chicken breast (10 oz/300 g)	1
2 tbsp	goat cheese, softened	30 mL
2 tbsp	chopped pitted kalamata olives	30 mL
1/3 cup	chopped sun-dried tomatoes	75 mL

1. Heat a large nonstick skillet over medium heat. Place the spinach in the skillet, cover, and cook, tossing occasionally, for 2 minutes, or until wilted. Drain off any excess water. Pat dry with paper towels. Set aside.

2. Lay the chicken breast on a work surface. If the fillet is attached, open it away from the breast, like opening a book. Using a sharp knife, cut through the thickest part of the chicken breast, without cutting through the edge. Open the breast like a book. With a heavy skillet or meat mallet, pound the chicken to 1/2 inch (1 cm) thickness. Spread the goat cheese evenly over the top side of the chicken. Scatter the reserved spinach, olives, and sun-dried tomatoes over the goat cheese.

3. Starting with a long side of the chicken, roll the chicken horizontally, jelly-roll style. Using 2 pieces of string, tie the chicken to secure. Transfer the chicken to the prepared baking sheet.

4. Bake in preheated oven for 40 minutes, or until an instant-read thermometer inserted in the center of the chicken pinwheel registers 165°F (74°C).

5. Remove and let stand for 10 minutes. Cut crosswise into 18 thin slices.

Kickin' Chicken "Wings"

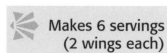 **Makes 6 servings (2 wings each)**

Prep time: 5 minutes • Total time: 40 minutes

3 tbsp	cayenne pepper sauce	45 mL
2 tbsp	barbecue sauce	30 mL
2	cloves garlic, minced	2
12	boneless skinless chicken breast tenderloins (12 oz/375 g total)	12
2 tbsp	low-fat blue cheese dressing (optional)	30 mL

Curb carbs: These "wings" make a tasty pre-dinner low-carb snack with only 1 gram of carbs from the sauce!

Fill up on fiber: Pair this kickin' chicken with carrot sticks for vitamin A and fiber!

Favor healthy fats: This recipe has almost no fat, so be sure to pump up your MUFAs and omega-3s with your entrée.

1. In a small bowl, mix the pepper sauce, barbecue sauce, and garlic. Place the chicken and half of the sauce in a large resealable bag. Close and shake to coat each piece. Refrigerate and allow the chicken to marinate for 30 minutes.

2. Heat a large skillet over medium heat. Remove the chicken from the bag, with any extra sauce in the bag, and cook for 4 minutes, turning once, or until browned and the internal temperature reaches 165°F (74°C).

3. Place the chicken on a serving plate and drizzle with the remaining sauce. Serve with the dressing, if using.

Makeover Magic		
Before		**After**
650	Calories	64
40 g	Fat	0 g
16 g	Sat Fat	0 g
48 g	Carbs	1 g
0 g	Fiber	0 g
28 g	Protein	13 g
900 mg	Sodium	326 mg

Greek Meatballs

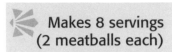

Makes 8 servings (2 meatballs each)

Prep time: 5 minutes • Total time: 35 minutes

Curb carbs: Use whole wheat bread crumbs to make these meatballs more wholesome.

Fill up on fiber: Pair with a dinner high in fiber to meet your fiber goals.

Favor healthy fats: Be sure to serve these meatballs only with a tomato sauce made from pure olive oil, not vegetable oil. This will guarantee you are favoring MUFAs.

- Preheat oven to 375°F (190°C)
- Large baking sheet, coated with nonstick cooking spray

10 oz	frozen spinach, thawed and squeezed dry	300 g
1 lb	extra-lean (99% fat-free) ground turkey	500 g
¾ cup	whole wheat bread crumbs	375 mL
2 tbsp	ground flaxseeds	30 mL
2	cloves garlic, minced	2
1 tsp	dried oregano	5 mL
¼ cup	crumbled feta cheese	60 mL
1	large egg, lightly beaten	1
1 cup	no-sugar-added marinara sauce (optional)	250 mL

1. In a large bowl, combine the spinach, turkey, bread crumbs, flaxseeds, garlic, oregano, feta cheese, and egg. With clean hands, roll the mixture into 16 meatballs. Place on the prepared sheet.

2. Bake in preheated oven for 15 minutes. Rotate the meatballs to ensure that they stay round. Bake for 15 minutes, or until the meatballs have reached an internal temperature of 165°F (74°C). Serve with marinara sauce, if using.

Makeover Magic		
Before		**After**
540	Calories	125
32 g	Fat	4 g
11 g	Sat Fat	1 g
31 g	Carbs	6 g
2 g	Fiber	3 g
31 g	Protein	18 g
900 mg	Sodium	126 mg

"Pigs" in a Blanket

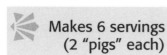 **Makes 6 servings (2 "pigs" each)**

Curb carbs: We swapped the average crescent roll dough for whole wheat pizza dough as the "blanket," to make this childhood favorite a blood-sugar-friendly option!

Fill up on fiber: The whole wheat pizza dough boosts the fiber to 3 grams, which is great for an appetizer!

Favor healthy fats: Using lean, 100% beef hot dogs helps to guarantee you are eating real meat with no filler, plus it decreases the saturated fat. Olive oil is the favored fat in this recipe.

Prep time: 13 minutes • Total time: 25 minutes

- Preheat the oven to 375°F (190°C)
- Baking sheet, lined with parchment paper

1 tbsp	whole wheat flour	15 mL
8 oz	store-bought whole wheat pizza dough	250 g
3	extra-lean nitrate-free 100% beef hot dogs, each cut into 4 pieces	3
1 tbsp	olive oil	15 mL
¼ cup	unsalted stone-ground mustard	60 mL

1. Lightly dust a clean work surface with the flour. Using a rolling pin, roll the dough into a circle, about 12 inches (30 cm) in diameter.

2. Using a pizza cutter or knife, slice the dough into 12 pizza-shaped slices.

3. Beginning at the base of each slice, add 1 piece of hot dog and roll up each triangle to the opposite point. Place on the prepared baking sheet. Repeat until all 12 slices have been filled. The ends of the hot dog may or may not be covered, depending on the size of each dough slice. Brush with the olive oil.

4. Bake in preheated oven for 12 minutes, or until the dough is golden brown and the hot dog is heated through. Serve with the mustard for dipping.

Makeover Magic		
Before		**After**
520	Calories	124
37 g	Fat	4 g
14 g	Sat Fat	0.5 g
29 g	Carbs	8 g
2 g	Fiber	3 g
17 g	Protein	5 g
1,250 mg	Sodium	401 mg

Vegetable-Tofu Wontons

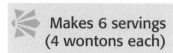 **Makes 6 servings (4 wontons each)**

Curb carbs: Who knew Chinese food could be healthy?

Fill up on fiber: Cruciferous vegetables like cabbage provide a great source of fiber. Serve over a bed of cabbage or broccoli slaw for even more filling fiber.

Prep time: 10 minutes • Total time: 40 minutes

- Preheat the oven to 425°F (220°C)
- Food processor
- Large baking sheet, coated with nonstick cooking spray

Sauce

2 tbsp	low-sodium soy sauce	30 mL
2 tsp	seasoned rice wine vinegar	10 mL
1/8 tsp	hot pepper flakes	0.5 mL

Wontons

3 oz	firm tofu, drained	90 g
2 tsp	grated fresh gingerroot (or 2/3 tsp/3 mL ground ginger)	10 mL
1	clove garlic, minced	1
1/8 tsp	ground black pepper	0.5 mL
2 tsp	peanut oil	10 mL
3	shiitake mushrooms, finely chopped	3
1 cup	packaged shredded green cabbage or coleslaw mix, finely chopped	250 mL
1	green onion, chopped	1
2 tbsp	chopped fresh cilantro	30 mL
24	3½-inch (8.5 cm) square wonton wrappers	24

1. *To make the sauce:* In a small bowl, whisk together the soy sauce, vinegar, and hot pepper flakes. Set aside.

2. *To make the wontons:* Place 1 folded-up paper towel on your work surface, place the tofu on it, and use another paper towel to gently press down on the tofu to release extra water. Do this on all sides of the tofu until much of the water has been released. You may need additional towels.

3. In a food processor, add the tofu, ginger, garlic, and pepper and pulse until the tofu is coarsely blended. There may be a few chunks in the mixture, but not many. Set aside.

Makeover Magic

Before		After
630	Calories	131
21 g	Fat	3 g
7 g	Sat Fat	0.5 g
77 g	Carbs	22 g
3 g	Fiber	1 g
32 g	Protein	5 g
980 mg	Sodium	398 mg

Favor healthy fats:
Peanut oil not only provides healthier fats than other oils, but it can be heated to a very high temperature without burning or smoking.

4. In a large nonstick skillet, heat the oil over medium-high heat. Cook the mushrooms, stirring, for 4 minutes or until starting to brown. Stir in the cabbage and cook, stirring occasionally, for 4 minutes, or until wilted. Add the green onion and cook for 1 minute. Transfer to a mixing bowl. Stir in the cilantro. Add the tofu mixture and stir to combine all ingredients.

5. Arrange the wonton wrappers on a clean work surface. Place a rounded teaspoon (5 mL) of the tofu filling in the center of each wonton. Dampen the edges with water and fold over to form a triangle. Press the edges with your fingers to seal. Place the wontons on the prepared baking sheet and lightly coat with cooking spray.

6. Bake in preheated for 10 minutes, or until lightly golden and crisp. Serve with seasoned soy sauce.

Salmon Slider Bites

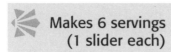 **Makes 6 servings (1 slider each)**

Prep time: 5 minutes • Total time: 15 minutes

1	large egg	1
1/8 tsp	salt	0.5 mL
1/8 tsp	ground black pepper	0.5 mL
1 tbsp	Dijon mustard	15 mL
2 tbsp	finely chopped fresh dill	30 mL
1/2	red onion, finely chopped	1/2
12 oz	wild salmon fillet, skin removed, finely chopped	375 g
1/3 cup	whole wheat bread crumbs	75 mL
2 tbsp	ground flaxseeds	30 mL

Curb carbs: Instead of serving the traditional slider on a bun, we chose to do without. Fancy this dish up by serving it over a bed of greens drizzled with balsamic vinegar. Now you can get most of your 45 grams of carbs from your entrée.

Fill up on fiber: These tasty sliders are mostly protein, so get your fiber with your entrée.

Favor healthy fats: Flaxseeds provide your daily dose of ALA omega-3s, while wild salmon is super-rich in DHA omega-3s.

1. In a bowl, whisk the egg until lightly beaten. Stir in the salt, pepper, and mustard. Add the dill, onion, salmon, bread crumbs, and flaxseeds and gently fold just until combined.

2. Divide the mixture into 6 parts. Roll into balls and press slightly to form 6 small patties.

3. Heat a large skillet over medium-high heat and coat with cooking spray. Cook for 8 minutes, turning once, or until the fish is opaque and patties are hot in the center.

Makeover Magic		
Before		**After**
220	Calories	133
7 g	Fat	6 g
2 g	Sat Fat	1 g
28 g	Carbs	6 g
4 g	Fiber	1 g
11 g	Protein	14 g
470 mg	Sodium	184 mg

Papaya-Tomato Bruschetta (page 120)

Guilt-Free Spinach-Artichoke Dip (page 140)

Steak Burrito Bowl
(page 151)

Beef Ragù Over Polenta (page 160)

Grilled Pork Tacos with Mango Salsa (page 168)

Asian Lettuce Cups (page 176)

Chicken Paprikash (page 190)

Chicken Pad Thai (page 197)

Sweet-'n'-Spicy Grilled Shrimp

 Makes 4 servings

Prep time: 10 minutes • Total time: 20 minutes

Curb carbs: We want the delicious flame-grilled shrimp flavor, so we opted to use real brown sugar and no breading on our shrimp, which curbs carbohydrates.

Fill up on fiber: To add fiber and vitamins to this protein-based dish, we recommend adding ½ cup (125 mL) steamed broccoli per serving on the side.

Favor healthy fats: Shrimp is a marine source of DHA, and using olive oil and olive oil–based mayonnaise gives this recipe a heart-healthy flair.

- Preheat barbecue grill to medium-high
- 4 metal skewers

Sauce
2 tbsp	olive oil mayonnaise	30 mL
¼ cup	plain nonfat (0%) Greek yogurt	60 mL
2 tbsp	lime juice	30 mL
2 tbsp	chopped fresh cilantro	30 mL

Shrimp
1 tbsp	brown sugar	15 mL
½ tsp	ground cumin	2 mL
¼ tsp	garlic powder	1 mL
¼ tsp	ground black pepper	1 mL
¼ tsp	cayenne pepper	1 mL
1 tbsp	olive oil	15 mL
12 oz	medium shrimp, peeled and deveined, patted dry	375 g

1. *To make the sauce:* In a small bowl, whisk together the mayonnaise, Greek yogurt, lime juice, and cilantro. Refrigerate.

2. *To make the shrimp:* In a small bowl, combine the brown sugar, ground cumin, garlic powder, black pepper, and cayenne. Add the oil and mix. Add the shrimp and toss to coat.

3. Thread the shrimp onto metal skewers, dividing equally and leaving ¼ inch (0.5 cm) between the pieces. Grill for 4 minutes, turning once, or until opaque. Serve with the dipping sauce.

Makeover Magic		
Before		**After**
560	Calories	165
29 g	Fat	7 g
6 g	Sat Fat	1 g
47 g	Carbs	6 g
4 g	Fiber	0 g
28 g	Protein	19 g
3,040 mg	Sodium	191 mg

Crab Cakes with Lemon-Dijon Sauce

**Makes 4 servings
(2 cakes each)**

Curb carbs: We added just enough whole wheat bread crumbs to act as a binder, leaving more room for the meaty crab and carbs with your entrée!

Prep time: 15 minutes • Total time: 30 minutes

- Preheat oven to 425°F (220°C)
- Nonstick baking sheet, coated with nonstick canola oil cooking spray

Lemon-Dijon Sauce

2 tbsp	canola oil mayonnaise	30 mL
1 tbsp	Dijon mustard	15 mL
1 tbsp	lemon juice	15 mL
1	clove garlic, minced	1

Crab Cakes

12 oz	cooked lump crabmeat	375 g
2	green onions, chopped	2
½	red bell pepper, finely chopped	½
¼ cup	plain nonfat (0%) Greek yogurt	60 mL
1	large egg, lightly beaten	1
2 tbsp	lemon juice	30 mL
¼ tsp	Old Bay seasoning	1 mL
½ cup	whole wheat panko bread crumbs, divided	125 mL

1. *To make the lemon-Dijon sauce:* In a small bowl, whisk together the mayonnaise, mustard, lemon juice, and garlic. Refrigerate.

2. *To make the crab cakes:* In a large bowl, combine the crabmeat, green onions, pepper, yogurt, egg, lemon juice, Old Bay seasoning, and ¼ cup (60 mL) bread crumbs.

3. Using your hands, loosely form the crab mixture into 8 patties.

Makeover Magic

Before		After
330	Calories	194
18 g	Fat	8 g
3 g	Sat Fat	1 g
20 g	Carbs	11 g
0 g	Fiber	2 g
22 g	Protein	19 g
690 mg	Sodium	407 mg

Fill up on fiber: The bread crumbs in the cakes provide the fiber in this recipe. To turn this appetizer into a meal, add fiber-full grilled veggies and spicy baked sweet potato fries on the side.

Favor healthy fats: Choosing a canola oil–based mayonnaise keeps the dip healthy. And crab contains omegas!

4. Spread the remaining bread crumbs on a plate and roll each crab cake over the crumbs to lightly coat. As the cakes are formed, place them on prepared baking sheet. If the patties are misshaped, use the palm of your hand to press them down into an evenly shaped circle, the size of a small hockey puck. Discard any excess crumbs.

5. Bake in preheated oven for 12 minutes, or until golden brown on the outside and hot in the center.

6. Top each crab cake with a heaping teaspoon (7 mL) of sauce.

Buffalo Chicken Quesadillas

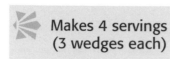

Makes 4 servings
(3 wedges each)

Curb carbs: Use whole wheat wraps instead of refined wheat. Look for wraps that have about 20 grams of carbs and 3 grams of fiber.

Fill up on fiber: Adding fiber with beans is easy! Remember, beans offer both carbs and protein.

Favor healthy fats: To make this dish truly comforting to your health, serve with guacamole.

Prep time: 10 minutes • Total time: 25 minutes

4	8-inch (20 cm) whole wheat tortillas	4
2	green onions, thinly sliced	2
1	stalk celery, finely chopped	1
1	cooked boneless skinless chicken breast (6 oz/175 g), finely shredded or chopped	1
1 tbsp	cayenne pepper sauce	15 mL
1 cup	no-salt-added canned black beans, drained and rinsed	250 mL
1/3 cup	crumbled blue cheese	75 mL
1/2 cup	blue cheese dressing (optional)	125 mL

1. Arrange the tortillas on a work surface.

2. In a small bowl, combine the green onions, celery, chicken, pepper sauce, beans, and cheese. Spread the mixture over the lower half of each tortilla. Fold the plain half over the filling to form a semicircle.

3. Heat a large nonstick skillet over medium heat until hot. Cook 2 of the tortillas for 8 minutes, turning once, until lightly browned and heated through. Transfer to a cutting board and repeat with the remaining tortillas. Cut each into 3 wedges and serve with blue cheese dressing, if using.

Smart Start

If eating this dish as an appetizer, serve 2 wedges per person. If eating as an entrée, serve 3 to 4 wedges each, with a side.

Makeover Magic		
Before		**After**
250	Calories	175
10 g	Fat	6 g
5 g	Sat Fat	3 g
27 g	Carbs	14 g
5 g	Fiber	2 g
13 g	Protein	16 g
590 mg	Sodium	389 mg

Mango-Tuna Spring Rolls

 Makes 8 servings

Prep time: 10 minutes • Total time: 45 minutes

Curb carbs: Rice paper wrappers are naturally low in carbohydrates.

Fill up on fiber: Choose a high-fiber dinner entrée to meet your fiber goals.

Favor healthy fats: Tuna is an outstanding source of omega-3 fatty acids. And while many spring rolls are fried, these are not! Instead, they are packed full of fresh flavor.

Dipping Sauce

1 tbsp	lime juice	15 mL
3 tbsp	low-sodium soy sauce	45 mL
1 tbsp	liquid honey	15 mL
1 tsp	Sriracha chili sauce	5 mL
1	clove garlic, minced	1

Spring Rolls

8	8-inch (20 cm) round rice paper wrappers	8
8	Bibb lettuce leaves	8
24	fresh mint leaves	24
2	cooked wild tuna steaks (each 5 oz/150 g), sliced very thin	2
1	red bell pepper, thinly sliced	1
1	mango, thinly sliced	1
2	green onions, thinly sliced	2

1. *To make the dipping sauce:* In a small dish, stir together the lime juice, soy sauce, honey, chili sauce, and garlic. Let stand for at least 20 minutes to allow the flavors to blend.

2. *To make the spring rolls:* Fill a large pie plate with very warm water. Set a clean towel nearby. Add 1 rice paper wrapper at a time and soak each for 30 to 45 seconds, or until softened. Place the rice papers in a stack on the towel and let stand for 2 minutes, or until soft and pliable.

3. Layer the ingredients in a 4-inch (10 cm) line in the center of each rice paper, starting 3 inches (7.5 cm) up from the edge closest to you. On each wrapper, arrange 1 leaf lettuce, 3 mint leaves, and one-eighth of the slices of tuna, pepper, mango, and green onions. Drizzle each spring roll with 1 tsp (5 mL) sauce. Fold in the sides and roll up, envelope-style. Set seam side down on a plate. Repeat with the remaining ingredients.

4. To serve, cut each roll in half on the diagonal and serve with the remaining dipping sauce.

Makeover Magic		
Before		**After**
210	Calories	108
6 g	Fat	1 g
0.5 g	Sat Fat	0 g
29 g	Carbs	16 g
1 g	Fiber	1 g
8 g	Protein	10 g
360 mg	Sodium	238 mg

Stuffed Potato Skins

Prep time: 5 minutes • Total time: 1 hour, 20 minutes

Curb carbs: By removing some of the flesh and filling the potato with protein and healthy fats, you can easily curb the carbs, leaving plenty of room for carbs with your entrée!

Fill up on fiber: In addition to the broccoli florets, the nutrient-dense skin of the potato packs a wallop of fiber.

Favor healthy fats: Top each potato with pine nuts or guacamole to keep your blood sugar balanced.

- Preheat oven to 400°F (200°C)
- Baking sheet, lined with foil

3	potatoes, scrubbed	3
3	slices turkey bacon, halved	3
2 tbsp	olive oil	30 mL
1 cup	frozen broccoli florets, thawed, finely chopped	250 mL
¼ cup	shredded Cheddar cheese	60 mL
¼ cup	plain nonfat (0%) Greek yogurt	60 mL
1	plum (Roma) tomato, finely chopped	1
1	green onion, thinly sliced	1

1. Prick the potatoes with a fork several times and place on a baking sheet. Bake for 45 minutes, or until the potatoes are cooked through and soft.

2. In a medium skillet over low heat, cook the bacon for 3 minutes, turning once, or until cooked through. Transfer to a plate lined with paper towels to drain. Crumble into small pieces. Set aside.

3. When the potatoes are done, transfer to a cooling rack for 10 minutes, or until cool enough to handle.

4. Increase the oven temperature to 450°F (230°C).

5. Cut each potato in half lengthwise. Using a spoon, scoop out the flesh, leaving ¼ inch (0.5 cm) of flesh in the skin. Reserve the flesh for another use.

6. Brush both sides of the potato skin halves with olive oil, place on the baking sheet, and bake for 10 minutes, or until golden and crisp.

7. In a small bowl, mix the bacon, broccoli, cheese, and yogurt. Remove the potato skins from the oven and fill each potato skin with the bacon mixture.

8. Bake for 5 minutes, until the cheese is melted. Top each with tomato and green onion.

Makeover Magic		
Before		**After**
338	Calories	119
17 g	Fat	7 g
8 g	Sat Fat	1 g
35 g	Carbs	9 g
3 g	Fiber	1 g
11 g	Protein	6 g
408 mg	Sodium	239 mg

Spiced Sweet Potato Chips

 Makes 4 servings

Prep time: 5 minutes • Total time: 25 minutes

Curb carbs: Did you know sweet potatoes have the same amount of carbs as white potatoes? Yes, they do! Our secret is leaving the skins on to get more fiber — plus, sweet potatoes are high in antioxidants that help prevent disease.

Fill up on fiber: Just 1 serving of these sweet potato chips packs 2 grams of fiber.

Favor healthy fats: Olive oil is an easy way to sneak in the day's worth of healthy fats — and baking these chips in the oven makes this a snack you can eat daily.

- Preheat the oven to 375°F (190°C)
- 2 large baking sheets, lined with parchment paper

2	sweet potatoes, cut crosswise into 1/8-inch (3 mm) thick slices	2
1 tbsp	olive oil	15 mL
1 tbsp	pure maple syrup	15 mL
1 tsp	ground cumin	5 mL
1/8 tsp	ground black pepper	0.5 mL
1/8 tsp	salt	0.5 mL

1. In a large bowl, toss the potato slices with the olive oil and maple syrup until coated. Add the cumin, pepper, and salt and toss again to coat.

2. Arrange the potato slices in a single layer on prepared baking sheets. Bake in preheated oven for 20 minutes, turning once, or until golden and crisp.

Makeover Magic		
Before		**After**
283	Calories	101
20 g	Fat	4 g
3 g	Sat Fat	0.5 g
25 g	Carbs	17 g
2 g	Fiber	2 g
3 g	Protein	1 g
1,283 mg	Sodium	110 mg

Salt-'n'-Vinegar Potato Chips

 Makes 4 servings

Prep time: 10 minutes • Total time: 1 hour, 25 minutes

Curb carbs: The key to curbing carbs here is portion control. This recipe makes a perfect snack or accompaniment to your sandwich at lunch!

Fill up on fiber: Keeping the skin on these potatoes is important, as the skin provides the bulk of the fiber.

Favor healthy fats: The olive oil coating douses the chips in healthy fats, and baking means no deep-frying in saturated fat.

- 2 large baking sheets, coated with nonstick cooking spray

2	russet potatoes	2
2½ cups	white vinegar	625 mL
1 tbsp	olive oil	15 mL
½ tsp	sea salt	2 mL

1. Using a mandoline or a knife, thinly slice potatoes crosswise.

2. In a large bowl, combine the potatoes and vinegar and cover for 1 hour.

3. After 50 minutes have passed, preheat the oven to 400°F (200°C).

4. Drain the potatoes and transfer to prepared baking sheets. Drizzle with the oil and toss to coat. Arrange in a single layer. Sprinkle with the salt.

5. Bake, one sheet at a time, for 8 minutes, turning once, or until the chips are golden and crisp.

Makeover Magic		
Before		**After**
193	Calories	116
9 g	Fat	4 g
1 g	Sat Fat	0.5 g
26 g	Carbs	19 g
3 g	Fiber	1 g
3 g	Protein	2 g
299 mg	Sodium	300 mg

Grand Slam Nachos

 Makes 6 servings

Prep time: 10 minutes • Total time: 25 minutes

Curb carbs: Beans provide complex carbs, making this dish blood sugar–friendly!

Fill up on fiber: You'll find fiber in the tortillas, beans, and corn.

Favor healthy fats: This is a lower-saturated-fat nacho recipe compared to most, because beans replace meat. Olives contribute our favored fats. Serve with 1 tablespoon (15 mL) of guacamole per serving to make this dish even higher in monounsaturated fatty acids.

• Preheat the oven to 425°F (220°C)

4 oz	unsalted blue corn tortilla chips	125 g
1½ tsp	olive oil	7 mL
½	red onion, diced	½
½	red bell pepper, finely chopped	½
1	jalapeño pepper, seeded and finely chopped	1
¼ cup	sliced pitted kalamata olives	60 mL
1 cup	rinsed drained canned black beans	250 mL
1 cup	frozen corn kernels, thawed	250 mL
½ tsp	ground cumin	2 mL
⅔ cup	shredded Cheddar cheese	150 mL
½ cup	plain nonfat (0%) Greek yogurt	125 mL
2 tbsp	lime juice	30 mL
¼ cup	finely chopped fresh cilantro	60 mL
⅔ cup	salsa	150 mL

1. Arrange the chips in a single layer on a large baking sheet. Set aside.
2. In a large skillet over medium-high heat, heat the oil. Cook the onion, bell pepper, and jalapeño pepper, stirring, for 5 minutes, or until softened.
3. In a bowl, combine the pepper mixture, olives, black beans, corn, and cumin. Scatter evenly over the tortilla chips. Sprinkle with the cheese.
4. Bake in preheated oven for 10 minutes, or until the cheese is melted and bubbling.
5. In a small bowl, combine the Greek yogurt, lime juice, and cilantro. Spoon over the nachos evenly. Top with salsa.

Makeover Magic		
Before		**After**
610	Calories	234
21 g	Fat	10 g
8 g	Sat Fat	3 g
76 g	Carbs	28 g
4 g	Fiber	4 g
30 g	Protein	9 g
1,240 mg	Sodium	396 mg

Fresh Guacamole with Vegetables

 Makes 6 servings

Prep time: 10 minutes • Total time: 10 minutes

Curb carbs: This naturally low-carb dip would pair well with nacho chips or toasted pita bread cut into triangles.

Fill up on fiber: Celery is mostly water and fiber, helping to keep carbs curbed and your tummy filled.

Favor healthy fats: Avocados are a prime source of healthy fats!

6	stalks celery, trimmed, halved lengthwise, and cut into 2-inch (5 cm) pieces	6
3	green bell peppers, cut into 1-inch (2.5 cm) slices	3
2	ripe avocados, pitted and peeled	2
1 tbsp	lemon juice	15 mL
2	plum (Roma) tomatoes, seeded and finely chopped	2
1	jalapeño pepper, seeded and finely chopped	1
½	red bell pepper, finely chopped	½
½	small red onion, finely chopped	½
1 tbsp	finely chopped fresh cilantro	15 mL

1. Arrange the celery and green bell pepper slices on a serving plate.

2. In a large bowl, mash the avocados with a fork until chunky. Add the lemon juice, tomatoes, jalapeño pepper, red pepper, onion, and cilantro and stir until all ingredients are combined.

3. Serve with the celery and peppers for dipping.

Makeover Magic		
Before		**After**
140	Calories	104
8 g	Fat	7 g
0 g	Sat Fat	1 g
18 g	Carbs	10 g
4 g	Fiber	5 g
2 g	Protein	2 g
400 mg	Sodium	136 mg

Mexican Dip

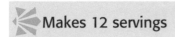Makes 12 servings

Prep time: 10 minutes • Total time: 35 minutes

Curb carbs: Blood sugar–friendly carbs come mainly from the corn and beans.

Fill up on fiber: Beans and corn are the fiber-boosting ingredients in this creamy dip!

Favor healthy fats: Top this dish with sliced avocado for healthy fats galore!

- Preheat oven to 350°F (180°C)
- 8-inch (20 cm) square glass baking dish, coated with nonstick cooking spray

4 oz	Neufchâtel cheese or reduced-fat cream cheese, softened	125 g
1 cup	plain nonfat (0%) Greek yogurt	250 mL
½ cup	shredded Cheddar cheese	125 mL
1	red bell pepper, finely chopped	1
1	jalapeño pepper, seeded and finely chopped	1
2	cloves garlic, minced	2
¾ cup	frozen corn kernels, thawed	175 mL
1	can (14 oz/398 mL) black beans, drained and rinsed	1
2	green onions, thinly sliced	2
2	plum (Roma) tomatoes, chopped	2
¼ cup	chopped fresh cilantro	60 mL
	Bell pepper slices, cucumber slices or whole-grain tortilla chips	

1. In a large bowl, stir the Neufchâtel cheese, yogurt, and Cheddar cheese to combine. Add the bell pepper, jalapeño pepper, garlic, corn, and black beans and stir until blended.

2. Transfer to baking dish. Bake in preheated oven for 15 minutes, or until bubbling.

3. Sprinkle with the green onions, tomatoes, and cilantro. Serve with bell pepper slices, cucumber slices, or whole-grain tortilla chips.

Makeover Magic		
Before		After
230	Calories	83
12 g	Fat	5 g
7 g	Sat Fat	2 g
24 g	Carbs	7 g
4 g	Fiber	2 g
9 g	Protein	5 g
1,200 mg	Sodium	140 mg

Guilt-Free Spinach-Artichoke Dip

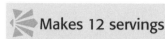
Prep time: 10 minutes • Total time: 40 minutes

Curb carbs: Choose to eat this dip with high-fiber vegetables and you'll save plenty of carbs for dinner and dessert!

Fill up on fiber: Artichokes are packed with fiber — as much as 2 grams per serving!

Favor healthy fats: Be sure to eat a dinner entrée high in MUFAs or omega-3s to get your daily dose of favored fats. Think fish fajitas!

- Preheat oven to 350°F (180°C)
- 8-inch (20 cm) square glass baking dish

1 cup	plain nonfat (0%) Greek yogurt	250 mL
6 oz	Neufchâtel cheese or reduced-fat cream cheese, softened	175 g
¼ cup	grated Parmesan cheese, divided	60 mL
3	cloves garlic, minced	3
2 tbsp	Dijon mustard	30 mL
⅛ tsp	paprika	0.5 mL
1	small red onion, finely chopped	1
9 oz	frozen artichoke hearts, thawed, squeezed dry, and chopped	270 g
10 oz	frozen chopped spinach, thawed and squeezed dry	300 g
	Veggies or unsalted tortilla chips	

1. In a large bowl, stir the yogurt, Neufchâtel cheese, 2 tbsp (30 mL) Parmesan cheese, garlic, mustard, and paprika to combine. Add the onion, artichoke hearts, and spinach to the mixture and stir to combine.

2. Pour into baking dish. Top with the remaining Parmesan cheese.

3. Bake in preheated oven for 20 minutes, or until bubbling hot. Serve with veggies or unsalted tortilla chips.

Makeover Magic		
Before		**After**
160	Calories	78
12 g	Fat	4 g
4 g	Sat Fat	2 g
5 g	Carbs	5 g
2 g	Fiber	2 g
7 g	Protein	5 g
300 mg	Sodium	189 mg

CHAPTER 7
Meat

Country-Fried Steak 142

Steak with Mushroom Sauce and Roasted Artichokes . . . 144

Traditional Slow-Cooker Pot Roast 146

Sizzlin' Beef Fajitas 147

Beef Stroganoff 148

Chinese Beef and Vegetables 150

Steak Burrito Bowl 151

Shepherd's Pie 152

Mom's Meat Loaf 154

Salisbury Steak 155

Un-Stuffed Peppers 156

Zesty Italian Cheeseburgers 157

Go-To Spaghetti and Meatballs 158

Beef Goulash 159

Beef Ragù over Polenta 160

Cobb Salad–Style Buffalo Dogs 161

Ground Bison with Spaghetti Squash 162

Lemon-Rosemary Lamb Chops 164

Lamb Burgers with Lemon-Yogurt Sauce 165

Slow-Cooker Pork Barbecue 166

Pork Chops with Apple Salad 167

Grilled Pork Tacos with Mango Salsa 168

Marinated Grilled Boneless Pork Ribs 169

Sweet Pork Tagine 170

Pork and Broccoli Stir-Fry 171

Rosemary Pork Medallions and Mashed Potatoes 172

Tangy Pork Kabobs 174

Italian Sausage and Linguine 175

Asian Lettuce Cups 176

Country-Fried Steak

Prep time: 5 minutes • Total time: 25 minutes

Curb carbs: Just coat the steaks once with whole wheat flour — it curbs carbs and gives the dish a slightly different look that sets it apart from the classic fried steak.

- Preheat oven to 350°F (180°C)
- Meat mallet
- Baking sheet, lined with foil

Steak

½ cup	whole wheat flour	125 mL
½ tsp	ground black pepper	2 mL
¼ tsp	cayenne pepper	1 mL
¼ tsp	garlic powder	1 mL
⅛ tsp	salt	0.5 mL
2	large egg whites	2
2 tbsp	1% milk	30 mL
4	pieces (each 4 oz/125 g) lean boneless top round steak	4
2 tbsp	canola oil	30 mL

Sauce

¾ cup	low-sodium ready-to-use beef broth	175 mL
2 tsp	cornstarch	10 mL
⅛ tsp	ground black pepper	0.5 mL

1. *To make the steak:* In a shallow bowl, combine the flour, black pepper, cayenne, garlic powder, and salt.

2. In another shallow bowl, whisk together the egg whites and milk.

3. On a cutting board, using a meat mallet, pound the steaks to ¼-inch (0.5 cm) thickness.

4. Dredge each steak in the flour mixture, then in the egg mixture, shaking off the excess, and back in the flour mixture to fully coat the steak. Transfer to a plate. Discard any excess egg and flour mixtures.

Makeover Magic		
Before		**After**
630	Calories	298
40 g	Fat	13 g
13 g	Sat Fat	3 g
32 g	Carbs	13 g
1 g	Fiber	2 g
34 g	Protein	31 g
670 mg	Sodium	183 mg

Fill up on fiber: Pair this recipe with a small baked sweet potato and 1 cup (250 mL) of steamed broccoli per serving to add 4 grams of fiber.

Favor healthy fats: Instead of frying in oil that is nearly 2 inches (5 cm) deep in the pan, we simply pan-fried our steaks in a small amount of canola oil, a source of MUFAs.

5. In a large nonstick skillet, heat the oil over medium-high heat. Cook the steaks, in batches as necessary, for 4 minutes, turning once, or until golden brown and crisp. Set aside the skillet and juices.

6. Transfer the steaks to the prepared baking sheet and bake in preheated oven for 10 minutes, or until a thermometer inserted in the center registers 145°F (63°C) for medium-rare.

7. *To make the sauce:* In the same skillet over medium-high heat, heat the broth for 30 seconds. In a small bowl, whisk together ¼ cup (60 mL) of the warmed broth and the cornstarch. Add the mixture into the skillet and whisk for 2 minutes, or until thickened. Stir in the black pepper. Serve the sauce over the steaks.

Steak with Mushroom Sauce and Roasted Artichokes

 Makes 4 servings

Prep time: 5 minutes • Total time: 1 hour, 5 minutes

Curb carbs: We kept the carbohydrates low by making a low-sugar red wine sauce instead of a heavier sauce.

- Preheat oven to 425°F (220°C)
- Baking sheet, lined with foil and lightly sprayed with nonstick cooking spray

Artichokes

4	artichokes, stems and tips removed	4
1 tbsp	olive oil	15 mL
1 tbsp	lemon juice	15 mL
2	cloves garlic, minced	2

Steak and Sauce

1 tbsp	olive oil, divided	15 mL
1 lb	lean beef flank steak	500 g
1/8 tsp	salt	0.5 mL
1/8 tsp	ground black pepper	0.5 mL
4 oz	cremini mushrooms, thinly sliced	125 mL
3/4 cup	dry red wine	175 mL
1/4 cup	balsamic vinegar	60 mL
2 tbsp	low-sodium ready-to-use beef broth	30 mL
2 tsp	chopped fresh thyme (or 2/3 tsp/ 3 mL dried)	10 mL
1 tbsp	finely chopped fresh rosemary (or 1 tsp/5 mL dried)	15 mL

1. *To make the artichokes:* Place the artichokes on the prepared baking sheet and drizzle with the oil and lemon juice. Sprinkle with the garlic. Bake in preheated oven for 1 hour, or until fork-tender and lightly golden.

2. *To make the steak and sauce:* After 30 minutes, in a large nonstick griddle or skillet, heat 1 1/2 tsp (7 mL) oil over medium heat. Season the steak with the salt and pepper. Cook the steak on the griddle, turning once, for 10 minutes, or until a thermometer inserted in the center registers 145°F (63°C) for medium-rare. Transfer the steak to a plate and cover.

Makeover Magic		
Before		**After**
847	Calories	346
49 g	Fat	14 g
22 g	Sat Fat	4 g
47 g	Carbs	20 g
6 g	Fiber	7 g
39 g	Protein	29 g
824 mg	Sodium	264 mg

Fill up on fiber:
Artichokes are full of fiber,
a great ingredient for
balancing blood sugar.

Favor healthy fats: This
dish often has bacon, but
we were able to cut that out,
along with using a lean cut
of beef to reduce saturated
fat. Olive oil provides flavor
and monounsaturated fats
in this savory recipe.

3. In the same skillet, heat the remaining oil over medium-high heat. Add the mushrooms and cook, stirring, for 3 minutes, or until golden brown. Add the wine, vinegar, and broth, stirring constantly, and bring to a boil. Reduce the heat to medium-low, add the thyme and rosemary, and simmer, stirring occasionally, for 10 minutes, or until the sauce reduces and thickens.

4. On a clean cutting board, slice the steak across the grain into $\frac{1}{2}$-inch (1 cm) thick slices and divide among 4 serving plates. Top with the sauce and serve with the artichokes.

Traditional Slow-Cooker Pot Roast

 Makes 4 servings

Prep time: 10 minutes • Total time: 8 hours, 25 minutes

Curb carbs: We love that the carbohydrate sources in this recipe are the vegetables. Vegetables provide healthy, energizing carbs while keeping this recipe comforting.

Fill up on fiber: Carrots and celery pumped up this recipe, taking it up to 5 grams of fiber per serving, which is great!

Favor healthy fats: Using broth with canola oil allows for a recipe with low saturated fat and more healthy fats.

- 4- to 6-quart slow cooker

6	carrots, cut into 1-inch (2.5 cm) pieces	6
1	onion, sliced lengthwise	1
3	stalks celery, coarsely chopped	3
1	small potato, cut into 1-inch (2.5 cm) pieces	1
½ cup	no-salt-added tomato purée or sauce	125 mL
1 cup	low-sodium ready-to-use beef broth	250 mL
2 tsp	chopped fresh thyme (or 1 tsp/ 5 mL dried)	10 mL
1 tbsp	canola oil	15 mL
1 lb	boneless beef chuck (blade) roast, trimmed of all visible fat	500 g
½ tsp	salt	2 mL
1 tsp	paprika	5 mL

1. In slow cooker stoneware, combine the carrots, onion, celery, potato, tomato purée, broth, and thyme.

2. In a large nonstick skillet, heat the oil over medium-high heat. Season the beef with the salt and paprika. Cook the beef for 4 minutes, turning occasionally, or until browned on all sides. Place on the vegetables.

3. Cover and cook on Low for 8 hours, or until the beef is fork-tender.

4. Remove the beef to a cutting board. Allow to sit for 10 minutes. Slice and serve with vegetables and broth.

Makeover Magic		
Before		**After**
595	Calories	279
29 g	Fat	9 g
11 g	Sat Fat	2 g
34 g	Carbs	24 g
4 g	Fiber	5 g
50 g	Protein	27 g
1,100 mg	Sodium	446 mg

Sizzlin' Beef Fajitas

 Makes 4 servings

Prep time: 10 minutes • Total time: 4 hours, 35 minutes (including marinating time)

Curb carbs: We opted for a 6-inch (15 cm) whole wheat tortilla instead of the traditional 8-inch (20 cm) white flour tortilla. Your fajita will be packed full with flavorful, juicy ingredients.

Fill up on fiber: We stuffed these whole wheat fajitas with more veggies than meat, a smart fiber-full move.

Favor healthy fats: Although the Before figure below represents a restaurant-size portion that may actually be 2 servings' worth, you can see the high amount of fat, calories, and carbs in the dish. Our homemade version is so delicious and so healthy. For more healthy fats, add a dollop of guacamole to your fajita or opt for fish instead of beef.

- Barbecue grill (optional)
- Broiler pan (if using broiler)

1 tbsp	olive oil	15 mL
4	cloves garlic, minced	4
2 tbsp	lime juice	30 mL
1 tsp	ground cumin	5 mL
12 oz	lean beef flank steak, trimmed of all visible fat	375 g
	Nonstick cooking spray	
1	green bell pepper, cut into ¼-inch (0.5 cm) wide strips	1
1	red bell pepper, cut into ¼-inch (0.5 cm) strips	1
1	small onion, cut into ¼-inch (0.5 cm) wide slices	1
4	6-inch (15 cm) whole wheat tortillas	4
¼ cup	salsa	60 mL

1. In a sealable plastic bag, combine the oil, garlic, lime juice, and cumin. Add the steak and toss well to coat. Refrigerate for 4 hours or overnight.

2. Coat a grill rack or broiler pan rack with cooking spray. Preheat the grill or broiler to medium-high.

3. Remove the steak from the marinade; discard marinade. Grill or broil 4 inches (10 cm) from the heat for 12 minutes, turning once, until a thermometer inserted in the center registers 145°F (63°C) for medium-rare. Transfer to a cutting board and cover loosely with foil.

4. Heat a nonstick skillet sprayed with cooking spray over medium-high heat. Cook the bell peppers and onion, stirring often, for 9 minutes, or until the vegetables are softened. Warm the tortillas according to the package directions. Thinly slice the steak across the grain on a slight angle.

5. To assemble a fajita, place 1 tortilla on a plate and top with one-quarter of the steak, one-quarter of the vegetable mixture, and 1 tbsp (15 mL) of the salsa.

Makeover Magic		
Before		After
1,433	Calories	261
73 g	Fat	9 g
26 g	Sat Fat	3 g
119 g	Carbs	22 g
13 g	Fiber	10 g
73 g	Protein	23 g
3,062 mg	Sodium	357 mg

Beef Stroganoff

 Makes 4 servings

Prep time: 10 minute • Total time: 45 minutes

Curb carbs: Who would have thought whole wheat egg noodles could be this good? As with all pasta-based dishes, keep an eye on the portions. We use just an ounce (30 g) of egg noodles per person, but you can increase it depending on your individual needs.

4 oz	whole wheat egg noodles	125 g
1 tbsp	canola oil (approx.)	15 mL
5 oz	white or cremini mushrooms, stems removed, halved	150 g
8 oz	asparagus, trimmed and cut into 1-inch (2.5 cm) pieces	250 g
1 lb	lean boneless beef sirloin steak, trimmed of visible fat, cut into thin strips	500 g
⅛ tsp	salt	0.5 mL
1	onion, finely chopped	1
2	cloves garlic, minced	2
½ cup	low-sodium ready-to-use beef broth	125 mL
2 tsp	cornstarch	10 mL
1 tbsp	tomato paste	15 mL
2 tbsp	plain nonfat (0%) Greek yogurt	30 mL
¼ cup	reduced-fat sour cream	60 mL
2	sprigs fresh parsley, chopped	2

1. Cook the noodles according to package directions, omitting the salt. Drain and set aside.

2. Meanwhile, in a large nonstick skillet, heat the oil over medium heat. Cook the mushrooms and asparagus, stirring, for 5 minutes, or until the asparagus is lightly golden and the mushrooms are caramelized. Remove to a large bowl and set aside.

3. Season the steak with salt. In the same skillet, adding more oil if necessary, cook the steak, stirring, for 5 minutes, until browned. Remove and set aside.

Makeover Magic		
Before		**After**
554	Calories	330
28 g	Fat	9 g
14 g	Sat Fat	4 g
44 g	Carbs	28 g
3 g	Fiber	4 g
26 g	Protein	35 g
797 mg	Sodium	229 mg

Fill up on fiber: Whole wheat egg noodles, mushrooms, and asparagus provide us with 4 grams of fiber per serving and will keep you satisfied.

Favor healthy fats: This dish gets its creaminess from Greek yogurt and reduced-fat sour cream, decreasing the fat without taking away the creaminess. Be sure to start with an appetizer high in healthy fats, like Mediterranean Chicken Pinwheels (page 122).

4. In the same skillet, cook the onion and garlic, stirring, for 5 minutes, or until softened. Stir in the broth, scraping the pan to release any browned bits. Transfer ¼ cup (60 mL) of the broth into a small measuring cup and stir in the cornstarch until smooth. Add the tomato paste and broth mixture to the skillet and stir until combined. Reduce the heat to low and simmer, stirring occasionally, for 12 minutes, or until the liquid thickens and reduces by half.

5. Return the asparagus, mushrooms, and steak to the skillet and cook for 2 minutes or until heated through. Remove from heat.

6. After the liquid cools just slightly, stir in the yogurt and sour cream. (If the mixture is too hot, the yogurt will separate.) Serve over the noodles and sprinkle with the parsley.

Chinese Beef and Vegetables

 Makes 4 servings

Prep time: 10 minutes • Total time: 20 minutes

Curb carbs: Takeout or premade sauces in Asian cuisine are often loaded with sugar. Here, we let the plentiful amount of vegetables be the main source of carbohydrates.

Fill up on fiber: The fibrous vegetables add bulk to this dish, making us full without loading on extra calories or carbs.

Favor healthy fats: We used just enough peanut oil, a source of MUFAs, to coat the steak for stir-frying, making this a dish that focuses on the right kinds of fats.

Sauce

3 tbsp	reduced-sodium soy sauce	45 mL
1 tbsp	packed brown sugar	15 mL
3 tbsp	low-sodium ready-to-use chicken broth	45 mL
½ tsp	cornstarch	2 mL

Stir-Fry

2 tsp	peanut oil	10 mL
1 lb	lean beef flank steak, thinly sliced across the grain	500 g
4	stalks broccoli, chopped into bite-size pieces	4
2 tbsp	water	30 mL
1	onion, halved and sliced	1
1	green bell pepper, sliced	1
1	red bell pepper, sliced	1
4 oz	cremini mushrooms, trimmed and sliced	125 g
1 tbsp	finely chopped fresh gingerroot (or 1 tsp/5 mL ground ginger)	15 mL
1	clove garlic, minced	1

1. *To make the sauce:* In a small saucepan over medium heat, combine the soy sauce and brown sugar.

2. In a small bowl, whisk together the broth and cornstarch until the cornstarch is dissolved. Whisk into the soy sauce. Cook, stirring, for 2 minutes, or until the sauce begins to thicken. Set aside.

3. *To make the stir-fry:* Heat a wok or large skillet over high heat for 1 minute. Add the oil. Cook the steak, stirring often, for 2 minutes, or until no longer pink. With a slotted spoon or tongs, transfer the meat to a plate and set aside. Reduce the heat to medium-high.

4. Add the broccoli and water. Cover and cook for 3 minutes, or until tender-crisp. Add the onion, green and red peppers, and mushrooms. Cook, stirring, for 5 minutes, or until the vegetables are tender-crisp.

5. Add the ginger and garlic. Cook, stirring, for 30 seconds. Add the reserved meat and sauce. Cook, stirring, for 2 minutes, or until heated through.

Makeover Magic

Before		After
670	Calories	272
35 g	Fat	9 g
8 g	Sat Fat	3 g
33 g	Carbs	19 g
4 g	Fiber	6 g
56 g	Protein	30 g
3,260 mg	Sodium	504 mg

Steak Burrito Bowl

 Makes 6 servings

Curb carbs: The trick to this dish is balancing the rice with all the other ingredients. Add just enough brown rice to give bulk to the dish, but leave most of the bowl for everything else.

Fill up on fiber: Between the beans, brown rice, and vegetables in this dish, you won't be surprised that each serving has 5 grams of fiber.

Favor healthy fats: Once again, guacamole is our star source of healthy fats. Using lean flank steak and reduced-fat cheese keeps the saturated fat within a reasonable range.

Prep time: 5 minutes • Total time: 25 minutes

- Preheat barbecue grill to medium-high
- Baking dish

1¼ cups	instant brown rice	300 mL
12 oz	lean beef flank steak, trimmed	375 g
1 tsp	chipotle seasoning	5 mL
½ tsp	ground black pepper	2 mL
1 tsp	olive oil	5 mL
1	can (15 oz/425 mL) black beans, drained and rinsed	1
3	romaine lettuce hearts, shredded	3
¼ cup	salsa	60 mL
¼ cup	guacamole	60 mL
¼ cup	reduced-fat shredded Cheddar cheese	60 mL

1. Prepare the rice according to package directions, omitting the salt. Set aside.

2. Place the steak in a baking dish and rub the steak on both sides with the chipotle seasoning and pepper. Rub the oil onto the steak.

3. Coat grill rack with cooking spray. Grill the steak for 12 minutes, turning once, or until a thermometer inserted in the center registers 145°F (63°C) for medium-rare.

4. Transfer the steak to a cutting board and let sit for 5 minutes. Slice into thin strips across the grain.

5. Evenly divide the rice, steak, beans, lettuce, salsa, guacamole, and cheese among 6 bowls.

Smart Start

If desired, another option to keep saturated fat low would be to use a leaner cut of steak while enjoying full-fat cheese.

Makeover Magic		
Before		**After**
480	Calories	252
25 g	Fat	8 g
12 g	Sat Fat	3 g
30 g	Carbs	26 g
5 g	Fiber	5 g
35 g	Protein	19 g
810 mg	Sodium	317 mg

Shepherd's Pie

 Makes 6 servings

Curb carbs: The carbohydrates in this recipe come from all the veggies. We reduced the potatoes and filled the rest of the crust mixture with delicious cauliflower.

Fill up on fiber: Shepherd's pie is such a classic recipe, and the basic contents of the recipe do not change much. There will always be meat, veggies, and potatoes to top a traditional shepherd's pie. We boosted the fiber of this dish by leaving the skins on our potatoes, packing in extra peas and adding carrots.

- Preheat oven to 350°F (180°C)
- 11- by 7-inch (28 by 18 cm) glass baking dish, sprayed with nonstick cooking spray

8 oz	russet potato (1 medium), cubed	250 g
2 cups	cauliflower florets	500 mL
	Cold water	
3 tbsp	low-fat (1%) buttermilk	45 mL
¼ cup	reduced-fat shredded Cheddar cheese	60 mL
	Nonstick cooking spray	
12 oz	boneless beef top round steak, cut into thin strips	375 g
3	carrots, chopped	3
2	cloves garlic, minced	2
1	can (14 to 15 oz/398 to 425 mL) no-salt-added diced tomatoes, with juice	1
1	onion, chopped	1
1½ cups	frozen peas, thawed	375 mL
2 tsp	reduced-sodium Worcestershire sauce	10 mL
2 tsp	cornstarch	10 mL
¼ cup	low-sodium ready-to-use beef broth	60 mL

1. Place the potato and cauliflower in a large saucepan. Add enough cold water to cover. Bring to a boil over high heat. Reduce the heat to medium and cook for 15 minutes, or until very tender. Drain and place in a medium bowl.

2. Mash well with an electric mixer or potato masher, adding the buttermilk and cheese.

Makeover Magic		
Before		**After**
548	Calories	252
30 g	Fat	5 g
14 g	Sat Fat	2 g
40 g	Carbs	33 g
4 g	Fiber	5 g
30 g	Protein	21 g
850 mg	Sodium	185 mg

Favor healthy fats: The comparison shepherd's pie uses canned cream of mushroom soup as its gravy, but we opted for the lighter version, using cornstarch to thicken beef broth for a flavorful bite. Be sure to serve a side high in healthy fats!

3. Heat a large nonstick skillet sprayed with cooking spray over medium-high heat. Cook the steak, carrots, and garlic for 5 minutes, stirring, until the steak is browned. Add the tomatoes with juice, onion, peas, and Worcestershire sauce. Bring to a boil.

4. In a small bowl, whisk together the cornstarch and broth. Add to the skillet and cook, stirring, for 3 minutes, or until the sauce thickens.

5. Spoon beef mixture into the prepared baking dish. Top with the mashed potato mixture.

6. Bake in preheated oven for 40 minutes, or until the top is golden brown. Let stand for 10 minutes before serving.

Mom's Meat Loaf

 Makes 8 servings

Prep time: 10 minutes • Total time: 1 hour, 25 minutes

Curb carbs: Many meat loaves are full of carbohydrates, not only from extra bread crumbs, but also from the sauces used for the glaze. We used flaxseeds and a thin glaze of ketchup, Worcestershire sauce, and spices to keep this a low-carb dinner option.

Fill up on fiber: The key to making a meat loaf dinner high in fiber is to pair it with tons of veggies! Check Appendix B for some high-fiber ideas. Or add oats, wheat germ, and chia seeds to your meat mixture.

Favor healthy fats: Flaxseeds are our healthy fat source in this dish. We're able to cut saturated fats by using extra-lean ground beef.

- Preheat oven to 350°F (180°C)
- 9- by 5-inch (23 by 12.5 cm) metal loaf pan, sprayed with nonstick cooking spray

Glaze

⅓ cup	ketchup	75 mL
2	cloves garlic, minced	2
1 tsp	dry mustard	5 mL
2 tbsp	reduced-sodium Worcestershire sauce	30 mL

Meat Loaf

1½ lbs	extra-lean ground beef	750 g
½ cup	ground flaxseeds	125 mL
1 tsp	dried oregano	5 mL
1 tbsp	reduced-sodium Worcestershire sauce	15 mL
1	small onion, finely chopped	1
1	large egg	1

1. *To make the glaze:* In a small bowl, mix together the ketchup, garlic, mustard, and Worcestershire sauce. Set aside.

2. *To make the meat loaf:* In a bowl, mix together the ground beef, flaxseeds, oregano, Worcestershire sauce, onion, egg, and 2 tbsp (30 mL) of the reserved ketchup mixture. Press the mixture into the prepared loaf pan.

3. Bake in preheated oven for 1 hour, or until a thermometer inserted in the center registers 160°F (71°C) and the meat is no longer pink.

4. Coat the top with the remaining ketchup mixture and bake for 10 additional minutes.

Smart Start
Add 2 tablespoons (30 mL) of wheat germ to this dish for a boost in B vitamins, fiber, protein, and MUFAs.

Makeover Magic		
Before		**After**
394	Calories	205
23 g	Fat	7 g
9 g	Sat Fat	3 g
17 g	Carbs	8 g
1 g	Fiber	1 g
28 g	Protein	26 g
1,094 mg	Sodium	307 mg

Salisbury Steak

 Makes 4 servings

Prep time: 5 minutes • Total time: 35 minutes

Curb carbs: Instead of egg noodles, we served our steak with half of a baked potato per serving to cut the carbs.

Fill up on fiber: The skin of the baked potato packs a wallop of fiber.

Favor healthy fats: Ground flaxseeds add ALA omega-3 fatty acids to this dish. To reduce the saturated fat, we used only egg whites and opted for lightly greasing the pan instead of using extra oil.

Steaks

1 lb	extra-lean ground beef	500 g
⅓ cup	ground flaxseeds	75 mL
1	clove garlic, minced	1
½ tsp	onion powder	2 mL
1 tbsp	reduced-sodium Worcestershire sauce	15 mL
1 tbsp	tomato paste	15 mL
2	large egg whites	2
	Nonstick cooking spray	

Gravy

½	onion, halved and thinly sliced	½
4 oz	cremini mushrooms, sliced	125 g
1½ cups	low-sodium ready-to-use beef broth, divided	375 mL
1½ tbsp	cornstarch	22 mL
2 tbsp	reduced-sodium Worcestershire sauce	30 mL
2	baked potatoes, halved	2

1. *To make the steaks:* In a large bowl, combine the beef, flaxseeds, garlic, onion powder, Worcestershire sauce, tomato paste, and egg whites and mix well. Form into 4 patties.

2. Heat a large nonstick skillet sprayed with cooking spray over medium-high heat. Cook the patties for 8 minutes, turning once, until browned. Transfer to a plate.

3. *To make the gravy:* In the same skillet over medium-high heat, cook the onion and mushrooms for 5 minutes, or until tender and golden brown. Add 1¼ cups (300 mL) broth and stir.

4. In a small bowl, whisk the remaining ¼ cup (60 mL) broth and the cornstarch until the cornstarch has dissolved. Add to the skillet and bring the mixture to a boil, whisking continuously. Reduce the heat to a simmer and whisk for 5 minutes, or until the gravy has reduced and thickened. Stir in the Worcestershire sauce.

5. In the skillet with the gravy, cook the patties for 5 minutes, or until a thermometer inserted in the center registers 160°F (71°C) and the meat is no longer pink.

6. Transfer to serving plates and top with gravy. Serve each with half of a baked potato.

Makeover Magic

Before		After
458	Calories	375
18 g	Fat	15 g
6 g	Sat Fat	5 g
42 g	Carbs	29 g
2 g	Fiber	6 g
31 g	Protein	31 g
767 mg	Sodium	300 mg

Un-Stuffed Peppers

 Makes 4 servings

Curb carbs: Whole-grain quinoa adds protein and fiber naturally lacking in white rice.

Fill up on fiber: The quinoa is a source of fiber, as are the peppers. Go ahead and add more quinoa on the side.

Favor healthy fats: Using extra-lean ground beef keeps saturated fat down, and we include healthy fats like olive oil in the marinara sauce. Quinoa gives a small dose of favored fats, too.

- Preheat oven to 350°F (180°C)
- 13- by 9-inch (33 by 23 cm) glass baking dish

⅔ cup	water	150 mL
⅓ cup	quinoa, rinsed well	75 mL
1 tsp	olive oil	5 mL
1 lb	extra-lean ground beef	500 g
2 cups	low-sodium marinara sauce, divided	500 mL
2	green bell peppers, sliced	2
2	red bell peppers, sliced	2
1	onion, halved and sliced	1
1	clove garlic, minced	1

1. In a saucepan, bring the water and quinoa to a boil over high heat. Reduce the heat to low, cover, and simmer for 15 minutes. Remove from the heat and cool for 5 minutes. Fluff the quinoa with a fork and set aside.

2. Meanwhile, in a large nonstick skillet, heat the oil over medium heat. Cook the ground beef for 5 minutes, or until lightly browned, stirring occasionally.

3. Add ½ cup (125 mL) of the sauce, the green and red peppers, onion, and garlic and cook, stirring, for 5 minutes, or until the peppers begin to soften.

4. Spoon ½ cup (125 mL) of the sauce on the bottom of the baking dish and add the beef mixture, quinoa, and remaining sauce. Mix until all ingredients are incorporated.

5. Bake in preheated oven for 10 minutes, or until heated through.

Smart Start

If available, choose grass-fed beef. Your choice helps to support sustainable agriculture.

Makeover Magic		
Before		**After**
390	Calories	275
17 g	Fat	8 g
7 g	Sat Fat	3 g
29 g	Carbs	25 g
4 g	Fiber	5 g
29 g	Protein	26 g
1,470 mg	Sodium	173 mg

Zesty Italian Cheeseburgers

 Makes 4 servings

Prep time: 5 minutes • Total time: 22 minutes

Curb carbs: Adding a whole wheat hamburger bun instead of Italian bread, which is popular with melts, worked wonders. With only 18 grams of carbs per bun, you can still add Spiced Sweet Potato Chips (page 135).

Fill up on fiber: Fresh vegetables boost the fiber in this juicy burger! Pair with a side of baked beans or sweet potato fries for a fiber-packed meal.

Favor healthy fats: Topping this burger with pesto not only adds Italian flair, but also provides healthy fats in the form of MUFAs. We love pesto for its olive oil and pine nuts.

1	large egg	1
1 lb	extra-lean ground beef	500 g
2	cloves garlic, minced	2
¼ cup	no-salt-added tomato sauce	60 mL
1 tsp	dried basil	5 mL
⅛ tsp	salt	0.5 mL
	Nonstick cooking spray	
4	whole wheat hamburger buns	4
4	slices part-skim mozzarella cheese	4
2 cups	fresh spinach	500 mL
1	plum (Roma) tomato, sliced	1
2 tbsp	pesto	30 mL

1. In a large bowl, whisk the egg. Add the beef, garlic, tomato sauce, basil, and salt, mixing with your hands until all ingredients are combined. Form into 4 patties.

2. Heat a grill pan or large nonstick skillet sprayed with cooking spray over medium-high heat. Cook the patties for 10 minutes, turning once, until a thermometer inserted in the center registers 160°F (71°C) and the meat is no longer pink.

3. Place each burger on a bun and top each with 1 slice of cheese, ½ cup (125 mL) of spinach, tomato slices, and 1½ tsp (7 mL) of pesto.

Makeover Magic		
Before		**After**
490	Calories	328
23 g	Fat	12 g
11 g	Sat Fat	4 g
37 g	Carbs	22 g
2 g	Fiber	3 g
32 g	Protein	33 g
785 mg	Sodium	476 mg

Go-To Spaghetti and Meatballs

 Makes 4 servings

Prep time: 5 minutes • Total time: 35 minutes

Curb carbs: Be careful to use just 8 oz (250 g) of whole wheat spaghetti in this dish — the key to curbing carbs with a pasta dish is always portion control!

Fill up on fiber: The spinach in the sauce boosts the fiber, and using whole wheat pasta instead of white spaghetti helps, too. Thanks to the magic carbs in this dish, we can serve more pasta per person than the usual 6 oz (175 g) for 4 servings.

Favor healthy fats: Packed with omega-3 fatty acids, flaxseeds are an easy substitute for bread crumbs in meat dishes, including meat loaf, meatballs, and breaded cutlets.

8 oz	whole wheat spaghetti	250 g
¼ cup	ground flaxseeds	60 mL
12 oz	extra-lean ground beef	375 g
2	cloves garlic, minced	2
2 tbsp	grated Parmesan cheese	30 mL
½ tsp	dried oregano	2 mL
1	large egg	1
	Nonstick cooking spray	
1	small onion, chopped	1
1½ cups	low-sodium pasta sauce with olive oil	375 mL
6 cups	fresh spinach (about 6 oz/175 g)	1.5 L

1. Cook the spaghetti according to package directions, omitting the salt.

2. Meanwhile, in a large bowl, mix the flaxseeds, beef, garlic, cheese, and oregano with your hands until all ingredients are combined. Add the egg and mix until all ingredients are again combined. Form into 16 meatballs.

3. Heat a large nonstick skillet sprayed with cooking spray over medium heat. Cook the meatballs for 6 minutes, turning often, or until browned. Transfer to a clean platter and set aside.

4. Return the skillet to medium-high heat and add the chopped onion. Cook for 5 minutes, stirring often, or until softened. Add the pasta sauce. Bring to a boil, reduce the heat to medium-low, cover, and simmer for 5 minutes, stirring often. Add the meatballs and cook for 8 minutes, or until a thermometer inserted in the center registers 160°F (71°C). Add the spinach to the sauce mixture, stir, and cook for 2 minutes.

5. Divide the spaghetti among 4 plates and top with the meatballs and sauce.

Makeover Magic		
Before		**After**
680	Calories	446
30 g	Fat	12 g
12 g	Sat Fat	4 g
63 g	Carbs	54 g
6 g	Fiber	9 g
39 g	Protein	36 g
1,320 mg	Sodium	393 mg

Beef Goulash

 Makes 4 servings

Curb carbs: Choose shirataki noodles, a widely available Japanese noodle made from yams, for a naturally low-carb alternative to the white pasta found in most goulashes.

Fill up on fiber: The veggies make this a really great fibrous meal to maximize that filling feeling while not raising your blood sugar. Feel free to add beans for more fiber and protein — just be sure to stay within your allotted grams of carbs.

Favor healthy fats: Personalize this dish by tossing in your favorite healthy fat source, such as veggies in an olive oil and garlic sauce.

- Preheat oven to 350°F (180°C)
- Ovenproof Dutch oven

8 oz	shirataki noodles	250 g
1 tbsp	canola oil	15 mL
1	onion, chopped	1
1	red bell pepper, chopped	1
1	green bell pepper, chopped	1
1¼ tsp	paprika	6 mL
12 oz	extra-lean ground beef	375 g
1	can (14 to 15 oz/398 to 425 mL) no-salt-added petite diced tomatoes, with juice	1
½ cup	reduced-sodium ready-to-use beef broth	125 mL
¼ tsp	salt	1 mL
¼ cup	plain nonfat (0%) Greek yogurt	60 mL
1½ tbsp	all-purpose flour	22 mL

1. Cook the noodles according to package directions and drain.

2. In ovenproof Dutch oven, warm the oil over medium-high heat. Cook the onion, peppers, and paprika, stirring, for 3 minutes. Crumble the beef into the pan. Cook, stirring, for 4 minutes, or until the beef is no longer pink. Stir in the tomatoes with juice, noodles, broth, and salt. Bring to a simmer.

3. Whisk the yogurt and flour in a small bowl. Whisk into the casserole. Stir over low heat for 2 minutes, or until thickened.

4. Cover tightly and bake in preheated oven for 15 minutes. Carefully remove the cover and stir. Bake, uncovered, for 10 minutes.

Makeover Magic		
Before		**After**
510	Calories	242
18 g	Fat	9 g
6 g	Sat Fat	2 g
53 g	Carbs	17 g
3 g	Fiber	5 g
33 g	Protein	23 g
850 mg	Sodium	307 mg

Beef Ragù over Polenta

 Makes 4 servings

Prep time: 5 minutes • Total time: 1 hour, 10 minutes

Curb carbs: Serving our ragù with an appropriate amount of higher-fiber polenta makes for a filling meal while meeting the goal of 45 to 60 grams of carbs per meal.

Fill up on fiber: With so many vegetables in the ragù, we aren't surprised that it has 6 grams of fiber.

Favor healthy fats: Olive oil is the favored fat in this cozy comfort dish.

2 tsp	olive oil, divided	10 mL
1 lb	extra-lean ground beef	500 g
2	zucchini, halved lengthwise and sliced	2
1	onion, chopped	1
3	carrots, sliced	3
2	cloves garlic, minced	2
¼ cup	tomato paste	60 mL
1 cup	dry red wine	250 mL
1	can (14 to 15 oz/398 to 425 mL) no-salt-added diced tomatoes, with juice	1
¾ cup	low-sodium ready-to-use chicken broth	175 mL
1½ tsp	dried Italian seasoning	7 mL
4 cups	water	1 L
1 cup	cornmeal	250 mL
⅛ tsp	salt	0.5 mL
¼ tsp	ground black pepper	1 mL
2 tbsp	grated Parmesan cheese	30 mL

1. In a large, heavy saucepan or Dutch oven, heat 1 tsp (5 mL) oil over medium heat. Cook the beef, stirring, for 5 minutes, or until lightly browned.

2. Add the remaining oil, zucchini, onion, carrots, and garlic, and cook, stirring, for 5 minutes, or until the onion softens. Stir in the tomato paste and wine and cook for 2 minutes, or until the liquid has reduced by half.

3. Add the tomatoes, broth, and Italian seasoning, stir to combine, and bring the mixture to a simmer. Reduce the heat to low, cover, and cook for 50 minutes, stirring occasionally, or until the sauce has thickened.

4. Meanwhile, in a saucepan, bring the water to a boil over high heat.

5. Add the cornmeal and salt, whisking constantly until the mixture comes to a boil. Reduce the heat to low and cover partially, allowing the steam to escape. Cook for 30 minutes, stirring every few minutes to avoid burning and clumps. Once thickened, stir in the pepper and cheese, cover, remove from the heat, and keep warm.

6. When the ragù is finished, serve over the polenta.

Makeover Magic		
Before		**After**
695	Calories	410
24 g	Fat	10 g
7 g	Sat Fat	3 g
84 g	Carbs	44 g
6 g	Fiber	6 g
34	Protein	29 g
736 mg	Sodium	391 mg

Cobb Salad–Style Buffalo Dogs

 Makes 4 servings

Prep time: 5 minutes • Total time: 12 minutes

Curb carbs: With a different spin on the average hot dog, we ran with the "wrap" craze and rested our dogs in a naturally lower-carb whole wheat tortilla. Our comparison recipe used a hearty sandwich roll, but we wanted minimal bread and lots of hot dog.

Fill up on fiber: Between the whole wheat wraps, lettuce, and tomatoes, this is an insanely high-fiber lunch!

Favor healthy fats: Buffalo hot dogs aren't a concession-stand staple, but they are so much better! Avocado is the source of healthy fats in this dish.

- Preheat barbecue grill to high, grill sprayed with nonstick cooking spray

4	buffalo wieners or 97% fat-free beef wieners	4
4	8-inch (20 cm) whole wheat tortillas	4
1 cup	shredded romaine lettuce	250 mL
¼	small onion, chopped	¼
½	avocado, thinly sliced	½
1	plum (Roma) tomato, chopped	1
¼ cup	crumbled reduced-fat blue cheese	60 mL
2	slices low-sodium bacon, cooked and crumbled	2

1. Grill the wieners, turning occasionally, for 7 minutes, or until browned.

2. Put 1 wiener in each tortilla and divide the lettuce, onion, avocado, tomato, cheese, and bacon among the wraps.

Makeover Magic		
Before		**After**
390	Calories	165
23 g	Fat	10 g
10 g	Sat Fat	3 g
31 g	Carbs	12 g
3 g	Fiber	8 g
15 g	Protein	15 g
1,020 mg	Sodium	303 mg

Ground Bison with Spaghetti Squash

Prep time: 5 minutes • Total time: 1 hour

Curb carbs: Spaghetti squash looks similar to pasta but is lower in carbs when compared serving for serving.

Fill up on fiber: The squash happens to be full of fiber, and all of the additional vegetables in the sauce add fiber as well.

- Preheat oven to 400°F (200°C)
- Roasting pan

1	medium (3- to 4-lb/1.5 to 2 kg) spaghetti squash	1
2 tsp	canola oil, divided	10 mL
1 lb	lean ground bison or beef	500 g
1	small onion, finely chopped	1
1	green bell pepper, cut into 1/4-inch (0.5 cm) thick slices	1
1	red bell pepper, cut into 1/4-inch (0.5 cm) thick slices	1
4 oz	cremini or white mushrooms, sliced	125 g
4 cups	fresh spinach	1 L
1/4 cup	water	60 mL
1/4 cup	no-salt-added tomato paste	60 mL
1	can (14 to 15 oz/398 to 425 mL) no-salt-added diced tomatoes, with juice	1
3	cloves garlic, minced	3
6	fresh basil leaves, finely chopped	6
1 tsp	dried oregano	5 mL
3/4 tsp	ground black pepper	3 mL
1/4 tsp	salt	1 mL
1/4 cup	grated Parmesan cheese	60 mL

1. Pierce the squash with a fork. Place in roasting pan. Bake in preheated oven for 55 minutes, or until fork-tender. When cool enough to handle, cut the squash in half, scoop it out, and discard the seeds. Scrape the flesh crosswise with a fork to separate the spaghetti-like strands. Place in a large serving bowl.

Makeover Magic		
Before		**After**
510	Calories	360
22 g	Fat	16 g
9 g	Sat Fat	5 g
42 g	Carbs	28 g
5	Fiber	7 g
38 g	Protein	27 g
1,552 mg	Sodium	364 mg

Favor healthy fats: Bison is not very common, but we wanted to use it because it is lean and the flavor is so unique. Add healthy fats to this dish by tossing in ground flaxseeds or adding more canola oil to the meat sauce.

2. Meanwhile, in a Dutch oven, heat 1 tsp (5 mL) oil over medium-high heat. Cook the bison, stirring, for 5 minutes, or until browned. Add the remaining oil and the onion, green and red peppers, and mushrooms and cook, stirring, for 3 minutes, or until the vegetables are lightly golden. Add the spinach, water, tomato paste, diced tomatoes, garlic, basil, oregano, pepper, and salt, and stir to combine. Reduce the heat and simmer for 30 minutes, stirring often, or until the sauce thickens and the vegetables are soft.

3. Divide the squash and sauce among 4 plates. Sprinkle with Parmesan cheese.

Lemon-Rosemary Lamb Chops

 Makes 4 servings

Prep time: 5 minutes • Total time: 1 hour, 20 minutes

Curb carbs: When eating pasta, choose whole wheat and portion no more than 2 oz (60 g) per person to keep within 45 grams of carbs.

Fill up on fiber: Using whole wheat orzo instead of white pasta adds fiber, as does the cucumber salad.

Favor healthy fats: Be sure to pair these chops with a side dish high in healthy fats.

- Barbecue grill
- Baking dish

8 oz	whole wheat orzo	250 g
¼ cup	lemon juice	60 mL
2	cloves garlic, minced	2
1 tbsp	finely chopped fresh rosemary (or 1 tsp/5 mL dried)	15 mL
8	lamb loin chops	8
½	cucumber, chopped	½
2	plum (Roma) tomatoes, chopped	2
1 tsp	olive oil	5 mL
2 tsp	balsamic vinegar	10 mL
	Nonstick cooking spray	

1. Cook the orzo according to package directions, omitting the salt.

2. In a small bowl, combine the lemon juice, garlic, and rosemary.

3. Place the lamb chops in baking dish and drizzle with the lemon mixture, massaging it into the meat. Cover the dish with plastic wrap and refrigerate for 40 minutes. Remove for 20 minutes before grilling to allow to come up to room temperature.

4. In a serving bowl, combine the orzo, cucumber, tomatoes, oil, and vinegar. Refrigerate.

5. Coat a grill rack with cooking spray. Preheat the grill to medium-high.

6. Remove lamb from marinade; discard marinade. Grill the lamb chops for 10 minutes, or until browned and a thermometer inserted in the center registers 145°F (63°C) for medium-rare.

7. Serve with the cucumber salad.

Makeover Magic		
Before		**After**
704	Calories	435
43 g	Fat	12 g
14 g	Sat Fat	4 g
40 g	Carbs	43 g
3 g	Fiber	10 g
37 g	Protein	37 g
306 mg	Sodium	160 mg

Lamb Burgers with Lemon-Yogurt Sauce

 Makes 4 servings

Prep time: 5 minutes • Total time: 20 minutes

Curb carbs: We chose to serve this Mediterranean burger in a heart-healthy whole wheat pita instead of a higher-carb bun. We also used honey in place of regular sugar. Since honey is sweeter, we're able to use less of it.

Fill up on fiber! The pita bread and fresh spinach add fiber here! Pair with a side salad and boost the fiber even more.

Favor healthy fats: We kept the oils and extra fat sources to a minimum here. For added healthy fats, smear on some olive tapenade, but watch your overall saturated fat intake for the entire day.

Sauce

¼ cup	plain fat-free (0%) Greek yogurt	60 mL
2 tbsp	lemon juice	30 mL
5	mint leaves, finely chopped	5
½ tsp	liquid honey	2 mL

Burgers

1 lb	lean ground lamb	500 g
1 cup	fresh spinach, chopped	250 mL
1	small red onion, finely chopped	1
⅓ cup	crumbled feta cheese	75 mL
¼ tsp	ground cumin	1 mL
1	large egg white	1
2	whole wheat pita breads, halved	2
2 cups	fresh spinach	500 mL
1	plum (Roma) tomato, thinly sliced	1

1. *To make the sauce:* In a small bowl, whisk together the yogurt, lemon juice, mint, and honey. Set aside.

2. *To make the burgers:* In a large bowl, mix together the lamb, chopped spinach, onion, cheese, cumin, and egg white. Form into 4 burgers.

3. In a large nonstick skillet over medium-high heat, cook the burgers for 10 minutes, turning once, or until a thermometer inserted in the center registers 160°F (71°C) and the meat is no longer pink.

4. Open a pita pocket and spread a spoonful of sauce inside. Cut each burger in half and place 2 halves into each pita pocket half. Fill each with ½ cup (125 mL) spinach leaves and a few tomato slices.

Makeover Magic		
Before		**After**
712	Calories	270
42 g	Fat	8 g
17 g	Sat Fat	3 g
43 g	Carbs	19 g
3 g	Fiber	3 g
40 g	Protein	32 g
1,150 mg	Sodium	414 mg

Slow-Cooker Pork Barbecue

 Makes 6 servings

Prep time: 15 minutes • Total time: 5 hours, 15 minutes

Note: To allow the spices to penetrate the pork, if time permits, rub the spice mixture over the pork and refrigerate for 4 to 8 hours before placing in the slow cooker.

Curb carbs: Replace bottled barbecue sauce with our simple vinegar- and tomato-based sauce to curb carbs deliciously.

Fill up on fiber: We added coleslaw to this sandwich, which boosted the fiber. If we could fit more coleslaw on top, we would. Whole wheat buns also add fiber.

Favor healthy fats: We used a lean pork tenderloin instead of pork shoulder, which cut the saturated fat. Add chia seeds to the coleslaw for a small helping of omega-3 fatty acids and fiber.

- 5- to 6-quart slow cooker, stoneware sprayed with nonstick cooking spray
- Large baking dish

½ tsp	salt	2 mL
½ tsp	chili powder	2 mL
2 tbsp	liquid honey	30 mL
1 tsp	olive oil	5 mL
2 lbs	pork tenderloin, trimmed	1 kg
1	onion, chopped	1
2	cloves garlic, minced	2
½ cup	apple cider vinegar	125 mL
3 tbsp	tomato paste	45 mL
3	whole wheat hamburger buns, split and toasted	3
1½ cups	store-bought coleslaw mix	375 mL
1 tbsp	lemon juice	15 mL
1 tsp	Dijon mustard	5 mL
¼ cup	plain nonfat (0%) Greek yogurt	60 mL

1. In a small bowl, combine the salt, chili powder, honey, and oil.

2. Place the pork in baking dish and rub the spice mixture on it.

3. Add the pork to prepared slow cooker stoneware. Add the onion, garlic, vinegar, and tomato paste, spreading over the pork to cover. Cover and cook on High for 5 hours or on Low for 8 hours, or until a thermometer inserted in the center reaches 145°F (63°C) and the juices run clear.

4. Meanwhile, in a bowl, stir together the coleslaw, lemon juice, mustard, and yogurt. Refrigerate.

5. When the pork is done, transfer it to a bowl and shred it. Stir in the juices from the slow cooker. Place half a bun on each of 6 plates. Divide the meat and juices among the buns. Top with the coleslaw.

Makeover Magic		
Before		**After**
470	Calories	287
19 g	Fat	5 g
7 g	Sat Fat	1 g
43 g	Carbs	25 g
2 g	Fiber	3 g
32 g	Protein	35 g
870 mg	Sodium	479 mg

Pork Chops with Apple Salad

 Makes 4 servings

Prep time: 10 minutes • Total time: 25 minutes

Curb carbs: We decided not to bread our pork chops. We just wanted to get a great sear on them to serve with our salad.

Fill up on fiber: Apples and all of the greens make this a really sweet and satisfying meal.

Favor healthy fats: Toss some flaxseeds or another nut or seed of your choice into the apple salad for a dose of healthy fats.

Apple Salad

2 tbsp	balsamic vinegar	30 mL
1 tbsp	Dijon mustard	15 mL
2	apples, thinly sliced lengthwise	2
1	head Bibb lettuce, chopped	1
2 cups	fresh spinach	500 mL
1	stalk celery, sliced	1
½	onion, sliced	½
¼ cup	crumbled reduced-fat blue cheese	60 mL

Pork Chops

4	bone-in pork loin chops (each 6 oz/175 g)	4
⅛ tsp	salt	0.5 mL
1 tbsp	chopped fresh thyme (or 1 tsp/5 mL dried)	15 mL
1	clove garlic, minced	1
	Nonstick cooking spray	

1. *To make the apple salad:* In a large bowl, whisk together the vinegar and mustard. Add the apples, lettuce, spinach, celery, and onion. Toss to coat. Sprinkle with the blue cheese. Set aside.

2. *To make the pork chops:* Season each pork chop with the salt, thyme, and garlic.

3. Heat a large nonstick skillet sprayed with cooking spray over medium heat. Cook the pork chops for 8 minutes, turning once, or until lightly browned and a thermometer inserted in the center of a chop registers 145°F (63°C) and the juices run clear. Serve with the apple salad.

Makeover Magic

Before		After
410	Calories	319
21 g	Fat	8 g
5 g	Sat Fat	3 g
21 g	Carbs	18 g
3 g	Fiber	4 g
35 g	Protein	42 g
860 mg	Sodium	381 mg

Grilled Pork Tacos with Mango Salsa

Makes 4 servings (2 tacos each)

Curb carbs: These tacos are packed with enough ingredients to be double-deckers, but instead of using 2 taco shells, we used just 1.

Fill up on fiber: Shredded lettuce is key in a good taco, but the mango salsa really boosts the fiber this time.

Favor healthy fats: We ditched cheese and sour cream to let the naturally low-fat mango salsa shine through. Remember, fats are key in balancing blood sugar, so be sure to pair with a side dish high in healthy fats.

Prep time: 10 minutes • Total time: 50 minutes

- Preheat barbecue grill to medium, grill sprayed with nonstick cooking spray

1	mango, diced	1
2	plum (Roma) tomatoes, diced	2
¼ cup	chopped fresh cilantro	60 mL
1	jalapeño pepper, seeded and finely chopped	1
½ tsp	paprika	2 mL
¼ tsp	salt	1 mL
2	cloves garlic, minced	2
1½ tsp	chipotle seasoning	7 mL
1¼ lbs	pork tenderloin, trimmed	625 g
1 tbsp	olive oil	15 mL
8	6-inch (15 cm) soft corn tortillas	8
1 cup	shredded lettuce	250 mL

1. In a bowl, stir together the mango, tomatoes, cilantro, and jalapeño. Set aside.

2. In a small bowl, mix the paprika, salt, garlic, and chipotle seasoning. Rub all over the pork and drizzle with the oil.

3. Grill the pork for 25 minutes, turning occasionally, or until a thermometer inserted in the center reaches 145°F (63°C) and the juices run clear. Let stand for 10 minutes before slicing. Cut the pork into thin slices.

4. Stack the tortillas and wrap them in foil. Place the tortillas on a cool corner of the grill to warm for 10 minutes.

5. Place the tortillas on a work surface. Arrange pork in the center of each tortilla. Top with lettuce and mango salsa.

Smart Start
For a bigger dose of healthy fats, try adding avocado to the mango salsa.

Makeover Magic		
Before		**After**
420	Calories	307
21 g	Fat	8 g
10 g	Sat Fat	2 g
38 g	Carbs	27 g
4 g	Fiber	4 g
21 g	Protein	32 g
900 mg	Sodium	211 mg

Marinated Grilled Boneless Pork Ribs

Prep time: 5 minutes • Total time: 4 hours, 25 minutes

Curb carbs: Instead of a thick, saucy glaze, we opted for a flavorful dry rub. The thick glazes often have many carbohydrates because of the barbecue sauce in them.

Fill up on fiber: This dish, while hearty, is low in fiber, so be sure to pair it with a salad of greens, or steamed veggies drizzled with lemon juice.

Favor healthy fats: There's enough olive oil in this dish to provide plentiful MUFAs.

- Barbecue grill
- Large rimmed baking sheet

2 tbsp	packed brown sugar	30 mL
1 tbsp	ground cumin	15 mL
1 tbsp	chili powder	15 mL
1 tsp	cayenne pepper	5 mL
1 tsp	garlic powder	5 mL
	Salt	
2 lbs	boneless lean country-style pork loin ribs	1 kg
4 tbsp	olive oil, divided	60 mL
	Nonstick cooking spray	
	Ground black pepper	

1. In a small bowl, combine the sugar, cumin, chili powder, cayenne pepper, garlic powder, and ¼ tsp (1 mL) salt.

2. Place the ribs on the baking sheet. Make crosswise slits halfway through the meat, without slicing through it completely. Rub 1 tbsp (15 mL) oil in the meat of the ribs and the dry rub all over the ribs on all sides, including into the cuts you made. Cover the baking sheet with plastic wrap and refrigerate at least 4 hours or up to 8 hours, turning occasionally.

3. Coat a grill rack with cooking spray. Preheat the grill to medium-high.

4. Sprinkle the ribs with salt and black pepper to taste. Grill the ribs for 20 minutes, turning once, or until a thermometer inserted in the center of a rib registers 145°F (63°C) and the juices run clear. Brush the ribs with the remaining oil and grill for 2 minutes.

Makeover Magic		
Before		After
890	Calories	389
62 g	Fat	17 g
23 g	Sat Fat	4 g
30 g	Carbs	9 g
1 g	Fiber	1 g
52 g	Protein	48 g
1,975 mg	Sodium	303 mg

Sweet Pork Tagine

 Makes 6 servings

Prep time: 10 minutes • Total time: 7 hours, 10 minutes

Curb carbs: Dried fruit adds flavor but also adds carbs. We use just enough dried fruit to add flavor without causing blood sugar to skyrocket.

Fill up on fiber: Dried fruits, fresh fruits, and vegetables provide 5 grams of fiber in this filling dish. Serve with whole wheat couscous, and the fiber will increase even more.

Favor healthy fats: Pine nuts and olive oil are the healthy fat sources in this succulent dish.

- 5- to 6-quart slow cooker, stoneware sprayed with nonstick cooking spray

⅔ cup	unsweetened apple juice	150 mL
½ cup	low-sodium ready-to-use chicken broth	125 mL
3 tbsp	olive oil	45 mL
1 tbsp	cornstarch	15 mL
¼ tsp	salt	1 mL
1 tsp	ground cumin	5 mL
1 tsp	ground cinnamon	5 mL
1 lb	pork tenderloin, trimmed and cut into 1-inch (2.5 cm) cubes	500 g
4	Granny Smith apples, cut into eighths	4
6	carrots, cut into 1-inch (2.5 cm) pieces	6
1	small onion, chopped	1
⅓ cup	pine nuts	75 mL
2 tbsp	raisins	30 mL
2	cloves garlic, minced	2
1 tsp	grated gingerroot	5 mL
½ cup	chopped fresh cilantro (optional)	125 mL

1. In prepared slow cooker stoneware, whisk together the juice, broth, olive oil, cornstarch, salt, cumin, and cinnamon until smooth. Add the pork, apples, carrots, onion, pine nuts, raisins, garlic, and ginger.

2. Cover and cook on Low for 7 to 8 hours or on High for 3 to 4 hours, or until a thermometer inserted in the center reaches 145°F (63°C) and the juices run clear. Stir in the cilantro, if using.

Makeover Magic		
Before		**After**
560	Calories	392
24 g	Fat	15 g
7 g	Sat Fat	2 g
51 g	Carbs	31 g
5 g	Fiber	5 g
35 g	Protein	34 g
1,850 mg	Sodium	229 mg

Pork and Broccoli Stir-Fry

 Makes 4 servings

Prep time: 10 minutes • Total time: 20 minutes

Curb carbs: The carbohydrates in our dish are primarily from the healthy brown rice, which we use less of thanks to bulky, delicious veggies.

Fill up on fiber: Using brown rice instead of white rice increases the fiber, as do the broccoli, bell pepper, and peas.

Favor healthy fats: This dish is low in fat compared to many similar dishes because we chose to use a minimal amount of oil and low-fat add-ins for flavor, such as the lime juice and a lean cut of meat.

Smart Start
Add ¼ cup (60 mL) crushed peanuts to this Asian favorite to get MUFAs!

Makeover Magic		
Before		**After**
589	Calories	329
24 g	Fat	7 g
4 g	Sat Fat	2 g
59 g	Carbs	37 g
5 g	Fiber	6 g
35 g	Protein	30 g
1,493 mg	Sodium	590 mg

Sauce		
3 tbsp	reduced-sodium soy sauce	45 mL
2 tbsp	lime juice	30 mL
1 tbsp	Asian chili paste	15 mL
1 tsp	liquid honey	5 mL
Stir-Fry		
3 tsp	sesame oil, divided	15 mL
1 lb	pork tenderloin, trimmed, cut into ¼-inch (0.5 cm) strips	500 g
1 tbsp	grated gingerroot (or 1 tsp/5 mL ground ginger)	15 mL
1	clove garlic, minced	1
3 cups	broccoli florets	750 mL
2	carrots, sliced	2
1	red bell pepper, thinly sliced	1
3 tbsp	water	45 mL
½ cup	snap peas (1 oz/30 g)	125 g
2 cups	hot cooked brown rice	500 mL

1. *To make the sauce:* In a small bowl, combine the soy sauce, lime juice, chili paste, and honey. Set aside.

2. *To make the stir-fry:* In a large nonstick skillet, heat 1 tsp (5 mL) oil over medium-high heat. Cook the pork, in batches if necessary so as not to overcrowd the skillet, stirring often, for 3 minutes, or until lightly browned. Transfer to a plate and set aside.

3. Return the skillet to medium-high heat and stir in the remaining oil. Cook the ginger and garlic, stirring, for 30 seconds, or until fragrant. Stir in the broccoli and cook, stirring, for 1 minute. Add the carrots, peppers, and water. Cover and simmer for 3 minutes, or until tender-crisp.

4. Uncover and stir in the peas, reserved soy sauce mixture, and pork. Cook, stirring, for 2 minutes, or until the sauce reduces and flavors blend. Remove from the heat and serve over the rice.

Rosemary Pork Medallions and Mashed Potatoes

 Makes 4 servings

Prep time: 10 minutes • Total time: 45 minutes

Curb carbs: We curbed the carbs in this recipe by not using breading or barbecue sauce on our pork. Potatoes and turnips are starchy vegetables that you can absolutely enjoy as part of a healthy, balanced diet for diabetes.

12 oz	Yukon gold potatoes, cut into 2-inch (5 cm) pieces	375 g
12 oz	turnips, peeled and cut into 2-inch (5 cm) pieces	375 g
4 tsp	olive oil, divided	20 mL
2 tbsp	plain nonfat (0%) Greek yogurt	30 mL
⅛ tsp	salt	0.5 mL
1 lb	pork tenderloin, trimmed, cut into 1-inch (2.5 cm) thick medallions	500 g
1½ tsp	cornstarch	7 mL
½ cup	low-sodium ready-to-use chicken broth, divided	125 mL
2 tbsp	chopped fresh rosemary (or 1 tsp/5 mL dried)	30 mL
2	cloves garlic, minced	2
1	small red onion, sliced	1

1. Place the potatoes and turnips in a large saucepan and fill with enough water to cover. Bring to a boil over medium-high heat, reduce the heat to a simmer, and cook for 15 minutes, or until the turnips and potatoes are fork-tender.

2. Remove from the heat and drain. With a potato masher, mash the potatoes and turnips. Add 1 tsp (5 mL) oil, the yogurt, and salt and continue to mash until well blended. Cover and keep warm.

3. In a large nonstick skillet, heat 1 tsp (5 mL) oil over medium-high heat. Cook the pork for 8 minutes, turning once, or until a thermometer inserted in the center reaches 145°F (63°C) and the juices run clear. Transfer to a plate and set aside.

Makeover Magic		
Before		**After**
520	Calories	321
15 g	Fat	7 g
6 g	Sat Fat	2 g
53 g	Carbs	34 g
4 g	Fiber	6 g
41 g	Protein	29 g
1,310 mg	Sodium	249 mg

Fill up on fiber: We kept the skins on our mashed potatoes and added an extra kick with turnips in our vegetable mixture to accompany the pork.

Favor healthy fats: We used lean pork tenderloin, minimal oil, and a vegetable mixture instead of cheese. The olive oil used in our recipe adds MUFA power. For even more MUFAs, serve this dish with roasted asparagus drizzled with olive oil.

4. In a small bowl, whisk together the cornstarch and ¼ cup (60 mL) broth.

5. In the same skillet over medium-high heat, add the remaining oil, rosemary, garlic, onion, and remaining broth. Whisk in the cornstarch mixture until combined and cook, stirring often, for 5 minutes, or until the broth is reduced by half and thickened and the onions are softened. Return the pork to the skillet and toss to combine.

6. Serve the pork over the mashed potatoes and top with the herbed onion mixture and sauce.

Tangy Pork Kabobs

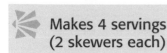 **Makes 4 servings
(2 skewers each)**

Curb carbs: Our recipe has just enough carbohydrates to satisfy you without going overboard. The grilled potatoes provide much of the carbohydrates.

Fill up on fiber: Along with this flavorful rubbed pork, we added bell pepper, mushrooms, and potatoes, with the skins, to make the dish fiber-full.

Favor healthy fats: The saturated fat in this recipe is so low thanks to the lean pork tenderloin we use. The olive oil contains MUFAs, but we suggest adding more healthy fats with a side dish like Quinoa Pilaf with Pistachios (page 255).

Makeover Magic		
Before		**After**
410	Calories	297
9 g	Fat	5 g
4 g	Sat Fat	1 g
68 g	Carbs	34 g
4 g	Fiber	5 g
17 g	Protein	30 g
1,045 mg	Sodium	149 mg

Prep time: 10 minutes • Total time: 1 hour, 5 minutes

- Barbecue grill
- Baking dish
- 8 metal skewers (7 to 8 inches/18 to 20 cm long), or wooden skewers soaked in water for 30 minutes

1 tbsp	packed brown sugar	15 mL
½ tsp	garlic powder	2 mL
½ tsp	chili powder	2 mL
½ tsp	onion powder	2 mL
¼ tsp	dry mustard	1 mL
⅛ tsp	salt	0.5 mL
1¼ lbs	red potatoes, cut into 1-inch (2.5 cm) pieces	625 g
1 lb	pork tenderloin, trimmed and cut into 1-inch (2.5 cm) pieces	500 g
2 tsp	olive oil, divided	10 mL
	Nonstick cooking spray	
1	onion, cut into 1-inch (2.5 cm) pieces	1
1	green bell pepper, cut into 1-inch (2.5 cm) pieces	1
12 oz	cremini mushrooms, halved	375 g

1. In a small bowl, combine the sugar, garlic, chili powder, onion powder, mustard, and salt.

2. In a large saucepan, add the potatoes and fill with enough water to cover. Bring to a boil over high heat and cook for 10 minutes, until nearly tender. Drain.

3. In baking dish, toss the pork, 1 tsp (5 mL) oil, and 1½ tbsp (22 mL) of the sugar mixture. Rub into the pork and allow to sit for 30 minutes.

4. Meanwhile, coat a grill rack with cooking spray. Preheat the grill to medium-high.

5. In a large bowl, toss the cooked potatoes, onion, pepper, and mushrooms with the remaining olive oil and remaining sugar mixture until coated.

6. Thread the skewers with pork, onion, potatoes, pepper, and mushrooms.

7. Grill for 10 minutes, turning once, or until the vegetables have softened and just a hint of pink remains in pork.

Italian Sausage and Linguine

 Makes 4 servings

Curb carbs: Eight ounces (250 g) of whole-grain linguine is a perfect portion for four people. This will keep within the recommended 45 grams of carbs.

Fill up on fiber: Whole-grain linguine, peppers, and broccoli provide 9 grams of fiber per serving. We like this dish because it has more going on than the average sausage and pasta dish.

Favor healthy fats: We reduced the amount of sausage in this recipe to just enough to enjoy with the pasta. We also used a light sauce made from chicken broth instead of heavy cream.

8 oz	whole-grain linguine	250 g
½ tsp	olive oil	2 mL
8 oz	sweet Italian sausage, sliced	250 g
6	cloves garlic, sliced	6
1	red bell pepper, thinly sliced	1
1	bag (10 oz/300 g) frozen chopped broccoli, thawed	1
1 cup	reduced-sodium, fat-free ready-to-use chicken broth	250 mL
1 tsp	hot pepper flakes	5 mL
¼ cup	grated Parmesan cheese	60 mL

1. Cook the linguine according to package directions, omitting the salt. Drain and set aside.

2. Meanwhile, in a large nonstick skillet, heat the oil over medium-high heat. Cook the sausage for 6 minutes, stirring. Reduce the heat to medium. Cook the garlic, bell pepper, and broccoli, stirring, for 4 minutes, or until lightly golden and softened.

3. Add the broth and bring to a boil. Cook for 4 minutes, or until reduced by half. Stir in the hot pepper flakes and cook for 2 minutes, stirring, until hot. Add the pasta and cheese and toss well.

Smart Start

If you are in the Repeating or Time stage (see page 13), swap the broth for a healthy fat source like pesto sauce, which is packed with MUFAs!

Makeover Magic		
Before		**After**
488	Calories	348
21 g	Fat	9 g
8 g	Sat Fat	3 g
55 g	Carbs	49 g
4 g	Fiber	9 g
22 g	Protein	20 g
694 mg	Sodium	541 mg

Asian Lettuce Cups

 Makes 4 servings
(3 wraps each)

Curb carbs: We used just enough brown rice to add bulk to these lettuce cups, making them a satisfying, heart-healthy meal.

Fill up on fiber: All of the vegetables in this dish pack fiber, as does the rice.

Favor healthy fats: To reduce saturated fat, we chose lean ground pork and used a small amount of oil, unlike many stir-fry-style dishes. Peanut oil is a great source of MUFAs and is best used when cooking over high heat.

2 tsp	peanut oil, divided	10 mL
1 lb	lean ground pork	500 g
1	clove garlic, minced	1
1	red bell pepper, thinly sliced	1
4 oz	shiitake mushrooms, trimmed, thinly sliced	125 g
2 tbsp	low-sodium soy sauce	30 mL
2 tbsp	Asian chili paste	30 mL
4	green onions, thinly sliced	4
1 cup	cooked brown rice	250 mL
12	leaves Bibb lettuce (1 to 2 large heads)	12
¼ cup	chopped fresh cilantro	60 mL

1. In a large nonstick skillet, heat 1 tsp (5 mL) oil over medium heat. Cook the pork for 5 minutes, stirring often, or until browned and cooked through. Add the remaining oil, garlic, pepper, and mushrooms and cook for 5 minutes, stirring often. Stir in the soy sauce, chili paste, green onions, and brown rice and cook for 2 minutes, or until heated through.

2. Arrange the lettuce leaves on a serving platter. Fill the leaves with the pork mixture, dividing evenly. Sprinkle with cilantro leaves.

> **Smart Start**
> *Try wild rice for even more fiber and flavor. And add ¼ cup (60 mL) chopped cashews for your favorite source of fat, MUFAs, and even more fiber.*

Makeover Magic		
Before		**After**
354	Calories	241
12 g	Fat	8 g
3 g	Sat Fat	2 g
43 g	Carbs	17 g
1 g	Fiber	3 g
20 g	Protein	27 g
1,025 mg	Sodium	517 mg

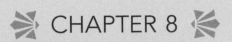

CHAPTER 8
Poultry

Chicken Piccata 178
Chicken and Waffles 179
Chicken Cacciatore 180
Chicken-Mushroom Bake 181
Quick, Creamy Chicken Lasagna 182
Chicken and Sausage Jambalaya 184
Chicken Pot Pie 185
Chicken and Dumplings 186
Baked Chicken with Mustard Sauce 187
Herb-Roasted Chicken Breasts with Vegetables 188
Orange-Sesame Chicken 189
Chicken Paprikash 190
Parmesan Chicken Fingers 191
Broccoli-Stuffed Chicken Roulade 192
Bacon-Wrapped Chicken 193
Layered Chicken and Bean Enchiladas 194
Chicken with Pinto Beans Skillet 195
Fried Chicken 196
Chicken Pad Thai 197
Broccoli-Chicken Casserole 198
Stuffed Turkey Tenderloin 199
Sweet Potato and Turkey Shepherd's Pie 200
Turkey Meat Loaf with Cranberry Chutney 202
Turkey Cheeseburgers 203
Turkey and Orzo Stuffed Peppers 204
Turkey and Bean Quesadillas 205
Turkey Meatballs and Zucchini Pasta 206
Baked Spaghetti with Turkey Meat Sauce 207
Baked Penne with Turkey 208
Turkey Swedish Meatballs 209
Sloppy Joes 210

Chicken Piccata

 Makes 4 servings

Prep time: 5 minutes • Total time: 15 minutes

Curb carbs: We cut the carbohydrates by using less flour and swapping out all-purpose flour for white whole wheat flour.

Fill up on fiber: White whole wheat flour has a good amount of fiber, but since we are using such a small amount, pair this dish with steamed vegetables or a salad to boost the fiber even more!

Favor healthy fats: We used our favorite heart-healthy olive oil and removed saturated fat by trading full-fat cream sauce for the flavorful lemon-caper broth.

- Meat mallet or rolling pin

1 lb	boneless skinless chicken breast tenderloins	500 g
4 tbsp	white whole wheat flour, divided	60 mL
1/4 cup	olive oil	60 mL
3 tbsp	low-sodium ready-to-use chicken broth	45 mL
2 tbsp	freshly squeezed lemon juice	30 mL
1	sprig fresh parsley, finely chopped	1
2 tsp	drained capers	10 mL

1. Lay the tenderloins on a work surface. With a smooth meat mallet or a rolling pin, flatten to 1/4-inch (0.5 cm) thickness. Dredge the cutlets lightly in 2 tbsp (30 mL) flour.

2. In a large skillet over medium heat, heat the oil. Cook the chicken, in batches as necessary, for 4 minutes, turning once, or until no longer pink inside. Transfer the chicken to a plate.

3. In a small bowl, whisk together the broth and the remaining flour until a smooth paste forms.

4. Add the lemon juice, parsley, and capers to the skillet. Bring to a boil. Whisk in the broth mixture. Reduce the heat and simmer for 2 minutes, whisking constantly until thickened. Serve chicken with sauce.

Makeover Magic		
Before		**After**
500	Calories	282
30 g	Fat	17 g
12 g	Sat Fat	2.5 g
15 g	Carbs	7 g
1 g	Fiber	1 g
40 g	Protein	25 g
980 mg	Sodium	178 mg

Chicken and Waffles

 Makes 4 servings

Prep time: 10 minutes • Total time: 20 minutes

Curb carbs: Using store-bought multigrain waffles is a quick, fiber-full fix that will keep portions of this comfort dish reasonable.

Fill up on fiber: Applying whole wheat pastry flour and corn flakes gives crunch and a satisfying fiber boost.

Favor healthy fats: Reduce saturated fat by using boneless skinless chicken tenderloins and smaller amounts of butter than a traditional version of this dish. For more healthy fats, try this dish with a smear of olive tapenade or avocado instead of the gravy.

6 tbsp	whole wheat pastry flour, divided	90 mL
2	large egg whites, lightly beaten	2
2 tbsp	1% milk	30 mL
1 cup	corn flakes cereal, finely crushed	250 mL
1 tbsp	canola oil	15 mL
1 lb	boneless skinless chicken breast tenderloins	500 g
2 tbsp	unsalted butter	30 mL
¾ cup	low-sodium ready-to-use chicken broth	175 mL
8	frozen multigrain waffles	8

1. Place ¼ cup (60 mL) flour in a shallow bowl. In another shallow bowl, whisk together the egg whites and milk. Place the crushed corn flakes in a third shallow bowl.

2. Dredge the chicken tenderloins in the flour to coat. Dip them into the egg mixture to coat, shaking off any excess, and transfer to the corn flakes to coat. Discard any excess flour, egg, and crumbs.

3. In a large nonstick skillet, heat the oil over medium-high heat. Cook the chicken, in batches as necessary, for 10 minutes, turning once, or until no longer pink inside. Transfer to a serving platter.

4. In the same skillet, melt the butter over medium heat. Whisk in the remaining flour until a smooth paste forms. Slowly whisk in the broth and cook, stirring, for 5 minutes, or until thickened. Remove from the heat.

5. Prepare the waffles according to package directions.

6. Top the waffles with the chicken and gravy.

> **Smart Start**
> *Switch from corn flakes to bran flakes.*

Makeover Magic		
Before		**After**
1,250	Calories	456
66 g	Fat	18 g
22 g	Sat Fat	5 g
94 g	Carbs	45 g
6 g	Fiber	9 g
69 g	Protein	32 g
3,950 mg	Sodium	424 mg

Chicken Cacciatore

 Makes 4 servings

Prep time: 10 minutes • Total time: 50 minutes

Curb carbs: We used whole wheat egg noodles to accompany this chicken dish instead of regular white pasta and used less of it than you typically would.

Fill up on fiber: Between the whole wheat egg noodles and all of the fresh vegetables added to this classic dish, we really boosted the fiber.

Favor healthy fats: Instead of coating our chicken in a heavy cream sauce, we opted for a savory sauce featuring olive oil.

4 oz	whole wheat egg noodles	125 g
2 tsp	olive oil	10 mL
1 lb	boneless skinless chicken breasts, about ½-inch (1 cm) thick	500 g
8 oz	cremini mushrooms, sliced	250 g
1	green bell pepper, sliced	1
1	red bell pepper, sliced	1
2	carrots, sliced	2
1	small onion, sliced	1
2	cloves garlic, minced	2
1	can (14 to 15 oz/398 to 425 mL) no-salt-added diced tomatoes, with juice	1
1 tsp	dried oregano	5 mL
¾ cup	dry white wine	175 mL

1. Cook the noodles according to package directions, omitting the salt. Drain and set aside.

2. Meanwhile, in a large nonstick skillet, heat the oil over medium-high heat. Cook the chicken, turning occasionally, for 6 minutes, or until browned on all sides. Transfer to a plate.

3. Add the mushrooms, green pepper, red pepper, carrots, onion, and garlic to the skillet and toss to combine. Reduce the heat to medium, cover, and cook, tossing occasionally, for 3 minutes, or until the mushrooms begin to release liquid. Uncover and cook to evaporate most of the liquid.

4. Add the tomatoes, oregano, wine, and the reserved chicken. Reduce the heat and simmer, stirring occasionally, for 30 minutes, until the mixture has thickened, and a thermometer inserted in the thickest portion of the chicken registers 165°F (74°C) and the juices run clear.

5. Serve the chicken over the noodles.

Makeover Magic		
Before		**After**
752	Calories	368
40 g	Fat	7 g
24 g	Sat Fat	1.5 g
48 g	Carbs	36 g
3 g	Fiber	6 g
45 g	Protein	32 g
842 mg	Sodium	183 mg

Chicken-Mushroom Bake

 Makes 6 servings

Prep time: 10 minutes • Total time: 45 minutes

Curb carbs: Sprouted whole-grain pasta is a lower-carb alternative to regular white pasta — it even beats out whole wheat!

Fill up on fiber: Sprouted grain pasta is also high in fiber, and the mushrooms give this recipe the final kick for fiber and nutrients.

Favor healthy fats: With such a creamy dish, instead of full-fat ingredients, we switched to reduced fat when we could. Top this dish with sliced olives to get favored fats.

- Preheat the oven to 400°F (200°C)
- 11- by 7-inch (28 by 18 cm) baking dish, sprayed with nonstick cooking spray

8 oz	sprouted whole-grain spaghetti	250 g
4 tsp	canola oil, divided	20 mL
1½ lbs	boneless skinless chicken breasts, cut crosswise into ¼-inch (0.5 cm) strips	750 g
8 oz	cremini mushrooms, sliced	250 g
1¾ cups	low-sodium ready-to-use chicken broth, divided	425 mL
½ cup	dry white wine or additional chicken broth	125 mL
1	bay leaf	1
2 tbsp	cornstarch	30 mL
¼ tsp	ground black pepper	1 mL
6 oz	Neufchâtel cheese or reduced-fat cream cheese, softened	175 g
½ cup	grated Parmesan cheese	125 mL

1. Cook the spaghetti according to package directions, omitting the salt. Drain well and transfer to a warm, large bowl.

2. In a large nonstick skillet, heat 1 tbsp (15 mL) oil over medium-high heat. Cook the chicken, stirring, for 6 minutes, or until no longer pink and the juices run clear. Transfer to the bowl with the pasta. In the skillet, heat remaining oil. Cook the mushrooms, stirring, for 5 minutes, or until tender and browned. Remove the mushrooms to the pasta bowl.

3. In the same skillet, bring 1½ cups (375 mL) broth, wine, and bay leaf to a boil.

4. In a cup or bowl, combine the cornstarch and the remaining broth. Whisk into the skillet and cook for 1 minute, whisking until thickened. Season with the pepper. Remove from the heat. Discard the bay leaf.

5. Add the Neufchâtel cheese to the sauce and whisk until melted. Pour over the pasta, tossing to mix. Pour into the prepared baking dish. Sprinkle with the Parmesan cheese.

6. Bake on top rack of preheated oven for 20 minutes, or until light brown and bubbling.

Makeover Magic		
Before		**After**
720	Calories	438
40 g	Fat	16 g
21 g	Sat Fat	6 g
58 g	Carbs	32 g
3 g	Fiber	5 g
31 g	Protein	37 g
1,240 mg	Sodium	358 mg

Quick, Creamy Chicken Lasagna

 Makes 8 servings

Prep time: 20 minutes • Total time: 1 hour, 15 minutes

Curb carbs: Marinara sauce can be a hidden carb bomb. This recipe uses the perfect amount for a moist dish that won't blow up your blood sugar.

Fill up on fiber: Oven-ready whole wheat lasagna noodles and nutrient-dense spinach make this dish hearty and filling.

- Preheat the oven to 400°F (200°C)
- 13- by 9-inch (33 by 23 cm) glass baking dish

9 oz	oven-ready whole wheat lasagna noodles (15 noodles)	270 g
	Warm water	
1 lb	boneless skinless chicken breasts	500 g
1½ tsp	dried basil	7 mL
8 oz	Neufchâtel cheese or reduced-fat cream cheese, softened, divided	250 g
1 tbsp	canola oil	15 mL
1½ cups	part-skim ricotta cheese	375 mL
¼ cup	grated Parmesan cheese	60 mL
1½ cups	shredded part-skim mozzarella cheese, divided	375 mL
½ cup	low-sodium ready-to-use chicken or vegetable broth	125 mL
3 cups	low-sodium marinara sauce, divided	750 mL
1	package (10 oz/300 g) frozen chopped spinach, thawed and drained	1

1. Place 3 of the noodles in a medium bowl. Cover with warm water and let stand for 5 minutes, or until pliable. Drain and reserve.

2. Meanwhile, in a large nonstick skillet over medium-high heat, bring 4 cups (1 L) water to a simmer. Cook the chicken for 10 minutes, or until a thermometer inserted in the thickest portion registers 165°F (74°C) and the juices run clear. Transfer to a cutting board and dice.

Makeover Magic		
Before		**After**
1,270	Calories	453
84 g	Fat	20 g
41 g	Sat Fat	10 g
54 g	Carbs	35 g
2 g	Fiber	4 g
60 g	Protein	32 g
3,520 mg	Sodium	523 mg

Favor healthy fats: It wouldn't be lasagna without cheesy goodness, so we made smart picks — part-skim products and hard cheeses like Parmesan decrease the saturated fat but keep our taste buds happy. Using canola oil and olive oil or canola oil–based marinara sauce ensures we incorporate our favored fats.

3. In a large bowl, combine the chicken, basil, 4 oz (125 g) Neufchâtel, oil, ricotta, Parmesan, and 1 cup (250 mL) mozzarella cheese.

4. In another bowl, whisk together the remaining Neufchâtel and broth until smooth.

5. Spread ⅓ cup (75 mL) marinara sauce in bottom of baking dish. Assemble 3 layers as follows: 4 noodles, ⅔ cup (150 mL) marinara sauce, one-third of the chicken mixture, and one-third of the spinach. Top with the softened noodles, the Neufchâtel sauce, the remaining marinara sauce, and the remaining mozzarella. Cover with foil.

6. Bake in preheated oven for 30 minutes. Uncover and bake for 15 minutes, or until the cheese melts. Let sit for 10 minutes before serving.

Smart Start
Look for jarred marinara sauce that has olive oil and no added sugar.

Chicken and Sausage Jambalaya

 Makes 4 servings

Prep time: 10 minutes • Total time: 55 minutes

Curb carbs: We added brown rice to our jambalaya to make a traditional dish more healthful and cut the amount of rice overall by adding beans, peppers, and more meat.

Fill up on fiber: Beans are the fiber star of this recipe!

Favor healthy fats: We reduced the saturated fat by subbing a mix of lean chicken breast and turkey sausage for the traditional pork sausage. This dish would pair well with an avocado and orange salad, full of healthy fats.

3 tsp	canola oil, divided	15 mL
8 oz	boneless skinless chicken breasts, cut crosswise into ¼-inch (0.5 cm) strips	250 g
4 oz	turkey sausage, casing removed, cut into small pieces	125 g
1	green bell pepper, chopped	1
4	green onions, sliced	4
1	jalapeño pepper, seeded and finely chopped	1
3	cloves garlic, minced	3
1 tbsp	salt-free Creole seasoning	15 mL
1	can (14 to 15 oz/398 to 425 mL) no-salt-added diced tomatoes, with juice	1
1 cup	rinsed drained no-salt-added canned black beans	250 mL
1½ cups	low-sodium ready-to-use chicken broth	375 mL
½ cup	long-grain brown rice	125 mL

1. In a Dutch oven or large nonstick skillet, heat 1 tsp (5 mL) oil over medium-high heat. Cook the chicken for 5 minutes, stirring. Add the sausage and cook, stirring often, for 6 minutes, or until the chicken and sausage are browned, cooked through, and the juices run clear.

2. Add the remaining oil, the bell pepper, green onions, jalapeño, garlic, and Creole seasoning. Cook for 3 minutes, stirring, or until the vegetables are browned and softened.

3. Add the tomatoes, beans, chicken broth, and rice and bring to a boil. Reduce the heat to medium-low, cover, and cook for 30 minutes, or until the rice is tender.

Makeover Magic		
Before		**After**
525	Calories	303
22 g	Fat	8 g
8 g	Sat Fat	2 g
47 g	Carbs	32 g
2 g	Fiber	4 g
35 g	Protein	23 g
830 mg	Sodium	411 mg

Chicken Pot Pie

Prep time: 5 minutes • Total time: 45 minutes

Curb carbs: Substituting whole wheat phyllo dough for store-bought piecrust is a simple trick to curb carbs when baking any kind of pie.

Fill up on fiber: In addition to the whole wheat phyllo dough, tons of vegetables add extra fiber to this classic comfort food.

Favor healthy fats: No store-bought gravy here. We thickened chicken broth with cornstarch to make a homemade, low-fat gravy to coat all of the veggies and chicken!

Smart Start

It's okay to have dessert to get your healthy fats. Pair this with Almond Rice Pudding (page 282).

Makeover Magic		
Before		**After**
430	Calories	222
22 g	Fat	5 g
8 g	Sat Fat	1 g
43 g	Carbs	20 g
1 g	Fiber	3 g
14 g	Protein	24 g
1,020 mg	Sodium	256 mg

- Preheat the oven to 350°F (180°C)
- 9-inch (23 cm) glass baking dish, sprayed with nonstick cooking spray

2 tsp	olive oil, divided	10 mL
1¼ lbs	boneless skinless chicken breasts, cut into ½- to ¾-inch (1 to 2 cm) cubes	625 g
2	carrots, thinly sliced	2
2	stalks celery, thinly sliced	2
1 tsp	dried rosemary, crushed	5 mL
2 cups	frozen corn, green bean and pea mix, thawed	500 mL
2 cups	low-sodium ready-to-use chicken broth, divided	500 mL
1 tbsp	cornstarch	15 mL
8	sheets whole wheat phyllo dough	8
	Nonstick cooking spray	

1. In a large nonstick skillet, heat 1 tsp (5 mL) oil over medium-high heat. Cook the chicken for 8 minutes, stirring, until no longer pink and the juices run clear. Transfer to a bowl and set aside.

2. In the same skillet, heat the remaining oil. Cook the carrots, celery, and rosemary, stirring, for 5 minutes, or until tender. Stir in the chicken and corn mixture. Transfer to the baking dish.

3. Add 1½ cups (375 mL) broth to the same skillet over medium-low heat and bring to a simmer. In a small bowl, whisk together the remaining broth and the cornstarch until smooth. Add the mixture to the broth in the skillet and whisk for 3 minutes, or until thickened. Pour into the chicken and vegetable mixture in the baking dish and stir to combine.

4. Lay 2 phyllo sheets across the top of the dish, tucking the edges into the pan. Lightly coat the sheets with cooking spray. Repeat to make 3 more layers.

5. Bake in preheated oven for 20 minutes, or until golden and bubbling.

Chicken and Dumplings

 Makes 6 servings

Curb carbs: We use half as much flour in this diabetes-friendly dish as the traditional recipe calls for, without sacrificing the flavor.

Fill up on fiber: Whole wheat dumplings help boost the fiber, but more importantly, we added a ton of fresh vegetables to pump up this recipe!

Favor healthy fats: Chicken and dumplings doesn't always have to be a diabetes disaster — we cut out butter and yet still created creamy gravy from light sour cream and broth. For a dose of healthy fats, serve a side salad dressed in flaxseed oil and sunflower seeds.

1 cup	whole wheat pastry flour	250 mL
1½ tsp	baking powder	7 mL
1	large egg, beaten	1
½ cup	buttermilk	125 mL
1 tbsp	olive oil	15 mL
1½ lbs	boneless skinless chicken breasts, cut into 1-inch (2.5 cm) pieces	750 g
1	onion, chopped	1
3	stalks celery, sliced	3
2	carrots, sliced	2
5 cups	low-sodium ready-to-use chicken broth, divided	1.25 L
2 tbsp	finely chopped fresh thyme (or 2 tsp/10 mL dried)	30 mL
1 tbsp	cornstarch or arrowroot starch	15 mL
½ cup	light sour cream	125 mL
1½ cups	frozen peas, thawed	375 mL

1. In a bowl, combine the flour and baking powder. Form a well in the center of the mixture.

2. In a liquid measuring cup, whisk together the egg and buttermilk. Pour into the dry ingredients. Stir just until combined. Set aside.

3. In a Dutch oven, heat the oil over medium-high heat. Cook the chicken, stirring often, for 8 minutes, or until no longer pink and the juices run clear.

4. Add the onion, celery, and carrots and cook, stirring, for 5 minutes, or until browned and softened. Add 4½ cups (1.125 L) broth and the thyme and bring to a simmer.

5. Reduce the heat to medium-low. In a small bowl, whisk together the remaining broth and cornstarch until smooth. Stir into the pot along with the sour cream and peas. Cook for 5 minutes, stirring often, until thickened.

6. Carefully drop spoonfuls of dumpling batter into the thickened sauce and cook for 10 minutes, or until the dumplings are firm on the inside and puffy.

Makeover Magic		
Before		After
721	Calories	338
27 g	Fat	9 g
11 g	Sat Fat	3 g
65 g	Carbs	30 g
3 g	Fiber	6 g
50 g	Protein	33 g
1,548 mg	Sodium	300 mg

Baked Chicken with Mustard Sauce

 Makes 4 servings

Prep time: 5 minutes • Total time: 35 minutes

Curb carbs: This dish is often glazed with maple-flavored pancake syrup, which has tons of carbs. Keep it sweet by using a touch of orange juice, which will enhance the mustard's flavor, too!

Fill up on fiber: Whole wheat panko bread crumbs add fiber to this cozy dish.

Favor healthy fats: Olive oil provides healthy fats, but for a bigger boost, pair this dish with the Broccoli-Walnut Farfalle Toss (page 257).

- Preheat the oven to 375°F (190°C)
- Rimmed baking sheet

Sauce		
3 tbsp	honey mustard	45 mL
3 tbsp	plain nonfat (0%) Greek yogurt	45 mL
2 tbsp	unsweetened orange juice	30 mL

Chicken		
2 tbsp	olive oil, divided	30 mL
1	large egg white	1
¼ cup	honey mustard	60 mL
½ tsp	ground black pepper	2 mL
¼ tsp	paprika	1 mL
4	boneless skinless chicken breasts (6 oz/175 each, ½ inch/1 cm thick)	4
¾ cup	whole wheat panko bread crumbs	175 mL

1. *To make the sauce:* In a small bowl, whisk together the mustard, yogurt, and orange juice. Place in the refrigerator until the chicken is finished.

2. *To make the chicken:* Using 1 tbsp (15 mL) oil, coat the baking sheet.

3. In a large bowl, whisk the egg white until foamy. Whisk in the mustard, pepper, and paprika. Add the chicken and turn to coat well.

4. Place the bread crumbs in a pie plate. One piece at a time, lift the chicken from the mustard mixture and roll in the crumbs, pressing them so they adhere. Place the chicken on the prepared baking sheet. Drizzle the chicken with the remaining oil. Discard any excess mustard mixture and crumbs.

5. Bake in preheated oven, turning once, for 25 minutes until crispy and browned, or until a thermometer inserted in the thickest portion registers 165°F (74°C) and the juices run clear. Serve with sauce.

Makeover Magic		
Before		**After**
560	Calories	347
22 g	Fat	12 g
6 g	Sat Fat	2 g
50 g	Carbs	17 g
0 g	Fiber	2 g
41 g	Protein	40 g
1,280 mg	Sodium	503 mg

Herb-Roasted Chicken Breasts with Vegetables

 Makes 4 servings

Prep time: 10 minutes • Total time: 1 hour

Curb carbs: Instead of filling up on traditional roasted potatoes, we mixed in some Brussels sprouts, though you could choose any non-starchy vegetable side.

Fill up on fiber: The fiber in this surefire favorite comes from keeping the skins on the potatoes and adding delicious Brussels sprouts.

Favor healthy fats: Olive oil and ground flaxseeds provide both MUFAs and ALA fatty acids in this dish.

- Preheat the oven to 400°F (200°C)
- 13- by 9-inch (33 by 23 cm) metal baking pan, sprayed with nonstick cooking spray
- Rimmed baking sheet, sprayed with nonstick cooking spray

Chicken

3 tbsp	lemon juice	45 mL
2 tbsp	ground flaxseeds	30 mL
2	cloves garlic, minced	2
1 tbsp	finely chopped fresh rosemary (or 1 tsp/5 mL dried)	15 mL
1 tbsp	olive oil	15 mL
4	small boneless skinless chicken breasts (4 oz/125 g each)	4

Vegetables

12 oz	Brussels sprouts, trimmed and halved lengthwise	375 g
12 oz	small red potatoes (1¾ to 2 inches/ 4.5 to 5 cm), halved	375 g
1 tbsp	olive oil	15 mL

1. *To make the chicken:* In a small bowl, stir together the lemon juice, flaxseeds, garlic, rosemary, and oil. Place the chicken breasts in the baking pan. Divide the herb mixture over the chicken breasts and rub on all sides.

2. Bake in preheated oven for 40 minutes, turning once, or until a thermometer inserted in the thickest portion registers 165°F (74°C) and the juices run clear.

3. *To make the vegetables:* While chicken is baking, place the Brussels sprouts and potatoes on the baking sheet. Toss with the oil to coat. Bake for 35 minutes, or until all the vegetables are tender.

4. Serve chicken with vegetables on the side.

Makeover Magic

Before		After
590	Calories	313
33 g	Fat	12 g
11 g	Sat Fat	2 g
40 g	Carbs	23 g
5 g	Fiber	6 g
34 g	Protein	29 g
220 mg	Sodium	169 mg

Orange-Sesame Chicken

 Makes 4 servings

Prep time: 5 minutes • Total time: 1 hour, 20 minutes

Curb carbs: Instead of using breading on our chicken, we kept it light with a tangy marinade to curb the carbs so that you can include brown rice in your dish — that's not even accounted for in the take-out version of this recipe.

Fill up on fiber: The brown rice and sesame seeds are the major contributors to fiber in this dish!

Favor healthy fats: We kept this dish low in saturated fats by grilling, not frying. Sesame seeds have some MUFAs, but you can add more by making a side salad dressed with olive oil.

- Barbecue grill

1½ cups	unsweetened orange juice, divided	375 mL
6 tbsp	reduced-sodium soy sauce, divided	90 mL
1	clove garlic, minced	1
1 lb	boneless skinless chicken breasts	500 g
1¾ cup	instant brown rice	425 mL
	Nonstick cooking spray	
2 tbsp	grated orange zest	30 mL
1 tsp	Asian sweet chili sauce (optional)	5 mL
3 tbsp	water	45 mL
1 tbsp	cornstarch	15 mL
2 tsp	sesame seeds	10 mL

1. In a resealable plastic bag, combine 1 cup (250 mL) orange juice, 2 tbsp (30 mL) soy sauce, and the garlic. Add the chicken, toss, and seal. Place in the refrigerator for 30 minutes, turning once. Remove from the refrigerator and bring to room temperature for 15 minutes.

2. Meanwhile, prepare the rice according to package directions, omitting the salt. Remove from the heat and keep covered.

3. Coat a grill rack with cooking spray. Heat the grill over high heat.

4. Remove the chicken from the marinade, discarding the marinade. Grill for 15 minutes, turning once, or until a thermometer inserted in the thickest portion registers 165°F (74°C) and the juices run clear.

5. Transfer the chicken to a clean cutting board and let it rest for 5 minutes.

6. In a small saucepan over medium-high heat, combine the remaining orange juice, remaining soy sauce, orange zest, and chili sauce, if using, and stir. Bring to a simmer.

7. In a small bowl, whisk together the water and cornstarch until a smooth paste forms. Whisk the mixture into the orange sauce and continue to cook, whisking, for 3 minutes, or until the orange sauce thickens.

8. Slice the chicken breasts crosswise into ½-inch (1 cm) thick pieces. Divide the rice, chicken, sauce, and sesame seeds among 4 plates.

Makeover Magic		
Before		**After**
860	Calories	326
41 g	Fat	5 g
7 g	Sat Fat	1 g
66 g	Carbs	39 g
3 g	Fiber	3 g
60 g	Protein	29 g
1,410 mg	Sodium	552 mg

Chicken Paprikash

Makes 4 servings

Prep time: 5 minutes • Total time: 45 minutes

Curb carbs: Our revamped recipe uses less flour. Serve it over a bed of lentils and greens instead of the typical pasta or rice to keep carbs curbed even further.

Fill up on fiber: This protein dish pairs naturally with high-fiber sides like whole wheat pasta or a bed of lentils and greens, such as Swiss chard or kale.

Favor healthy fats: Use a small amount of canola oil to lightly fry this dish. Cook your lentils and greens in olive oil for MUFAs, with a bit of garlic for more flavor and a slew of other health benefits.

1 tbsp	canola oil, divided	15 mL
1 lb	boneless skinless chicken thighs	500 g
1½ tbsp	paprika, divided	22 mL
1	large onion, sliced lengthwise	1
1	clove garlic, minced	1
1 cup	low-sodium ready-to-use chicken broth	250 mL
1 tbsp	no-salt-added tomato paste	15 mL
½ cup	light sour cream	125 mL
1 tbsp	white whole wheat flour or whole wheat flour	15 mL
	Chopped parsley (optional)	

1. In a large nonstick skillet, heat 2 tsp (10 mL) oil over medium-high heat. Season the chicken with 1 tsp (5 mL) paprika. Cook in the skillet for 6 minutes, turning once, or until lightly golden. Transfer to a plate and set aside.

2. Heat the remaining oil in the skillet. Cook the onion and garlic, stirring often, for 6 minutes, or until softened and browned.

3. In a small bowl, whisk together the broth, tomato paste, and remaining paprika until thoroughly combined. Pour into the skillet. Reserve the bowl.

4. Add the chicken pieces back to the skillet. Reduce the heat to low to bring the mixture to a simmer. Cover and cook for 20 minutes, or until a thermometer inserted in the thickest portion registers 165°F (74°C) and the juices run clear.

5. Transfer the chicken to a plate and keep warm.

6. In the reserved bowl, whisk together the sour cream and flour. Whisk the mixture into the skillet. Cook, stirring constantly, for 4 minutes, or until thickened and bubbling. Serve the chicken topped with the sauce and garnished with the parsley (if using).

Makeover Magic		
Before		**After**
400	Calories	247
20 g	Fat	12 g
11 g	Sat Fat	4 g
16 g	Carbs	10 g
2 g	Fiber	2 g
37 g	Protein	25 g
230 mg	Sodium	145 mg

Parmesan Chicken Fingers

 Makes 4 servings

Prep time: 10 minutes • Total time: 25 minutes

Curb carbs: Instead of a thick breading, we used a thin, blood sugar–friendly coating of bran flakes, Parmesan cheese, flaxseeds, and spices!

Fill up on fiber: Bran flakes provide some fiber in this dish, but you can add more by serving it with a green salad with sunflower seeds, grated carrots, and baked sweet potato rounds (leave the skins on).

Favor healthy fats: The ground flaxseeds serve up essential omega-3s. Using natural hard cheeses like Parmesan keeps the saturated fats down in this recipe.

- Preheat oven to 450°F (230°C)
- Baking sheet, sprayed with nonstick cooking spray

1 lb	boneless skinless chicken breast tenderloins	500 g
¼ tsp	ground black pepper	1 mL
3	large egg whites, lightly beaten	3
¾ cup	bran flakes cereal, finely crushed	175 mL
⅓ cup	grated Parmesan cheese	75 mL
2½ tbsp	ground flaxseeds	37 mL
1 tsp	dried basil	5 mL
½ tsp	garlic powder	2 mL

1. Season the chicken with the pepper.

2. Whisk the egg whites in a shallow bowl. Combine the crushed bran flakes, cheese, flaxseeds, basil, and garlic powder on a plate.

3. Dip the chicken tenderloins into the egg, shaking off any excess, and toss in the bran flake mixture. Discard any excess egg and bran flake mixture. Place on the prepared baking sheet.

4. Bake in preheated oven for 12 minutes, or until no longer pink and the juices run clear.

Makeover Magic		
Before		**After**
340	Calories	199
14 g	Fat	5 g
6 g	Sat Fat	2 g
26 g	Carbs	9 g
1 g	Fiber	3 g
27 g	Protein	33 g
1,350 mg	Sodium	247 mg

Broccoli-Stuffed Chicken Roulade

 Makes 6 servings

Curb carbs: Instead of breaded and fried chicken, we pan-fried chicken cutlets without breading!

Fill up on fiber: We boosted the fiber in this recipe by adding extra broccoli to fill you up while keeping the overall carb count low.

Favor healthy fats: With such a small amount of oil in this recipe, most of the fat is found in the chicken and naturally lower-saturated-fat Parmesan cheese. The ground flaxseeds provide some omega-3 fatty acids.

Makeover Magic		
Before		**After**
480	Calories	204
22 g	Fat	7 g
9 g	Sat Fat	2 g
39 g	Carbs	7 g
1 g	Fiber	2 g
32 g	Protein	27 g
1,190 mg	Sodium	204 mg

Prep time: 20 minutes • Total time: 45 minutes

2 tsp	olive oil, divided	10 mL
1	shallot, finely chopped	1
2	cloves garlic, minced, divided	2
¾ tsp	hot pepper flakes, divided	3 mL
2 tbsp	ground flaxseeds	30 mL
¼ cup	grated Parmesan cheese	60 mL
1	package (10 oz/300 g) frozen chopped broccoli, thawed, drained and finely chopped	1
4	chicken breast cutlets (6 oz/175 g each), pounded to ¼ inch (0.5 cm) thick	4
¾ cup	low-sodium ready-to-use chicken broth, divided	175 mL
2 tsp	cornstarch	10 mL

1. In a medium nonstick skillet, heat 1 tsp (5 mL) oil over medium heat. Cook the shallot, half of the garlic, and ¼ tsp (1 mL) hot pepper flakes, stirring, for 3 minutes, or until softened.

2. In a small bowl, combine the shallot mixture, flaxseeds, Parmesan, and broccoli. Lay the chicken on a work surface, smooth side down. Divide the broccoli mixture evenly among the cutlets, spreading it down the center of each. Loosely roll up the sides of the cutlets around the broccoli mixture and secure with testers.

3. Add the remaining oil to the skillet set over medium heat. Cook the chicken for 5 minutes, turning occasionally, or until golden brown on all sides. Add ⅔ cup (150 mL) broth. Cover and cook over low heat for 10 minutes, or until a thermometer inserted in the thickest portion registers 165°F (74°C) and the juices run clear. Transfer to a serving platter. Cover to keep warm.

4. Bring the pan juices to a simmer. Add the remaining garlic. In a small bowl, whisk together the remaining broth and the cornstarch until smooth. Whisk into the juices in the skillet and cook, stirring, for 3 minutes, or until the mixture thickens slightly. Stir in the remaining hot pepper flakes. Remove from the heat.

5. Cut the roulades into diagonal slices. Drizzle with sauce.

Baked Penne with
Turkey (page 208)

Asian Fish Packets (page 214)

Tuna Tetrazzini (page 220)

Wild Mushroom and
White Bean Risotto (page 226)

Asparagus Swiss Quiche (page 234)

Caramelized Onion and Fennel Pizza (page 242)

Scalloped Red Potatoes (page 251)

Whipped Sweet Potato Casseroles (page 252)

Bacon-Wrapped Chicken

 Makes 4 servings

Prep time: 5 minutes • Total time: 20 minutes

Curb carbs: We decided not to use a glaze on our chicken, as glaze often contains syrups with many carbs. Instead, we let the jalapeño and bacon speak for themselves. We also used simple grilled chicken without any breading.

Fill up on fiber: Serve this on top of romaine hearts to add not only a good crunch, but fiber, too!

Favor healthy fats: Turkey bacon is much leaner than regular bacon, and cooking with olive oil provides MUFAs.

- Preheat barbecue grill to medium-high, grill sprayed with nonstick cooking spray

1 lb	boneless skinless chicken breast tenderloins	500 g
1	jalapeño pepper, seeded and finely chopped	1
8	slices turkey bacon, halved	8
1 tbsp	olive oil	15 mL
4	romaine hearts, halved lengthwise	4
¼ cup	crumbled reduced-fat blue cheese	60 mL

1. Lay the chicken on a clean cutting board. Top each tenderloin with a small spoonful of jalapeños. Wrap 1 slice of bacon around the length of each chicken tenderloin. Use a tester to pierce and hold the bacon, if needed.

2. Grill for 12 minutes, turning once, or until no longer pink and the juices run clear.

3. Brush the olive oil over the cut side of the romaine hearts. Place the romaine hearts, cut side down, on the grill, sear quickly until there are grill marks, and transfer to a serving platter. Sprinkle with the blue cheese. Serve alongside the chicken tenderloins.

Makeover Magic		
Before		**After**
660	Calories	314
34 g	Fat	8 g
15 g	Sat Fat	2 g
61 g	Carbs	8 g
1 g	Fiber	3 g
33 g	Protein	55 g
690 mg	Sodium	579 mg

Layered Chicken and Bean Enchiladas

 Makes 8 servings

Prep time: 10 minutes • Total time: 1 hour, 5 minutes

Curb carbs: Using 6-inch (15 cm) corn tortillas instead of a larger size helps curb carbs — especially since we use just one tortilla layer instead of two.

Fill up on fiber: We added beans to the traditional chicken enchiladas to boost the fiber in this casserole.

Favor healthy fats: The fat in this recipe comes from the Cheddar cheese and small amounts in the chicken, sour cream, and olive oil. Healthy fats come from the olives.

- Preheat the oven to 350°F (180°C)
- 13- by 9-inch (33 by 23 cm) glass baking dish

	Nonstick cooking spray	
1 lb	boneless skinless chicken breasts, cut into bite-size pieces	500 g
2 tsp	olive oil	10 mL
1	large onion, chopped	1
1	jalapeño pepper, seeded and finely chopped	1
1	large green bell pepper, chopped	1
¾ cup	pitted black olives	175 mL
2¼ cups	medium red enchilada sauce	550 mL
1	can (15 oz/425 mL) no-salt-added black beans, drained and rinsed	1
10	6-inch (15 cm) corn tortillas	10
1 cup	shredded Cheddar cheese, divided	250 mL
½ cup	light sour cream	125 mL
1	large tomato, chopped	1

1. In a large nonstick skillet sprayed with cooking spray, cook the chicken over medium heat, stirring, for 5 minutes, or until a thermometer inserted in the thickest portion registers 165°F (74°C) and the juices run clear. Transfer chicken to a plate and set aside.

3. In the same skillet, heat the oil over medium heat. Cook the onion and jalapeño, stirring, for 5 minutes, or until tender. Stir in the bell pepper, olives, and enchilada sauce. Add the chicken. Reduce the heat and simmer for 5 minutes. Stir in the beans.

4. Spread half of the chicken mixture evenly in baking dish. Place the tortillas on top, overlapping them to cover the entire surface. Sprinkle with ½ cup (125 mL) cheese. Top with the remaining chicken mixture.

5. Cover with foil and bake in preheated oven for 35 minutes, or until heated through. Uncover. Sprinkle with the remaining cheese. Bake for 5 minutes, or until the cheese is melted.

6. Serve topped with the sour cream and tomato.

Makeover Magic		
Before		After
651	Calories	286
38 g	Fat	12 g
18 g	Sat Fat	4 g
37 g	Carbs	24 g
1 g	Fiber	4 g
37 g	Protein	21 g
1,392 mg	Sodium	563 mg

Chicken with Pinto Beans Skillet

 Makes 4 servings

Prep time: 5 minutes • Total time: 40 minutes

Curb carbs: The majority of carbs in this dish come from the fresh veggies, a hearty substitute for the tortilla chips often used in this type of recipe.

Fill up on fiber: Pinto beans and broccoli work together to bulk up the fiber in this recipe.

Favor healthy fats: Serve with sliced avocado for a creamy topping of healthy fats!

3 tsp	canola oil, divided	15 mL
1 tsp	ground cumin, divided	5 mL
1 lb	boneless skinless chicken breasts	500 g
1	package (10 oz/300 g) frozen broccoli florets, thawed	1
1	red or yellow bell pepper, chopped	1
1	small onion, chopped	1
3	cloves garlic, finely chopped	3
1	can (15 oz/425 mL) pinto beans, drained and rinsed	1
1	can (14 to 15 oz/398 to 425 mL) no-salt-added diced tomatoes	1
½ cup	low-sodium ready-to-use chicken broth	125 mL

1. On a plate, combine 1 tsp (5 mL) oil and ½ tsp (1 mL) cumin. Add the chicken and rub to coat evenly.

2. In a large nonstick skillet over medium-high heat, cook the chicken for 10 minutes, turning once, or until browned and a thermometer inserted in the thickest portion registers 165°F (74°C) and the juices run clear. Remove to a cutting board. Let rest.

3. In the same skillet, heat the remaining oil over medium-high heat for 1 minute. Add the broccoli, pepper, onion, garlic, and the remaining cumin. Cover and cook, stirring occasionally, for 5 minutes, or until the vegetables are golden. Add the beans, tomatoes, and broth. Cover, reduce the heat, and simmer for 10 minutes to flavor the beans.

4. Divide the chicken and bean mixture among 4 plates.

Makeover Magic		
Before		**After**
374	Calories	292
15 g	Fat	7 g
7 g	Sat Fat	1 g
44 g	Carbs	23 g
5 g	Fiber	7 g
13 g	Protein	30 g
1,117 mg	Sodium	254 mg

Fried Chicken

 Makes 8 servings

Prep time: 5 minutes • Total time: 4 hours, 25 minutes (including marinating time)

Curb carbs: We curbed the carbs by using a smaller amount of flour to bread our chicken pieces.

Fill up on fiber: For just 1 serving of fried chicken, you get 2 grams of fiber, thanks to using white whole wheat flour instead of the traditional white flour.

Favor healthy fats: Instead of submerging the chicken in oil, we used just enough to make the chicken crispy! Canola oil adds heart-healthy MUFAs to this traditionally artery-clogging dish.

Smart Start

Serve with a high-fiber side to get your 22 grams of fiber daily.

- Baking sheet, lined with a double layer of paper towels

1½ cups	buttermilk	375 mL
3	large cloves garlic, crushed	3
½ tsp	ground black pepper, divided	2 mL
1¼ lbs	boneless skinless chicken breasts (¾-inch/2 cm thick)	625 g
1¼ lbs	boneless skinless chicken thighs (¾-inch/2 cm thick)	625 g
¼ cup	canola oil	60 mL
1 cup	white whole wheat flour or whole wheat flour	250 mL
2 tsp	paprika	10 mL
½ tsp	cayenne pepper (optional)	2 mL
1 tbsp	cornstarch	15 mL
½ cup	1% milk	125 mL

1. In a resealable plastic bag, combine the buttermilk, garlic, and ¼ tsp (1 mL) black pepper. Add the chicken pieces and turn to coat. Seal and refrigerate for at least 4 or for up to 24 hours.

2. Preheat the oven to 250°F (120°C).

3. In a large, heavy skillet, heat the oil over medium-low heat.

4. In a large, shallow bowl, combine the flour, paprika, and cayenne, if using. Remove the chicken from the marinade and dredge in the flour mixture. Place on a large platter or a baking sheet. Discard the marinade.

5. When the oil is hot, add the chicken, in batches if necessary, and cook for 6 minutes, or until deep brown on the first side. Turn the pieces, cover the skillet loosely with foil, and cook for 5 minutes, or until the chicken is golden, the juices run clear, and a meat thermometer registers 165°F (74°C). Remove to the lined baking sheet and keep warm in the oven.

6. Using a slotted spoon, remove most of the loose browned bits from the pan. Stir the cornstarch into the oil left in the pan. Cook, stirring, for 1 minute. Gradually whisk in the milk and cook, stirring, for 3 minutes, or until thickened. Season with the remaining pepper. Serve the gravy with the chicken.

Makeover Magic		
Before		**After**
616	Calories	308
35 g	Fat	12 g
9 g	Sat Fat	2 g
24 g	Carbs	15 g
1 g	Fiber	2 g
50 g	Protein	32 g
613 mg	Sodium	162 mg

Chicken Pad Thai

 Makes 4 servings

Curb carbs: With so many great toss-ins, we don't need to use such a large portion of noodles.

Fill up on fiber: Using brown rice noodles instead of white boosts the fiber, as does a generous serving of bean sprouts!

Favor healthy fats: Peanut butter, peanut oil, and chopped peanuts are all great sources of healthy MUFAs!

Prep time: 5 minutes • Total time: 15 minutes

4 oz	flat brown rice noodles	125 g
2 tbsp	low-sodium soy sauce	30 mL
2 tbsp	peanut butter, warmed	30 mL
1 tbsp	Sriracha sauce	15 mL
1 tsp	low-sodium fish sauce	5 mL
1 tbsp	peanut oil	15 mL
12 oz	boneless skinless chicken breasts, cut into 1½-inch (4 cm) strips	375 g
2	cloves garlic, minced	2
3	green onions, sliced	3
1 cup	bean sprouts	250 mL
¼ cup	peanuts, chopped	60 mL
1	lime, quartered, for garnish	1

1. Cook the noodles according to package directions, omitting the salt.

2. In a small bowl, combine the soy sauce, peanut butter, Sriracha sauce, and fish sauce.

3. In a large nonstick skillet, heat the oil over medium-high heat. Cook the chicken, stirring often, for 5 minutes, or until no longer pink and the juices run clear.

4. Add the garlic and cook, stirring, for 30 seconds. Stir in the noodles and cook for 1 minute, or until hot. Add the soy sauce mixture and cook, tossing, for 1 minute. Stir in the green onions and remove from the heat.

5. Divide among 4 plates, garnishing each with ¼ cup (60 mL) bean sprouts and sprinkling with the peanuts. Serve with the lime wedges.

Makeover Magic		
Before		**After**
650	Calories	355
19 g	Fat	15 g
2 g	Sat Fat	3 g
83 g	Carbs	32 g
5 g	Fiber	5 g
38	Protein	26 g
2,280 mg	Sodium	560 mg

Broccoli-Chicken Casserole

 Makes 6 servings

Prep time: 10 minutes • Total time: 1 hour

Curb carbs: We swapped out pasta and added wild rice, which has 10 grams fewer carbs than even healthy brown rice!

Fill up on fiber: Broccoli, onions, and whole grains all boost the fiber.

Favor healthy fats: We used ground flaxseeds to boost healthy fats and reduced saturated fat by thickening our sauce with milk and sour cream instead of using a canned cream soup.

- Preheat the oven to 350°F (180°C)
- 8-inch (20 cm) square glass baking dish, sprayed with nonstick cooking spray

1½ cups	wild rice	375 mL
1 tbsp	canola oil	15 mL
12 oz	boneless skinless chicken breasts	375 g
1	package (10 oz/300 g) frozen chopped broccoli, thawed	1
1	small onion, chopped	1
2	cloves garlic, minced	2
1¼ cups	1% milk, divided	300 mL
¾ cup	light sour cream	175 mL
¾ cup	reduced-fat shredded Cheddar cheese	175 mL
2 tbsp	whole wheat panko bread crumbs	30 mL
2 tbsp	ground flaxseeds	30 mL

1. In a saucepan, cook the rice according to package directions, omitting the salt. Remove from the heat and set aside.

2. Meanwhile, in a large nonstick skillet, heat the oil over medium-high heat. Cook the chicken for 10 minutes, turning once, or until browned and a thermometer inserted in the thickest portion registers 165°F (74°C) and the juices run clear. Transfer to a clean cutting board and let rest for 5 minutes. Using a fork, shred the chicken into small pieces.

3. In the same skillet, cook the broccoli, onion, and garlic, stirring, for 5 minutes, or until the onion softens. Stir into the rice.

4. Add ¾ cup (175 mL) milk to the skillet and bring to a simmer over medium-low heat.

5. Whisk the remaining milk, sour cream, and cheese into the skillet and stir for 5 minutes, or until thickened. Pour the mixture into the baking dish. Add the reserved rice mixture and chicken. Stir until all ingredients are combined. In a bowl, combine the bread crumbs and flaxseeds. Sprinkle this mixture over the rice mixture.

6. Bake in preheated oven for 20 minutes, or until the cheese is melted and the mixture is thickened.

Makeover Magic		
Before		After
526	Calories	267
17 g	Fat	11 g
8 g	Sat Fat	4 g
51 g	Carbs	19 g
4 g	Fiber	3 g
39 g	Protein	23 g
845 mg	Sodium	246 mg

Stuffed Turkey Tenderloin

 Makes 4 servings

Prep time: 10 minutes • Total time: 40 minutes

Curb carbs: Instead of using a ready-made stuffing mix, we created our own with apples, onions, and pecans — no bread needed!

Fill up on fiber: Leave the skins on the apples for added fiber.

Favor healthy fats: Ground flaxseeds provide omega-3s, and pecans are a delicious source of MUFAs.

1 tbsp	canola oil, divided	15 mL
½	small onion, finely chopped	½
1	Granny Smith apple, chopped	1
3 tbsp	finely chopped pecans	45 mL
2 tbsp	ground flaxseeds	30 mL
2	cloves garlic, minced	2
1 lb	turkey breast tenderloins (2 tenderloins)	500 g
1 cup	low-sodium ready-to-use chicken broth	250 mL
2 tbsp	plain nonfat (0%) Greek yogurt	30 mL
2 tsp	finely chopped fresh thyme (or ⅔ tsp/3 mL dried)	10 mL

1. In a large nonstick skillet, heat 1½ tsp (7 mL) oil over medium heat. Cook the onion, stirring, for 5 minutes, or until softened. Add the apple, pecans, flaxseeds, and garlic and cook, stirring, for 2 minutes, or until the garlic is fragrant and the apples are slightly softened. Transfer the mixture to a bowl; reserve skillet.

2. On a clean cutting board, pat the tenderloins dry with a paper towel. Cut a slit, or a pocket, in the tenderloins lengthwise across the side of the tenderloin three-quarters of the way through, to make a deep enough pocket. Stuff each pocket with the apple mixture.

3. In the same skillet, heat the remaining oil over medium heat. Cook the turkey for 4 minutes, turning once, until browned. Add the broth. Cover, reduce the heat, and simmer for 15 minutes, or until a thermometer inserted in the thickest portion registers 165°F (74°C) and the juices run clear.

4. Transfer the turkey to a plate and keep warm. Increase the heat and cook the broth for 3 minutes, or until reduced by half. Whisk in the yogurt and thyme.

5. Cut tenderloins in half and spoon sauce over top to serve.

Makeover Magic		
Before		**After**
440	Calories	235
15 g	Fat	10 g
2 g	Sat Fat	1 g
38 g	Carbs	9 g
2 g	Fiber	3 g
37 g	Protein	31 g
710 mg	Sodium	87 mg

Sweet Potato and Turkey Shepherd's Pie

 Makes 6 servings

Prep time: 10 minutes • Total time: 50 minutes

Curb carbs: We turned a bread-based casserole into one filled with meat and vegetables with a sweet potato "crust."

- Preheat the oven to 350°F (180°C)
- 8-inch (20 cm) square glass baking dish, sprayed with nonstick cooking spray

2	sweet potatoes (each 8 oz/250 g), peeled and cut into ½-inch (1 cm) pieces	2
1 tbsp	olive oil	15 mL
	Nonstick cooking spray	
1	onion, chopped	1
2 tsp	dried thyme	10 mL
12 oz	extra-lean (99% fat-free) ground turkey	375 g
1 cup	low-sodium ready-to-use chicken broth	250 mL
3 tbsp	whole wheat flour	45 mL
3	carrots, chopped	3
1 cup	frozen peas, thawed	250 mL
1 cup	frozen corn, thawed	250 mL
1 cup	frozen cut green beans, thawed	250 mL
¼ cup	dried cranberries	60 mL

1. Place sweet potatoes in a large saucepan; fill halfway with water and bring to a boil over high heat. Cook the sweet potatoes for 15 minutes, or until tender. Remove from the heat. Drain. Place the potatoes back in the saucepan and drizzle with the oil. Using a potato masher, mash the potatoes until smooth. Set aside.

2. Coat a nonstick skillet with cooking spray and heat over medium-high heat. Cook the onion and thyme, stirring occasionally, for 4 minutes, or until starting to soften. Add the turkey and cook, breaking up with a spoon, for 5 minutes, or until no longer pink.

Makeover Magic		
Before		**After**
460	Calories	228
23 g	Fat	6 g
10 g	Sat Fat	2 g
37 g	Carbs	29 g
2 g	Fiber	5 g
25 g	Protein	15 g
980 mg	Sodium	119 mg

Fill up on fiber: The veggies, dried fruit, and whole wheat flour help this nostalgic recipe to not only feel like Thanksgiving, but also give you a 5-gram dose of fiber.

Favor healthy fats: Olive oil adds MUFAs to this dinner.

3. Combine the broth and flour and pour into the skillet. Bring the mixture to a boil, stirring constantly. Reduce the heat to medium-low and simmer for 5 minutes, or until thickened. Stir in the carrots, peas, corn, beans, and cranberries.

4. Pour the filling into the baking dish. Spread the mashed sweet potatoes over the top of the mixture.

5. Bake in preheated oven for 20 minutes, or until the top is browned and the filling is hot and bubbly.

Turkey Meat Loaf with Cranberry Chutney

 Makes 8 servings

Prep time: 10 minutes • Total time: 1 hour, 35 minutes

Curb carbs: Many meat loaves are high in carbohydrates because of the thick sauces in and on top of them. We went with a basic meat loaf base with the addition of quinoa to add texture and healthy carbs.

Fill up on fiber: The cranberries and quinoa give this meat loaf a kick of fiber!

Favor healthy fats: Instead of the traditional, and more fatty, ground beef, we used extra-lean ground turkey with only a small amount of fat. The olive oil and flaxseeds provide the healthy fats!

- Preheat the oven to 350°F (180°C)
- 13- by 9-inch (33 by 23 cm) glass baking dish

1½ tsp	olive oil	7 mL
1	shallot, finely chopped	1
2 cups	cranberries	500 mL
½ cup	quinoa	125 mL
1 cup	water	250 mL
1 tbsp	olive oil	15 mL
1	onion, chopped	1
2	cloves garlic, minced	2
3 lbs	extra-lean (99% fat-free) ground turkey	1.5 kg
¼ cup	ketchup	60 mL
2	large egg whites, lightly beaten	2
2 tbsp	ground flaxseeds	30 mL

1. In a saucepan, heat the oil over medium-high heat. Cook the shallot, stirring, for 5 minutes. Add the cranberries and cook, stirring often, for 10 minutes.

2. Meanwhile, in a saucepan, bring the quinoa and water to a boil. Reduce the heat to low, cover, and cook for 15 minutes. Remove from the heat, transfer to a large bowl, and set aside.

3. In a skillet, heat the oil over medium heat. Cook the onion and garlic, stirring, for 5 minutes, or until lightly browned. Transfer to the bowl with the quinoa.

4. Add the turkey, ketchup, egg whites, and flaxseeds to the bowl with the onion mixture. Stir to combine.

5. Transfer the meat loaf into a baking dish and loosely form into a rectangular log. Cover with half of the chutney.

6. Bake in preheated oven for 60 minutes, or until a thermometer inserted in the center registers 165°F (74°C) and the meat is no longer pink. Serve the meat loaf with the remaining chutney.

Makeover Magic		
Before		**After**
515	Calories	288
26 g	Fat	6 g
10 g	Sat Fat	0.5 g
29 g	Carbs	16 g
1 g	Fiber	3 g
39 g	Protein	46 g
948 mg	Sodium	198 mg

Turkey Cheeseburgers

 Makes 4 servings

Prep time: 5 minutes • Total time: 20 minutes

Curb carbs: We used an average-size whole wheat hamburger bun instead of an oversize white bun, which helped us to maintain proper portion sizes.

Fill up on fiber: A whole wheat bun loaded with mushrooms, pepper, and onion — we made sure you got a good amount of fiber from this burger!

Favor healthy fats: Add a thin slice of avocado for a creamy burger topping that's full of MUFAs. Or pair with a salad drizzled in olive oil.

- Preheat barbecue grill to medium, grill sprayed with nonstick cooking spray
- Grill basket or cast-iron skillet

1 lb	extra-lean (99% fat-free) ground turkey	500 g
2	large egg whites	2
1½ tbsp	reduced-sodium Worcestershire sauce	22 mL
8 oz	mushrooms, trimmed and sliced	250 g
2 tsp	olive oil	10 mL
4	slices onion, each ¼ inch (0.5 cm) thick	4
1	green bell pepper, sliced	1
4	whole wheat hamburger buns	4
2 oz	reduced-fat Cheddar cheese, sliced	60 g
¼ cup	barbecue sauce	60 mL

1. In a large bowl, combine the turkey, egg whites, and Worcestershire sauce. Gently form into 4 burgers, pressing down to create a shallow well in the center of each.

2. Toss the mushrooms with the oil and cook in a grill basket (or cast-iron skillet) for 6 minutes, stirring, until golden brown. Remove from the heat and keep warm.

3. Coat the onion and bell pepper with olive oil spray. Grill the onion and pepper, turning, for 4 minutes, or until tender. Grill the buns cut side down for 2 minutes, or until marked. Grill the burgers for 8 minutes, turning once, or until a thermometer inserted in the center registers 165°F (74°C) and the meat is no longer pink. Top with cheese and grill, covered, for 30 seconds, or until melted.

4. Serve the burgers on buns and top with the onion, pepper, mushrooms, and barbecue sauce.

Makeover Magic		
Before		**After**
578	Calories	367
37 g	Fat	10 g
6 g	Sat Fat	3 g
51 g	Carbs	36 g
3 g	Fiber	5 g
29 g	Protein	39 g
896 mg	Sodium	591 mg

Turkey and Orzo Stuffed Peppers

Makes 4 servings

Prep time: 5 minutes • Total time: 40 minutes

Curb carbs: This dish's carbs come primarily from the vegetables and orzo. But our makeover dish is so high in fiber that the magic carbs come out to just 29 grams!

Fill up on fiber: Kale and whole wheat orzo are great sources of fiber that set this recipe apart from more traditional stuffed peppers.

Favor healthy fats: Add olives and pine nuts for flavor and some favored fats.

- Preheat oven to 350°F (180°C)
- 8-inch (20 cm) glass baking dish

1/3 cup	whole wheat orzo	75 mL
16 cups	water	4 L
4	large red bell peppers	4
2 tsp	canola oil	10 mL
1 lb	extra-lean (99% fat-free) ground turkey	500 g
1	small onion, chopped	1
2	cloves garlic, minced	2
1 tbsp	finely chopped fresh thyme	15 mL
1 lb	baby kale	500 g
1/2 cup	frozen peas, thawed	125 mL
1	can (14 to 15 oz/398 to 425 mL) no-salt-added tomato sauce	1

1. Cook the orzo according to package directions, omitting the salt. Drain well.

2. In a large pot, bring water to a boil over high heat. Cut off and discard the stems of the bell peppers. Seed the peppers, being careful not to puncture them. Cook the whole peppers in the boiling water for 2 minutes, or until slightly softened. Drain the peppers on paper towels. Place in baking dish, standing the peppers upright. Set aside.

3. In a large nonstick skillet, heat the oil over medium-high heat until hot but not smoking. Cook the turkey, stirring, for 3 minutes, breaking up any clumps with a spoon. Add the onion, garlic, and thyme. Cook, stirring, for 3 minutes, or until the onion is softened. Add the kale and peas. Cover and cook for 3 minutes, or until the kale is wilted. Remove the pan from the heat.

4. Add the reserved orzo to the kale mixture and stir to combine. Spoon the mixture into the bell peppers. Pour the tomato sauce into the baking dish in and around the peppers.

5. Bake in the preheated oven for 15 minutes, or until the peppers and filling are hot.

Makeover Magic		
Before		**After**
560	Calories	353
28 g	Fat	6 g
14 g	Sat Fat	0.5 g
42 g	Carbs	40 g
6 g	Fiber	11 g
34 g	Protein	37 g
990 mg	Sodium	215 mg

Turkey and Bean Quesadillas

 Makes 8 servings

Prep time: 5 minutes • Total time: 30 minutes

Curb carbs: Use a sprouted grain wrap when trying to find ways to decrease carbs and increase fiber.

Fill up on fiber: The sprouted grain wrap, vegetables, and beans we added set this quesadilla apart from the rest because it is a superstar in fiber! This recipe has a whopping 17 grams of fiber, which you can subtract from the total carbs to count this dish as just 14 grams of carbs.

Favor healthy fats: Using 50% reduced-fat cheese allowed us to make these quesadillas very cheesy, with only 5 grams of fat from the cheese. The avocado is the heart-healthy fat of choice in this recipe.

- Preheat barbecue grill to medium, grill sprayed with nonstick cooking spray

1 lb	turkey breast cutlets	500 g
1 tsp	canola oil	5 mL
1	green bell pepper, finely chopped	1
1	small onion, finely chopped	1
½ cup	frozen corn kernels, thawed	125 mL
1	jalapeño pepper, seeded and finely chopped	1
1	can (15 oz/425 mL) black beans, drained and rinsed	1
16	7 inch (18 cm) sprouted whole wheat tortillas	16
8 oz	reduced-fat Cheddar cheese, shredded	250 g
1 cup	salsa	250 mL
½	avocado, chopped	½

1. On the grill, cook the turkey cutlets for 10 minutes, turning once, or until no longer pink. Transfer to a cutting board and use a fork to shred the meat. (Leave grill on.)

2. In a nonstick skillet, heat the oil over medium-high heat. Cook the bell pepper and onion, stirring, for 5 minutes, or until tender. Add the corn, jalapeño, black beans, and turkey and cook, stirring, for 5 minutes, or until heated through. Remove from the heat.

3. On a clean work surface, lay out 8 tortillas. Sprinkle half of the cheese on the 8 tortillas and top them with the turkey mixture. Sprinkle the remaining cheese on top of the turkey mixture and top with the remaining tortillas.

4. Place the tortillas on the grill, working in batches if necessary, and cook for 6 minutes, turning once, or until the cheese is melted and the tortillas are golden brown. Adjust the heat if necessary to prevent burning. Transfer the quesadillas to serving plates. Top with salsa and avocado.

Makeover Magic		
Before		**After**
520	Calories	307
28 g	Fat	11 g
12 g	Sat Fat	4 g
41 g	Carbs	31 g
4 g	Fiber	17 g
27 g	Protein	34 g
1,210 mg	Sodium	445 mg

Turkey Meatballs and Zucchini Pasta

Prep time: 5 minutes • Total time: 35 minutes

Curb carbs: We replaced traditional linguine with succulent strands of zucchini for a dramatic cut in carbs.

Fill up on fiber: Zucchini is the main source of fiber in this recipe.

Favor healthy fats: Flaxseeds create a great foundation of healthy fats. Add olives and pine nuts for flavor and even more good fats.

- Preheat oven to 400°F (200°C)
- Baking sheet, sprayed with nonstick cooking spray

1 lb	extra-lean (99% fat-free) ground turkey	500 g
3	cloves garlic, minced, divided	3
1	large egg white	1
¼ cup	ground flaxseeds	60 mL
1 tbsp	canola oil	15 mL
1	onion, chopped	1
2 tsp	dried Italian seasoning	10 mL
1	can (28 oz/796 mL) whole tomatoes, chopped, with juice	1
1 tbsp	no-salt-added tomato paste	15 mL
3	large zucchini, cut into matchsticks	3

1. In a bowl, combine the turkey, one-third of the garlic, the egg white, and the ground flaxseeds. With slightly damp hands, form the mixture into sixteen 1½-inch (4 cm) balls and set them 1 inch (2.5 cm) apart on the prepared baking sheet.

2. Bake in preheated oven, turning once, for 25 minutes, or until a thermometer inserted in the center registers 165°F (74°C) and the meat is no longer pink.

3. In a large saucepan, heat the oil over medium-high heat. Cook the remaining garlic, onion, and Italian seasoning, stirring occasionally, for 3 minutes, or until the onion begins to soften. Stir in the tomatoes and tomato paste. Bring to a boil. Reduce the heat to medium-low and simmer, partially covered, for 15 minutes, or until the sauce starts to thicken. Stir in the meatballs and simmer for 5 minutes, or until the sauce has thickened and the meatballs are hot.

4. Place the zucchini in a large microwave-safe bowl and cook in the microwave oven on High for 1 minute, or until slightly softened.

5. Divide the zucchini among 4 shallow bowls and top each with 4 meatballs and sauce.

Makeover Magic		
Before		**After**
510	Calories	298
22 g	Fat	9 g
9 g	Sat Fat	1 g
42 g	Carbs	21 g
5 g	Fiber	7 g
38 g	Protein	36 g
1,552 mg	Sodium	467 mg

Baked Spaghetti with Turkey Meat Sauce

 Makes 8 servings

Prep time: 5 minutes • Total time: 1 hour, 15 minutes

Curb carbs: Our dish uses whole wheat spaghetti instead of regular pasta — and less of it than a traditional baked spaghetti.

Fill up on fiber: The pasta is a great source of fiber. Pair this dish with a side salad to boost the fiber even more!

Favor healthy fats: We swapped out ground beef and went with 99% lean ground turkey, which is less fatty but just as tasty. Top with olives for added healthy fats.

- Preheat oven to 350°F (180°C)
- 13- by 9-inch (33 by 23 cm) glass baking dish

8 oz	whole wheat spaghetti, broken into 2-inch (5 cm) pieces	250 g
1/3 cup	grated Parmesan cheese	75 mL
2	large egg whites	2
1 tbsp	canola oil	15 mL
1 lb	extra-lean (99% fat-free) ground turkey	500 g
2 cups	low-sodium olive oil–based pasta sauce	500 mL
1/2 tsp	dried oregano	2 mL
1	clove garlic, minced	1
1 cup	reduced-fat (2%) cottage cheese	250 mL
4 oz	part-skim mozzarella cheese, shredded	125 g

1. Cook the spaghetti according to package directions, omitting the salt. Drain.

2. Place the spaghetti in baking dish. Stir in the Parmesan cheese and egg whites until thoroughly combined. Spread the mixture evenly in the dish.

3. In a large skillet, heat the oil over medium-high heat. Cook the turkey for 5 minutes, breaking up with a spoon, until the meat is brown. Drain. Stir in the pasta sauce, oregano, and garlic.

4. Spread the cottage cheese over the spaghetti layer and top with the meat mixture.

5. Bake in preheated oven for 30 minutes. Sprinkle the mozzarella cheese over the top and bake for 10 minutes, or until the cheese is melted and just begins to brown. Let stand for 15 minutes before cutting.

Makeover Magic		
Before		**After**
434	Calories	312
17 g	Fat	9 g
8 g	Sat Fat	4 g
43 g	Carbs	32 g
3 g	Fiber	5 g
26 g	Protein	28 g
732 mg	Sodium	330 mg

Baked Penne with Turkey

 Makes 4 servings

Prep time: 10 minutes • Total time: 55 minutes

Curb carbs: The carbohydrates in our recipe are similar to our comparison, but by upping the fiber, we're able to use magic carbs to bring the recipe down to 36 grams.

Fill up on fiber: Kale and whole wheat penne raise the fiber!

Favor healthy fats: For a dose of healthy fats, add a side salad drizzled with olive oil, canola oil, or even flaxseed oil.

- Preheat the oven to 375°F (190°C)
- 12-cup (3 L) shallow baking dish, sprayed with nonstick cooking spray

1½ cups	whole wheat penne pasta (5 oz/150 g)	375 mL
6 oz	lean Italian-style turkey sausage (sweet or mild), cut into 4-inch (10 cm) pieces	175 g
8 oz	extra-lean (99% fat-free) ground turkey	250 g
1	large green bell pepper, chopped	1
1	small onion, chopped	1
4 oz	mushrooms, trimmed and chopped	125 g
3	cloves garlic, minced	3
2 tsp	dried Italian seasoning	10 mL
2 cups	low-sodium pasta sauce	500 mL
8 oz	baby kale	250 g
¾ cup	shredded part-skim mozzarella cheese	175 mL

1. Cook the pasta according to package directions, omitting the salt. Drain and set aside.

2. Heat a large nonstick skillet over medium heat. Cook the sausage and ground turkey, stirring and breaking up turkey with a spoon, for 10 minutes, or until browned and no longer pink. Transfer the meat mixture to a clean plate and allow to cool while preparing the rest of the sauce.

3. In the same skillet, cook the bell pepper, onion, mushrooms, garlic, and Italian seasoning, stirring occasionally, for 7 minutes, or until the onion is almost soft. Stir in the pasta sauce and kale.

4. Cut the sausage into ¼-inch (0.5 cm) slices and place in the prepared baking dish along with the sauce and pasta. Toss to combine. Sprinkle with the cheese.

5. Bake in preheated oven for 25 minutes, or until heated through and the cheese is melted and slightly browned.

Makeover Magic		
Before		**After**
630	Calories	407
30 g	Fat	11 g
15 g	Sat Fat	4 g
45 g	Carbs	43 g
3 g	Fiber	7 g
45 g	Protein	34 g
878 mg	Sodium	573 mg

Turkey Swedish Meatballs

 Makes 4 servings

Prep time: 5 minutes • Total time: 25 minutes

Curb carbs: Instead of using bread crumbs, we opted for ground flaxseeds, which dramatically cut the carbohydrates.

Fill up on fiber: This dish is low in fiber, so be sure to serve it with a whole grain or other fiber superstar.

Favor healthy fats: We love lean ground turkey because it really cuts the saturated fat compared to most Swedish meatball recipes. Serve with toasted almonds and pine nuts over a spinach salad for a delicious serving of healthy fats.

1 lb	extra-lean (99% fat-free) ground turkey	500 g
1	small onion, finely chopped	1
1	large egg	1
1/4 cup	ground flaxseeds	60 mL
1/4 tsp	ground allspice	1 mL
3/4 cup	low-sodium ready-to-use chicken broth	175 mL
2 tsp	cornstarch	10 mL
2 tsp	Worcestershire sauce	10 mL
2 tsp	canola oil	10 mL
1/2 cup	light sour cream	125 mL

1. In a large bowl, combine the turkey, onion, egg, flaxseeds, and allspice. Mix until well combined and form into twenty-four 1-inch (2.5 cm) meatballs.

2. In a small bowl, combine the broth, cornstarch, and Worcestershire sauce and set aside.

3. In a large nonstick skillet, heat the oil over medium heat. Cook the meatballs for 14 minutes, turning occasionally, until browned, a thermometer inserted in the center registers 165°F (74°C), and the meat is no longer pink inside. Transfer the meatballs to paper towels to drain.

4. Increase the heat to medium-high and add the broth mixture to the skillet. Bring to a boil, shaking the pan often, and cook for 2 minutes to thicken. Remove from the heat and stir in the sour cream until well blended.

5. Return the meatballs to the pan and gently turn to coat with the sauce.

Makeover Magic		
Before		**After**
710	Calories	260
42 g	Fat	11 g
20 g	Sat Fat	3 g
45 g	Carbs	8 g
2 g	Fiber	3 g
35 g	Protein	34 g
1,580 mg	Sodium	147 mg

Sloppy Joes

Prep time: 10 minutes • Total time: 25 minutes

Curb carbs: We chose a whole wheat bun over the average white bun. Instead of fries, serve with a non-starchy side like asparagus to keep carbs curbed.

Fill up on fiber: We added pepper, onion, and celery to give this classic sandwich an extra kick of fiber!

Favor healthy fats: Serve this classic dish with grilled asparagus coated in olive oil and slivered almonds for favored fats.

	Nonstick cooking spray	
1	onion, chopped	1
1	green bell pepper, chopped	1
1	stalk celery, chopped	1
2	cloves garlic, chopped	2
1 lb	extra-lean (99% fat-free) ground turkey	500 g
1½ cups	no-salt-added crushed tomatoes	375 mL
2 tbsp	pure maple syrup	30 mL
1 tbsp	cider vinegar	15 mL
2 tsp	Worcestershire sauce	10 mL
4	whole wheat sandwich buns	4

1. Heat a large nonstick skillet sprayed with cooking spray to medium. Cook the onion, bell pepper, celery, and garlic, stirring, for 7 minutes, or until soft.

2. Add the turkey. Cook for 5 minutes, breaking the meat up with a spoon, or until no longer pink.

3. Add the crushed tomatoes, maple syrup, vinegar, and Worcestershire sauce. Cook, stirring occasionally, for 5 minutes, or until hot and bubbly. Spoon into the buns.

Makeover Magic		
Before		**After**
439	Calories	315
16 g	Fat	4 g
6 g	Sat Fat	0.5 g
46 g	Carbs	40 g
2 g	Fiber	6 g
27 g	Protein	34 g
1,360 mg	Sodium	324 mg

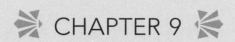

CHAPTER 9
Seafood

Fish Po' Boy with Cajun Slaw 212

Fish and Chips 213

Asian Fish Packets 214

Cornmeal Catfish with Black-Eyed Peas 215

Trout Paella. 216

Salmon Pasta Casserole 217

Salmon with Avocado Salsa 218

Salmon-Barley Bake. 219

Tuna Tetrazzini 220

Tuna Steaks on Greens 221

Shrimp Tacos 222

Shrimp Scampi Linguine 223

Sweet and Sour Shrimp. 223

Scallops with Beans and Arugula. 224

Fish Po' Boy with Cajun Slaw

 Makes 4 servings

Prep time: 20 minutes • Total time: 35 minutes

Curb carbs: Most po' boys are breaded and fried, adding carbs, fat, and calories. This seasoned version is a fresh, flavorful take on the comfort food favorite.

Fill up on fiber: Adding coleslaw to this dish boosts the fiber while adding tanginess.

Favor healthy fats: Baking the fish instead of frying it greatly reduces the trans fats. Cod is a great source of the omega-3 fatty acids EPA and DHA.

- Preheat oven to 350°F (180°C)
- Baking sheet, sprayed with nonstick cooking spray

3 tbsp	plain nonfat (0%) Greek yogurt	45 mL
2 tbsp	olive oil mayonnaise	30 mL
2 tbsp	agave syrup or honey	30 mL
1 tbsp	cider vinegar	15 mL
¼ tsp	hot pepper sauce (optional)	1 mL
1	bag (14 oz/420 g) shredded coleslaw mix	1
1	red bell pepper, cut into 1-inch (2.5 cm) strips, each halved	1
½	small onion, grated	½
2 tsp	blackening seasoning	10 mL
4	thick cod fillets (each 5 oz/150 g)	4
1 cup	mixed greens	250 mL
1	large tomato, thinly sliced	1
1	whole wheat baguette (12 oz/375 g), sliced lengthwise in half and cut crosswise into 4 pieces	1

1. In a large bowl, whisk together the yogurt, mayonnaise, agave syrup, vinegar, and hot pepper sauce (if using). Add the coleslaw mix, bell pepper, and onion. Toss to coat well. Cover and refrigerate until ready to serve.

2. Rub the seasoning over the fish. Place the fish on the baking sheet and bake in preheated oven, turning once, for 15 minutes, or until the fish flakes easily.

4. Divide the greens and tomato on the baguettes. Top each with a fish fillet, folding the fish to fit, if necessary. Serve with the coleslaw.

Makeover Magic		
Before		**After**
1,041	Calories	347
55 g	Fat	6 g
8 g	Sat Fat	1 g
82 g	Carbs	43 g
10 g	Fiber	8 g
56 g	Protein	33 g
2,562 mg	Sodium	405 mg

Fish and Chips

 Makes 4 servings

Prep time: 20 minutes • Total time: 1 hour

Curb carbs: Each serving of "chips" equals just half a potato, a plentiful amount alongside the fish fillets.

Fill up on fiber: Both the panko breading and the sweet potatoes contribute fiber to this pub favorite.

Favor healthy fats: Halibut is full of marine omega-3s. By baking the fillets, we avoid frying in saturated fats.

- Preheat oven to 425°F (220°C)

2	medium sweet potatoes, peeled and cut into large wedges	2
1 tbsp	canola oil	15 mL
1 tsp	salt, divided	5 mL
1 tsp	ground black pepper, divided	5 mL
2	large egg whites	2
1 tbsp	Dijon mustard	15 mL
1 cup	whole wheat panko bread crumbs	250 mL
½ tsp	dried thyme	2 mL
4	wild halibut fillets (each 6 oz/175 q), skin removed	4
	Malt vinegar	

1. Place the potatoes on a large baking sheet and drizzle with the oil and ½ tsp (2 mL) each of the salt and pepper. Toss to coat. Bake in preheated oven for 15 minutes.

2. Meanwhile, in a shallow bowl, whisk together the egg whites, mustard, and the remaining salt and pepper. In another shallow bowl, combine the bread crumbs and thyme. Dip the fish into the egg whites and then into the crumbs. Discard any excess egg and crumb mixtures.

3. Add the fish to the baking sheet and return to the oven. Bake for 15 minutes, or until the fish flakes easily. Serve with the vinegar.

Makeover Magic		
Before		**After**
579	Calories	350
33 g	Fat	8 g
4 g	Sat Fat	1 g
53 g	Carbs	26 g
3 g	Fiber	4 g
14 g	Protein	41 g
759 mg	Sodium	413 mg

Asian Fish Packets

Prep time: 15 minutes • Total time: 25 minutes

Curb carbs: Instead of a sweet, sugary sauce, these fish packets are flavored with fresh ginger and a touch of rice wine vinegar.

Fill up on fiber: Bok choy offers not just fiber, but also a lovely, sweet flavor.

Favor healthy fats: Halibut is our source of EPA and DHA omega-3 fatty acids.

- Preheat oven to 450°F (230°C)
- Four 20- by 12-inch (50 by 30 cm) sheets of parchment, one side sprayed with nonstick cooking spray

4	baby bok choy	4
2	carrots, cut into matchsticks	2
1	onion, cut into thin wedges	1
2 tsp	low-sodium soy sauce, divided	10 mL
1 tsp	rice wine vinegar, divided	5 mL
2 tsp	grated gingerroot, divided	10 mL
4	wild halibut fillets (each 6 oz/175 g)	4

1. Place prepared parchment sheets on work surface, sprayed side up. Divide the bok choy, carrots, and onion among the sheets. Drizzle each with ½ tsp (2 mL) soy sauce, ¼ tsp (1 mL) vinegar, and ½ tsp (2 mL) ginger. Add the fillets.

2. Fold the other half of each sheet over the filling and fold the edges to make a tight seal.

3. Arrange the packets on a large baking sheet. Bake in preheated oven for 10 minutes, or until the packets are puffed. Check to make sure the fish flakes easily; return to oven and bake longer, if necessary. Transfer each packet to a serving plate. Carefully slit the top of each to allow the steam to escape. After a minute, peel back the paper.

Makeover Magic		
Before		**After**
830	Calories	233
60 g	Fat	4 g
9 g	Sat Fat	0.5 g
16 g	Carbs	10 g
5 g	Fiber	4 g
58 g	Protein	39 g
810 mg	Sodium	280 mg

Cornmeal Catfish with Black-Eyed Peas

 Makes 4 servings

Prep time: 15 minutes • Total time: 30 minutes

Curb carbs: Nothing says southern comfort like catfish! This dish is typically fried and dredged in flour and cornmeal, adding unnecessary carbs. Our version cuts straight to the cornmeal, using smaller amounts of the blood sugar–busting ingredients overall.

Fill up on fiber: Topping the fish with corn and black beans adds classic flavor — and lots of fiber.

Favor healthy fats: Catfish contains heart-healthy omega-3 fatty acids. Plus, using our simple skillet sauté method takes saturated fats from deep-frying out of the equation.

4 tsp	canola oil, divided	20 mL
1 cup	fresh or thawed frozen corn kernels	250 mL
1	clove garlic, minced	1
½ tsp	dried thyme	2 mL
1	can (15 oz/425 mL) black-eyed peas, drained and rinsed	1
1	roasted red bell pepper, patted dry and chopped	1
1 cup	yellow cornmeal	250 mL
¼ tsp	salt	1 mL
4	catfish fillets (each 6 oz/175 g)	4

1. In a medium saucepan, heat 1 tsp (5 mL) oil over medium-high heat. Cook the corn, garlic, and thyme for 5 minutes, stirring occasionally, until lightly browned. Add the peas and red pepper and cook for 1 minute, or until heated through. Keep warm.

2. On a large plate, combine the cornmeal and salt. Dredge the fillets in the cornmeal, pressing to adhere. Discard any excess cornmeal mixture.

3. In a large nonstick skillet, heat the remaining oil over medium heat. Cook the catfish, in batches as necessary, for 8 minutes, turning once, or until golden and the fish flakes easily. Serve the fish topped with the black-eyed pea mixture.

Makeover Magic		
Before		**After**
764	Calories	426
42 g	Fat	18 g
7 g	Sat Fat	3 g
46 g	Carbs	40 g
4 g	Fiber	5 g
47 g	Protein	29 g
1,369 mg	Sodium	115 mg

Trout Paella

 Makes 4 servings

Curb carbs: We use ½ cup (125 mL) of quinoa in this dish instead of a cup (250 mL) or more of white rice.

Fill up on fiber: Quinoa and kale both pack fiber — enough to use the magic carbs effect!

Favor healthy fats: Trout is an underappreciated fish when it comes to dining, but just as great a source of healthy fats as the more common salmon and tuna.

1 tsp	canola oil	5 mL
1	small onion, chopped	1
1	red bell pepper, chopped	1
3	cloves garlic, finely chopped	3
1 tsp	paprika	5 mL
½ tsp	ground turmeric	2 mL
¼ tsp	dried thyme	1 mL
1 cup	rinsed drained no-salt-added canned chickpeas	250 mL
2 cups	reduced-sodium ready-to-use chicken broth	500 mL
½ cup	quinoa, rinsed well	125 mL
3 cups	chopped trimmed kale or collard leaves	750 mL
1 lb	wild rainbow trout fillets, cut into 2-inch (5 cm) chunks	500 g

1. In a large saucepan, heat the oil over medium-high heat. Cook the onion, bell pepper, garlic, paprika, turmeric, and thyme, stirring occasionally, for 5 minutes, or until lightly browned. Stir in the chickpeas, broth, and quinoa. Cover and simmer for 10 minutes, or until most of the broth is absorbed.

2. Stir in the kale or collards. Cook for 1 minute, or until partially wilted. Stir in the trout. Cover and simmer for 5 minutes, or until the trout flakes easily.

Makeover Magic		
Before		**After**
540	Calories	350
23 g	Fat	8 g
9 g	Sat Fat	1 g
56 g	Carbs	36 g
2 g	Fiber	10 g
28 g	Protein	33 g
1,420 mg	Sodium	304 mg

Salmon Pasta Casserole

 Makes 4 servings

Prep time: 10 minutes • Total time: 50 minutes

Curb carbs: Going with a moderate amount of whole-grain pasta (6 ounces/175 g in this case) is an easy way to curb carbs.

Fill up on fiber: While whole-grain pasta is naturally higher in fiber, the real stars of this recipe are the spinach and artichokes, which add a whopping 5 grams!

Favor healthy fats: Typically a dish like this is laden with heavy cream and butter. Here, we substituted MUFA-rich canola oil mayonnaise and replaced the high-carb bread crumbs with golden flaxseeds to keep the crunch but add more MUFAs and ALA omega-3s. Plus, salmon is naturally plentiful in the EPA and DHA forms of omega-3s, which you should aim to get into your diet through marine sources twice per week.

- Preheat oven to 350°F (180°C)
- 8-inch (20 cm) square glass baking dish, sprayed with nonstick cooking spray

6 oz	whole-grain farfalle pasta (bow ties)	175 g
2	pouches (each 5 oz/142 g) wild pink salmon, drained	2
1	package (10 oz/300 g) frozen artichoke hearts, thawed and chopped	1
1	package (10 oz/300 g) frozen chopped spinach, thawed and drained	1
¼ cup	canola oil mayonnaise	60 mL
¼ cup	grated Parmesan cheese, divided	60 mL
1 tbsp	lemon juice	15 mL
¼ cup	ground golden flaxseeds	60 mL

1. Cook the pasta according to package directions, omitting the salt. Drain and set aside.

2. Meanwhile, in a large bowl, combine the salmon, artichokes, spinach, mayonnaise, 2 tbsp (30 mL) cheese, and the lemon juice. Toss gently until blended. Stir in the pasta and spread in the prepared baking dish. Top with the flaxseeds and remaining cheese.

3. Bake in preheated oven for 30 minutes, or until heated through.

Smart Start
You can add a lower-carb dessert or a cup (250 mL) of berries to this dinner dish if you are craving sweets.

Makeover Magic		
Before		**After**
650	Calories	371
31 g	Fat	12 g
17 g	Sat Fat	2 g
46 g	Carbs	42 g
2 g	Fiber	12 g
43 g	Protein	26 g
440 mg	Sodium	500 mg

Salmon with Avocado Salsa

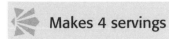 **Makes 4 servings**

Prep time: 15 minutes • Total time: 30 minutes + standing time

Curb carbs: Ditch the taco shell and pair this naturally low-carb dish with a higher-carb side like Baked Risotto (page 256) or Scalloped Red Potatoes (page 251).

Fill up on fiber: Avocado is a great source of fiber, and the bell pepper adds fiber as well.

Favor healthy fats: While this dish seems high in fat, most of that represents good fats from both the salmon and the avocado.

1	avocado, chopped	1
1	red bell pepper, chopped	1
1	small red onion, chopped	1
3 tbsp	freshly squeezed lime juice	45 mL
¼ cup	chopped fresh cilantro	60 mL
1	clove garlic, minced	1
¼ tsp	salt	1 mL
1 tbsp	canola oil	15 mL
2	wild salmon fillets (each 6 oz/175 g)	2

1. In a small bowl, combine the avocado, pepper, onion, lime juice, cilantro, garlic, and salt. Cover and let stand for at least 30 minutes to blend the flavors.

2. In a large nonstick skillet, heat the oil over medium-high heat. Sear the fillets for 10 minutes, turning once, or until opaque. Divide the salmon among 4 plates. Serve with the salsa.

Makeover Magic		
Before		**After**
830	Calories	375
45 g	Fat	22 g
10 g	Sat Fat	3 g
61 g	Carbs	10 g
7 g	Fiber	4 g
44 g	Protein	35 g
1,920 mg	Sodium	372 mg

Salmon-Barley Bake

 Makes 4 servings

Prep time: 15 minutes • Total time: 45 minutes

Curb carbs: Barley is a delicious whole grain. Using just ½ cup (125 mL) in this recipe gives the casserole body without affecting blood sugar.

Fill up on fiber: Barley and peas are the main sources of fiber in this dish.

Favor healthy fats: Wild canned salmon is an excellent source of healthy fats — choose the darker-color variety for more omega-3s.

- Preheat oven to 400°F (200°C)
- 6-cup (1.5 L) shallow glass baking dish, sprayed with nonstick cooking spray

1 cup	water	250 mL
½ cup	quick-cooking barley	125 mL
¾ cup	reduced-sodium ready-to-use chicken broth	175 mL
3	medium carrots, sliced diagonally	3
1	onion, finely chopped	1
1½ cups	1% milk	375 mL
¼ tsp	ground black pepper	1 mL
1 tbsp	arrowroot, dissolved in 2 tbsp (30 mL) cold water	15 mL
1	can (14.7 oz/420 g) wild red salmon, drained, with skin and bones removed	1
1	package (9 oz/270 g) frozen peas, thawed	1
2 tbsp	chopped fresh tarragon (or 2 tsp/ 10 mL dried)	30 mL

1. In a small saucepan, bring the water to a boil over medium-high heat. Stir in the barley, reduce the heat to medium low, cover, and cook for 10 minutes, or just until tender. Remove from the heat.

2. Meanwhile, in a large skillet over medium heat, bring the broth to a boil. Add the carrots and onion, cover, and cook, stirring often, for 3 minutes, or until crisp-tender. Transfer to the prepared baking dish with a slotted spoon.

3. Add the milk and pepper to the broth in the skillet and bring to a boil. Stir the arrowroot mixture and add it to the milk mixture. Cook, stirring constantly, until thickened. Reduce the heat to medium and stir in the salmon, barley, peas, and tarragon. Bring to a simmer and pour into the prepared baking dish.

4. Bake in preheated oven for 15 minutes, or until bubbly.

Makeover Magic		
Before		**After**
480	Calories	329
22 g	Fat	6 g
13 g	Sat Fat	2 g
53 g	Carbs	40 g
2 g	Fiber	8 g
20 g	Protein	31 g
560 mg	Sodium	464 mg

Tuna Tetrazzini

 Makes 4 servings

Curb carbs: We use less pasta in our version than standard tetrazzinis, bumping up the volume with lower-carb vegetables instead.

Fill up on fiber: Adding broccoli to this mix adds delicious fiber.

Favor healthy fats: Typically dishes like this are made with a cream high in saturated fat. We've switched to 1% milk, and it's just as delicious. Tuna is the source of omega-3 fatty acids in this dish.

- Preheat oven to 350°F (180°C)
- Medium glass baking dish, sprayed with nonstick cooking spray

8 oz	multigrain spaghetti	250 g
	Nonstick cooking spray	
4 cups	broccoli florets	1 L
4 oz	mushrooms, sliced	125 g
1	onion, chopped	1
¼ cup	water	60 mL
1	jar (2 oz/57 g) diced pimientos, drained	1
1½ tsp	dried Italian seasoning	7 mL
⅓ cup	whole-grain pastry flour	75 mL
2½ cups	1% milk	625 mL
⅓ cup	grated Parmesan cheese	75 mL
2	cans (each 5 oz/142 g) light tuna packed in water, drained	2

1. Cook the spaghetti according to package directions, omitting the salt, and drain.

2. In a large saucepan sprayed with cooking spray over medium-high heat, cook the broccoli, mushrooms, onion, and water, stirring occasionally, for 5 minutes, or until the broccoli is tender-crisp. Stir in the pimientos and Italian seasoning. Place in a bowl.

3. In the same saucepan, add the flour. Gradually add the milk, whisking constantly, until smooth. Cook, whisking constantly, over medium heat for 6 minutes, or until slightly thickened and bubbling.

4. Remove from the heat. Stir in the Parmesan until smooth. Stir in the tuna, the reserved broccoli mixture, and the spaghetti. Toss to mix. Pour into the prepared baking dish.

5. Cover and bake in preheated oven for 20 minutes. Uncover and bake for 10 minutes, or until bubbly. Remove from the oven and let stand for 5 minutes before serving.

Makeover Magic		
Before		**After**
520	Calories	309
13 g	Fat	5 g
7 g	Sat Fat	2 g
60 g	Carbs	41 g
6 g	Fiber	5 g
40 g	Protein	25 g
940 mg	Sodium	310 mg

Tuna Steaks on Greens

 Makes 4 servings

Prep time: 5 minutes • Total time: 15 minutes

Curb carbs: No need to serve these steaks on a roll — the flavor is so strong and delicious that a bed of greens makes a perfect platter. Plus, at only 8 grams of carbs, you've got room to add a higher-carb side dish or enjoy a slice of cake for dessert!

Fill up on fiber: Our fiber comes from the mixed greens, cucumber, and avocado. The roll in the comparison recipe adds fiber — but also lots of carbs.

Favor healthy fats: This dish is full of amazing fats! Tuna is a nice source of omega-3 fatty acids, while canola oil mayonnaise and avocado are both full of MUFAs.

- Preheat barbecue grill to medium-high heat or preheat broiler
- Broiler pan (if using broiler)

¼ cup	canola oil mayonnaise	60 mL
2	green onions, thinly sliced	2
1 tbsp	lime juice	15 mL
1	small clove garlic, minced	1
½ tsp	ground cumin	2 mL
	Nonstick cooking spray	
4	yellowfin tuna steaks (each 4 oz/125 g)	4
2 tsp	canola oil	10 mL
¼ tsp	salt	1 mL
4 cups	mixed greens	1 L
1	small cucumber, sliced	1
1	avocado, thinly sliced	1
2 tbsp	chopped fresh cilantro (optional)	30 mL

1. In a medium bowl, stir together the mayonnaise, green onions, lime juice, garlic, and cumin until well blended. Refrigerate until serving.

2. Coat the grill rack or broiler pan with nonstick cooking spray. Brush the tuna steaks with the oil and sprinkle with the salt. Set on the grill rack or broiler pan. Grill or broil for 4 minutes, turning once, or until well marked and opaque.

3. Divide the greens, cucumber, and avocado among 4 plates. Top each with 1 tuna steak and a dollop of the mayonnaise mixture. Sprinkle with the cilantro, if using.

Makeover Magic		
Before		**After**
460	Calories	327
12 g	Fat	20 g
6 g	Sat Fat	2 g
45 g	Carbs	8 g
7 g	Fiber	5 g
42 g	Protein	19 g
780 mg	Sodium	296 mg

Shrimp Tacos

 Makes 4 servings

Curb carbs: The best way to make a taco healthy and satisfying is to select 6-inch (15 cm) corn tortillas over the larger white flour ones. This move cuts the carbs while adding some fiber.

Fill up on fiber: The fiber in this dish comes not just from the tortillas, but also the avocado.

Favor healthy fats: Shrimp and avocado team up in this recipe to bring you both omega-3 fatty acids and essential MUFAs.

1	Hass avocado, cubed	1
3 tbsp	finely chopped red onion	45 mL
2 tbsp	chopped fresh cilantro (or 2 tsp/10 mL ground coriander)	30 mL
½	jalapeño pepper, seeded and finely chopped	½
1 tbsp	freshly squeezed lime juice	15 mL
½ tsp	salt, divided	2 mL
1 lb	medium shrimp, peeled and deveined	500 g
1½ tsp	chili powder	7 mL
1 tbsp	olive oil	15 mL
8	6-inch (15 cm) corn tortillas	8
1 cup	shredded romaine	250 mL

1. In a small bowl, toss together the avocado, onion, cilantro, jalapeño, lime juice, and ¼ tsp (1 mL) salt. Set aside.

2. In a medium bowl, combine the shrimp, chili powder, and remaining salt.

3. In a large nonstick skillet, heat the oil over medium-high heat. Cook the shrimp, stirring, for 5 minutes, or until opaque. Transfer to a plate and keep warm.

4. One at a time, heat the tortillas in a dry skillet over medium-high heat for 1 minute, turning once, or until hot and lightly toasted. Place 2 tortillas on each of 4 plates. Divide the romaine, shrimp, and avocado mixture among the tortillas.

Makeover Magic Shrimp Tacos		
Before		**After**
400	Calories	320
10 g	Fat	12 g
2 g	Sat Fat	2 g
56 g	Carbs	27 g
4 g	Fiber	6 g
22 g	Protein	27 g
560 mg	Sodium	484 mg

Makeover Magic Shrimp Scampi Linguine		
Before		**After**
587	Calories	336
28 g	Fat	12 g
10 g	Sat Fat	3 g
45 g	Carbs	19 g
7 g	Fiber	7 g
34 g	Protein	33 g
554 mg	Sodium	446 mg

Makeover Magic Sweet and Sour Shrimp		
Before		**After**
483	Calories	283
29 g	Fat	6 g
4 g	Sat Fat	1 g
46 g	Carbs	31 g
1 g	Fiber	3 g
13 g	Protein	27 g
1,928 mg	Sodium	283 mg

Shrimp Scampi Linguine

Makes 4 servings

Prep time: 10 minutes • Total time: 20 minutes

Curb carbs: Using shirataki noodles in place of wheat-based linguine cuts the carbs dramatically while still serving up satisfying, slurpable noodles.

Fill up on fiber: Adding lentils and spinach to this classic dish pumps up the fiber, as well as other important nutrients, like iron.

Favor healthy fats: Shrimp is very low in saturated fats and high in omega-3s. As for the topping, no need to bathe this dish in lots of butter. Instead, we flavor the sauce with wine, lemon, and fresh tomatoes.

8 oz	shirataki fettuccine	250 g
2 tbsp	canola oil	30 mL
1 lb	medium shrimp, peeled and deveined	500 g
4	cloves garlic, minced	4
½ tsp	hot pepper flakes	2 mL
2 cups	cherry tomatoes, halved	500 mL
½ cup	dry white wine	125 mL
	Juice of 1 lemon	
4 cups	packed baby spinach leaves	1 L
1	can (15 oz/425 mL) lentils, drained and rinsed	1
½ cup	grated Parmesan cheese	125 mL

1. Cook the fettuccine according to package directions, omitting the salt, and drain.

2. Meanwhile, in a large skillet, heat the oil over medium heat. Cook the shrimp, garlic, and hot pepper flakes for 2 minutes, stirring, or until the shrimp start to turn pink.

3. Add the tomatoes, wine, and lemon juice. Cook for 2 minutes, or until the tomatoes start to soften. Add the spinach and lentils and cook, stirring, for 1 minute, or until the spinach wilts. Stir in the fettuccine and toss to coat well. Divide among 4 plates and sprinkle each with 2 tbsp (30 mL) cheese.

Sweet and Sour Shrimp

Makes 2 servings

Prep time: 5 minutes • Total time: 10 minutes

Curb carbs: Instead of a sugary sauce, all-fruit jam adds natural sweetness.

Fill up on fiber: Steamed broccoli and pepper strips contribute fiber.

Favor healthy fats: Instead of deep-frying the shrimp, we cut out saturated fat by cooking the shrimp right in the pan.

2 tsp	canola oil	10 mL
2 cups	frozen bell pepper strips (about 8 oz/250 g)	500 mL
⅓ cup	apricot all-fruit jam	75 mL
2 tsp	red wine vinegar	10 mL
6 oz	cooked peeled deveined shrimp	175 g
4 cups	hot steamed broccoli	1 L

1. In a large nonstick skillet, heat the oil over medium-high heat. Cook the peppers for 3 minutes, stirring, until lightly browned. Stir in the jam, vinegar, and shrimp. Cook, stirring, for 2 minutes, or until bubbly. Serve with the broccoli.

Scallops with Beans and Arugula

 Makes 4 servings

Prep time: 5 minutes • Total time: 20 minutes

Curb carbs: The scallops are so flavorful there's no need for extra breading. Enjoy them au naturel with the beans and arugula for company.

Fill up on fiber: Adding beans to any dish pumps up the fiber.

Favor healthy fats: There's no need to fry scallops — searing them in healthy canola oil adds good fats and nice flavor.

2 tbsp	canola oil, divided	30 mL
1	red onion, finely chopped	1
1	clove garlic, minced	1
1½	cans (each 15 oz/425 mL) white beans, drained and rinsed	1½
4 cups	baby arugula	1 L
1 lb	large sea scallops, side muscles removed	500 g
	Pinch of salt	
	Pinch of ground black pepper	

1. In a large skillet, heat 1 tbsp (15 mL) oil over medium heat. Cook the onion and garlic, stirring, for 3 minutes, or until the onion is softened. Add the beans and arugula and cook, stirring, for 3 minutes, or until the beans are hot and the arugula is wilted. Place on a serving plate. Cover and keep warm.

2. In the same skillet, heat the remaining oil over medium-high heat. Blot the scallops dry with a paper towel and sprinkle with salt and pepper. Cook the scallops for 5 minutes, turning once, or until browned and opaque.

3. Place over the bean mixture.

Makeover Magic		
Before		**After**
386	Calories	298
19 g	Fat	12 g
5 g	Sat Fat	3 g
36 g	Carbs	22 g
0 g	Fiber	6 g
16 g	Protein	28 g
919 mg	Sodium	267 mg

Quinoa Pilaf with Pistachios (page 255)

Mexican Fried Rice (page 258)

Lemon-Raspberry
Cheesecake (page 264)

Chocolate Layer Cake with Maple Frosting (page 268)

Rich Chocolate Cream
Pie (page 272)

Southern Pecan Bread Pudding (page 275)

Oatmeal-Apple Cookies (page 280)

Creamy Pumpkin Mousse (page 283)

CHAPTER 10

Vegetarian

Wild Mushroom and White Bean Risotto 226

Vegetable Sauté with Quinoa 227

Pasta with Summer Vegetables 228

Roasted Vegetable Mac and Cheese 229

Broccoli Penne 230

Baked Pasta and Vegetables 231

Vegetable Lo Mein 232

Veggie Burger Wraps 233

Asparagus Swiss Quiche 234

Broccoli-Cheddar Strata 235

African Stew 236

Fire-Roasted Chili 237

Bean Enchiladas 238

Black Bean Burgers 239

Vegetable Pizza 240

Caramelized Onion and Fennel Pizza 242

Wild Mushroom and White Bean Risotto

 Makes 4 servings

Prep time: 10 minutes • Total time: 40 minutes

Curb carbs: By "beefing up" this vegetarian classic with porcinis, shiitakes, and cannellini beans, we were able to use less rice.

Fill up on fiber: Brown rice and cannellini beans work together to pack fiber into this savory dish.

Favor healthy fats: Olive oil provides some MUFAs, but for more healthy fats, try adding a side salad drizzled with flaxseed oil or a salad Niçoise.

1 cup	brown rice	250 mL
½ oz	dried porcini mushrooms	15 g
¾ cup	boiling water	175 mL
2 tbsp	olive oil	30 mL
1	onion, chopped	1
8 oz	shiitake mushrooms, stems discarded, caps thinly sliced	250 g
2	cloves garlic, minced	2
1 tsp	chopped fresh rosemary (or ⅓ tsp/1.5 mL dried)	5 mL
¼ tsp	salt	1 mL
¼ cup	dry white wine	60 mL
1	can (14 to 19 oz/398 to 540 mL) low-sodium cannellini beans, drained and rinsed	1
2 tbsp	grated Parmesan cheese	30 mL

1. Cook the rice according to package directions, omitting the salt.

2. Meanwhile, in a small bowl, combine the dried mushrooms and boiling water. Let the mushrooms stand for 10 minutes, or until softened. With a slotted spoon, remove the mushrooms to a sieve. Rinse and coarsely chop. Reserve the mushroom soaking liquid.

3. In a large nonstick skillet, heat the oil over medium-high heat. Cook the onion for 6 minutes, stirring, or until softened. Add the chopped porcinis, shiitake mushrooms, garlic, rosemary, and salt. Cook for 6 minutes, stirring occasionally, or until tender.

4. Add the wine and bring to a boil. Boil for 30 seconds, scraping any browned bits from the bottom of the pan, or until the wine is almost evaporated. Carefully pour in the reserved soaking liquid, leaving any grit in the bottom of the bowl. Bring to a boil. Reduce the heat and simmer for 5 minutes, or until the liquid is reduced by half. Stir in the beans and the rice and cook for 2 minutes, or until hot. Sprinkle with the Parmesan.

Makeover Magic		
Before		**After**
590	Calories	273
22 g	Fat	7 g
10 g	Sat Fat	2 g
83 g	Carbs	35 g
2 g	Fiber	4 g
14 g	Protein	8 g
1,140 mg	Sodium	352 mg

Vegetable Sauté with Quinoa

 Makes 4 servings

Prep time: 20 minutes • Total time: 50 minutes

Curb carbs: Quinoa has fewer carbs and more fiber and protein than white rice.

Fill up on fiber: Don't forget asparagus when selecting vegetables — it offers 5 grams of fiber per serving.

Favor healthy fats: Avocado not only adds MUFAs but is also a good source of fiber.

1½ cups	water	375 mL
¾ cup	quinoa, rinsed	175 mL
¼ tsp	salt	1 mL
1 tbsp	canola oil	15 mL
1	onion, cut into wedges	1
1 lb	asparagus, trimmed and cut in half	500 g
1	bunch radishes, trimmed and halved	1
2	cloves garlic, minced	2
¼ cup	low-sodium ready-to-use vegetable broth	60 mL
2 tbsp	apricot all-fruit spread	30 mL
1 tbsp	balsamic vinegar	15 mL
8 oz	baby spinach	250 g
1	avocado, cubed	1

1. In a large skillet, bring the water to a boil over high heat. Stir in the quinoa and salt and return to a boil. Reduce the heat to low, cover, and simmer for 20 minutes, or until all of the water is absorbed and the quinoa is tender.

2. Meanwhile, in a large nonstick skillet, heat the oil over medium-high heat. Cook the onion, stirring, for 3 minutes, or until tender. Stir in the asparagus, radishes, and garlic and cook, stirring, for 2 minutes. Add the broth, apricot spread, and vinegar and stir for 1 minute to deglaze the pan. Add the spinach, cover, and cook for 3 minutes, or until wilted.

3. Divide the quinoa and vegetables among 4 plates. Sprinkle with the avocado.

Makeover Magic		
Before		**After**
450	Calories	315
20 g	Fat	13 g
4 g	Sat Fat	2 g
60 g	Carbs	44 g
2 g	Fiber	11 g
7 g	Protein	9 g
700 mg	Sodium	379 mg

Pasta with Summer Vegetables

 Makes 4 servings

Prep time: 15 minutes • Total time: 35 minutes

Curb carbs: Cutting the pasta with veggies helps to bring down the carbs.

Fill up on fiber: By using whole wheat pasta and high-fiber veggies, there's enough fiber in this dish to bring the magic carbs down to 41 grams per serving!

Favor healthy fats: Sneak in some extra healthy fats by using omega-3-enriched pasta! Reduce saturated fat by using fresh mozzarella balls instead of a thick cheese sauce.

8 oz	whole-grain shell pasta with added protein and omega-3s	250 g
1 tbsp	olive oil	15 mL
1	small red onion, thinly sliced	1
2	cloves garlic, sliced	2
1	medium zucchini, cut into 1-inch (2.5 cm) chunks	1
1	yellow summer squash, cut into 1-inch (2.5 cm) chunks	1
1 cup	cherry tomatoes, halved	250 mL
1 cup	drained small fresh mozzarella balls (ciliegini), halved	250 mL
¼ cup	chopped fresh basil (or 8 tsp/ 40 mL dried)	60 mL

1. Cook the pasta according to package directions, omitting the salt, and drain.

2. Meanwhile, in a large nonstick skillet, heat the oil over medium-high heat. Cook the onion and garlic for 2 minutes, stirring occasionally, or until softened. Stir in the zucchini and squash and cook for 8 minutes, stirring occasionally, or until the vegetables are tender-crisp. Stir in the tomatoes and cook for 3 minutes, or just until the tomatoes begin to burst.

3. Stir in the pasta and mozzarella. Cook for 2 minutes, stirring, or until the pasta is hot and the mozzarella just begins to melt. Remove the skillet from the heat and stir in the basil.

Makeover Magic		
Before		**After**
670	Calories	390
27 g	Fat	7 g
9 g	Sat Fat	1 g
91 g	Carbs	49 g
5 g	Fiber	8 g
17 g	Protein	34 g
100 mg	Sodium	490 mg

Roasted Vegetable Mac and Cheese

 Makes 6 servings

Prep time: 20 minutes • Total time: 1 hour, 15 minutes

Curb carbs: We halved the typical amount of pasta and tossed in cauliflower, onion, and bell pepper.

Fill up on fiber: Whole-grain pasta and vegetables add fiber, not to mention a satisfying, sophisticated flavor, to a childhood favorite!

Favor healthy fats: We used reduced-fat dairy to minimize the saturated fat and relied on canola oil for a helping of MUFAs. Add more by tossing in some toasted pine nuts.

- Preheat oven to 350°F (180°C)
- Rimmed baking sheet
- 11- by 7-inch (28 by 18 cm) glass baking dish, sprayed with nonstick cooking spray

1	head cauliflower, cut into large florets	1
1	large onion, cut into wedges	1
1	yellow or red bell pepper, cut into eighths	1
2 tsp	canola oil	10 mL
8 oz	whole-grain elbow macaroni	250 g
2 cups	1% milk	500 mL
2 tbsp	whole wheat flour	30 mL
½ tsp	dried mustard	2 mL
¼ tsp	salt	1 mL
1½ cups	shredded reduced-fat sharp (old) Cheddar cheese	375 mL
2 tbsp	grated Romano cheese	30 mL

1. On a rimmed baking sheet, toss the cauliflower, onion, and bell pepper with oil, then spread out in a single layer. Roast in preheated oven for 30 minutes, stirring once, or until the cauliflower is golden brown. Remove from the oven to a cutting board, leaving the oven on, and chop the roasted vegetables coarsely. Add to the prepared baking dish.

2. Meanwhile, cook the macaroni according to package directions, omitting the salt. Drain and place in the dish with the roasted vegetables.

3. In a medium saucepan, whisk together the milk, flour, mustard, and salt. Cook over medium heat for 4 minutes, whisking, or until the mixture begins to thicken. Stir in the Cheddar and Romano and cook for 2 minutes, or until melted. Pour over the pasta and vegetables, tossing to coat.

4. Bake for 20 minutes, or until bubbling.

Makeover Magic		
Before		**After**
630	Calories	346
34 g	Fat	13 g
21 g	Sat Fat	7 g
55 g	Carbs	42 g
2 g	Fiber	6 g
27 g	Protein	22 g
850 mg	Sodium	470 mg

Broccoli Penne

 Makes 4 servings

Prep time: 15 minutes • Total time: 25 minutes

Curb carbs: This dish uses half the pasta thanks to added broccoli and tomatoes.

Fill up on fiber: We used multigrain pasta for a fiber boost. Broccoli adds both fiber and flavor.

Favor healthy fats: Pesto sauce, full of healthy MUFAs, is a great substitute for saturated fat–laden Alfredo sauce. The multigrain pasta adds some omega-3 fatty acids to the dish.

6 oz	multigrain penne pasta	175 g
2 cups	fresh broccoli florets	500 mL
1 cup	grape tomatoes, halved	250 mL
6 oz	fresh mozzarella cheese, cubed	175 g
1/4 cup	pesto sauce	60 mL
1 tbsp	lemon juice	15 mL

1. Cook the pasta according to package directions, omitting the salt. Add the broccoli to the pot for the last 2 minutes of cooking. Drain, reserving 1/2 cup (125 mL) of the pasta water.

2. In a large bowl, combine the pasta, broccoli, tomatoes, cheese, pesto, and lemon juice. Add the reserved water, 1 tbsp (15 mL) at a time, stirring gently, until smooth.

Makeover Magic		
Before		**After**
800	Calories	341
48 g	Fat	15 g
30 g	Sat Fat	5 g
69 g	Carbs	34 g
4 g	Fiber	5 g
24 g	Protein	20 g
810 mg	Sodium	228 mg

Baked Pasta and Vegetables

 Makes 4 servings

Prep time: 10 minutes • Total time: 45 minutes

Curb carbs: This creamy dish is lower in carbs because we substituted vegetables for half of the pasta.

Fill up on fiber: Aside from the whole-grain pasta, the main sources of fiber in this recipe are asparagus, carrots, and red onion.

Favor healthy fats: Canola oil and flaxseeds are our sources of favored fats. We used reduced-fat cream cheese to keep this dish heart-healthy.

- Preheat oven to 450°F (230°C)
- 8-inch (20 cm) square glass baking dish, sprayed with nonstick cooking spray

4 oz	whole-grain spaghetti	125 g
1 lb	asparagus, trimmed and cut into 3-inch (7.5 cm) pieces	500 g
2	carrots, sliced	2
2 tbsp	canola oil	30 mL
1	red onion, cut into thin wedges	1
½ tsp	dried basil	2 mL
2 tbsp	whole-grain pastry flour	30 mL
1 cup	1% milk	250 mL
2 oz	reduced-fat cream cheese, cut into cubes	60 g
¼ cup	grated Parmesan cheese	60 mL
¼ cup	ground golden flaxseeds	60 mL

1. Cook the pasta according to package directions, omitting the salt. Add the asparagus and carrots during the last 3 minutes of cooking. Drain.

2. Meanwhile, in a large skillet, heat the oil over medium heat. Cook the onion and basil, stirring, for 5 minutes, or until soft. Add the flour and cook, stirring constantly with a wooden spoon, for 2 minutes, or until lightly browned. Gradually whisk in the milk.

3. Cook, whisking, for 5 minutes, or until thickened. Remove from the heat and stir in the cream cheese until blended. Add the pasta mixture and toss to coat well. Pour into the prepared dish. Sprinkle with the cheese and flaxseeds.

4. Bake in preheated oven for 15 minutes, or until lightly browned.

Makeover Magic		
Before		**After**
550	Calories	257
20 g	Fat	6 g
11 g	Sat Fat	2 g
69 g	Carbs	38 g
4 g	Fiber	8 g
23 g	Protein	6 g
960 mg	Sodium	243 mg

Vegetable Lo Mein

 Makes 4 servings

Prep time: 15 minutes • Total time: 20 minutes

Curb carbs: Cutting the vegetables into matchstick-thin pieces allows them to replace some of the pasta without losing any of the flavor.

Fill up on fiber: In addition to using whole wheat spaghetti instead of white lo mein noodles, we use lots of fibrous vegetables for a dish bursting with flavor.

Favor healthy fats: Canola oil and sesame oil both have healthy fats. For additional MUFAs, sprinkle on a few tablespoons (45 mL) of sesame seeds.

8 oz	whole wheat spaghetti	250 g
1 tbsp	canola oil	15 mL
1	red onion, thinly sliced	1
3	baby bok choy, thinly sliced	3
2	carrots, thinly sliced	2
½ cup	low-sodium ready-to-use vegetable broth	125 mL
2	cloves garlic, minced	2
3 tbsp	reduced-sodium soy sauce	45 mL
2 tbsp	rice wine vinegar	30 mL
2 tsp	cornstarch	10 mL
1 tsp	toasted sesame oil	5 mL
4 oz	snow peas, sliced lengthwise	125 g

1. Cook the pasta according to package directions, omitting the salt, and drain.

2. Meanwhile, in a large skillet, heat the canola oil over medium-high heat. Cook the onion, bok choy, and carrots, stirring, for 3 minutes, or until tender-crisp.

3. In a small bowl, whisk together the broth, garlic, soy sauce, vinegar, cornstarch, and sesame oil and add it to the skillet. Add the snow peas and cook, stirring constantly, for 3 minutes, or until the sauce is thickened. Add the pasta and toss to combine.

Makeover Magic		
Before		**After**
490	Calories	292
6 g	Fat	6 g
0.5 g	Sat Fat	0.5 g
94 g	Carbs	49 g
6 g	Fiber	11 g
19 g	Protein	11 g
2,870 mg	Sodium	458 mg

Veggie Burger Wraps

 Makes 2 servings

Prep time: 5 minutes • Total time: 15 minutes

Curb carbs: Who said a burger has to be on a bun? Cut the burger in half and it fits perfectly into a wrap!

Fill up on fiber: Between the tortilla, veggie burger, and fresh toppings, this meal comes in at an awesome 13 grams of fiber!

Favor healthy fats: The avocado in this dish provides MUFAs as well as a creamy, flavorful condiment for this veggie burger wrap.

2	frozen vegetarian garden burgers, thawed	2
2	6-inch (15 cm) whole wheat tortillas	2
1 cup	baby spinach	250 mL
1	plum (Roma) tomato, sliced	1
1	green onion, thinly sliced	1
2 tbsp	unsalted stone-ground mustard	30 mL
½	avocado, sliced	½

1. In a nonstick skillet over medium-high heat, cook the burgers for 6 minutes, turning once, until browned and heated through.

2. Cut the burgers in half and place 2 halves in each tortilla. Top with the spinach, tomato, green onion, mustard, and avocado slices.

Makeover Magic		
Before		**After**
420	Calories	238
20 g	Fat	11 g
4 g	Sat Fat	1 g
28 g	Carbs	25 g
4 g	Fiber	13 g
30 g	Protein	18 g
1,310 mg	Sodium	377 mg

Asparagus Swiss Quiche

 Makes 4 servings

Prep time: 10 minutes • Total time: 1 hour, 5 minutes

Curb carbs: Eliminating the crust typical of quiche reduces both carbs and fat in this recipe, without losing the gooey goodness.

Fill up on fiber: Asparagus adds some fiber to the dish. Serve it with a green salad with apple wedges and a sprinkle of walnuts for more fiber and nutrients.

Favor healthy fats: Dusting the quiche pan with flaxseeds creates a slight crust while adding good fats. We also boost healthy fats by using omega-3–rich eggs.

- Preheat oven to 350°F (180°C)
- 9-inch (23 cm) quiche dish or glass pie plate, sprayed with nonstick cooking spray

3 tbsp	ground golden flaxseeds	45 mL
1 tbsp	water	15 mL
1 lb	asparagus, trimmed and cut into 1½-inch (4 cm) pieces	500 g
4	green onions, thinly sliced	4
1½ cups	1% milk	375 mL
1 cup	shredded reduced-fat Swiss cheese	250 mL
4	large egg whites	4
2	large omega-3-enriched eggs	2
2 tsp	Dijon mustard	10 mL
¼ tsp	ground black pepper	1 mL
⅛ tsp	salt	0.5 mL
2 tbsp	grated Parmesan cheese	30 mL

1. Sprinkle flaxseeds in prepared quiche dish.

2. In a nonstick skillet, heat the water over medium-high heat. Cook the asparagus and green onions, stirring, for 5 minutes, or until tender-crisp.

3. Meanwhile, in a large bowl, whisk together the milk, Swiss cheese, egg whites, eggs, mustard, pepper, and salt. Stir in the asparagus mixture. Pour into the quiche dish and sprinkle with the Parmesan.

4. Bake in preheated oven for 40 minutes, or until a knife inserted in the center comes out clean. Let stand for 10 minutes before serving.

Makeover Magic		
Before		**After**
620	Calories	217
52 g	Fat	8 g
25 g	Sat Fat	3 g
20 g	Carbs	15 g
0 g	Fiber	4 g
17 g	Protein	23 g
580 mg	Sodium	387 mg

Broccoli-Cheddar Strata

 Makes 4 servings

Prep time: 10 minutes • Total time: 50 minutes

Curb carbs: We use less bread in this strata and fill in the rest with savory vegetables.

Fill up on fiber: Multigrain bread is chock-full of fiber.

Favor healthy fats: Kalamata olives provide healthy fats in this dish.

- Preheat oven to 350°F (180°C)
- 11- by 7-inch (28 by 18 cm) glass baking dish, sprayed with nonstick cooking spray

5	slices low-carb multigrain bread, toasted and broken into 2-inch (5 cm) pieces	5
2 cups	1% milk	500 mL
4	large eggs	4
3	large egg whites	3
2 tbsp	all-purpose flour	30 mL
½ tsp	ground black pepper	2 mL
2 cups	frozen broccoli florets	500 mL
½ cup	frozen or fresh chopped onion	125 mL
2 tbsp	chopped kalamata olives	30 mL
1½ cups	shredded reduced-fat low-sodium Cheddar cheese	375 mL

1. Place the bread in prepared baking dish.

2. In a large bowl, whisk together the milk, eggs, egg whites, flour, and pepper. Stir in the broccoli, onion, and olives. Pour over the bread. Top with the cheese. Let stand at room temperature for 10 minutes.

3. Bake in preheated oven for 35 minutes, or until a knife inserted in the center comes out clean.

Makeover Magic		
Before		**After**
450	Calories	345
25 g	Fat	16 g
14 g	Sat Fat	5 g
35 g	Carbs	24 g
2 g	Fiber	4 g
21 g	Protein	30 g
780 mg	Sodium	570 mg

African Stew

Prep time: 15 minutes • Total time: 50 minutes

Curb carbs: By mixing 1 sweet potato with other lower-carb veggies, we're able to curb carbs in this dish while boosting fiber.

Fill up on fiber: This hearty stew is full of fiber-toting veggies, including white beans, sweet potato, eggplant, and zucchini.

Favor healthy fats: The omega-3-enriched peanut butter and chopped nuts add healthful MUFAs and omega-3 fats.

	Nonstick cooking spray	
1	large onion, chopped	1
1	Japanese eggplant, chopped	1
1	small zucchini, chopped	1
1	clove garlic, minced	1
1 tsp	ground ginger	5 mL
1 tsp	dried thyme	5 mL
4 cups	low-sodium ready-to-use vegetable or chicken broth	1 L
1	can (14 to 15 oz/398 to 425 mL) diced tomatoes, drained	1
1	large sweet potato, peeled and cut into ½-inch (1 cm) pieces	1
⅓ cup	omega-3-enriched peanut butter	75 mL
1	can (14 oz/398 mL) white beans, drained and rinsed	1
½ cup	unsalted peanuts, coarsely chopped	125 mL

1. In a large saucepan sprayed with cooking spray over medium-high heat, cook the onion, eggplant, zucchini, garlic, ginger, and thyme for 5 minutes, stirring, or until the vegetables are lightly browned.

2. Stir in the broth, tomatoes, and sweet potato and bring to a boil. Reduce the heat to low, cover, and simmer for 15 minutes, or until the potatoes are just tender.

3. Place the peanut butter in a small bowl. Remove 1 cup (250 mL) of the simmering broth and whisk into the peanut butter. Return to the pan with the beans and cook for 10 minutes, or until the flavors are blended.

4. Divide the stew among 4 bowls and sprinkle with the peanuts.

Makeover Magic		
Before		**After**
639	Calories	355
23 g	Fat	17 g
5 g	Sat Fat	3 g
55 g	Carbs	41 g
7 g	Fiber	10 g
53 g	Protein	13 g
866 mg	Sodium	283 mg

Fire-Roasted Chili

 Makes 4 servings

Curb carbs: All the carbs in this hearty dish come from high-fiber legumes and veggies.

Fill up on fiber: Beans, corn, and tomatoes pump up the fiber in this dish. Serve with ½ cup (125 mL) cooked brown rice or quinoa per serving for added flavor and fiber.

Favor healthy fats: Choosing this vegetarian chili over a meaty version cuts out saturated fat. Canola oil provides some healthy fats, but you could top with sliced avocado in addition to the yogurt to get even more MUFAs.

2 tbsp	canola oil	30 mL
1	large onion, chopped	1
1	green bell pepper, chopped	1
3	cloves garlic, minced	3
1	can (14 to 15 oz/398 to 425 mL) fire-roasted diced tomatoes with green chiles	1
1	can (14 to 15 oz/398 to 425 mL) no-salt-added diced tomatoes, with juice	1
1	can (14 to 19 oz/398 to 540 mL) no-salt-added red kidney beans, drained and rinsed	1
1 cup	frozen shelled edamame	250 mL
1 cup	fresh or thawed frozen corn kernels	250 mL
1	can (4 oz/113 g) chopped mild green chiles, drained	1
2 tbsp	chili powder	30 mL
1 tsp	ground cumin	5 mL
¼ cup	chopped fresh cilantro	60 mL
¼ cup	plain nonfat (0%) Greek yogurt	60 mL

1. In a Dutch oven or large pot, heat the oil over medium-high heat. Cook the onion, bell pepper, and garlic for 8 minutes, stirring occasionally, or until tender. Stir in both cans of tomatoes, beans, edamame, corn, chiles, chili powder, and cumin.

2. Bring to a boil. Reduce the heat to low, cover, and simmer, stirring occasionally, for 25 minutes, or until the flavors are blended. Stir in the cilantro. Serve with the yogurt.

Makeover Magic		
Before		**After**
400	Calories	276
28 g	Fat	10 g
8 g	Sat Fat	1 g
14 g	Carbs	38 g
0 g	Fiber	12 g
23 g	Protein	14 g
1,050 mg	Sodium	305 mg

Bean Enchiladas

 Makes 4 servings

Prep time: 15 minutes • Total time: 1 hour, 5 minutes

Curb carbs: Choose smaller 6-inch (15 cm) corn tortillas over the huge flour ones to cut the carbs while adding nice flavor.

Fill up on fiber: Black beans and kale work together in this dish for a great source of fiber.

Favor healthy fats: Ground flaxseeds and avocado are the favored fats in this recipe. Serve with mixed greens drizzled with olive oil, vinegar, and pepitas.

- Preheat oven to 350°F (180°C)
- 13- by 9-inch (33 by 23 cm) glass baking dish, sprayed with nonstick cooking spray

2 tsp	canola oil	10 mL
1	onion, chopped	1
2	cloves garlic, finely chopped	2
½ tsp	ground cumin	2 mL
3 cups	chopped fresh trimmed kale	750 mL
1	can (15 oz/425 mL) no-salt-added black beans, drained and rinsed	1
2 tbsp	ground flaxseeds	30 mL
1	can (15 oz/425 mL) no-salt-added diced tomatoes, drained	1
½ cup	loosely packed chopped fresh cilantro	125 mL
8	6-inch (15 cm) corn tortillas	8
4	slices reduced-sodium pepper Jack cheese, halved	4
½	avocado, thinly sliced into 8 pieces	½

1. In a large nonstick skillet, heat the oil over medium heat. Cook the onion, garlic, and cumin, stirring occasionally, for 3 minutes, or until softened. Add the kale and cook for 5 minutes, stirring, or until wilted. Stir in the beans and flaxseeds. Cook for 5 minutes, or until simmering. Smash some of the beans with the back of a spoon to thicken the mixture.

2. In a medium bowl, stir together the tomatoes and cilantro. Set aside.

3. Wrap the tortillas in paper towels and microwave on High for 1 minute, or until softened. Remove to a work surface. Evenly divide the bean mixture down the center of each tortilla. Roll each into a tube. Place seam side down in the prepared baking dish. Spoon the tomato mixture over the enchiladas. Cover tightly with foil.

4. Bake in preheated oven for 20 minutes. Carefully remove the foil and place 1 piece of the cheese over each enchilada. Bake for 10 minutes, or until the cheese melts. Remove from the oven and allow the enchiladas to sit for 5 minutes before serving.

5. Place 2 enchiladas on 4 plates, along with 2 slices of avocado.

Makeover Magic		
Before		**After**
505	Calories	366
27 g	Fat	16 g
14 g	Sat Fat	4 g
35 g	Carbs	45 g
3 g	Fiber	10 g
30 g	Protein	14 g
760 mg	Sodium	243 mg

Black Bean Burgers

 Makes 4 servings

Curb carbs: Using sandwich thins instead of white burger buns not only lowers carbs, but ensures each bite is full of juicy burger instead of mostly bread.

Fill up on fiber: The beans and whole-grain sandwich thins mean the magic carbs in this dish come out to just 33 — still allowing room for a starchy vegetable side like an ear of corn, if desired.

Favor healthy fats: Going meatless cuts saturated fat, as does using reduced-fat cheese. Add healthy fats by spreading some olive tapenade or guacamole on your burger.

• Food processor

6 oz	mushrooms, quartered	175 g
½	red onion, quartered	½
½ cup	chopped fresh cilantro	125 mL
¼ cup	ground flaxseeds	60 mL
2	cloves garlic	2
1	large egg white	1
1 tsp	salt	5 mL
1	can (15 oz/425 mL) no-salt-added black beans, drained and rinsed	1
1 tbsp	canola oil	15 mL
4	slices reduced-fat pepper Jack cheese	4
4	whole-grain sandwich thins, split	4
4	lettuce leaves	4
1	small tomato, sliced	1

1. In a food processor, process the mushrooms, onion, cilantro, flaxseeds, garlic, egg white, and salt until finely chopped. Add the beans and pulse 15 times, or until coarsely chopped. Evenly divide the mixture into 4 burgers.

2. In a large skillet, heat the oil over medium heat. Cook the burgers for 6 minutes, turning once or until both sides are golden and burgers are hot in the center. Top each burger with a slice of cheese. Cover the skillet and cook for 3 minutes, or until the cheese melts.

3. Place on the sandwich thins and top with the lettuce and tomato.

Makeover Magic		
Before		**After**
550	Calories	290
32 g	Fat	8 g
15 g	Sat Fat	2 g
40 g	Carbs	44 g
2 g	Fiber	11 g
27 g	Protein	17 g
690 mg	Sodium	389 mg

Vegetable Pizza

 Makes 8 servings

Prep time: 20 minutes • Total time: 1 hour, 20 minutes

Curb carbs: Making this delicious, doughy whole wheat pizza crust from scratch eliminates extra sugars and processed ingredients that can drive the carb count way up and wreak havoc on your health.

- Food processor
- 14-inch (35 cm) round pizza pan, sprayed with nonstick cooking spray

Crust

	Nonstick cooking spray	
⅔ cup	warm water (105° to 115°F/ 41° to 46°C)	150 mL
1	envelope (¼ oz/8 g) active dry yeast (2¼ tsp/11 mL)	1
2 tsp	olive oil	10 mL
2 cups	whole wheat pastry or white whole wheat flour, divided	500 mL
¼ tsp	salt	1 mL

Topping

1 tbsp	olive oil	15 mL
1½ cups	frozen mixed bell peppers, thawed	375 mL
1	package (10 oz/300 g) frozen chopped spinach, thawed and drained well	1
1	clove garlic, minced	1
1	can (14 to 15 oz/398 to 425 mL) diced tomatoes, well drained	1
4 oz	fresh mozzarella cheese, sliced	125 g

1. *To make the crust:* Coat a large bowl with cooking spray. Set aside.

2. In a glass measuring cup, mix the water and the yeast to dissolve. Stir in the oil.

3. In a food processor, pulse 1¾ cups (425 mL) flour and the salt to mix. With the machine running, add the yeast water through the feed tube. Process for 2 minutes, or until the mixture forms a moist ball. Transfer the dough to a work surface lightly floured with some of the remaining flour. Knead for 1 minute, or until the dough is smooth. Place the dough in the prepared bowl. Coat lightly with cooking spray. Cover with plastic wrap. Set aside to rise for about 30 minutes, or until doubled in size.

Makeover Magic		
Before		**After**
330	Calories	243
11 g	Fat	8 g
6 g	Sat Fat	3 g
39 g	Carbs	27 g
3 g	Fiber	5 g
14 g	Protein	14 g
890 mg	Sodium	452 mg

Fill up on fiber:
Whole-grain pizza dough contributes the bulk of fiber in this recipe — add on your own homemade sauce and you have a great, fresh, fiber-full pizza.

Favor healthy fats:
Olive oil provides plenty of MUFAs, but for more healthy fats, you can always top with sliced olives.

4. Punch down the dough. Transfer to a lightly floured surface. Let stand for 5 minutes. With floured hands or a rolling pin, pat or roll into a 14-inch (35 cm) circle. Transfer to the prepared pan. Pinch the edges to make a border. Cover with plastic wrap and let stand for 15 minutes.

5. Preheat the oven to 375°F (190°C).

6. *To make the topping:* In a large skillet, heat the oil over medium-high heat. Cook the peppers, stirring, for 3 minutes or until lightly browned. Stir in the spinach and garlic and cook, stirring, for 3 minutes. Add the tomatoes and cook, stirring, for 3 minutes, or until any liquid evaporates.

7. Spread the tomato mixture over the crust. Sprinkle with the cheese. Bake for 17 minutes, or until golden and bubbly. Cut into 8 slices.

Caramelized Onion and Fennel Pizza

 Makes 6 servings

Prep time: 10 minutes • Total time: 45 minutes

Curb carbs: A thin 11-inch (28 cm) pizza crust makes a delicious and crunchy low-carb pizza.

Fill up on fiber: We chose a whole wheat crust, and using beans as a pizza sauce pumps up both the fiber and protein in this dish.

Favor healthy fats: We use olive oil in this delicious slice of the Mediterranean; for a bigger boost of healthy fats, top the pizza with sliced kalamata olives.

- Preheat oven to 450°F (230°C)
- Rimmed baking sheet or roasting pan

1	large red onion, cut into 8 wedges	1
1	small fennel bulb, thinly sliced	1
2	plum (Roma) tomatoes, chopped	2
3	cloves garlic, thinly sliced	3
1 tbsp	olive oil	15 mL
1 tbsp	chopped fresh rosemary (or 1 tsp/5 mL dried)	15 mL
¼ tsp	hot pepper flakes	1 mL
1 cup	rinsed drained no-salt-added cannellini beans	250 mL
1	11-inch (28 cm) thin whole wheat pizza crust	1
2 oz	reduced-fat goat cheese, crumbled	60 g

1. On baking sheet, combine the onion, fennel, tomatoes, and garlic. Add the oil, rosemary, and hot pepper flakes. Toss to coat well. Roast in preheated oven for 25 minutes, stirring occasionally, or until the vegetables are tender and lightly browned. Remove from oven, leaving oven on.

2. In a medium bowl, mash the beans until coarsely mashed. Spread evenly over the pizza crust, leaving a ½-inch (1 cm) border all around. Scatter the vegetables over the top. Sprinkle with the cheese.

3. Bake for 10 minutes, or until the topping is hot and the crust is crisp. Let stand for 5 minutes before cutting into 6 slices.

Makeover Magic		
Before		**After**
548	Calories	240
19 g	Fat	8 g
10 g	Sat Fat	4 g
69 g	Carbs	35 g
3 g	Fiber	8 g
22 g	Protein	10 g
1,022 mg	Sodium	315 mg

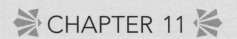

CHAPTER 11
Sides

Stir-Fried Asparagus with Ginger, Sesame and Soy . . . 244

Green Bean Casserole. 245

Creamed Spinach and Artichokes 246

Creamed Sweet Corn 247

Garlic Oven Fries 247

Chili Cheese Fries 248

Cheese and Vegetable Bake 249

Creamy Mashed Potatoes. 250

Scalloped Red Potatoes 251

Whipped Sweet Potato Casseroles 252

Mushroom-Barley Stuffing 253

Barley Pilaf with Artichokes and Kale. 254

Quinoa Pilaf with Pistachios 255

Baked Risotto. 256

Broccoli-Walnut Farfalle Toss 257

Mexican Fried Rice 258

Fettuccine with Basil-Walnut Sauce 259

Tex-Mex Pasta and Beans. 260

Stir-Fried Asparagus with Ginger, Sesame, and Soy

Prep time: 15 minutes • Total time: 25 minutes

Curb carbs: This naturally low-carb dish was made over to raise the fiber and get healthy fats into your meal. It would pair well with Tuna Tetrazzini (page 220) or Chicken Pad Thai (page 197).

Fill up on fiber: Asparagus contributes the bulk of the fiber in this dish at nearly 4 grams.

Favor healthy fats: Sesame seeds, sesame oil, and canola oil are all full of diabetes-friendly fats, making this a great side to pair with low-in-fat main course recipes.

1½ lbs	thin asparagus, trimmed and cut into 2-inch (5 cm) pieces	750 g
2 tsp	canola oil	10 mL
1	red bell pepper, cut into strips	1
1 tbsp	chopped gingerroot (or 1 tsp/5 mL ground ginger)	15 mL
1 tbsp	reduced-sodium soy sauce	15 mL
1 tsp	toasted sesame oil	5 mL
1 tsp	sesame seeds	5 mL

1. In a large nonstick skillet, bring ¼ inch (0.5 cm) of water to a boil over high heat. Add the asparagus and return to a boil. Reduce the heat to low, cover, and simmer for 5 minutes, or until tender-crisp. Drain and cool briefly under cold running water. Wipe the skillet dry with a paper towel.

2. In the same skillet, heat the oil over high heat. Cook the pepper, stirring constantly, for 3 minutes, or until tender-crisp. Add the asparagus, ginger, and soy sauce and cook for 2 minutes, or until heated through. Remove from the heat and stir in the sesame oil and sesame seeds.

Makeover Magic		
Before		**After**
175	Calories	86
7 g	Fat	4 g
1 g	Sat Fat	0.5 g
16 g	Carbs	11 g
4 g	Fiber	5 g
3 g	Protein	4 g
550 mg	Sodium	135 mg

Green Bean Casserole

 Makes 8 servings

Prep time: 15 minutes • Total time: 1 hour, 5 minutes

Curb carbs: For an autumnal feel, pair this naturally low-carb dish with a turkey-centered main, like Sweet Potato and Turkey Shepherd's Pie (page 200).

Fill up on fiber: Green beans are a fiber boss! Using homemade onion rings with panko breading instead of the prepackaged kind also adds fiber.

Favor healthy fats: Almonds are a great source of healthy MUFAs for this holiday favorite!

- Preheat oven to 500°F (260°C)
- Baking sheet, sprayed with nonstick cooking spray
- Medium glass or ceramic baking dish, sprayed with nonstick cooking spray

½ cup	buttermilk	125 mL
½ cup	whole wheat panko bread crumbs	125 mL
1	onion, cut crosswise into ¼-inch (0.5 cm) thick slices and separated into rings	1
	Nonstick cooking spray	
8 oz	mushrooms, sliced	250 mL
1	small onion, chopped	1
½ tsp	dried thyme	2 mL
¼ tsp	salt	1 mL
¼ cup	whole wheat pastry flour	60 mL
3 cups	1% milk	750 mL
1	bag (1 lb/500 g) frozen French-cut green beans, thawed and drained	1
¼ cup	almonds, sliced	60 mL

1. Place the buttermilk in a shallow bowl. Place the bread crumbs in another shallow bowl. Dip the onion rings in buttermilk, dredge in bread crumbs, and place on the baking sheet. Spray lightly with cooking spray. Bake in preheated oven for 20 minutes, or until tender and golden brown. Remove from oven and reduce the oven temperature to 400°F (200°C).

2. Meanwhile, coat a large saucepan with cooking spray. Set over medium heat. Add the mushrooms, chopped onion, thyme, and salt. Coat with cooking spray. Cook, stirring occasionally, for 5 minutes, or until the mushrooms give off liquid. Sprinkle with the flour. Cook, stirring, for 1 minute. Add the milk. Cook, stirring constantly, for 4 minutes, or until thickened. Add the green beans and almonds. Stir to mix.

3. Pour the bean mixture into the prepared baking dish. Scatter the onion rings over the top. Bake for 30 minutes, or until hot and bubbly.

Makeover Magic		
Before		**After**
315	Calories	115
22 g	Fat	2 g
11 g	Sat Fat	0.5 g
23 g	Carbs	20 g
4 g	Fiber	4 g
11 g	Protein	7 g
711 mg	Sodium	146 mg

Creamed Spinach and Artichokes

 Makes 4 servings

Prep time: 10 minutes • Total time: 20 minutes

Curb carbs: While this dish is not typically high in carbs, we've still worked our magic on it by eliminating flour from the sauce and instead using cream cheese to thicken it. While our carbs are slightly higher than typical creamed spinach, we make up for it with a huge boost in the fiber content!

Fill up on fiber: Spinach is already a great source of fiber. Toss in artichokes and you'll be surprised how high the fiber count rises in this classic dish.

Favor healthy fats: Sautéing in healthy olive oil instead of butter adds MUFAs to this dish. Be sure to serve this with a main dish high in healthy fats to get enough to reap the benefits on your blood sugar.

1 tbsp	olive oil	15 mL
1	onion, chopped	1
1	clove garlic, minced	1
¼ cup	ready-to-use vegetable broth	60 mL
1 lb	baby spinach	500 g
1	box (9 oz/270 g) frozen artichokes, thawed and chopped	1
3 oz	reduced-fat cream cheese, cubed	90 g
⅛ tsp	ground black pepper	0.5 mL
⅛ tsp	ground nutmeg	0.5 mL

1. In a large nonstick skillet, heat the oil over medium-high heat. Cook the onion and garlic for 5 minutes, stirring occasionally, or until softened. Add the broth and bring to a simmer. Cook the spinach for 4 minutes, tossing frequently, or just until wilted.

2. Stir in the artichokes, cream cheese, pepper, and nutmeg and cook for 1 minute, or until the cream cheese melts and is well blended.

Makeover Magic Creamed Spinach and Artichokes		
Before		**After**
190	Calories	120
13 g	Fat	6 g
8 g	Sat Fat	2 g
13 g	Carbs	15 g
2 g	Fiber	7 g
6 g	Protein	4 g
660 mg	Sodium	216 mg

Makeover Magic Creamed Sweet Corn		
Before		**After**
378	Calories	150
26 g	Fat	6 g
16 g	Sat Fat	1 g
34 g	Carbs	22 g
4 g	Fiber	3 g
8 g	Protein	6 g
439 mg	Sodium	492 mg

Makeover Magic Garlic Oven Fries		
Before		**After**
500	Calories	221
25 g	Fat	4 g
4 g	Sat Fat	2 g
63 g	Carbs	27 g
6 g	Fiber	2 g
6 g	Protein	3 g
350 mg	Sodium	97 mg

Creamed Sweet Corn

Makes 4 servings

Prep time: 5 minutes • Total time: 25 minutes

Curb carbs: We use less corn than a typical creamed corn recipe and fill the remainder with fresh bell pepper, onion, and celery.

Fill up on fiber: The fiber in this recipe comes from a riot of veggies tossed together here. The comparison has more fiber only because it contains twice the amount of corn.

Favor healthy fats: Ground flaxseeds add ALA omega-3s to this dish. Using evaporated milk means there's no need for added butter and sugar.

1 tbsp	olive oil	15 mL
1	small onion, diced	1
1	red bell pepper, diced	1
2	stalks celery, diced	2
2 cups	fresh or frozen corn kernels	500 mL
1	clove garlic, minced	1
¾ tsp	salt	3 mL
½ cup	2% evaporated milk	125 mL
1 tbsp	ground flaxseeds	15 mL

1. Heat the oil in a medium saucepan over medium heat. Cook the onion, pepper, and celery for 4 minutes, stirring often, or until soft. Add the corn, garlic, and salt and cook for 10 minutes, stirring often.

2. Pour in the milk and the ground flaxseeds. Cook over low heat, stirring, for 2 minutes, or until the mixture is creamy.

Garlic Oven Fries

Makes 4 servings

Prep time: 10 minutes • Total time: 40 minutes

Curb carbs: Carrots may seem an unlikely choice for fries, but this root vegetable is a delicious low-carb choice that fits in great with the russet potatoes.

Fill up on fiber: The potatoes take the lead when it comes to fiber — just remember to include the skins! The comparison has higher fiber only because it uses solely potatoes instead of including carrots.

Favor healthy fats: Instead of deep-frying, use a small amount of canola oil, our favored fat for this recipe.

- Preheat oven to 450°F (230°C)
- 2 large baking sheets, sprayed with nonstick cooking spray

1 lb	russet (baking) potatoes, cut into 3½- by ½-inch (8.5 by 1 cm) sticks	500 g
3	carrots, quartered lengthwise and cut into 3½-inch (8.5 cm) sticks	3
2 tbsp	canola oil	30 mL
¼ tsp	garlic salt	1 mL
¼ tsp	ground black pepper	1 mL

1. In a large bowl, combine the potatoes, carrots, oil, garlic salt, and pepper, tossing to coat well. On the baking sheets, arrange the potatoes and carrots in a single layer.

2. Bake in preheated oven for 30 minutes, turning once, or until golden and crisp.

Chili Cheese Fries

 Makes 4 servings

Prep time: 10 minutes • Total time: 40 minutes

Curb carbs: The homemade version of this fast-food favorite is still high in carbs, so be sure to pair it with a low-carb, high-fiber main dish such as Cobb Salad–Style Buffalo Dogs (page 161).

Fill up on fiber: The best way to keep fiber in a potato-based dish is to keep the skin on the potatoes.

Favor healthy fats: Instead of using real chili on these fries, get the same flavor without all the saturated fat by using chili powder and Cheddar cheese. Using olive oil to cook the fries adds MUFA power!

- Preheat oven to 450°F (230°C)
- 2 large rimmed baking sheets, sprayed with nonstick cooking spray

2 tbsp	olive oil	30 mL
2 tsp	chili powder	10 mL
½ tsp	ground cumin	2 mL
2	medium russet potatoes, each cut into 16 wedges	2
¼ cup	shredded reduced-fat Cheddar cheese	60 mL

1. In a large bowl, combine the oil, chili powder, and cumin until blended. Add the potatoes and toss to coat well. Arrange the potatoes in a single layer on the prepared baking sheets.

2. Bake in preheated oven for 30 minutes, turning once, or until golden brown and crisp. Sprinkle with the cheese and bake for 1 minute, or until the cheese is melted.

Makeover Magic		
Before		**After**
570	Calories	303
30 g	Fat	9 g
11 g	Sat Fat	2 g
58 g	Carbs	48 g
8 g	Fiber	5 g
18 g	Protein	8 g
1,200 mg	Sodium	77 mg

Cheese and Vegetable Bake

 Makes 6 servings

Prep time: 15 minutes • Total time: 1 hour, 25 minutes

Curb carbs: This clever spaghetti squash swap means fewer carbs and way more nutrients than basic spaghetti has to offer.

Fill up on fiber: Flaxseeds, kale, and squash all work together to bring fiber to this side dish.

Favor healthy fats: Keeping saturated fat low is easy when you choose reduced-fat cheese or simply use less of the full-fat variety. For MUFAs, almonds and canola oil go a long way!

- Preheat oven to 400°F (200°C)
- Baking sheet, sprayed with nonstick cooking spray
- 13- by 9-inch (33 by 23 cm) glass baking dish, sprayed with nonstick cooking spray

1	spaghetti squash, halved and seeded	1
2 tbsp	canola oil	30 mL
4 cups	chopped trimmed kale leaves	1 L
2	plum (Roma) tomatoes, chopped	2
2	cloves garlic, chopped	2
1 cup	low-fat (1%) cottage cheese	250 mL
½ cup	shredded low-fat mozzarella cheese	125 mL
¼ tsp	salt	1 mL
¼ cup	grated Parmesan cheese	60 mL
3 tbsp	ground flaxseeds	45 mL
¼ cup	finely chopped almonds	60 mL

1. Place the squash, cut side down, on the prepared baking sheet. Bake in preheated oven for 30 minutes, or until tender. Remove from oven, leaving oven on, and, using a fork, scrape the squash strands into a large bowl.

2. Meanwhile, in a medium skillet, heat the oil over medium heat. Cook the kale for 10 minutes, stirring, or until tender. Add the tomatoes and garlic and cook, stirring, for 3 minutes.

3. Add the cottage cheese, mozzarella, salt, and tomato mixture to the squash. Toss to coat. Place in the prepared baking dish. Sprinkle the Parmesan, flaxseeds, and almonds over the top.

4. Bake for 30 minutes, or until hot and bubbly.

Makeover Magic		
Before		**After**
520	Calories	226
27 g	Fat	14 g
14 g	Sat Fat	4 g
59 g	Carbs	13 g
2 g	Fiber	4 g
12 g	Protein	15 g
350 mg	Sodium	353 mg

Creamy Mashed Potatoes

 Makes 6 servings

Curb carbs: This is the ultimate in sneaky substitutions — by substituting cauliflower for half of the potatoes, we also cut the carbs in half while adding a rich, creamy flavor.

Fill up on fiber: One little cauliflower head contributes twice as much fiber as a whole pound of potatoes. To up the fiber more, leave the potato peels intact and go for "smashed" potatoes instead.

Favor healthy fats: Typically, mashed potatoes are full of butter. Adding olive oil for healthy fat and Greek yogurt for creaminess is a healthier alternative.

• Electric mixer

1 lb	russet (baking) potatoes, peeled and halved	500 g
1	small head cauliflower, cut into florets	1
1/3 cup	ready-to-use vegetable broth	75 mL
2 tbsp	olive oil	30 mL
1/2 cup	plain nonfat (0%) Greek yogurt	125 mL

1. In a large pot, combine the potatoes and cauliflower and cover with water. Over high heat, bring to a boil. Reduce the heat to medium and simmer for 20 minutes, or until the potatoes and cauliflower are easily pierced with a fork. Drain.

2. In a large bowl, place the drained potatoes, cauliflower, broth, and oil. With an electric mixer on medium speed, beat until creamy. Add the yogurt and beat just until blended.

Makeover Magic		
Before		**After**
250	Calories	132
8 g	Fat	5 g
5 g	Sat Fat	1 g
39 g	Carbs	19 g
2 g	Fiber	3 g
5 g	Protein	5 g
370 mg	Sodium	347 mg

Scalloped Red Potatoes

Makes 4 servings

Curb carbs: We reduced the flour in this dish and added chia seeds to help thicken the milk.

Fill up on fiber: Chia seeds are an excellent source of fiber, but of course the potatoes provide the most fiber here.

Favor healthy fats: By using a smaller amount of cheese, we reduced the saturated fat, while adding chia seeds offers up ALA omega-3 fatty acids.

- Preheat oven to 400°F (200°C)
- 11- by 7-inch (28 by 18 cm) glass baking dish, sprayed with nonstick cooking spray

3 tbsp	whole wheat flour	45 mL
2 tbsp	white chia seeds	30 mL
¼ tsp	ground nutmeg	1 mL
6	medium red potatoes, scrubbed and cut into ½-inch (1 cm) slices	6
6	green onions, chopped	6
1 cup	shredded 4-cheese Italian blend, divided	250 mL
1 cup	1% milk	250 mL

1. In a small bowl, stir together the flour, chia seeds, and nutmeg.

2. Arrange one-third of the potatoes in the prepared baking dish. Sprinkle with one-third of the flour mixture, one-third of the green onions, and one-third of the cheese. Repeat the layers twice. Pour the milk over the top.

3. Cover and bake in preheated oven for 25 minutes. Uncover and bake for 20 minutes, or until the potatoes are tender and browned.

Smart Start
Serve with wild salmon or grilled chicken.

Makeover Magic		
Before		**After**
740	Calories	256
46 g	Fat	5 g
28 g	Sat Fat	3 g
54 g	Carbs	42 g
11 g	Fiber	5 g
3 g	Protein	12 g
1,260 mg	Sodium	181 mg

Whipped Sweet Potato Casseroles

 Makes 6 servings

Prep time: 10 minutes • Total time: 35 minutes

Curb carbs: There's no need to sweeten this side with sugar — pumpkin pie spice adds nice flavor to these already sweet potatoes.

Fill up on fiber: Walnuts are our main source of fiber in this dish.

Favor healthy fats: This dish is full of beneficial fats. MUFAs come from the canola oil and walnuts, while ALA omega-3 fatty acids come from the ground flaxseeds.

- Preheat oven to 400°F (200°C)
- Six 4-oz (125 mL) ramekins, sprayed with nonstick cooking spray
- Steamer basket
- Electric mixer

8 tbsp	finely chopped walnuts, divided	120 mL
2 tbsp	ground flaxseeds	30 mL
2½ tbsp	canola oil, divided	37 mL
1½ lbs	sweet potatoes, peeled and cut into ½-inch (1 cm) cubes	750 g
⅓ cup	orange juice	75 mL
2 tbsp	fat-free half-and-half	30 mL
½ tsp	pumpkin pie spice	2 mL
⅛ tsp	salt	0.5 mL
⅛ tsp	ground black pepper	0.5 mL

1. Place prepared ramekins on a baking sheet.

2. In a small bowl, combine 6 tbsp (90 mL) walnuts, the flaxseeds, and 1½ tbsp (22 mL) oil until blended. Divide the mixture among the ramekins and press with a fork to cover the bottoms of the ramekins. Set aside.

3. In a large saucepan with a steamer basket inserted, bring 2 inches (5 cm) of water to a boil over high heat. Add the sweet potatoes, cover, and cook over medium heat for 15 minutes, or until very tender.

4. Place the potatoes in a medium bowl. Add the orange juice, half-and-half, pumpkin pie spice, salt, pepper, and the remaining oil. With an electric mixer, beat the mixture until smooth. Divide among the ramekins. Sprinkle with the remaining walnuts.

5. Bake in preheated oven for 10 minutes, or until golden brown.

Makeover Magic		
Before		**After**
480	Calories	222
22 g	Fat	13 g
10 g	Sat Fat	1 g
69 g	Carbs	24 g
4 g	Fiber	5 g
5 g	Protein	4 g
190 mg	Sodium	112 mg

Mushroom-Barley Stuffing

 Makes 8 servings

Prep time: 15 minutes • Total time: 1 hour, 20 minutes

Curb carbs: Turn this dish into a blood sugar buster by switching from a base of bread (usually low-fiber white) to barley. Thanks to the rule of magic carbs, this makes a great side dish to just about any main course recipe.

Fill up on fiber: Barley and mushrooms both lead to a high fiber count.

Favor healthy fats: Canola oil and chia seeds provide delicious healthy fats.

- Preheat oven to 400°F (200°C)
- 3-quart (3 L) ceramic or glass baking dish, sprayed with nonstick cooking spray

1 oz	dried porcini mushrooms	30 g
2 cups	hot water	500 mL
2 tbsp	canola oil	30 mL
8 oz	sliced mushrooms	250 g
2	stalks celery, chopped	2
1	large red onion, chopped	1
2	cloves garlic, minced	2
1/2 tsp	dried rosemary	2 mL
1/2 tsp	dried thyme	2 mL
2 cups	pearl barley	500 mL
3 cups	low-sodium ready-to-use chicken broth	750 mL
1/4 cup	chia seeds	60 mL
2 tbsp	grated Romano cheese	30 mL
1/4 tsp	salt	1 mL
1/4 tsp	ground black pepper	1 mL

1. In a small bowl, combine the porcini mushrooms and water and let stand for 20 minutes, or until the mushrooms are soft. Using a slotted spoon, remove the mushrooms. Chop and set aside. Strain the liquid into a small bowl through a fine sieve lined with cheesecloth or a coffee filter. Set aside.

2. Meanwhile, in a medium saucepan, heat the oil over medium-high heat. Cook the sliced mushrooms, celery, onion, garlic, rosemary, and thyme, stirring, for 10 minutes, or until the mushroom liquid has evaporated.

3. Add the reserved porcini mushrooms and the barley. Cook, stirring, for 4 minutes. Add the reserved mushroom liquid and the broth and bring to a boil. Remove from the heat. Stir in the chia seeds, cheese, salt, and pepper. Place in the prepared baking dish.

4. Cover and bake in preheated oven for 40 minutes, or until the barley is tender.

Makeover Magic		
Before		**After**
310	Calories	196
11 g	Fat	4 g
6 g	Sat Fat	1 g
46 g	Carbs	35 g
3 g	Fiber	7 g
6 g	Protein	7 g
500 mg	Sodium	238 mg

Barley Pilaf with Artichokes and Kale

 Makes 6 servings

Prep time: 15 minutes • Total time: 1 hour, 5 minutes

Curb carbs: Barley is much more nutritious than white rice. To reduce carbs, reduce the amount of grain and bulk the dish up with vegetables.

Fill up on fiber: Artichokes, kale, and barley work together to give this dish 8 grams of fiber! Using the magic carbs rule makes this a perfect accompaniment to a low-carb main dish recipe.

Favor healthy fats: Artichokes and canola oil are the healthy fat stars in this pilaf.

1 tbsp	canola oil	15 mL
1	onion, chopped	1
1	carrot, chopped	1
1	stalk celery, chopped	1
½ cup	barley	125 mL
1	clove garlic, minced	1
2½ cups	low-sodium ready-to-use vegetable or chicken broth	625 mL
½ cup	water	125 mL
¼ cup	bulgur wheat	60 mL
4 cups	chopped trimmed kale leaves	1 L
1	package (9 oz/270 g) frozen artichoke hearts	1
½ tsp	grated lemon zest	2 mL

1. In a medium saucepan, heat the oil over medium-high heat. Cook the onion, carrot, and celery for 5 minutes, stirring, or until softened. Add the barley and garlic and cook, stirring, for 3 minutes.

2. Stir in the broth and water and bring to a boil over high heat. Reduce the heat to low, cover, and simmer for 25 minutes. Stir in the bulgur and kale, cover, and cook for 5 minutes. Stir in the artichokes and lemon zest, cover, and cook for 10 minutes, or until all of the broth is absorbed and the barley is al dente.

Makeover Magic		
Before		**After**
260	Calories	162
7 g	Fat	4 g
3 g	Sat Fat	0.5 g
42 g	Carbs	30 g
0 g	Fiber	8 g
7 g	Protein	6 g
700 mg	Sodium	262 mg

Quinoa Pilaf with Pistachios

 Makes 6 servings

Curb carbs: Quinoa has fewer carbs per serving than rice and is always a smart pick for blood sugar control.

Fill up on fiber: Quinoa is also high in fiber, bringing this meal over the "magic carbs" number all on its own at more than 7 grams per serving.

Favor healthy fats: Pistachios are a great source of MUFAs. Meanwhile, olive oil is a smart pick over vegetable oil to keep saturated fat low and healthy fats abundant.

2 tbsp	olive oil	30 mL
1 cup	quinoa, rinsed	250 mL
4	green onions, chopped	4
1	clove garlic, minced	1
1½ cups	water	375 mL
1 cup	ready-to-use vegetable broth	250 mL
¼ tsp	ground cardamom	1 mL
½ cup	pistachios, chopped	125 mL

1. In a medium saucepan, heat the oil over medium heat. Cook the quinoa, green onions, and garlic for 3 minutes, stirring, or until the vegetables are softened.

2. Add the water, broth, and cardamom and bring to a boil. Reduce the heat to low, cover, and simmer for 20 minutes, or until the quinoa is tender. Remove from the heat and set aside for 5 minutes. Stir in the pistachios.

Makeover Magic		
Before		**After**
470	Calories	235
18 g	Fat	12 g
8 g	Sat Fat	1 g
71 g	Carbs	26 g
3 g	Fiber	9 g
11 g	Protein	7 g
440 mg	Sodium	295 mg

Baked Risotto

 Makes 4 servings

Prep time: 10 minutes • Total time: 1 hour, 10 minutes

Curb carbs: Using half wild and half brown rice cuts down on the carbs while adding variety to the flavor and texture of this risotto.

Fill up on fiber: Rice and peas are both packed with fiber.

Favor healthy fats: Typically this dish would be cooked in lots of butter, but using canola oil cuts down on saturated fat while boosting your dose of good fats.

- Preheat oven to 425°F (220°C)
- Large ovenproof saucepan or Dutch oven

2 tbsp	canola oil	30 mL
1	onion, chopped	1
1	medium red bell pepper, chopped	1
½ cup	brown rice, preferably short- or medium-grain	125 mL
½ cup	wild rice	125 mL
1	clove garlic, minced	1
3 cups	ready-to-use vegetable broth	750 mL
1 cup	frozen peas, thawed	250 mL
⅓ cup	grated Romano cheese	75 mL

1. In saucepan, heat the oil over medium heat. Cook the onion and pepper, stirring, for 3 minutes. Add the brown rice, wild rice, and garlic and cook, stirring, for 2 minutes, or until the rice is coated. Add the broth and bring to a boil.

2. Cover and bake in preheated oven for 55 minutes, or until the broth is absorbed and the rice is just tender. Remove from the oven and stir in the peas and cheese. Cover and let stand for 5 minutes.

Makeover Magic		
Before		**After**
470	Calories	236
23 g	Fat	8 g
12 g	Sat Fat	2 g
50 g	Carbs	32 g
2 g	Fiber	3 g
18 g	Protein	8 g
970 mg	Sodium	383 mg

Broccoli-Walnut Farfalle Toss

 Makes 4 servings

Prep time: 10 minutes • Total time: 25 minutes

Curb carbs: We reduced the pasta in this recipe by half and tossed in broccoli, which — while also high in carbs — packs more fiber.

Fill up on fiber: Using whole-grain varieties is an easy way to up the fiber in any pasta recipe. Toss in high-fiber veggies like broccoli and you're all set!

Favor healthy fats: Walnuts and canola oil bring the MUFAs and omega-3 fatty acids to this dish. Goat cheese is a delicious gourmet dairy item that's also relatively low in saturated fat.

4 oz	whole-grain farfalle (bow-tie) pasta	125 g
1	bunch broccoli, cut into florets	1
2 tbsp	canola oil	30 mL
1	small red onion, thinly sliced	1
¼ tsp	salt	1 mL
⅛ tsp	ground black pepper	0.5 mL
1½ oz	goat cheese, crumbled	45 g
⅓ cup	walnuts, toasted and coarsely chopped	75 mL

1. Cook the pasta according to package directions, omitting the salt. Add the broccoli during the last 1 minute of cooking time. Drain, reserving ¼ cup (60 mL) of the cooking water. Transfer the pasta and broccoli to a bowl.

2. In the same pot, heat the oil over medium heat. Cook the onion for 5 minutes, stirring occasionally, or until softened.

3. Stir in the drained pasta and broccoli, reserved pasta cooking water, salt, and pepper. Cook for 1 minute, stirring, or until heated through. Remove from the heat and stir in the goat cheese. Sprinkle with the walnuts.

Makeover Magic		
Before		**After**
680	Calories	307
39 g	Fat	16 g
6 g	Sat Fat	3 g
63 g	Carbs	32 g
5 g	Fiber	7 g
19 g	Protein	13 g
830 mg	Sodium	249 mg

Mexican Fried Rice

 Makes 8 servings

Curb carbs: We can use less rice in this side because of the large amount of vegetables tossed in.

Fill up on fiber: Brown rice is higher in fiber than the white rice typically used in this type of recipe. The chopped veggies also add fiber.

Favor healthy fats: Pumpkin seeds are a delicious source of diabetes-friendly fats that add unexpected flavor to fried rice.

1 tbsp	olive oil	15 mL
1	onion, chopped	1
1	medium zucchini, chopped	1
1	chayote squash, peeled, seeded and chopped	1
1	red bell pepper, chopped	1
1 tsp	ground cumin	5 mL
1½ cups	cooked brown rice, chilled	375 mL
1 cup	green pumpkin seeds, toasted	250 mL
½ tsp	salt	2 mL
2 tbsp	chopped fresh cilantro	30 mL
1 tsp	freshly grated lime zest	5 mL

1. In a large nonstick skillet, heat the oil over medium-high heat. Cook the onion, zucchini, squash, pepper, and cumin, stirring, for 5 minutes, or until tender-crisp.

2. Add the rice and cook, stirring often, for 2 minutes, or until lightly toasted.

3. Stir in the pumpkin seeds and salt and cook, stirring, for 1 minute. Remove from the heat and stir in the cilantro and lime zest.

Makeover Magic		
Before		**After**
260	Calories	118
8 g	Fat	6 g
2 g	Sat Fat	1 g
33 g	Carbs	14 g
2 g	Fiber	3 g
14 g	Protein	6 g
700 mg	Sodium	106 mg

Fettuccine with Basil-Walnut Sauce

 Makes 4 servings

Prep time: 20 minutes • Total time: 20 minutes

Curb carbs: Shirataki noodles are naturally low in carbs and make a great swap for traditional wheat pasta.

Fill up on fiber: Spinach adds fiber and flavor to this blood sugar–friendly pasta dish.

Favor healthy fats: Walnuts, rich in ALAs, are the base of this sauce that's so rich and delicious you'd swear it was loaded with heavy cream.

- Food processor or blender

8 oz	shirataki fettuccine	250 g
½ cup	walnuts, toasted and coarsely chopped	125 mL
¼ cup	fresh basil (or 8 tsp/40 mL dried)	60 mL
2	cloves garlic	2
2 tbsp	olive oil	30 mL
3 cups	baby spinach	750 mL
½ cup	plain low fat (1%) Greek yogurt	125 mL
¼ cup	grated Romano cheese	60 mL

1. In a medium saucepan, cook the fettuccine according to package directions, omitting the salt. Drain and return to the saucepan.

2. Meanwhile, in a food processor, process the walnuts, basil, and garlic until blended. Add the oil and pulse until well blended.

3. Add the pesto and spinach to the pan with the fettuccine. Over low heat, cook for 3 minutes, stirring, or until the spinach wilts. Remove from the heat and stir in the yogurt and cheese.

Makeover Magic		
Before		**After**
730	Calories	219
43 g	Fat	18 g
21 g	Sat Fat	3 g
63 g	Carbs	8 g
3 g	Fiber	3 g
22 g	Protein	7 g
370 mg	Sodium	154 mg

Tex-Mex Pasta and Beans

 Makes 4 servings

Prep time: 10 minutes • Total time: 25 minutes

Curb carbs: We use half the amount of pasta called for in typical dishes of this type and pump up the volume with vegetables like pepper and onion.

Fill up on fiber: Adding beans increases the fiber, as does switching from white pasta to whole wheat.

Favor healthy fats: Not all pasta has to be bathed in rich, saturated fat–laden cheese sauce. Here, avocado adds favored fats and creaminess to this dish.

1 cup	whole wheat rotelle pasta	250 mL
	Nonstick cooking spray	
1	red onion, chopped	1
1	green bell pepper, chopped	1
½ tsp	ground cumin	2 mL
1 cup	canned black beans, drained and rinsed	250 mL
¾ cup	salsa	175 mL
2 tbsp	chopped fresh cilantro	30 mL
½	avocado, chopped	½

1. Cook the pasta according to package directions, omitting the salt, and drain.

2. Meanwhile, in a large nonstick skillet sprayed with cooking spray over medium-high heat, cook the onion and pepper for 5 minutes, stirring occasionally, or until softened. Add the cumin and cook for 1 minute, stirring, or until fragrant.

3. Stir in the pasta, beans, salsa, and cilantro. Cook, stirring, for 1 minute, or until hot. Top with the avocado.

Makeover Magic		
Before		**After**
460	Calories	230
17 g	Fat	5 g
9 g	Sat Fat	0.5 g
60 g	Carbs	41 g
4 g	Fiber	8 g
17 g	Protein	8 g
940 mg	Sodium	275 mg

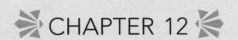

CHAPTER 12
Desserts

Orange-Pecan Tea Bread 262

Chocolate-Almond Cake 263

Lemon-Raspberry Cheesecake. 264

Maple-Walnut Cake. 266

Coconut-Lime Pudding Cake 267

Chocolate Layer Cake with Maple Frosting 268

Three-Berry Pie 270

Rich Chocolate Cream Pie 272

Double Oat–Blueberry Crisp 273

Pear-Ginger Cobbler. 274

Southern Pecan Bread Pudding. 275

Fruit and Nut Clusters. 276

Pistachio Kisses 277

Rich Brownies. 278

Fig Bars. 279

Oatmeal-Apple Cookies 280

Crispy Oat Squares 281

Almond Rice Pudding 282

Creamy Pumpkin Mousse 283

Frozen Mocha Parfaits 284

Chocolate Malt 285

Orange-Pecan Tea Bread

 Makes 9 servings

Prep time: 15 minutes • Total time: 50 minutes

Curb carbs: The average coffee cake recipe uses over 1 cup (250 mL) of sugar! Get delicious results with just 4 tablespoons (60 mL) of honey instead.

Fill up on fiber: Adding nuts and whole wheat flour boosts the fiber.

Favor healthy fats: Pecans and canola oil are high in MUFAs. We cut the standard amount of butter from this recipe, which decreases saturated fat.

- Preheat oven to 350°F (180°C)
- 9- by 5-inch (23 by 12.5 cm) metal loaf pan, sprayed with nonstick cooking spray

1 cup	whole-grain pastry flour	250 mL
½ cup	finely chopped pecans	125 mL
2 tbsp	ground flaxseeds	30 mL
1 tsp	baking powder	5 mL
½ tsp	grated orange zest	2 mL
¼ tsp	ground cardamom	1 mL
½ cup	1% milk	125 mL
1	large egg, lightly beaten	1
2 tbsp	canola oil	30 mL
4 tbsp	liquid honey, divided	60 mL
1 tbsp	unsweetened orange juice	15 mL

1. In a medium bowl, whisk together the flour, pecans, flaxseeds, baking powder, orange zest, and cardamom.

2. In a small bowl, whisk together the milk, egg, oil, and 2 tbsp (30 mL) honey. Stir into the flour mixture just until combined. Spread the batter in the prepared pan.

3. Bake in preheated oven for 30 minutes, or until a tester inserted in the center comes out clean. Cool in the pan on a rack for 10 minutes.

4. In a small saucepan, heat the remaining honey and the orange juice until warm.

5. Using the tines of a fork, poke holes over the surface of the cake. Spoon on the honey mixture. Remove the cake from the pan and cut into 9 slices.

Smart Start
Serve with a cup of green or black tea for added antioxidants.

Makeover Magic		
Before		**After**
499	Calories	151
27 g	Fat	8 g
4 g	Sat Fat	1 g
60 g	Carbs	18 g
2 g	Fiber	2 g
5 g	Protein	3 g
407 mg	Sodium	61 mg

Chocolate-Almond Cake

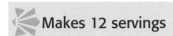 **Makes 12 servings**

Prep time: 15 minutes • Total time: 45 minutes

Curb carbs: Choose this cake over a frosted chocolate cake, which is loaded with carbs. By eliminating the flour and using nuts instead, not only did we curb the carbs, but we added healthy fats and pumped up the vitamins and minerals.

Fill up on fiber: The combination of chocolate with almonds is delicious and also adds fiber.

Favor healthy fats: Canola oil offers up both omega-3 fatty acids and MUFAs, and almonds add MUFAs, too.

- Preheat oven to 350°F (180°C)
- Food processor
- Electric mixer
- 8- or 9-inch (20 or 23 cm) springform pan, sprayed with nonstick cooking spray

3 oz	bittersweet (60% to 75%) chocolate, coarsely chopped	90 g
½ cup	blanched almonds	125 mL
8 tbsp	granulated sugar, divided	120 mL
½ cup	reduced-fat sour cream	125 mL
¼ cup	ground flaxseeds	60 mL
3	large omega-3-enriched egg yolks	3
2 tbsp	canola oil	30 mL
1 tsp	vanilla extract	5 mL
½ tsp	almond extract	2 mL
3 tbsp	unsweetened cocoa powder	45 mL
5	large omega-3-enriched egg whites, at room temperature	5
¼ tsp	salt	1 mL

1. In a glass bowl, microwave the chocolate on High for 2 minutes, stirring every 30 seconds, or until smooth.

2. In a food processor, finely grind the almonds with 1 tbsp (15 mL) sugar.

3. In a large bowl, stir together the melted chocolate, sour cream, flaxseeds, egg yolks, oil, vanilla, almond extract, 5 tbsp (75 mL) sugar, and the cocoa powder until well blended.

4. In another large bowl, with an electric mixer on high speed, beat the egg whites and salt until foamy. Gradually add the remaining sugar, beating, until stiff peaks are formed.

5. Stir one-quarter of the beaten whites into the chocolate mixture. Gently fold in the remaining whites. Spoon into the prepared pan. Smooth the top.

6. Bake in preheated oven for 30 minutes, or until the cake is dry on the top, and a tester inserted in the center comes out with a few moist crumbs. Cool in the pan on a rack. The cake will fall dramatically. Loosen the edges of the cake with a knife and remove the pan sides.

Makeover Magic		
Before		**After**
490	Calories	184
33 g	Fat	12 g
14 g	Sat Fat	3 g
47 g	Carbs	18 g
3 g	Fiber	3 g
6 g	Protein	5 g
292 mg	Sodium	80 mg

Lemon-Raspberry Cheesecake

 Makes 8 servings

Prep time: 15 minutes • Total time: 55 minutes + standing and chilling time

Curb carbs: Cut carbs by using a small amount of honey instead of sugar. Replacing cream cheese with cottage cheese adds protein, which is ideal for blood sugar control.

- Preheat oven to 350°F (180°C)
- 8-inch (20 cm) springform pan, bottom and sides buttered
- Food processor
- Electric mixer

¼ cup	oat bran	60 mL
¼ cup	ground golden flaxseeds	60 mL
½ tsp	ground cinnamon	2 mL
1½ cups	low-fat (1%) cottage cheese	375 mL
¼ cup	buttermilk	60 mL
6 tbsp	honey	90 mL
3 tbsp	whole-grain flour	45 mL
½ tsp	grated orange zest	2 mL
1½ tsp	grated lemon zest	7 mL
	Juice of 1 lemon	
1 tbsp	vanilla extract	15 mL
4	large eggs, separated	4
2 cups	raspberries	500 mL
½ cup	raspberry all-fruit jam	125 mL

1. In a medium bowl, combine the oat bran, flaxseeds, and cinnamon. Sprinkle the mixture into the prepared pan, tilting the pan to lightly coat the sides. Press the crumbs into the bottom of the pan.

2. In a food processor, combine the cottage cheese, buttermilk, honey, flour, orange zest, lemon zest, lemon juice, and vanilla; purée until smooth. Add the egg yolks and pulse to combine. Transfer to a large bowl.

Makeover Magic		
Before		**After**
636	Calories	229
43 g	Fat	5 g
26 g	Sat Fat	1 g
52 g	Carbs	38 g
1 g	Fiber	6 g
9 g	Protein	11 g
387 mg	Sodium	214 mg

Fill up on fiber: Oat bran gives the crust a boost in fiber.

Favor healthy fats: Ground flaxseeds serve up favored fats.

3. In another large bowl, with an electric mixer on high speed, beat the egg whites until stiff peaks form. Gently fold the egg whites and raspberries into the cottage cheese mixture.

4. Pour the batter into the pan. Drop the jam by tablespoons (15 mL) on top of the batter. With a knife, swirl the jam into the batter.

5. Bake in preheated oven for 40 minutes, or until puffed and set. Turn off the oven and open the door for 1 minute to reduce the heat. Close the door and let the cheesecake remain in the oven for 1 hour. Refrigerate for 4 hours or overnight. Remove the pan sides before serving.

Maple-Walnut Cake

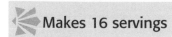 **Makes 16 servings**

Prep time: 30 minutes • Total time: 2 hours

Curb carbs: To cut the overall total grams of carbs per serving in this recipe, we substituted flaxseeds for some of the flour and used maple syrup as the main sweetener.

Fill up on fiber: Whole wheat pastry flour provides most of the fiber in this cake recipe.

Favor healthy fats: Walnuts and flaxseeds add healthy fats. Instead of relying on butter, we used applesauce and whole eggs to give this cake a moist tenderness.

- Preheat oven to 300°F (150°C)
- Electric mixer
- 9- by 5-inch (23 by 12.5 cm) loaf pan, sprayed with nonstick cooking spray

½ cup	canola oil	125 mL
¾ cup	pure maple syrup	175 mL
½ cup	unsweetened applesauce	125 mL
4	large omega-3-enriched eggs	4
1 tsp	vanilla extract	5 mL
1½ cups	whole wheat pastry flour	375 mL
¾ cup	chopped walnuts	175 mL
¼ cup	ground golden flaxseeds	60 mL
½ tsp	baking soda	2 mL
¼ tsp	salt	1 mL
⅔ cup	reduced-fat sour cream	150 mL

1. In a large bowl, using an electric mixer on medium speed, beat the oil, syrup, and applesauce until light in color. Add the eggs, one at a time, beating well after each addition. Beat in the vanilla.

2. In a medium bowl, whisk together the flour, walnuts, flaxseeds, baking soda, and salt. Alternately stir the flour mixture and the sour cream into the maple mixture, beginning and ending with the flour mixture.

3. Pour the batter into the pan. Bake in preheated oven for 90 minutes, or until lightly browned and a tester inserted in the center comes out clean. Cool in the pan on a rack for 10 minutes. Run a spatula around the edges and invert the cake onto the rack. Turn upright and let cool completely on the rack.

Makeover Magic		
Before		**After**
420	Calories	229
16 g	Fat	14 g
4 g	Sat Fat	2 g
64 g	Carbs	22 g
1 g	Fiber	3 g
6 g	Protein	5 g
300 mg	Sodium	115 mg

Coconut-Lime Pudding Cake

 Makes 4 servings

Prep time: 15 minutes • Total time: 50 minutes

Curb carbs: Enjoy the delicious flavors of a coconut cream pie — without all the carbs and calories.

Fill up on fiber: Coconut is a great source of fiber.

Favor healthy fats: Be sure to use omega-3-enriched eggs and canola oil — they add diabetes-friendly fats.

- Preheat oven to 350°F (180°C)
- Electric mixer
- 8-inch (20 cm) square glass baking dish, sprayed with nonstick cooking spray
- Large roasting pan

3	limes	3
1 cup	1% milk	250 mL
2 tbsp	canola oil	30 mL
2	large omega-3-enriched eggs, separated	2
1/8 tsp	salt	0.5 mL
1/3 cup	whole-grain pastry flour	75 mL
1/2 cup	unsweetened shredded coconut	125 mL
1	large omega-3-enriched egg white	1
1/4 cup	granulated sugar	60 mL
	Boiling water	

1. From the limes, grate 1½ tsp (7 mL) of zest and squeeze ⅓ cup (75 mL) of juice.

2. In a large bowl, whisk together the milk, lime zest, lime juice, oil, egg yolks, and salt. Whisk in the flour and coconut until smooth.

3. In a separate large bowl, using an electric mixer on high speed, beat the 3 egg whites until soft peaks form. Gradually add the sugar while beating until stiff, glossy peaks form. Fold into the lime mixture. The batter will be lumpy and thin. Pour into the prepared baking dish.

4. Place the baking dish in a large roasting pan. Fill with boiling water until it reaches halfway up the baking dish.

5. Bake in preheated oven for 35 minutes, or until puffed and browned and the center of the cake is set. Cool on a rack for 15 minutes.

Makeover Magic		
Before		**After**
580	Calories	203
41 g	Fat	12 g
27 g	Sat Fat	7 g
47 g	Carbs	19 g
1 g	Fiber	2 g
5 g	Protein	4 g
270 mg	Sodium	82 mg

Chocolate Layer Cake with Maple Frosting

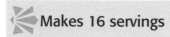

Prep time: 15 minutes • Total time: 1 hour, 30 minutes

Curb carbs: Replacing sugar with maple syrup in the frosting is one quick way to curb carbs and make this cake diabetes-friendly.

- Preheat oven to 350°F (180°C)
- Electric mixer
- Two 8-inch (20 cm) round metal cake pans, sprayed with nonstick cooking spray
- Double boiler

1½ cups	whole-grain pastry flour	375 mL
½ cup	unsweetened cocoa powder	125 mL
1 tbsp	instant espresso powder	15 mL
1 tsp	baking soda	5 mL
½ cup	butter, softened	125 mL
1 cup	granulated sugar	250 mL
1	large egg	1
1 tsp	vanilla extract	5 mL
½ cup	low-fat (1%) buttermilk	125 mL
½ cup	hot tap water	125 mL
¾ cup	pure maple syrup	175 mL
3	large egg whites	3
½ tsp	cream of tartar	2 mL

1. In a medium bowl, mix the flour, cocoa powder, espresso powder, and baking soda.

2. In a large bowl, using an electric mixer on medium speed, beat the butter and sugar for 3 minutes, or until creamy. Add the egg and vanilla. Beat on low speed until creamy.

3. With the mixer on low speed, beat in half of the flour mixture and all of the buttermilk. Beat in half of the remaining flour mixture and all of the water. Beat in the remaining flour mixture. Pour into the prepared pans.

Makeover Magic		
Before		**After**
790	Calories	188
42 g	Fat	7 g
25 g	Sat Fat	4 g
104 g	Carbs	31 g
5 g	Fiber	2 g
10 g	Protein	3 g
670 mg	Sodium	104 mg

Fill up on fiber: Whole-grain pastry flour is a high-fiber alternative to white flour for this type of dessert.

Favor healthy fats: Be sure to serve this dessert following a dinner high in healthy fats.

4. Bake in preheated oven for 25 minutes, or until a tester inserted in the center comes out clean. Cool in the pans on a rack for 10 minutes. Remove to the rack and cool completely.

5. In the top of a double boiler, combine the syrup, egg whites, and cream of tartar. Using an electric mixer on medium-high speed, beat until well blended. Place over rapidly boiling water. Beat for 7 minutes, or until stiff peaks form. Remove the top of the double boiler from the water and continue beating for 5 minutes, or until thickened and fluffy.

6. Place 1 cake layer on a serving plate. Spread 1 cup (250 mL) of the frosting over the cake. Top with the second cake layer. Spread the remaining frosting over the top and sides of the cake.

Three-Berry Pie

Prep time: 45 minutes • Total time: 1 hour, 30 minutes

Curb carbs: Curb carbs by using just one crust, rather than a double pie crust, and sprinkling crumbs on top.

- Food processor
- 9-inch (23 cm) pie plate, sprayed with nonstick cooking spray
- Baking sheet, lined with foil

Crust

¾ cup	whole-grain pastry flour	175 mL
¼ cup	oat bran	60 mL
¼ tsp	salt	1 mL
¼ cup	chilled butter, cut into small pieces	60 mL
3 tbsp	light sour cream	45 mL
1½ tbsp	ice water, divided	22 mL
¼ tsp	almond extract	1 mL

Filling

2 cups	raspberries	500 mL
1 cup	blackberries	250 mL
1 cup	blueberries	250 mL
3 tbsp	lemon juice	45 mL
¼ cup	liquid honey	60 mL
3 tbsp	cornstarch	45 mL
3 tbsp	instant tapioca	45 mL

Crumb Topping

¼ cup	whole-grain pastry flour	60 mL
1 tbsp	canola oil	15 mL
2 tsp	liquid honey	10 mL

1. *To make the crust:* In a food processor, pulse together the flour, oat bran, and salt until blended. Add the butter. Pulse until the mixture resembles coarse crumbs.

2. Add the sour cream, 1 tbsp (15 mL) water, and the almond extract. Pulse just until the dough forms large clumps. (If the dough seems too dry, add a few more drops of remaining ice water.) Form into a ball and flatten into a disk. Cover and refrigerate for at least 15 minutes, or up to 1 day.

Makeover Magic		
Before		**After**
410	Calories	205
19 g	Fat	7 g
5 g	Sat Fat	2 g
57 g	Carbs	35 g
4 g	Fiber	5 g
4 g	Protein	3 g
270 mg	Sodium	207 mg

Fill up on fiber: Oat bran and whole-grain flour add fiber.

Favor healthy fats: Eat this dessert following a meal high in healthy fats.

3. Preheat the oven to 400°F (200°C).

4. On a well-floured surface, roll out dough into a 10-inch (25 cm) circle. Fit the dough into the pie plate, leaving the overhang.

5. *To make the filling:* In a large bowl, combine the raspberries, blackberries, blueberries, and lemon juice.

6. In a small bowl, combine the honey, cornstarch, and tapioca. Pour over the fruit, mix well, and let stand at room temperature for 15 minutes. Spoon into the pie plate.

7. *To make the topping:* Combine the flour, oil, and honey. Lightly sprinkle over the fruit filling.

8. Place the pie on the prepared baking sheet and bake in preheated oven for 40 minutes, or until the crust is golden brown and the juices bubble. Cool on a rack.

Smart Start
Add toasted oats to the crumb topping for an even more fiber-full recipe.

Rich Chocolate Cream Pie

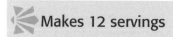 **Makes 12 servings**

Prep time: 20 minutes • Total time: 30 minutes + cooling time

Curb carbs: Relying on a small amount of honey and bittersweet chocolate for sweetness reduces the carbs in this recipe.

Fill up on fiber: Almond meal and oat bran add fiber to the crust.

Favor healthy fats: Almonds and canola oil provide healthy fats.

- Preheat oven to 350°F (180°C)
- 9-inch (23 cm) metal pie plate
- Food processor

¾ cup	almond meal or almond flour	175 mL
¾ cup	oat bran	175 mL
¼ tsp	baking powder	1 mL
¼ tsp	salt	1 mL
2 tbsp	canola oil	30 mL
1 tbsp	liquid honey	15 mL
2	packages (12 oz/340 g each) silken tofu, drained	2
2 tbsp	unsweetened cocoa powder	30 mL
1 tbsp	vanilla extract	15 mL
8 oz	bittersweet (60% to 75%) chocolate, melted	250 g
1 cup	plain nonfat (0%) Greek yogurt	250 mL

1. In a large bowl, whisk together the almond meal, oat bran, baking powder, and salt. Stir in the oil and honey until blended. Press into pie plate.

2. Bake in preheated oven for 10 minutes, or until set and lightly browned. Remove to a rack and cool completely.

3. Meanwhile, in a food processor, place the tofu, cocoa, and vanilla and blend until smooth. Add the chocolate and blend for 1 minute. Scrape the sides with a rubber spatula and blend for 1 minute, or until incorporated. Pour into a large bowl.

4. Fold in the yogurt just until blended. Refrigerate.

5. When the pie shell is cooled, spread the chocolate mixture into the shell.

Makeover Magic		
Before		**After**
305	Calories	206
19 g	Fat	12 g
10 g	Sat Fat	6 g
31 g	Carbs	21 g
1 g	Fiber	2 g
3 g	Protein	6 g
90 mg	Sodium	87 mg

Double Oat–Blueberry Crisp

 Makes 6 servings

Prep time: 15 minutes • Total time: 1 hour, 5 minutes

Curb carbs: We cut back the amount of sweetener and let the natural flavor of the berries come through.

Fill up on fiber: Steel-cut oats are higher in fiber than regular or instant oats. Combining steel-cut oats and oat bran adds even more fiber and texture.

Favor healthy fats: Sliced almonds serve up a dish with MUFAs.

- Preheat oven to 350°F (180°C)
- 8-inch (20 cm) glass baking dish, sprayed with cooking spray

2 tbsp	liquid honey	30 mL
1½ tbsp	arrowroot powder or cornstarch	22 mL
3 cups	blueberries	750 mL
⅛ tsp	ground nutmeg	0.5 mL
1½ tsp	almond extract	7 mL
½ cup	steel-cut oats	125 mL
¼ cup	oat bran	60 mL
¼ cup	sliced almonds	60 mL
1 tbsp	packed light brown sugar	15 mL
2 tbsp	canola oil	30 mL
	Light whipped topping (optional)	

1. In a large bowl, stir together the honey and arrowroot powder. Add the blueberries, nutmeg, and almond extract. Toss to coat the berries thoroughly. Transfer to the prepared baking dish.

2. In the same bowl, combine the oats, oat bran, almonds, brown sugar, and oil. Toss to coat well. Sprinkle over the berry mixture.

3. Bake in preheated oven for 45 minutes, or until bubbling. Remove and let stand at room temperature for 5 minutes. Serve with a dollop of light whipped topping, if desired.

Smart Start

Add lots of cinnamon to the crisp topping for glycemic balance!

Makeover Magic		
Before		**After**
650	Calories	169
24 g	Fat	6 g
15 g	Sat Fat	1 g
104 g	Carbs	29 g
7 g	Fiber	4 g
5 g	Protein	3 g
270 mg	Sodium	32 mg

Pear-Ginger Cobbler

 Makes 4 servings

Prep time: 25 minutes • Total time: 1 hour

Curb carbs: This dish uses honey instead of sugar for a major carb reduction.

Fill up on fiber: Switching out some of the flour for oat bran increases the fiber. Pears are naturally a good source of fiber.

Favor healthy fats: Be sure to use omega-3-enriched eggs. They are the secret source in this recipe.

- Preheat oven to 425°F (220°C)
- 9-inch (23 cm) round ceramic baking dish, sprayed with nonstick cooking spray

4 cups	sliced pears	1 L
2 tbsp	liquid honey	30 mL
1	large omega-3-enriched egg, well beaten	1
1 tbsp	quick-cooking tapioca	15 mL
1 tsp	grated gingerroot	5 mL
½ cup	whole wheat pastry flour	125 mL
½ cup	oat bran	125 mL
1 tsp	baking soda	5 mL
⅓ cup	buttermilk	75 mL
1 tbsp	butter, at room temperature	15 mL

1. In a medium bowl, combine the pears, honey, egg, tapioca, and ginger. Spread evenly over the bottom of the prepared baking dish.

2. In another medium bowl, combine the flour, oat bran, baking soda, buttermilk, and butter to make a dough.

3. On a well-floured surface, roll out the dough into a 9-inch (23 cm) round, about ½ inch (1 cm) thick. Prick the dough with a fork and place loosely over the pears.

4. Bake in preheated oven for 25 minutes, until the filling is set and the topping is golden brown.

Makeover Magic		
Before		**After**
300	Calories	196
9 g	Fat	3 g
5 g	Sat Fat	2 g
51 g	Carbs	39 g
5 g	Fiber	6 g
2 g	Protein	6 g
90 mg	Sodium	237 mg

Southern Pecan Bread Pudding

 Makes 9 servings

Prep time: 15 minutes • Total time: 50 minutes

Curb carbs: We reduced the amount of bread from a traditional recipe to keep carbs in check, but the pudding is still gooey and comforting.

Fill up on fiber: Whole-grain bread and pecans add fiber.

Favor healthy fats: Pecans add MUFAs to this classic southern dish.

- Preheat oven to 350°F (180°C)
- Electric mixer
- 8-inch (20 cm) glass baking dish, sprayed with nonstick cooking spray

2	large eggs, separated	2
2	large egg whites	2
Pinch	salt	Pinch
1½ cups	1% milk	375 mL
7 tbsp	liquid honey, divided	105 mL
1 tbsp	vanilla extract	15 mL
1 tbsp	canola oil	15 mL
⅛ tsp	ground nutmeg	0.5 mL
3 cups	cubed whole-grain bread	750 mL
¼ cup	finely chopped pecans	60 mL
1 tbsp	bourbon (optional)	15 mL
Pinch	ground cinnamon	Pinch

1. In a large bowl, using an electric mixer on high speed, beat the egg whites and salt until stiff, glossy peaks form.

2. In another bowl, beat the egg yolks with a fork. Add the milk, 3 tbsp (45 mL) honey, vanilla, oil, and nutmeg. Beat to blend. Add the bread and pecans. Press with the back of a fork until the bread absorbs the liquid. Gently pour into the bowl with the beaten whites. Fold to incorporate. Transfer to the prepared baking dish.

3. Bake in preheated oven for 35 minutes, or until a knife inserted in the center comes out clean. If the top is browning too fast, cover lightly with a sheet of foil.

4. Meanwhile, in a microwave-safe bowl, combine the remaining honey, bourbon (if using), and cinnamon. Microwave on High for 40 seconds, or until bubbling. Whisk until smooth. Spoon the warm pudding onto dessert plates. Drizzle with the honey mixture.

Makeover Magic		
Before		**After**
976	Calories	156
64 g	Fat	5 g
30 g	Sat Fat	1 g
95 g	Carbs	22 g
3 g	Fiber	1 g
11 g	Protein	5 g
558 mg	Sodium	139 mg

Fruit and Nut Clusters

Prep time: 10 minutes • Total time: 1 hour

Curb carbs: Classic candied nuts are coated in sugar. Here, we lightly sweetened the nut mixture with honey, cinnamon, and cardamom.

Fill up on fiber: Dried apples, pecans, and almonds add fiber to this dish.

Favor healthy fats: Nuts and pumpkin seeds are all great sources of desirable fats.

- Preheat oven to 350°F (180°C)
- Baking sheet, lined with parchment paper

1	large egg white	1
1 tbsp	liquid honey	15 mL
1 tsp	ground cinnamon	5 mL
1 tsp	ground ginger	5 mL
¼ tsp	ground cardamom	1 mL
½ cup	pecans	125 mL
½ cup	almonds	125 mL
½ cup	raw green pumpkin seeds (pepitas)	125 mL
½ cup	chopped dried apples	125 mL

1. In a medium bowl, whisk the egg white, honey, cinnamon, ginger, and cardamom. Add the pecans, almonds, pumpkin seeds, and apples and toss to coat well. Spread the mixture onto the parchment paper.

2. Bake in preheated oven for 20 minutes, or until browned. Cool on a rack for 30 minutes, or until cooled. Break into bite-size pieces.

Makeover Magic		
Before		**After**
255	Calories	172
18 g	Fat	12 g
2 g	Sat Fat	2 g
22 g	Carbs	11 g
3 g	Fiber	3 g
6 g	Protein	7 g
233 mg	Sodium	25 mg

Pistachio Kisses

 Makes 6 servings

Prep time: 15 minutes • Total time: 2 hours, 15 minutes

Curb carbs: Using nuts instead of flour in these cookies obliterates carbs while leaving snackers satisfied.

Fill up on fiber: The pistachios provide half the belly-filling fiber in this recipe.

Favor healthy fats: Pistachios are also a source of MUFAs

- Preheat oven to 250°F (120°C)
- Electric mixer
- 2 large baking sheets, lined with parchment paper

2	large egg whites, at room temperature	2
¼ tsp	cream of tartar	1 mL
¼ cup	maple sugar	60 mL
½ cup	unsalted roasted pistachios, chopped	125 mL
⅛ tsp	ground cardamom	0.5 mL

1. In a large bowl, using an electric mixer on high speed, beat the egg whites and cream of tartar until soft peaks form. Continue beating while gradually adding the maple sugar until very stiff and glossy peaks form. Gently fold in the pistachios and cardamom. Drop by tablespoons (15 mL) onto the parchment paper.

2. Bake in preheated oven for 1 hour. Turn off the oven and leave in the oven for 1 hour without opening the oven door.

3. Remove from the oven and store in an airtight container.

Makeover Magic		
Before		**After**
130	Calories	120
6 g	Fat	5 g
2 g	Sat Fat	1 g
18 g	Carbs	11 g
0 g	Fiber	2 g
2 g	Protein	5 g
55 mg	Sodium	30 mg

Rich Brownies

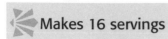

Prep time: 10 minutes • Total time: 50 minutes

Curb carbs: This is one cool trick — instead of flour, use high-fiber black beans and watch half the carbs disappear!

Fill up on fiber: Black beans, pecans, and cocoa powder all add fiber to this dish.

Favor healthy fats: Dark chocolate and pecans add MUFAs.

- Preheat oven to 350°F (180°C)
- Food processor or blender
- 8-inch (20 cm) square metal baking pan, sprayed with nonstick cooking spray

1	can (14 oz/398 mL) no-salt-added black beans, drained and rinsed	1
3	large eggs	3
½ cup	honey	125 mL
⅓ cup	canola oil	75 mL
¼ cup	unsweetened cocoa powder	60 mL
2 tsp	ground cinnamon	10 mL
6 oz	bittersweet (60% to 75%) chocolate, broken into pieces	175 g
½ cup	chopped pecans	125 mL

1. In a food processor, combine the black beans, eggs, honey, oil, cocoa, and cinnamon. Pulse until smooth. Add the chocolate and pulse until coarsely chopped.

2. Pour the batter into the pan. Sprinkle with the pecans.

3. Bake in preheated oven for 45 minutes, or until a tester inserted in the center comes out clean.

Makeover Magic		
Before		**After**
310	Calories	180
18 g	Fat	11 g
8 g	Sat Fat	4 g
32 g	Carbs	19 g
2 g	Fiber	2 g
4 g	Protein	3 g
70 mg	Sodium	26 mg

Fig Bars

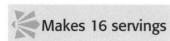

Prep time: 15 minutes • Total time: 40 minutes

Curb carbs: Honey is sweeter than sugar, so you can use less of it!

Fill up on fiber: Up the fiber with oats, walnuts, flaxseeds, and dried fruit. Just remember that dried fruit adds to your carb count quickly.

Favor healthy fats: Walnuts and ground flaxseeds are a great source of ALA omega-3 fatty acids.

- Preheat oven to 350°F (180°C)
- 8-inch (20 cm) metal baking pan, sprayed with nonstick cooking spray

½ cup	honey	125 mL
⅓ cup	plain nonfat (0%) Greek yogurt	75 mL
3 tbsp	canola oil	45 mL
1	large omega-3-enriched egg	1
1½ tsp	vanilla extract	7 mL
1½ cups	chopped dried figs	375 mL
¾ cup	large-flake (old-fashioned) rolled oats	175 mL
½ cup	whole wheat pastry flour	125 mL
⅓ cup	ground golden flaxseeds	75 mL
2 tbsp	chopped walnuts	30 mL
½ tsp	baking soda	2 mL
1 tbsp	ground cinnamon	15 mL

1. In a large bowl, whisk together the honey, yogurt, oil, egg, and vanilla until smooth.

2. In another bowl, stir together the figs, oats, flour, flaxseeds, walnuts, baking soda, and cinnamon. Add to the first bowl. Stir to combine. Spread into the prepared pan.

3. Bake in preheated oven for 25 minutes, or until the top is browned and a tester inserted in the center comes out with a few moist crumbs. Do not overbake. Remove to a rack to cool. Cut into 16 squares.

Makeover Magic		
Before		**After**
279	Calories	149
11 g	Fat	5 g
11 g	Sat Fat	0.5 g
45 g	Carbs	25 g
3 g	Fiber	3 g
3 g	Protein	3 g
157 mg	Sodium	49 mg

Oatmeal-Apple Cookies

**Makes 8 cookies
(2 per serving)**

Prep time: 10 minutes • Total time: 20 minutes

Curb carbs: No need to add flour or too much sugar to these cookies. Honey and oats keep carbs curbed by removing flour and decreasing the overall sugar content.

Fill up on fiber: Oats, apple (with the skin on) and chia seeds all add fiber!

Favor healthy fats: Olive oil and chia seeds provide MUFAs and omega-3 fatty acids to these sweet treats.

- Preheat oven to 350°F (180°C)
- Baking sheet, sprayed with nonstick cooking spray

¾ cup	large-flake (old-fashioned) rolled oats	175 mL
1	apple, shredded	1
2	large egg whites	2
2 tbsp	liquid honey	30 mL
2 tbsp	white chia seeds	30 mL
1 tbsp	1% milk	15 mL
1 tbsp	olive oil	15 mL
1 tsp	ground cinnamon	5 mL
½ tsp	baking powder	2 mL
Pinch	salt	Pinch

1. In a large bowl, combine the oats, apple, egg whites, honey, chia seeds, milk, oil, cinnamon, baking powder, and salt. Stir together until well blended.

2. Divide the dough into 8 equal pieces. Place on the prepared baking sheet and flatten with the bottom of a glass.

3. Bake in preheated oven for 12 minutes, or until golden brown on the edges.

Makeover Magic		
Before		**After**
300	Calories	125
14 g	Fat	4 g
8 g	Sat Fat	0.5 g
39 g	Carbs	20 g
0 g	Fiber	2 g
3 g	Protein	3 g
230 mg	Sodium	102 mg

Crispy Oat Squares

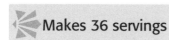
Prep time: 10 minutes • Total time: 1 hour, 10 minutes

Curb carbs: This is essentially a crispy rice treat, but our version uses honey instead of marshmallows and adds peanut butter for body and protein, while cutting carbs.

Fill up on fiber: Oat cereal adds just 1 gram of fiber, so this dessert would be great following a higher-fiber meal.

Favor healthy fats: Nut butter is the favored fat providing MUFAs.

- 8-inch (20 cm) square metal baking pan, sprayed with nonstick cooking spray

3 cups	oat "O" cereal	750 mL
½ cup	natural peanut or cashew butter	125 mL
⅓ cup	honey	75 mL
1 tbsp	vanilla extract	15 mL

1. Place the oat cereal in a large bowl.

2. In a medium saucepan over medium heat, stir the peanut butter, honey, and vanilla constantly for 3 minutes, or until melted. Remove from the heat and stir into the cereal.

3. Spread into the prepared pan. Cover and refrigerate for 1 hour. Cut into 36 squares.

Makeover Magic		
Before		**After**
180	Calories	100
5 g	Fat	4 g
1 g	Sat Fat	0.5 g
29 g	Carbs	13 g
1 g	Fiber	1 g
4 g	Protein	2 g
160 mg	Sodium	72 mg

Almond Rice Pudding

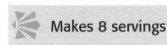

Makes 8 servings

Curb carbs: Use unsweetened soy milk or even unsweetened almond milk to prevent this from being a blood-sugar bomb.

Fill up on fiber: Brown rice and chia seeds provide a small amount of fiber.

Favor healthy fats: Chia seeds can serve as fiber and fat. Sprinkling with sliced almonds adds the ultimate nutty flavor and favored fat.

3 cups	unsweetened soy milk	750 mL
1/2 cup	brown rice	125 mL
2 tbsp	white chia seeds	30 mL
2 tbsp	honey	30 mL
1 tsp	almond extract	5 mL
1/8 tsp	salt	0.5 mL
1/8 tsp	ground cinnamon	0.5 mL
2	large eggs	2
1/4 cup	sliced almonds, toasted	60 mL

1. In a medium saucepan, stir together the milk, rice, chia seeds, honey, almond extract, salt, and cinnamon. Bring to a boil over medium heat. Reduce the heat to low, cover, and simmer, stirring occasionally, for 1 1/2 hours, or until the rice is very tender. Remove from the heat and let cool for 5 minutes.

2. In a small bowl, lightly beat the eggs with a fork. Stir 1/2 cup (125 mL) of the hot rice mixture into the eggs. Gradually stir the egg mixture into the saucepan.

3. Place over medium-low heat and cook, stirring constantly, for 5 minutes, or until thickened. Remove from the heat and cool for 10 minutes. Pour into a serving bowl and cover the surface with plastic wrap. Refrigerate until cold. Sprinkle with almonds and serve.

Makeover Magic		
Before		**After**
436	Calories	190
18 g	Fat	7 g
4 g	Sat Fat	1 g
59 g	Carbs	23 g
1 g	Fiber	2 g
12 g	Protein	8 g
159 mg	Sodium	119 mg

Creamy Pumpkin Mousse

 Makes 4 servings

Curb carbs: Using Greek yogurt instead of sweetened whipped cream takes the carbs down in this sweet autumnal dish.

Fill up on fiber: Pumpkin is naturally high in fiber — each serving has 3 grams!

Favor healthy fats: Chia seeds provide healthy fats in this dish.

1	can (15 oz/425 mL) pumpkin purée (not pie filling)	1
1 tbsp	chia seeds	15 mL
2 tbsp	liquid honey	30 mL
1½ tsp	pumpkin pie spice	7 mL
1½ cups	plain nonfat (0%) Greek yogurt	375 mL
2 oz	bittersweet (60 to 75%) chocolate, shaved	60 g

1. In a large bowl, combine the pumpkin, chia seeds, honey, and pumpkin pie spice. Gently fold in the yogurt until blended. Transfer to 4 individual serving bowls and top with the chocolate shavings.

2. Refrigerate for at least 1 hour before serving.

Makeover Magic		
Before		**After**
552	Calories	204
42 g	Fat	6 g
29 g	Sat Fat	4 g
41 g	Carbs	32 g
2 g	Fiber	5 g
6 g	Protein	9 g
172 mg	Sodium	52 mg

Frozen Mocha Parfaits

 Makes 4 servings

Curb carbs: Streamlining the ingredients of a classic parfait helps cut calories. Layering nuts instead of cookies eliminates carbs — as does using bittersweet chocolate instead of milk chocolate.

Fill up on fiber: Even dessert can have fiber. Use sliced almonds for a combo of healthy fiber and fat.

Favor healthy fats: Get rid of the unhealthy saturated fat in whipped cream by replacing it with a topping of slivered almonds, which are packed with MUFAs. Not only does bittersweet chocolate have less sugar than milk chocolate, but it is also a good source of antioxidants and MUFAs.

- 4 parfait glasses

1 tsp	instant espresso powder	5 mL
¼ cup	bittersweet (60% to 75%) chocolate chips	60 mL
2 cups	low-fat chocolate frozen yogurt	500 mL
4 tbsp	sliced almonds, toasted	60 mL

1. Place the espresso powder and chocolate chips in a small glass bowl. Microwave on Medium (50%) power for 2 minutes, stirring every 30 seconds, or until smooth. Let cool for 5 minutes.

2. Place 1 small scoop (¼ cup/60 mL) of the yogurt in each of 4 parfait glasses. Drizzle each with 1 tsp (5 mL) of the chocolate mixture and ½ tbsp (7 mL) almonds. Repeat the layers. Serve immediately or freeze for up to 1 hour.

Makeover Magic		
Before		**After**
694	Calories	216
41 g	Fat	10 g
23 g	Sat Fat	5 g
80 g	Carbs	29 g
3 g	Fiber	3 g
7 g	Protein	7 g
170 mg	Sodium	59 mg

Chocolate Malt

 Makes 1 serving

Prep time: 5 minutes • Total time: 5 minutes

Curb carbs: Milk contains about 12 grams of carbs per cup (250 mL). By using unsweetened cocoa and malted milk powder, you can keep the carbs curbed. You may need to halve this recipe if your snacks are limited to 15 grams of carbs.

Fill up on fiber:
Surprised to see fiber in this drink? It comes from the cocoa powder, which adds almost 2 grams per tablespoon (15 mL).

Favor healthy fats:
Add a tablespoon (15 mL) of chia seeds for a dose of omega-3 and omega-6 fatty acids.

- Blender
- Frosted glass

2 tbsp	unsweetened cocoa powder	30 mL
1 tbsp	unsweetened malted milk powder	15 mL
¼ cup	warm water	60 mL
¾ cup	1% milk	175 mL
2 tsp	vanilla extract	10 mL
⅓ cup	crushed ice	75 mL

1. In a blender, pulse the cocoa powder, malted milk powder, and water until well blended. Blend in the milk, vanilla, and ice for 1 minute, or until the mixture is thick and frothy.

2. Pour into a frosted glass and serve immediately.

Makeover Magic		
Before		**After**
496	Calories	156
23 g	Fat	4 g
14 g	Sat Fat	3 g
64 g	Carbs	21 g
3 g	Fiber	4 g
10 g	Protein	9 g
211 mg	Sodium	119 mg

Meal Plans

You have reached the Repeating step. You are ready to consistently implement everything you have learned, whether it is journaling in your food log, observing your hunger/fullness cues, or curbing your carbs. To make this stage easy for you, we have created a delicious and comforting 2-week meal plan. So grab your sneakers and your canvas bags and head to the grocery store to get your ingredients for success.

Keep in mind that all meals curb carbohydrates to 45 grams. Men, feel free to add 15 grams of carbs to each of your three main meals per day to ensure that they are nutritionally adequate and you don't feel deprived. Each individual may add one to three snacks per day. This will depend on your internal regulation system, personal weight-loss goals, level of physical activity, and the quantity of food you were previously eating. Your meal plan is created with three meals and one snack. Add or reduce planned snack times depending on how feasible three meals and one snack are. Ask yourself, "Am I satiated? Can I wait 2 to 4 hours between snacks or meals?" Consider whether you are eating less than before. In most cases, you should be eating less than you were when you started reading this lifestyle cookbook. If you are choosing snacks, we recommend a mid-

morning snack, a mid-afternoon snack, and/or a nighttime snack, each equal to 15 grams of carbs for women and 30 grams of carbs for men.

If you have already been diagnosed with diabetes and use a glucometer, you can take your meal plan a step further. Be proactive in achieving optimal blood sugar management by taking your blood sugar before eating and then 2 hours after your meal. This will help to ensure that the amounts and combinations of foods you are eating work for your body. In other words, check to be sure your blood sugar is generally less than 180 mg/dl 2 hours after meals. Remember that this number varies for each individual and is best determined with your personal diabetes care team when discussing diabetes self-management education.

Finally, if you love a particular recipe or food — especially one that is high in grams of carbohydrates per serving — learn to spread this food choice throughout the day to prevent a sugar roller coaster. So if you can't get enough of the Fruit and Nut Clusters (page 276), feel free to have one at breakfast and one at lunch, just not two at the same meal. This action plan will keep you happy and your body healthy.

All portions are equal to 1 serving unless otherwise noted.

Week 1

Sunday

Breakfast

¾ cup (175 mL) plain nonfat (0%) Greek yogurt

¼ cup (60 mL) cooked wheat berries

1 small apple, cubed

2 tbsp (30 mL) chopped walnuts

2 tbsp (30 mL) mixed berries

Lunch

Chicken-Veggie Bowl: 4 oz (125 g) grilled and shredded chicken strips and 2 cups (500 mL) cooked vegetables (½ cup/125 mL sliced onion; 1½ cups/375 mL chopped red, orange, and yellow bell peppers; 1 clove garlic, minced; and 2 tsp/10 mL canola oil sautéed over medium heat). Serve in a bowl and, on the side, include a whole wheat tortilla spread with 1 tbsp (15 mL) olive hummus.

Chocolate-Almond Cake (page 263)

Dinner

Pasta with Summer Vegetables (page 228)

Baked Salmon: 4 oz (125 g) wild salmon fillet spread with 2 tsp (10 mL) Dijon mustard and sprinkled with 2 tsp (10 mL) ground flaxseeds. Bake at 375°F (190°C) for 10 minutes, or until the salmon is opaque.

Snack

15 grams of carbs: 2 tbsp (30 mL) almonds and ½ large orange

30 grams of carbs: ¼ cup (60 mL) almonds and 1 large orange

Monday

Breakfast

1 cup (250 mL) plain nonfat (0%) Greek yogurt

1 cup (250 mL) mixed berries

1 tbsp (15 mL) wheat germ

1 Fruit and Nut Cluster (page 276)

Lunch

Broccoli-Walnut Farfalle Toss (page 257)

1 Fruit and Nut Cluster (page 276)

Dinner

1½ servings Herb-Roasted Chicken Breasts with Vegetables (page 188)

Cheese and Vegetable Bake (page 249)

Snack

15 grams of carbs: 10 to 15 olives and 5 high-fiber crackers (1 oz/30 g total)

30 grams of carbs: ¼ cup (60 mL) guacamole with 10 to 15 low-sodium baked tortilla chips (1 oz/30 g total) and 1 cup (250 mL) carrot sticks for dipping

Tuesday

Breakfast

Eggs Un-Benedict: 2 large poached eggs, ¼ cup (60 mL) steamed spinach, and 2 toasted English muffins. Spread half the spinach over each muffin bottom, and top with 1 poached egg and the muffin top.

1 clementine

Lunch

Turkey and Bean Quesadillas (page 205)

1 small apple

Dinner

Beef Ragù over Polenta (page 160)

Spinach Salad: 2 cups (500 mL) spinach dressed with 1 tbsp (15 mL) slivered almonds, 1 tsp (5 mL) grated Parmesan cheese, and 1 tbsp (15 mL) Lemon–Olive Oil Dressing (1 tsp/5 mL lemon juice mixed with 2 tsp/10 mL olive oil and salt and ground black pepper to taste).

Snack

15 grams of carbs: ¾ cup (175 mL) plain nonfat (0%) Greek yogurt sprinkled with 1 crushed small cookie

30 grams of carbs: ¾ cup (175 mL) fruit-flavored nonfat (0%) Greek yogurt mixed with ½ cup (125 mL) berries and 1 tbsp (15 mL) wheat germ

Wednesday

Breakfast

1 cup (250 mL) higher-fiber, moderate-carbohydrate cereal

¾ cup (175 mL) blueberry nonfat (0%) Greek yogurt

Lunch

Asparagus Swiss Quiche (page 234)

Spiced Sweet Potato Chips (page 135)

Dinner

6 oz (175 g) grilled wild trout fillet

1 cup (250 mL) Brussels sprouts roasted with 1 tsp (5 mL) olive oil and 1 tsp (5 mL) garlic

1 cup (250 mL) steamed yellow summer squash

Pear-Ginger Cobbler (page 274)

Snack

15 grams of carbs: 2 tbsp (30 mL) chopped pecans and 1 small banana

30 grams of carbs: ¼ cup (60 mL) chopped pecans and 1 banana

Thursday

Breakfast

Peanut Butter and Strawberry Sandwich:
2 slices multigrain toast sandwiched
with 4 tsp (20 mL) no-salt-added natural
peanut butter and 1/4 cup (60 mL) sliced
strawberries.

Lunch

Corn, Black Bean, and Edamame Salad
(page 106)

Turkey Wrap with Hummus: 4 oz (125 g)
cooked turkey breast, 1 tbsp (15 mL)
hummus, and 1/3 cup (75 mL) spinach
wrapped in a whole wheat tortilla.

Dinner

Italian Sausage and Linguine (page 175)

(Optional: pesto sauce for MUFAs)

Snack

15 grams of carbs: 1 higher-fiber, lower-
carb, higher-protein bar (~5 grams fiber,
15 grams carbs, 7 to 14 grams protein)

30 grams of carbs: 1 granola bar (~6 grams
fiber, 25 to 28 grams carbs, 10 to 14 grams
protein or healthy fats)

Friday

Breakfast

Lox Omelet: Combine 1 large egg and
2 large egg whites with 1/4 cup (60 mL)
chopped bell peppers, 1 oz (30 g) lox, and
1/2 oz (15 g) feta cheese, crumbled. Cook
in a skillet sprayed with canola oil spray.

1 toasted pita (whole wheat, oat bran, or
spelt)

1/2 cup (125 mL) orange slices

Lunch

MUFA Salad: Toss together 3 cups (750 mL)
mixed greens, 1/2 cucumber, chopped,
8 olives; 1/8 avocado, diced; and 1 tbsp
(15 mL) sunflower seeds. Top with 2 tbsp
(30 mL) olive oil balsamic vinaigrette.

1 oat bran pita

Dinner

Mom's Meat Loaf (page 154)

Roasted Vegetable Mac and Cheese
(page 229)

Snack

15 grams of carbs: Upside-Down Ambrosia:
1/2 cup (125 mL) low-sodium, low-fat (1%)
cottage cheese and 1 tsp (5 mL) shredded
coconut sprinkled over 3/4 cup (175 mL)
chopped fresh pineapple.

30 grams of carbs: Upside-Down Ambrosia:
1/2 cup (125 mL) low-sodium, low-fat
(1%) cottage cheese, 8 chopped nuts,
and 1 tsp (5 mL) shredded coconut
sprinkled over 1 1/4 cups (300 mL) chopped
fresh pineapple.

Saturday

Breakfast

Sunrise Oatmeal (page 83)

¾ cup (175 mL) plain nonfat (0%) Greek yogurt

Lunch

Citrus–Grilled Shrimp Salad (page 103)

Coconut-Lime Pudding Cake (page 267)

Dinner

4 oz (125 g) beef filet mignon or top sirloin, grilled

1 small sweet potato, baked

1½ cups (375 mL) chopped broccoli cooked in 1 tsp (5 mL) olive oil with 2 tsp (10 mL) minced garlic

Snack

15 grams of carbs: 2 tbsp (30 mL) guacamole and ½ toasted whole wheat pita

30 grams of carbs: ¼ cup (60 mL) hummus and 20 to 25 whole-grain pretzels (1½ oz/45 g total)

Sunday

Breakfast

Spiced Apple Pancakes (page 79)

½ cup (125 mL) low-fat (1%) cottage cheese

Lunch

Grilled Cheese: 2 slices sodium-free whole wheat bread sandwiched with 2 slices provolone cheese. Cook in a skillet coated with canola oil spray.

1 cup (250 mL) low-sodium, low-fat cream of tomato soup

Dinner

Beef Stroganoff (page 148)

2 cups (500 mL) spinach, steamed

1 Pistachio Kiss (page 277)

Snack

15 grams of carbs: 10 to 23 almonds and ½ large orange

30 grams of carbs: 15 to 25 almonds and 1 large orange

Monday

Breakfast

2 frozen whole-grain waffles, toasted (should equal 20 grams carbs, using magic carbs), spread with 1 tbsp (15 mL) no-salt-added natural peanut butter and 2 tsp (10 mL) agave nectar or honey and sprinkled with ground cinnamon

Lunch

Tuna Salad Wrap (page 117)

¼ cup (60 mL) hummus

½ apple

½ cup (125 mL) baby carrots

Dinner

Asian Lettuce Cups (page 176)

⅔ cup (150 mL) cooked wild rice

Snack

15 grams of carbs: ¾ cup (175 mL) fruit-flavored nonfat (0%) Greek yogurt

30 grams of carbs: ¾ cup (175 mL) plain nonfat (0%) Greek yogurt with 1 small apple and ½ cup (125 mL) berries

Tuesday

Breakfast

Tex-Mex Breakfast Pizza (page 75)

2 tbsp (30 mL) chopped avocado

Lunch

Almond Butter Sandwich: 2 slices sprouted wheat bread sandwiched with 4 tsp (20 mL) no-salt-added natural almond butter and ½ green apple, thinly sliced.

¾ cup (175 mL) plain nonfat (0%) Greek yogurt

Dinner

2 oz (60 g) sprouted grain pasta, cooked, combined with ½ cup (125 mL) tomato sauce (made with olive oil, no sugar); 4 oz (125 g) extra-lean (99% fat-free) ground turkey, browned; and ¼ cup (60 mL) diced carrot, cooked; and sprinkled with 8 olives, sliced

1½ cups (375 mL) steamed broccoli

Snack

15 grams of carbs: ¼ cup (60 mL) hummus with 1 cup (250 mL) cauliflower florets and ½ apple, sliced

30 grams of carbs: ¼ cup (60 mL) hummus with 1 cup (250 mL) carrots and ¾ whole wheat or spelt pita, toasted and cut into triangles

Wednesday

Breakfast

1 Raspberry-Lemon Muffin (page 81)

¾ cup (175 mL) fruit-flavored nonfat (0%) Greek yogurt

Lunch

Turkey Sandwich: 2 slices sprouted wheat bread sandwiched with 1 tbsp (15 mL) olive tapenade and 4 oz (125 g) cooked turkey breast.

1 cup (250 mL) watermelon chunks

Dinner

5 oz (150 g) wild salmon fillet, grilled or broiled

Chilled Cilantro–Soba Noodle Salad (page 108)

1½ cups (375 mL) steamed mixed vegetables: Tuscan kale, carrots, and broccoli

Snack

15 grams of carbs: 1 oz (30 g) hard cheese and 15 grapes

30 grams of carbs: 1½ oz (45 g) hard cheese, 15 grapes, and 1 slice sprouted wheat toast

Thursday

Breakfast

1 cup (250 mL) bran flakes topped with ¾ cup (175 mL) unsweetened almond milk, 2 tbsp (30 mL) slivered almonds, 1 tsp (5 mL) chia seeds, 1 tsp (5 mL) wheat germ, and 1 cup (250 mL) blueberries

Lunch

Tuna Sandwich: 4 oz (125 g) low-sodium chunk light tuna in water mixed with 1 tbsp (15 mL) canola oil mayonnaise on a toasted English muffin.

1 cup (250 mL) baby carrots and/or cauliflower florets

¼ cup (60 mL) hummus

Dinner

4 oz (125 g) herbed pork tenderloin, cooked

8 stalks asparagus, grilled

Barley Pilaf with Artichokes and Kale (page 254)

Chocolate Malt (page 285)

Snack

15 grams of carbs: Upside-Down Ambrosia: ½ cup (125 mL) low-sodium, low-fat (1%) cottage cheese and 1 tsp (5 mL) shredded coconut sprinkled over ¾ cup (175 mL) chopped fresh pineapple.

30 grams of carbs: Upside-Down Ambrosia: ½ cup (125 mL) low-sodium, low-fat (1%) cottage cheese, 8 chopped nuts, and 1 tsp (5 mL) shredded coconut sprinkled over 1¼ cups (300 mL) chopped fresh pineapple.

Friday

Breakfast

Grilled Steak and Eggs (page 68)

2 pieces whole-grain toast spread with
   2 tbsp (30 mL) mashed avocado

Lunch

Apple and Blue Cheese Salad (page 100)

Veggie Burger Wrap (page 233)

Dinner

5 oz (150 g) roasted chicken (no skin)

1 baked potato with 2 tsp (10 mL) olive oil
   (instead of butter)

1 cup (250 mL) steamed broccoli

1 Pistachio Kiss (page 277)

Snack

15 grams of carbs: ¾ cup (175 mL) plain
   nonfat (0%) Greek yogurt topped with
   1 crushed small cookie

30 grams of carbs: ¾ cup (175 mL) fruit-
   flavored nonfat (0%) Greek yogurt mixed
   with ½ cup (125 mL) berries and 1 tbsp
   (15 mL) wheat germ

Saturday

Breakfast

Salmon Breakfast Burrito (page 69)

1 cup (250 mL) mixed berries

2 tbsp (30 mL) chopped walnuts

Lunch

1½ servings Vegetable Pizza (page 240)

Dinner

Vegetable Stir-Fry: 3 cups (750 mL) mixed
   vegetables, ½ cup (125 mL) shelled
   edamame, 1 cup (250 mL) cubed firm
   tofu, and 2 tbsp (30 mL) low-sodium
   teriyaki sauce, stir-fried and served over
   ¾ cup (175 mL) whole wheat couscous
   and sprinkled with 1 tbsp (15 mL) toasted
   sesame seeds.

Snack

15 grams of carbs: 1 higher-fiber, lower-
   carb, higher-protein bar (~5 grams fiber,
   15 grams carbs, 7 to 14 grams protein)

30 grams of carbs: 1 granola bar (~6 grams
   fiber, 25 to 28 grams carbs, 10 to 14 grams
   protein or healthy fats)

APPENDIX B

Calories, Carbs, and Fiber of Common Foods

Use this list to design your own meals, modify your favorite comfort food recipes, and build your own meal plans to follow the Diabetes Comfort Food Diet. The serving size of each food is included, as well as the total calories, carbohydrates, and fiber, so that you can take the "magic carbs" effect into account.

Food	Serving	Calories	Carbs (g)	Fiber (g)
VEGETABLES				
Artichokes:				
Whole	1 medium	60	13	7
Hearts, marinated	4	35	7	1
Asparagus	4 spears	25	3	1
Bamboo shoots	½ cup (125 mL)	12	2	1
Beans, green	½ cup (125 mL)	41	5	2
Beans, yellow wax	½ cup (125 mL)	22	5	2
Beets	½ cup (125 mL)	24	6	1
Bok choy	½ cup (125 mL)	5	1	0.5
Broccoli:				
Raw	½ cup (125 mL)	12	2	1
Cooked	½ cup (125 mL)	26	5	3
Broccoli rabe	½ cup (125 mL)	4	1	0.5
Brussels sprouts	½ cup (125 mL)	32	6	3
Cabbage:				
Chinese	½ cup (125 mL)	8	1	1
Green	½ cup (125 mL)	17	3	2
Red	½ cup (125 mL)	14	3	1
Savoy	½ cup (125 mL)	20	4	2
Carrots:				
Whole, raw	1, 7½ inches (19 cm) long	30	7	2
Sliced	½ cup (125 mL)	43	6	2

Food	Serving	Calories	Carbs (g)	Fiber (g)
Cauliflower:				
Raw	½ cup (125 mL)	13	3	1
Steamed	½ cup (125 mL)	19	4	2
Celeriac	½ cup (125 mL)	5	1	21
Celery:				
Raw	1 rib	6	1	1
Cooked	½ cup (125 mL)	14	3	1
Chard	½ cup (125 mL)	14	3	2
Collards	½ cup (125 mL)	22	4	2
Corn:				
On the cob	1 ear	58	14	2
Cream-style	½ cup (125 mL)	92	23	2
Kernels	½ cup (125 mL)	66	15	2
Cucumber	½ cup (125 mL)	7	1	0.5
Dandelion greens	½ cup (125 mL)	17	3	2
Eggplant	½ cup (125 mL)	14	3	1
Endive	½ cup (125 mL)	4	1	1
Fennel:				
Raw	½ cup (125 mL)	13	3	1
Cooked	½ cup (125 mL)	12	3	1
Garlic cloves	1	3	1	0.5
Jerusalem artichoke	½ cup (125 mL)	57	13	1
Jicama, raw	½ cup (125 mL)	25	6	3
Kale	½ cup (125 mL)	18	4	1
Kohlrabi	½ cup (125 mL)	24	6	1
Lettuce:				
Boston/Bibb	½ cup (125 mL)	4	1	0.5
Iceberg	½ cup (125 mL)	4	1	0.5
Mixed greens	½ cup (125 mL)	5	1	0.5
Romaine	½ cup (125 mL)	4	1	0.5

Food	Serving	Calories	Carbs (g)	Fiber (g)
Mushrooms:				
Portobello	4 oz (125 g)	40	6	3
Shiitake, cooked	½ cup (125 mL)	40	10	2
Straw, canned	½ cup (125 mL)	29	4	2
Whole white, raw	½ cup (125 mL)	1	2	0.5
Mustard greens	½ cup (125 mL)	14	2	2
Okra	½ cup (125 mL)	23	5	2
Onions, raw	½ cup (125 mL)	32	8	1
Parsnips	½ cup (125 mL)	55	13	3
Peas, snow	½ cup (125 mL)	34	6	2
Peas	½ cup (125 mL)	55	10	3
Peppers:				
Green bell, raw	½ cup (125 mL)	15	4	1
Red bell, raw	½ cup (125 mL)	19	5	2
Potatoes:				
Baked	½ cup (125 mL)	78	15	2
Boiled	½ cup (125 mL)	83	16	1
Radicchio	½ cup (125 mL)	5	1	0.5
Radishes	10	9	2	1
Rutabaga	½ cup (125 mL)	33	7	2
Sauerkraut	½ cup (125 mL)	14	3	2
Scallions	½ cup (125 mL)	6	4	1
Shallots	½ cup (125 mL)	58	13	1
Sorrel, cooked	½ cup (125 mL)	0	2	1
Spinach:				
Frozen, steamed	½ cup (125 mL)	33	5	4
Raw	½ cup (125 mL)	3	0.5	0.5
Summer squash:				
Raw	½ cup (125 mL)	9	2	1
Cooked	½ cup (125 mL)	18	4	1

Food	Serving	Calories	Carbs (g)	Fiber (g)
Sweet potatoes:				
Baked	½ medium	51	12	2
Boiled	½ cup (125 mL)	76	18	3
Tomatoes:				
Cherry	10	31	7	2
Plum	1	11	2	1
Small field	1	16	4	1
Sun-dried, in oil	5 pieces	32	4	1
Turnip greens	½ cup (125 mL)	5	4	3
Turnips	½ cup (125 mL)	16	4	2
Water chestnuts	½ cup (125 mL)	40	10	2
Watercress	½ cup (125 mL)	2	0.5	0.5
Winter squash:				
Acorn, baked	½ cup (125 mL)	57	15	5
Butternut, baked	½ cup (125 mL)	41	11	3
Hubbard, boiled	½ cup (125 mL)	35	8	3
Pumpkin, boiled	½ cup (125 mL)	5	6	1
Pumpkin, canned	½ cup (125 mL)	58	10	4
Spaghetti, cooked	½ cup (125 mL)	21	5	1
Zucchini:				
Raw	½ cup (125 mL)	9	2	1
Steamed	½ cup (125 mL)	17	4	1
FRUIT				
Apple	½ medium	36	10	2
Applesauce:				
Sweetened	½ cup (125 mL)	97	25	2
Unsweetened	½ cup (125 mL)	52	14	2
Apricots:				
Canned in juice	3 halves	52	13	2
Dried	6 halves	50	13	2
Fresh	3 whole	50	12	2

Food	Serving	Calories	Carbs (g)	Fiber (g)
Avocado:				
Hass	½ cup (125 mL)	192	10	8
Florida	½ cup (125 mL)	138	9	6
Bananas	1 small	90	23	3
Blackberries:				
Fresh	½ cup (125 mL)	31	7	4
Frozen, sweetened	½ cup (125 mL)	93	25	2
Frozen, unsweetened	½ cup (125 mL)	48	12	4
Blueberries:				
Fresh	½ cup (125 mL)	41	11	2
Frozen, sweetened	½ cup (125 mL)	93	25	2
Frozen, unsweetened	½ cup (125 mL)	40	9	2
Boysenberries:				
Fresh	½ cup (125 mL)	31	7	4
Frozen, unsweetened	½ cup (125 mL)	33	8	4
Cherries:				
Sour, canned in water	½ cup (125 mL)	44	11	1
Sour, fresh	½ cup (125 mL)	26	6	1
Sweet, canned in water	½ cup (125 mL)	57	15	2
Sweet, fresh	½ cup (125 mL)	42	10	1
Cranberries, fresh	½ cup (125 mL)	23	6	2
Dates:				
Dry, chopped	½ cup (125 mL)	240	62	6
Fresh	3	68	18	2
Figs:				
Canned in water	½ cup (125 mL)	30	17	3
Fresh	1 small	30	8	1
Fruit cocktail:				
Canned in heavy syrup	½ cup (125 mL)	91	24	1
Canned in water	½ cup (125 mL)	38	10	1

Food	Serving	Calories	Carbs (g)	Fiber (g)
Gooseberries	½ cup (125 mL)	33	8	3
Grapefruit	½ cup (125 mL)	37	10	2
Grapes:				
Green seedless	½ cup (125 mL)	57	14	1
Red seedless	½ cup (125 mL)	57	14	1
Guava	½ cup (125 mL)	56	12	5
Kiwi	1	46	11	3
Kumquats	4	54	12	5
Loganberries	½ cup (125 mL)	37	9	4
Mango:				
Dried	1 piece	16	4	0.5
Fresh	½ cup (125 mL)	54	14	2
Melons:				
Cantaloupe, cubes	½ cup (125 mL)	31	7	1
Cantaloupe	¼ melon	97	12	1
Crenshaw melon, cubes	½ cup (125 mL)	22	5	1
Honeydew, cubes	½ cup (125 mL)	30	8	1
Watermelon, cubes	½ cup (125 mL)	25	6	0.5
Nectarine	1 medium	60	14	2
Oranges:				
Sections	½ cup (125 mL)	42	11	2
Fresh	1 medium	64	16	3
Papaya:				
Dried	1 piece	59	15	3
Fresh	½ small	59	15	3
Passion fruit	¼ cup (60 mL)	57	14	6
Peaches:				
Canned in water	½ cup (125 mL)	29	8	2
Dried	2 halves	62	16	2
Fresh	1 small	31	8	1

Food	Serving	Calories	Carbs (g)	Fiber (g)
Pears:				
Canned in water	½ cup (125 mL)	35	10	2
Fresh, Bartlett	1 whole	98	25	4
Fresh, Bosc	1 whole	82	21	3
Persimmon	½ cup (125 mL)	59	16	3
Pineapples:				
Canned in water	½ cup (125 mL)	39	10	1
Fresh, chunks	½ cup (125 mL)	38	10	1
Plums:				
Fresh	1 whole	16	4	0.5
Canned in water	½ cup (125 mL)	51	14	1
Pomegranate	¼ medium	26	7	0.5
Prunes:				
Fresh	4 whole	80	21	2
Canned in heavy syrup	½ cup (125 mL)	123	33	5
Raisins:				
Golden	1 tbsp (15 mL)	31	8	0.5
Seedless	1 tbsp (15 mL)	31	8	1
Raspberries:				
Fresh	½ cup (125 mL)	30	7	4
Frozen, sweetened	½ cup (125 mL)	129	33	6
Rhubarb	½ cup (125 mL)	13	3	1
Strawberries:				
Fresh	½ cup (125 mL)	24	6	1
Frozen, sweetened	½ cup (125 mL)	122	33	2
Frozen, unsweetened	½ cup (125 mL)	39	10	2
Tangerine	1 medium	37	9	1
BEANS (LEGUMES) AND TOFU				
Black beans	½ cup (125 mL)	114	20	8
Black-eyed peas	½ cup (125 mL)	111	20	5
Chickpeas	½ cup (125 mL)	147	25	7

Food	Serving	Calories	Carbs (g)	Fiber (g)
Fava beans	½ cup (125 mL)	94	17	5
Great Northern beans	½ cup (125 mL)	130	20	6
Kidney beans	½ cup (125 mL)	110	20	8
Lentils	½ cup (125 mL)	110	19	8
Lima beans	½ cup (125 mL)	115	21	7
Navy beans	½ cup (125 mL)	127	24	10
Pink beans	½ cup (125 mL)	126	24	5
Pinto beans	½ cup (125 mL)	117	22	7
Soybeans, green	½ cup (125 mL)	127	10	4
Soybeans, roasted	¼ cup (60 mL)	133	10	5
Split peas	½ cup (125 mL)	116	21	8
Tofu:				
Firm	½ cup (125 mL)	183	5	3
Regular	½ cup (125 mL)	94	2	0.5
Silken, firm	½ cup (125 mL)	70	3	0.5
Silken, soft	½ cup (125 mL)	62	3	0.5
GRAINS				
Barley, cooked	½ cup (125 mL)	97	22	3
Bran, oat	2 tbsp (30 mL)	10	3	1
Bran, wheat	2 tbsp (30 mL)	16	5	3
Bulgur, cooked	½ cup (125 mL)	76	17	4
Cornmeal	2 tbsp (30 mL)	63	13	1
Kasha, cooked	½ cup (125 mL)	77	17	2
Millet, cooked	½ cup (125 mL)	104	21	1
Noodles and pasta (cooked):				
Couscous	½ cup (125 mL)	88	18	1
Egg noodles	½ cup (125 mL)	106	20	1
Japanese somen	½ cup (125 mL)	115	24	1
Plain pasta	½ cup (125 mL)	88	20	3
Rice noodles	½ cup (125 mL)	96	22	1
Thai rice noodles	½ cup (125 mL)	105	25	1

Food	Serving	Calories	Carbs (g)	Fiber (g)
Noodles and pasta (cooked) (continued):				
Udon (brown rice noodles)	½ cup (125 mL)	103	20	2
Whole wheat pasta	½ cup (125 mL)	100	27	3
Pasta from other grains (cooked):				
Corn pasta	½ cup (125 mL)	100	23	3
Quinoa pasta	½ cup (125 mL)	90	18	1
Rice pasta	½ cup (125 mL)	105	22	0.5
Semolina pasta	½ cup (125 mL)	300	61	3
Spelt pasta	½ cup (125 mL)	95	20	3
Quinoa, dry	1¼ cups (300 mL)	159	29	3
Rice:				
Arborio, cooked	½ cup (125 mL)	121	27	1
Basmati, dry	¼ cup (60 mL)	160	36	0
Brown, cooked	½ cup (125 mL)	108	22	2
White, cooked	½ cup (125 mL)	121	27	0
Wild, cooked	½ cup (125 mL)	83	18	2
NUTS, NUT BUTTERS, SEEDS AND SEED BUTTERS				
Almond butter	2 tbsp (30 mL)	203	7	1
Almonds, slivered	2 tbsp (30 mL)	102	3	2
Almonds, whole	24	166	6	3
Brazil nuts	7	186	3	2
Cashew butter	2 tbsp (30 mL)	188	9	1
Cashews, whole	18	161	9	1
Chestnuts, roasted	6	138	30	3
Hazelnuts, whole	12	177	5	3
Macadamia nut butter	2 tbsp (30 mL)	230	5	0
Macadamia nuts, whole	12	203	4	2
Peanut butter	2 tbsp (30 mL)	190	6	2
Peanuts, whole	35	164	6	2
Pecans, whole	15	191	4	3
Pine nuts	2 tbsp (30 mL)	96	2	1

Food	Serving	Calories	Carbs (g)	Fiber (g)
Pistachio nuts, whole (no shells)	49	161	8	3
Pumpkin seeds, hulled	2 tbsp (30 mL)	36	4	0.5
Sesame seeds	2 tbsp (30 mL)	103	4	2
Sunflower seeds, hulled	3 tbsp (45 mL)	165	7	3
Sunflower seed butter	2 tbsp (30 mL)	200	7	4
Walnut halves	14	185	4	2
OILS				
Canola	1 tbsp (15 mL)	124	0	0
Coconut	1 tbsp (15 mL)	116	0	0
Corn	1 tbsp (15 mL)	120	0	0
Olive	1 tbsp (15 mL)	119	0	0
Peanut	1 tbsp (15 mL)	119	0	0
Safflower	1 tbsp (15 mL)	120	0	0
Sesame	1 tbsp (15 mL)	120	0	0
Soybean	1 tbsp (15 mL)	120	0	0
DAIRY PRODUCTS				
Cheese:				
Blue, hunk	1 oz (30 g)	100	1	0
Blue, crumbled	½ cup (125 mL)	238	2	0
Brie	1 oz (30 g)	95	0.5	0
Cheddar, sliced	1 oz (30 g)	114	0.5	0
Cheddar, shredded	½ cup (125 mL)	288	1	0
Colby, sliced	1 oz (30 g)	110	1	0
Colby, shredded	½ cup (125 mL)	223	1	0
Cottage cheese, 1%	1 cup (250 mL)	163	6	0
Cream cheese	1 tbsp (15 mL)	50	1	0
Feta, crumbled	½ cup (125 mL)	198	3	0
Fontina, sliced	1 oz (30 g)	109	0.5	0
Fontina, shredded	½ cup (125 mL)	210	1	0
Gouda, sliced	1 oz (30 g)	101	1	0
Monterey, sliced	1 oz (30 g)	104	0.5	0

Food	Serving	Calories	Carbs (g)	Fiber (g)
Cheese (continued):				
Mozzarella, sliced	1 oz (30 g)	85	1	0
Mozzarella, shredded	½ cup (125 mL)	168	1	0
Muenster, sliced	1 oz (30 g)	103	0.5	0
Parmesan, hard	1 oz (30 g)	111	1	0
Provolone, sliced	1 oz (30 g)	98	1	0
Ricotta, part-skim	½ cup (125 mL)	170	6	0
Sour cream, reduced fat	1 tbsp (15 mL)	22	1	0
Swiss, sliced	1 oz (30 g)	106	2	0
Swiss, shredded	½ cup (125 mL)	205	3	0
Cream:				
Half-and-half	1 tbsp (15 mL)	20	1	0
Heavy cream	1 tbsp (15 mL)	51	0.5	0
Nondairy creamer	1 tbsp (15 mL)	20	2	0
Whipped heavy cream	2 tbsp (30 mL)	52	0.5	0
Whipped light cream	1 tbsp (15 mL)	29	1	0
Milk:				
Buttermilk, 1%	1 cup (250 mL)	110	13	0
Condensed	2 tbsp (30 mL)	123	21	0
Evaporated, 2%	2 tbsp (30 mL)	29	4	0
Evaporated, whole	2 tbsp (30 mL)	42	3	0
Low-fat (1%)	1 cup (250 mL)	102	12	0
Nonfat (skim)	1 cup (250 mL)	83	12	0
Reduced-fat (2%)	1 cup (250 mL)	122	11	0
Whole (homogenized)	1 cup (250 mL)	146	13	0
FISH (COOKED UNLESS NOTED)				
Bass, sea	6 oz (175 g)	252	0	0
Bass, striped	6 oz (175 g)	211	0	0
Bluefish	6 oz (175 g)	270	0	0
Catfish	6 oz (175 g)	313	0	0
Cod	6 oz (175 g)	208	0	0

Food	Serving	Calories	Carbs (g)	Fiber (g)
Flounder	6 oz (175 g)	225	0	0
Haddock	6 oz (175 g)	208	0	0
Haddock, smoked	6 oz (175 g)	197	0	0
Halibut	6 oz (175 g)	238	0	0
Herring in sour cream	1¼ cups (300 mL)	120	8	0
Mackerel	6 oz (175 g)	377	0	0
Mahi-mahi	6 oz (175 g)	193	0	0
Perch	6 oz (175 g)	199	0	0
Salmon	6 oz (175 g)	291	0	0
Salmon, canned	6 oz (175 g)	245	0	0
Salmon, smoked	6 oz (175 g)	199	0	0
Sardines, canned in mustard	6 oz (175 g)	316	1	0
Sardines, canned in oil	6 oz (175 g)	354	0	0
Scrod	6 oz (175 g)	218	0	0
Shad	6 oz (175 g)	429	0	0
Swordfish	6 oz (175 g)	301	1	0
Trout	6 oz (175 g)	319	0	0
Tuna	6 oz (175 g)	259	0	0
Whitefish, canned in oil	6 oz (175 g)	316	0	0
Whitefish, canned in water	6 oz (175 g)	194	0	0
SHELLFISH				
Clams	6 oz (175 g)	157	6	0
Crab	6 oz (175 g)	174	0	0
Crawfish	6 oz (175 g)	122	0	0
Lobster	6 oz (175 g)	167	2	0
Mussels	6 oz (175 g)	293	13	0
Oysters	6 oz (175 g)	104	6	0
Scallops	6 oz (175 g)	228	5	0
Shrimp	6 oz (175 g)	241	2	0
Squid	6 oz (175 g)	36	6	0
Surimi	6 oz (175 g)	174	17	0

Food	Serving	Calories	Carbs (g)	Fiber (g)
CHICKEN				
Breast, skinless	6 oz (175 g)	243	0	0
Breast, with skin	6 oz (175 g)	335	0	0
Drumstick, skinless	6 oz (175 g)	348	0	0
Drumstick, with skin	6 oz (175 g)	367	0	0
Light and dark meat only	6 oz (175 g)	379	0	0
Thigh, boneless, with skin	6 oz (175 g)	420	0	0
OTHER POULTRY				
Duck breast, no skin	6 oz (175 g)	238	0	0
Turkey breast, no skin	6 oz (175 g)	230	0	0
Turkey jerky	½ oz (15 g)	50	1	0
PORK				
Center cut, bone-in	6 oz (175 g)	344	0	0
Loin chop, bone-in	6 oz (175 g)	549	0	0
Loin roast	6 oz (175 g)	422	0	0
Pancetta	1 oz (30 g)	200	0	0
Prosciutto	6 oz (175 g)	331	1	0
Sausage, Italian	2 oz (60 g)	192	2	0
Spare ribs	6 oz (175 g)	427	0	0
Tenderloin	6 oz (175 g)	279	0	0
BEEF				
Brisket	6 oz (175 g)	563	0	0
Calf liver	6 oz (175 g)	240	5	0
Chuck	6 oz (175 g)	498	0	0
Eye round	6 oz (175 g)	410	0	0
Ground chuck	6 oz (175 g)	562	0	0
Ground round	6 oz (175 g)	454	0	0
Jerky stick	5 oz (150 g)	39	1	0
Prime rib	6 oz (175 g)	667	0	0
Rib-eye roast	6 oz (175 g)	667	0	0
Roast	6 oz (175 g)	576	0	0

Food	Serving	Calories	Carbs (g)	Fiber (g)
Short ribs	6 oz (175 g)	660	0	0
Sirloin steak	6 oz (175 g)	344	0	0
Skirt steak	6 oz (175 g)	276	0	0
Tenderloin	6 oz (175 g)	258	0	0
Top loin	6 oz (175 g)	332	0	0
Top sirloin	6 oz (175 g)	342	0	0
Veal cutlet	6 oz (175 g)	483	0	0
LAMB				
Lamb chops	6 oz (175 g)	614	0	0
Leg of lamb	6 oz (175 g)	325	0	0
PROCESSED MEATS				
Bacon	3 pieces	81	0.5	0
Beef bologna	3 slices	129	2	0
Beef hot dog	1	194	3	0
Canadian bacon	3 pieces	129	1	0
Ham	6 oz (175 g)	174	2	0
Liverwurst	6 oz (175 g)	556	5	0
Pastrami	6 oz (175 g)	248	0	0
Pepperoni	5 pieces	128	1	0
Salami	3 slices	110	1	0
Sausage:				
Breakfast sausage	1 link	90	0	0
Chorizo	2 oz (60 g)	258	1	0
Kielbasa	2 oz (60 g)	126	2	0
Pork and beef sausage	1 link	51	0.5	0
Pork sausage	1 piece	82	0.5	0
Turkey sausage	2 oz (60 g)	97	0.5	0
SWEETENERS				
Natural sweeteners:				
Agave nectar	1 tsp (5 mL)	20	4	0
Brown rice syrup	1 tsp (5 mL)	20	5	0

Food	Serving	Calories	Carbs (g)	Fiber (g)
Natural sweeteners *(continued)*:				
Evaporated cane juice	1 tsp (5 mL)	15	4	0
Honey	1 tsp (5 mL)	21	6	0
Maple syrup, pure	1 tsp (5 mL)	22	5	0
Molasses	1 tsp (5 mL)	16	4	0
Sugar, brown	1 tsp (5 mL)	17	5	0
Sugar, raw (turbinado)	1 tsp (5 mL)	16	4	0
Sugar, white	1 tsp (5 mL)	16	4	0
Noncaloric sweeteners:				
Equal	1 packet	0	0	0
Splenda	1 packet	4	1	0
Stevia	1 packet	4	1	0
Sugar Twin	1 packet	0	0.5	0
Sweet'N Low	1 packet	0	<1	0
BEVERAGES				
Beer:				
Beer, light	12 oz (341 mL)	99	0–5	0
Beer, regular	12 oz (341 mL)	154	13	0
Wine/liquor:				
Hard liquor (all)	1 oz (30 mL)	82	0	0
Red wine	5 oz (150 mL)	88	3	0
Sherry, dry	3½ oz (100 mL)	72	1	0
Sherry, sweet	3½ oz (100 mL)	158	12	0
White wine	5 oz (150 mL)	85	3	0
Wine cooler	5 oz (150 mL)	49	6	0
Tea:				
Brewed (black, green, white)	1 cup (250 mL)	2	1	0
Herbal, brewed	1 cup (250 mL)	2	1	0
Soda:				
Cola	12 oz (341 mL)	153	36	0
Diet soda	12 oz (341 mL)	0	0	0

Food	Serving	Calories	Carbs (g)	Fiber (g)
Ginger ale	12 oz (341 mL)	124	32	0
Grape	12 oz (341 mL)	124	32	0
Lemon-lime	12 oz (341 mL)	147	38	0
Root beer	12 oz (341 mL)	152	39	0
Seltzer/club soda	12 oz (341 mL)	0	0	0
Fruit juice:				
Apple	½ cup (125 mL)	58	15	0.5
Apricot	½ cup (125 mL)	70	18	1
Cranberry juice cocktail	½ cup (125 mL)	72	18	0.5
Grape	½ cup (125 mL)	77	19	0.5
Grapefruit, sweetened	½ cup (125 mL)	58	14	0.5
Grapefruit, unsweetened	½ cup (125 mL)	47	11	0.5
Guava	½ cup (125 mL)	74	19	1
Lemon	2 tbsp (30 mL)	6	2	0.5
Lime	2 tbsp (30 mL)	6	2	0.5
Mango	½ cup (125 mL)	73	19	1
Orange	½ cup (125 mL)	56	13	0.5
Passion fruit	½ cup (125 mL)	63	17	0.5
Peach	½ cup (125 mL)	67	17	1
Pear	½ cup (125 mL)	66	16	0.5
Pineapple	½ cup (125 mL)	66	16	0.5
Prune	½ cup (125 mL)	91	22	1
Vegetable juice:				
Carrot	½ cup (125 mL)	47	11	1
Tomato	½ cup (125 mL)	21	5	1
Vegetable juice cocktail	½ cup (125 mL)	23	6	1

References

American Diabetes Association. Nutrition recommendations and interventions for diabetes: A position statement of the American Diabetes Association. *Diabetes Care*, 2008 Jan; 31 Suppl 1: S61–78.

American Diabetes Association. Standards of medical care in diabetes — 2012. *Diabetes Care*, 2012 Jan; 35 Suppl 1: S11–S63.

American Diabetes Association and the American Dietetic Association. *Exchange Lists for Meal Planning*. Alexandria, VA: American Diabetes Association, 1995.

Anderson JW, Spencer DB, Hamilton CC, et al. Oat-bran cereal lowers serum total and LDL cholesterol in hypercholesterolemic men. *American Journal of Clinical Nutrition*, 1990 September; 52 (3): 495–99.

Bozzetto L, De Natale C, Di Capua L, et al. The association of hs-CRP with fasting and postprandial plasma lipids in patients with type 2 diabetes is disrupted by dietary monounsaturated fatty acids. *Acta Diabetologica*, 2013 April; 50 (2): 273–76.

Bozzetto L, Prinster A, Annuzzi G, et al. Liver fat is reduced by an isoenergetic MUFA diet in a controlled randomized study in type 2 diabetic patients. *Diabetes Care*, 2012 July; 35 (7): 1429–35.

Brand-Miller J, Wolever T, Foster-Powell K, Colagiuri S. *The New Glucose Revolution: The Authoritative Guide to the Glycemic Index — The Dietary Solution for Lifelong Health*. New York, NY: Marlowe & Company, 2007.

Breneman CB, Tucker L. Dietary fibre consumption and insulin resistance — The role of body fat and physical activity. *British Journal of Nutrition*, 2013 July 28; 110 (2): 375–83.

Brostow DP, Odegaard AO, Koh WP, et al. Omega-3 fatty acids and incident type 2 diabetes: The Singapore Chinese health study. *American Journal of Clinical Nutrition*, 2011 August; 94 (2): 520–26.

Chandalia M, Garg A, Lutjohann D, et al. Beneficial effects of high dietary fiber intake in patients with type 2 diabetes mellitus. *New England Journal of Medicine*, 2000 May 11; 342 (19): 1392–98.

Colberg S. Increasing insulin sensitivity. *Diabetes Self-Management*. December 3, 2008. Available at http://www.diabetesselfmanagement.com/ articles/insulin/increasing_insulin_sensitivity (accessed December 21, 2012).

Colberg SR, Sigal RJ, Fernhall B, et al. Exercise and type 2 diabetes: The American College of Sports Medicine and the American Diabetes Association: Joint position statement executive summary. *Diabetes Care*, 2010 December; 33 (12): 2692–96.

Diabetes Prevention Program's Lifestyle Change Program, Appendix A: Session 4 or 2: Be a fat detective, page 6. Available at http://www.bsc. gwu.edu/dpp/lifestyle/dpp_dcor.html.

Djoussé L, Biggs ML, Lemaitre RN, et al. Plasma omega-3 fatty acids and incident diabetes in older adults. *American Journal of Clinical Nutrition*, 2011 August; 94 (2): 527–33.

Duncan GE, Perri MG, Theriaque DW, et al. Exercise training, without weight loss, increases insulin sensitivity and postheparin plasma lipase activity in previously sedentary adults. *Diabetes Care*, 2003 March; 26 (3): 557–62.

Fowler SP, Williams K, Resendez RG, et al. Fueling the obesity epidemic? Artificially sweetened beverage use and long-term weight gain. *Obesity* (Silver Spring, MD), 2008 August; 16 (8): 1894–1900.

Franz MJ, Powers MA, Leontos C, et al. The evidence for medical nutrition therapy for type 1 and type 2 diabetes in adults. *Journal of the American Dietetic Association*, 2010 December; 110 (12): 1852–89.

Greene GW, Rossi SR, Rossi JS, et al. Dietary applications of the stages of change model. *Journal of the American Dietetic Association*, 1999 June; 99 (6): 673–78.

Haas L, Maryniuk M, Beck J, et al. National standards for diabetes self-management education and support. *Diabetes Educator*, 2012 September–October; 38 (5): 619–29.

Hu FB, Stampfer MJ, Manson JE, et al. Dietary fat intake and the risk of coronary heart disease in women. *New England Journal of Medicine*, 1997 November 20; 337 (21): 1491–99.

Kiehm TG, Anderson JW, Ward K. Beneficial effects of a high carbohydrate, high fiber diet on hyperglycemic diabetic men. *American Journal of Clinical Nutrition*, 1976 August; 29 (8): 895–99.

Larson R. *The American Dietetic Association's Complete Food and Nutrition Guide*. New York, NY: American Dietetic Association, 1998: 160–68.

Magistrelli A, Chezem J. Effect of ground cinnamon on postprandial blood glucose concentration in normal-weight and obese adults. *Journal of the Academy of Nutrition and Dietetics*, 2012 November; 112 (11): 1806–9.

Margens S. *The Wellness Encyclopedia of Food and Nutrition*. New York, NY: Health Letter Association, 1992: 271–82.

May AM, Romaguera D, Travier N, et al. Combined impact of lifestyle factors on prospective change in body weight and waist circumference in participants of the EPIC-PANACEA study. *PLoS One*, 2012; 7 (11): e50712.

Melanson KJ, Zukley L, Lowndes J, et al. Effects of high-fructose corn syrup and sucrose consumption on circulating glucose, insulin, leptin, and ghrelin and on appetite in normal-weight women. *Nutrition*, 2007 February; 23 (2): 103–12.

Meyer KA, Kushi LH, Jacobs DR Jr, et al. Carbohydrates, dietary fiber, and incident type 2 diabetes in older women. *American Journal of Clinical Nutrition*, 2000 April; 71 (4): 921–30.

Montonen J, Knekt P, Järvinen R, et al. Whole-grain and fiber intake and the incidence of type 2 diabetes. *American Journal of Clinical Nutrition*, 2003 March; 77 (3): 622–29.

National Diabetes Information Clearinghouse (NDIC). Insulin resistance and prediabetes. Available at http://diabetes.niddk.nih.gov/dm/pubs/insulinresistance/index.aspx#what (accessed January 21, 2013).

National Diabetes Information Clearinghouse. Diabetes Prevention Program (DPP). Available at http:/diabetes.niddk.nih.gov/dm/pubs/preventionprogram (updated November 6, 2012).

National Institutes of Health. Third report of the National Cholesterol Education Program (NECP) expert panel on Detection, Evaluation, and Treatment of High Blood Cholesterol in Adults (Adult Treatment Panel III). Bethesda, MD: National Institutes of Health, 2001. NIH Publication 01–3670.

National Pesticide Information Center. Pesticides and pregnancy. October 8, 2012. Available at http://npic.orst.edu/health/preg.html (accessed January 21, 2013).

Ng SW, Slining MM, Popkin BM. Use of caloric and noncaloric sweeteners in US consumer packaged foods, 2005–2009. *Journal of the Academy of Nutrition and Dietetics*, 2012 November; 112 (11): 1828–34.

Rico C. Is agave nectar safe for people with diabetes? American Diabetes Association. Available at http://www.diabetes.org/living-with-diabetes/treatment-and-care/ask-the-expert/ask-the-dietitian/archives/is-agave-nectar-safe-for.html (accessed December 28, 2012).

Sinha R, Kulldorff M, Chow WH, et al. Dietary intake of heterocyclic amines, meat-derived mutagenic activity, and risk of colorectal adenomas. *Cancer Epidemiology, Biomarkers & Prevention*, 2001 May; 10 (5): 559–62.

United States Environmental Protection Agency. What should I know about eating fish that might contain mercury or other pollutants? Where can I find information about eating fish caught in a particular body of water? November 22, 2012. Available at http://publicaccess.supportportal.com/link/portal/23002/23012/Article/24361/What-should-I-know-about-eating-fish-that-might-contain-mercury-or-other-pollutants-Where-can-I-find-information-about-eating-fish-caught-in-a-particular-body-of-water (accessed January 21, 2013).

Van Ittersum K, Wansink B. Plate size and color suggestibility: The Delboeuf illusion's bias on serving and eating behavior. *Journal of Consumer Research*, 2012 August; 39 (2): 215–28.

Yang Q. Gain weight by "going diet"? Artificial sweeteners and the neurobiology of sugar cravings: Neuroscience 2010. *Yale Journal of Biology and Medicine*, 2010 June; 83 (2): 101–8.

Library and Archives Canada Cataloguing in Publication

Cipullo, Laura, author
   The diabetes comfort food diet / Laura Cipullo, RD, CDE, and the editors of Prevention.

Includes index.
Previously published: Emmaus, Pennsylvania : Rodale, ©2013.
ISBN 978-0-7788-0518-2 (paperback)

   1. Diabetes—Diet therapy—Recipes. 2. Weight loss. 3. Comfort food. 4. Cookbooks. I. Title.

RC662.C58 2015   641.5'6314   C2015-903332-2

Index

Note: SS = Smart Start tips

A

acanthosis nigricans, 11
acesulfame K, 27
African Stew, 236
ALA (alpha-linolenic acid), 36, 37
alcohol, 17, 32, 54, 308
almonds. *See also* milks, nondairy;
    nut butters
    Almond Rice Pudding, 282
    Belgian Waffles, 80
    Cheese and Vegetable Bake, 249
    Chocolate-Almond Cake, 263
    Double Oat–Blueberry Crisp, 273
    Frozen Mocha Parfaits, 284
    Fruit and Nut Clusters, 276
    Green Bean Casserole, 245
    Hearty Fruit and Nut Granola, 84
    Rich Chocolate Cream Pie, 272
A1C (hemoglobin A1C) test, 12,
    59, 63
apples and applesauce, 29
    Apple, Sausage and Potato
      Casserole, 71
    Apple and Blue Cheese Salad, 100
    Apple–Sweet Potato Soup, 99
    Bacon and Apple Grilled Cheese,
      116
    Fruit and Nut Clusters, 276
    Maple-Walnut Cake, 266
    Oatmeal-Apple Cookies, 280
    Pork Chops with Apple Salad, 167
    Spiced Apple Pancakes, 79
    Stuffed Turkey Tenderloin, 199
    Sweet Pork Tagine, 170
artichokes
    Barley Pilaf with Artichokes and
      Kale, 254
    Creamed Spinach and Artichokes,
      246
    Guilt-Free Spinach-Artichoke
      Dip, 140
    Salmon Pasta Casserole, 217
    Steak with Mushroom Sauce and
      Roasted Artichokes, 144
Asian Fish Packets, 214
Asian Lettuce Cups, 176
asparagus
    Asparagus Swiss Quiche, 234
    Baked Pasta and Vegetables, 231
    Beef Stroganoff, 148
    Stir-Fried Asparagus with Ginger,
      Sesame, and Soy, 244
    Vegetable Sauté with Quinoa, 227

aspartame, 27
avocado
    Bean Enchiladas, 238
    Cobb Salad–Style Buffalo Dogs,
      161
    Fiesta Turkey Soup, 90
    Fresh Guacamole with
      Vegetables, 138
    Grilled Pork Tacos with Mango
      Salsa (SS), 168
    Salmon with Avocado Salsa, 218
    Shrimp Tacos, 222
    Tex-Mex Breakfast Pizza (SS), 75
    Tex-Mex Pasta and Beans, 260
    Tuna Steaks on Greens, 221
    Turkey and Bean Quesadillas, 205
    Vegetable Sauté with Quinoa, 227
    Veggie Burger Wraps, 233

B

bacon, 307
    Bacon and Apple Grilled Cheese,
      116
    Bacon-Wrapped Chicken, 193
    Cobb Salad–Style Buffalo Dogs,
      161
    Manhattan Clam Chowder, 95
    Stuffed Potato Skins, 134
    Warm German Potato Salad, 105
bananas, 29
    Chocolate-Banana-Stuffed French
      Toast, 78
    Sundae Breakfast Smoothie, 86
barley
    Barley Pilaf with Artichokes and
      Kale, 254
    Beef Barley Soup, 92
    Mushroom-Barley Stuffing, 253
    Salmon-Barley Bake, 219
beans, 27, 40, 300–301. *See also*
    beans, green; edamame
    African Stew, 236
    Bean Enchiladas, 238
    Black Bean Burgers, 239
    Buffalo Chicken Quesadillas, 132
    Caramelized Onion and Fennel
      Pizza, 242
    Chicken and Sausage Jambalaya,
      184
    Chicken with Pinto Beans Skillet,
      195
    Corn, Black Bean, and Edamame
      Salad, 106
    Fiesta Turkey Soup, 90
    Fire-Roasted Chili, 237

    Grand Slam Nachos, 137
    Kicked-Up Tomato Soup, 97
    Layered Chicken and Bean
      Enchiladas, 194
    Mexican Dip, 139
    Rich Brownies, 278
    Scallops with Beans and Arugula,
      224
    Steak Burrito Bowl, 151
    Tex-Mex Pasta and Beans, 260
    Turkey and Bean Quesadillas, 205
    Wild Mushroom and White Bean
      Risotto, 226
beans, green
    Green Bean Casserole, 245
    Sweet Potato and Turkey
      Shepherd's Pie, 200
beef, 306–7
    Beef Barley Soup, 92
    Beef Goulash, 159
    Beef Ragù over Polenta, 160
    Beef Stroganoff, 148
    Chinese Beef and Vegetables, 150
    Country-Fried Steak, 142
    Grilled Steak and Eggs, 68
    Ground Bison with Spaghetti
      Squash, 162
    Meat Loaf, Mom's, 154
    Philly Cheese Steaks, 110
    Roast Beef Rolls, 117
    Salisbury Steak, 155
    Shepherd's Pie, 152
    Sizzlin' Beef Fajitas, 147
    Slow-Cooker Pot Roast,
      Traditional, 146
    Spaghetti and Meatballs, Go-To,
      158
    Steak Burrito Bowl, 151
    Steak with Mushroom Sauce and
      Roasted Artichokes, 144
    Un-Stuffed Peppers, 156
    Zesty Italian Cheeseburgers, 157
beer, 32, 308
Belgian Waffles, 80
berries, 29
    Belgian Waffles, 80
    Double Oat–Blueberry Crisp, 273
    Good Morning "Grits," 72
    Hearty Fruit and Nut Granola, 84
    Lemon-Raspberry Cheesecake,
      264
    PB&J Stuffed French Toast, 77
    Peach-Blueberry Yogurt Parfait,
      85
    Raspberry-Lemon Muffins, 81

berries *(continued)*
  Spinach-Cranberry Salad, 101
  Sunrise Oatmeal, 83
  Sweet Potato and Turkey
    Shepherd's Pie, 200
  Three-Berry Pie, 270
  Turkey Meat Loaf with Cranberry
    Chutney, 202
beverages, 59, 86–87, 285, 308–9.
    See also beer; wine
  alcoholic, 17, 32, 54, 308
  diet soda, 16
  glasses for, 44, 53, 59
  juices, 29, 309
  sugar-sweetened, 17
Bison, Ground, with Spaghetti
    Squash, 162
blood pressure, 11
blood sugar, 9–10. *See also* glucose
  exercise and, 18
  fiber and, 33–34
  foods and, 49, 51
  monitoring, 17, 52, 58, 62
  nutrients and, 15, 16
  physical effects, 49, 51, 61
blood tests, 12, 59, 63
BMI (body mass index), 17–18
bok choy
  Asian Fish Packets, 214
  Vegetable Lo Mein, 232
breads, 24–26
breads (as ingredient). *See also*
    burgers; sandwiches; tortillas
  Broccoli-Cheddar Strata, 235
  Chocolate-Banana-Stuffed
    French Toast, 78
  Papaya-Tomato Bruschetta, 120
  PB&J Stuffed French Toast, 77
  Southern Pecan Bread Pudding,
    275
breakfasts, 59, 62, 67–87
broccoli
  Broccoli-Cheddar Strata, 235
  Broccoli-Chicken Casserole, 198
  Broccoli Penne, 230
  Broccoli-Stuffed Chicken
    Roulade, 192
  Broccoli-Walnut Farfalle Toss,
    257
  Cheesy Vegetable Chowder, 94
  Chicken with Pinto Beans Skillet,
    195
  Chinese Beef and Vegetables, 150
  Italian Sausage and Linguine,
    175
  Pork and Broccoli Stir-Fry, 171
  Stuffed Potato Skins, 134
  Sweet and Sour Shrimp, 223
  Tuna Tetrazzini, 220
Buffalo Chicken Quesadillas, 132

Buffalo Grilled Cheese Sandwiches,
    115
burgers, 157, 165, 203, 239, 307
buttermilk
  Chicken and Dumplings, 186
  Chocolate Layer Cake with
    Maple Frosting, 268
  Fried Chicken, 196
  Green Bean Casserole, 245
  Lox-Cheddar Scones, 82

C

cabbage
  Fish Po' Boy with Cajun Slaw,
    212
  Minestrone, 91
  Open-Faced Asian Chicken
    Sandwiches, 113
  Slow-Cooker Pork Barbecue,
    166
  Tricolor Slaw and Potato Salad,
    104
  Vegetable-Tofu Wontons, 126
calcium, 38
canola oil, 41
carbohydrates, 9, 11, 15, 16. *See also*
    sugars
  in common foods, 294–309
  curbing, 22–32, 53, 58, 63
  in fat-free foods, 28
  intake of, 15, 17, 62
  magic, 32–33, 62
  mixing, 41
  net, 33
carrots. *See also* vegetables (mixed)
  Beef Ragù over Polenta, 160
  Garlic Oven Fries, 247
  Salmon-Barley Bake, 219
  Sweet Pork Tagine, 170
cauliflower
  Creamy Mashed Potatoes, 250
  Roasted Vegetable Mac and
    Cheese, 229
  Shepherd's Pie, 152
celery. *See also* vegetables (mixed)
  Barbecue Shrimp Wraps, 118
  Buffalo Grilled Cheese
    Sandwiches, 115
  Creamed Sweet Corn, 247
  Mushroom-Barley Stuffing, 253
  Tuna Salad Wraps, 117
  Warm German Potato Salad, 105
cellulose, 11, 25
cereals, 24, 34
cereals (as ingredient)
  Chicken and Waffles, 179
  Crispy Oat Squares, 281
  Parmesan Chicken Fingers, 191
  Peach-Blueberry Yogurt Parfait,
    85

change, 55, 58–60, 61
cheese, 38, 41, 303–4. *See also* pasta;
    pizzas; *specific cheeses (below)*
  Apple and Blue Cheese Salad,
    100
  Asparagus Swiss Quiche, 234
  Baked Risotto, 256
  Bean Enchiladas, 238
  Black Bean Burgers, 239
  Buffalo Chicken Quesadillas, 132
  Buffalo Grilled Cheese
    Sandwiches, 115
  Cheese and Vegetable Bake, 249
  Cheesy Vegetable Chowder, 94
  Cobb Salad–Style Buffalo Dogs,
    161
  Guilt-Free Spinach-Artichoke
    Dip, 140
  Mexican Dip, 139
  Monte Cristos, 112
  Parmesan Chicken Fingers, 191
  Roasted Vegetable Mac and
    Cheese, 229
  Scalloped Red Potatoes, 251
  Sweet Turkey Paninis, 114
  Zesty Italian Cheeseburgers, 157
cheese, Cheddar. *See also* cheese
  Bacon and Apple Grilled Cheese,
    116
  Broccoli-Cheddar Strata, 235
  Broccoli-Chicken Casserole, 198
  Cheesy Scrambled Eggs and
    Ham, 70
  Chili Cheese Fries, 248
  Grand Slam Nachos, 137
  Layered Chicken and Bean
    Enchiladas, 194
  Lox-Cheddar Scones, 82
  Philly Cheese Steaks, 110
  Turkey and Bean Quesadillas,
    205
  Turkey Cheeseburgers, 203
cheese, cottage/cream/ricotta, 27.
    See also cheese
  Chocolate Cake Smoothie, 86
  Creamed Spinach and Artichokes,
    246
  Lemon-Raspberry Cheesecake,
    264
chia seeds. *See also* seeds
  Almond Rice Pudding, 282
  Belgian Waffles, 80
  Creamy Pumpkin Mousse, 283
  Mushroom-Barley Stuffing, 253
  Oatmeal-Apple Cookies, 280
  Raspberry-Lemon Muffins, 81
  Scalloped Red Potatoes, 251
  Spiced Apple Pancakes, 79
chicken, 305–6
  Bacon-Wrapped Chicken, 193

Baked Chicken with Mustard Sauce, 187
Broccoli-Chicken Casserole, 198
Broccoli-Stuffed Chicken Roulade, 192
Buffalo Chicken Quesadillas, 132
Chicken and Dumplings, 186
Chicken and Sausage Jambalaya, 184
Chicken and Waffles, 179
Chicken Cacciatore, 180
Chicken-Mushroom Bake, 181
Chicken Pad Thai, 197
Chicken Paprikash, 190
Chicken Piccata, 178
Chicken Pot Pie, 185
Chicken with Pinto Beans Skillet, 195
Fried Chicken, 196
Hawaiian Chicken Skewers, 121
Herb-Roasted Chicken Breasts with Vegetables, 188
Kickin' Chicken "Wings," 123
Layered Chicken and Bean Enchiladas, 194
Mediterranean Chicken Pinwheels, 122
Open-Faced Asian Chicken Sandwiches, 113
Orange-Sesame Chicken, 189
Parmesan Chicken Fingers, 191
Quick, Creamy Chicken Lasagna, 182
Scalloped Red Potatoes (SS), 251
chickpeas
    Couscous and Chickpea Salad, 107
    Minestrone, 91
    Trout Paella, 216
Chili Cheese Fries, 248
Chilled Cilantro–Soba Noodle Salad, 108
Chinese Beef and Vegetables, 150
chocolate
    Chocolate-Almond Cake, 263
    Chocolate-Banana-Stuffed French Toast, 78
    Chocolate Layer Cake with Maple Frosting, 268
    Chocolate Malt, 285
    Creamy Pumpkin Mousse, 283
    Frozen Mocha Parfaits, 284
    Rich Brownies, 278
    Rich Chocolate Cream Pie, 272
cholesterol, 11, 18, 19, 33, 37–38
cinnamon, 30
Citrus–Grilled Shrimp Salad, 103
Cobb Salad–Style Buffalo Dogs, 161
Coconut-Lime Pudding Cake, 267

coffee
    Chocolate Cake Smoothie, 86
    Chocolate Layer Cake with Maple Frosting, 268
    Frozen Mocha Parfaits, 284
condiments, 40
corn
    Cheesy Vegetable Chowder, 94
    Corn, Black Bean, and Edamame Salad, 106
    Cornmeal Catfish with Black-Eyed Peas, 215
    Creamed Sweet Corn, 247
    Fiesta Turkey Soup, 90
    Fire-Roasted Chili, 237
    Grand Slam Nachos, 137
    Mexican Dip, 139
    South-of-the-Border Shrimp Soup, 96
    Sweet Potato and Turkey Shepherd's Pie, 200
    Tricolor Slaw and Potato Salad, 104
    Turkey and Bean Quesadillas, 205
cornmeal
    Beef Ragù over Polenta, 160
    Cornmeal Catfish with Black-Eyed Peas, 215
    Lox-Cheddar Scones, 82
Country-Fried Steak, 142
Country-Style Hash Browns, 73
Couscous and Chickpea Salad, 107
cucumber
    Lemon-Rosemary Lamb Chops, 164
    Open-Faced Asian Chicken Sandwiches, 113
    Tuna Steaks on Greens, 221

D

dairy and alternatives, 27–28, 38, 40, 303–4. See also cheese; milk; yogurt
desserts, 29, 261–85
dextrin, 11
DHA (docosahexaenoic acid), 36, 37
diabetes, 10–11, 14, 49
    gestational, 11, 20
    reactions to diagnosis, 8, 9, 13, 49
Diabetes Comfort Food Diet, 9, 54–55
    food logging, 52, 56–57
    getting support, 50–51, 52, 55
    reinforcing, 62–63
Diabetes Prevention Program (DPP), 14–15
dining out, 55, 59, 62, 65
disaccharides, 11
dishware, 41, 44, 53, 59

E

eating, 21. See also foods; meal planning
    planning, 17, 62
    quantities, 17, 24, 28
    reasons for, 20, 44, 45, 59
    in restaurants, 55, 59, 62, 65
    timing, 17, 45
edamame
    Chilled Cilantro–Soba Noodle Salad, 108
    Corn, Black Bean, and Edamame Salad, 106
    Fire-Roasted Chili, 237
eggs, 39–41
    Apple, Sausage and Potato Casserole, 71
    Asparagus Swiss Quiche, 234
    Broccoli-Cheddar Strata, 235
    Cheesy Scrambled Eggs and Ham, 70
    Grilled Steak and Eggs, 68
    Pistachio Kisses, 277
    Southern Pecan Bread Pudding, 275
    Tex-Mex Breakfast Pizza, 75
EPA (eicosapentaenoic acid), 36, 37
Equal, 27, 308
erythritol, 27, 32
exercise, 10, 18–19, 38, 54, 65
    continuing, 62, 63
    enjoying, 20, 51
    frequency of, 17, 59
    starting up, 51, 52

F

fat (body), 18
fats (dietary), 15
    healthy, 22, 35–38, 53, 59, 63
    intake of, 17, 62
    unhealthy, 27, 37–38
fiber (dietary), 17, 65
    added, 24, 25
    in common foods, 294–309
    filling up on, 22, 32–35, 53, 59, 63
Fiesta Turkey Soup, 90
Fig Bars, 279
Fire-Roasted Chili, 237
fish, 36, 62, 304–5. See also salmon; seafood; tuna
    Asian Fish Packets, 214
    Cornmeal Catfish with Black-Eyed Peas, 215
    Fish and Chips, 213
    Fish Po' Boy with Cajun Slaw, 212
    Trout Paella, 216
flaxseeds (ground). See also seeds
    Asparagus Swiss Quiche, 234
    Baked Pasta and Vegetables, 231

flaxseeds (*continued*)
  Black Bean Burgers, 239
  Chocolate-Almond Cake, 263
  Fig Bars, 279
  Lemon-Raspberry Cheesecake, 264
  Maple-Walnut Cake, 266
  Meat Loaf, Mom's, 154
  Orange-Pecan Tea Bread, 262
  Parmesan Chicken Fingers, 191
  Peach-Blueberry Yogurt Parfait, 85
  Salisbury Steak, 155
  Salmon Pasta Casserole, 217
  Spaghetti and Meatballs, Go-To, 158
  Turkey Meatballs and Zucchini Pasta, 206
  Turkey Swedish Meatballs, 209
foods. *See also* eating; meal planning
  and blood sugar, 49, 51
  calorie and carb content, 294–309
  combining, 65
  cooking, 41, 54
  fat content, 27–28
  fiber content, 294–309
  logging, 52, 56–57, 59, 61
  organic, 30
  pantry staples, 39–41, 53, 59
  plating, 41–44, 53, 59
  shopping for, 36, 53, 62
FPG (fasting plasma glucose) test, 12
Frozen Mocha Parfaits, 284
fructose, 11
fruit, dried
  Fruit and Nut Clusters, 276
  Hearty Fruit and Nut Granola, 84
  Sweet Pork Tagine, 170
  Sweet Potato and Turkey Shepherd's Pie, 200
fruit, fresh, 28–29, 30, 31, 40, 297–300. *See also* berries; *specific fruits*
  Hawaiian Chicken Skewers, 121
  Papaya-Tomato Bruschetta, 120
  Peach-Blueberry Yogurt Parfait, 85
  Sundae Breakfast Smoothie, 86
  Tuna Salad Wraps, 117

G

galactose, 11
garlic
  Barbecue Shrimp Wraps, 118
  Garlic Oven Fries, 247
  Italian Sausage and Linguine, 175
  Shrimp Scampi Linguine, 223
  Sizzlin' Beef Fajitas, 147
  South-of-the-Border Shrimp Soup, 96

ginger
  Asian Fish Packets, 214
  Chinese Beef and Vegetables, 150
  Hawaiian Chicken Skewers, 121
  Pear-Ginger Cobbler, 274
  Pork and Broccoli Stir-Fry, 171
  Stir-Fried Asparagus with Ginger, Sesame, and Soy, 244
  Sweet Pork Tagine, 170
  Vegetable-Tofu Wontons, 126
glassware, 44, 53, 59
glucometer, 52, 58, 62
glucose, 9, 11. *See also* blood sugar
glycogen, 9, 11
Good Morning "Grits," 72
Go-To Spaghetti and Meatballs, 158
grains, 24–26, 40, 301–2. *See also* barley; oats; quinoa
  Hearty Fruit and Nut Granola, 84
Grand Slam Nachos, 137
Greek Meatballs, 124
Green Bean Casserole, 245
greens, bitter, 39. *See also* spinach
  Baked Penne with Turkey, 208
  Barley Pilaf with Artichokes and Kale, 254
  Bean Enchiladas, 238
  Cheese and Vegetable Bake, 249
  Trout Paella, 216
  Turkey and Orzo Stuffed Peppers, 204
greens, salad. *See also* lettuce
  Fish Po' Boy with Cajun Slaw, 212
  Scallops with Beans and Arugula, 224
  Sweet Turkey Paninis, 114
  Tuna Salad Wraps, 117
  Tuna Steaks on Greens, 221
Ground Bison with Spaghetti Squash, 162
Guilt-Free Spinach-Artichoke Dip, 140

H

ham, 307
  Cheesy Scrambled Eggs and Ham, 70
  Creamy Potato, Lentil, and Ham Chowder, 93
  Monte Cristos, 112
Hawaiian Chicken Skewers, 121
Hearty Fruit and Nut Granola, 84
Herb-Roasted Chicken Breasts with Vegetables, 188
herbs, 40
high blood pressure, 11
high-fructose corn syrup, 27, 30
Homemade Breakfast Sausage, 76

honey, 307
  Crispy Oat Squares, 281
  Fig Bars, 279
  Rich Brownies, 278
hot dogs. *See* wieners
hunger/fullness scale, 44–46
hyperglycemia (high blood sugar), 9, 10
hyperinsulinemia, 19

I

IFG (impaired fasting glucose) test, 11
IGT (impaired glucose tolerance) test, 11
insulin, 9
insulin resistance, 10
inulin, 11, 25
IRS (Internal Regulation System), 44–46, 61, 63
Italian Sausage and Linguine, 175

J

journaling, 20, 50
juices, 29, 309

K

kale. *See* greens, bitter
Kicked-Up Tomato Soup, 97
Kickin' Chicken "Wings," 123

L

lactose, 11
lamb, 307
  Lamb Burgers with Lemon-Yogurt Sauce, 165
  Lemon-Rosemary Lamb Chops, 164
Layered Chicken and Bean Enchiladas, 194
lemon
  Crab Cakes with Lemon-Dijon Sauce, 130
  Lamb Burgers with Lemon-Yogurt Sauce, 165
  Lemon-Raspberry Cheesecake, 264
  Lemon-Rosemary Lamb Chops, 164
  Raspberry-Lemon Muffins, 81
lentils
  Creamy Potato, Lentil, and Ham Chowder, 93
  Lentil–Broccoli Rabe Soup, 98
  Shrimp Scampi Linguine, 223
lettuce
  Apple and Blue Cheese Salad, 100
  Asian Lettuce Cups, 176
  Bacon-Wrapped Chicken, 193

Barbecue Shrimp Wraps, 118
Cobb Salad–Style Buffalo Dogs,
  161
Creamy Pasta Salad, 109
Grilled Pork Tacos with Mango
  Salsa, 168
Mango-Tuna Spring Rolls, 133
Pork Chops with Apple Salad,
  167
Roast Beef Rolls, 117
Shrimp Tacos, 222
Steak Burrito Bowl, 151
lime
  Citrus–Grilled Shrimp Salad, 103
  Coconut-Lime Pudding Cake, 267
  Salmon with Avocado Salsa, 218
liquor, 17, 32, 54, 308
Lox-Cheddar Scones, 82

M

macronutrients, 15
maltose, 11
mango
  Grilled Pork Tacos with Mango
    Salsa, 168
  Mango-Tuna Spring Rolls, 133
Manhattan Clam Chowder, 95
maple syrup/sugar, 307
  Chocolate Layer Cake with Maple
    Frosting, 268
  Hearty Fruit and Nut Granola, 84
  Maple-Walnut Cake, 266
  Pistachio Kisses, 277
  Sloppy Joes, 210
  Spiced Sweet Potato Chips, 135
meal planning, 17, 39–41, 54, 59, 61.
    See also eating; foods
  chart for, 42–43
  makeover guidelines, 53
  weekly, 286–93
meatballs, 124, 158, 206, 209
Mediterranean Chicken Pinwheels,
  122
Mediterranean diet, 35
Mexican Dip, 139
Mexican Fried Rice, 258
milk, 28, 304. See also buttermilk;
    milks, nondairy
  Apple, Sausage and Potato
    Casserole, 71
  Asparagus Swiss Quiche, 234
  Belgian Waffles, 80
  Broccoli-Cheddar Strata, 235
  Broccoli-Chicken Casserole, 198
  Cheesy Vegetable Chowder, 94
  Chocolate Malt, 285
  Creamed Sweet Corn, 247
  Creamy Potato, Lentil, and Ham
    Chowder, 93
  Green Bean Casserole, 245

Roasted Vegetable Mac and
  Cheese, 229
Salmon-Barley Bake, 219
Southern Pecan Bread Pudding,
  275
Tuna Tetrazzini, 220
milks, nondairy, 27, 28
  Almond Rice Pudding, 282
  Chocolate Cake Smoothie, 86
  Spiced Apple Pancakes, 79
mindfulness, 20, 46, 53, 59
Minestrone, 91
Mom's Meat Loaf, 154
monosaccharides, 11
Monte Cristos, 112
MUFAs (monounsaturated fats),
  35, 37
mushrooms, 39. See also vegetables
    (mixed)
  Baked Penne with Turkey, 208
  Beef Stroganoff, 148
  Black Bean Burgers, 239
  Chicken-Mushroom Bake, 181
  Green Bean Casserole, 245
  Ground Bison with Spaghetti
    Squash, 162
  Mushroom-Barley Stuffing, 253
  Salisbury Steak, 155
  Steak with Mushroom Sauce and
    Roasted Artichokes, 144
  Tangy Pork Kabobs, 174
  Tuna Tetrazzini, 220
  Turkey Cheeseburgers, 203
  Wild Mushroom and White Bean
    Risotto, 226

N

Nachos, Grand Slam, 137
National Standards for Diabetes
    Self-Management Education
    and Support, 12
Nectresse, 27
noodles, 301. See also pasta
  Beef Goulash, 159
  Beef Stroganoff, 148
  Chicken Cacciatore, 180
  Chicken Pad Thai, 197
  Chilled Cilantro–Soba Noodle
    Salad, 108
nut butters
  African Stew, 236
  Chicken Pad Thai, 197
  Chocolate Cake Smoothie, 86
  Crispy Oat Squares, 281
  PB&J Stuffed French Toast, 77
NutraSweet, 27
nutrition labels, 23, 55
nuts, 40, 302. See also nut butters;
    specific types of nuts
  Asian Lettuce Cups (SS), 176

Barbecue Shrimp Wraps, 118
Chocolate Cake Smoothie, 86
Pistachio Kisses, 277
Quinoa Pilaf with Pistachios, 255
Sweet Turkey Paninis (SS), 114

O

oat bran. See also oats
  Lemon-Raspberry Cheesecake,
    264
  Pear-Ginger Cobbler, 274
  Rich Chocolate Cream Pie, 272
  Three-Berry Pie, 270
oats. See also oat bran
  Double Oat–Blueberry Crisp, 273
  Fig Bars, 279
  Hearty Fruit and Nut Granola, 84
  Oatmeal-Apple Cookies, 280
  Sunrise Oatmeal, 83
  Three-Berry Pie (SS), 270
OGTT (oral glucose tolerance test),
  12
oils, 35, 303
omega 3 fatty acids, 36, 37
onions. See also onions, green;
    vegetables (mixed)
  Caramelized Onion and Fennel
    Pizza, 242
  Hawaiian Chicken Skewers, 121
  Tangy Pork Kabobs, 174
onions, green
  Asian Lettuce Cups, 176
  Asparagus Swiss Quiche, 234
  Chicken and Sausage Jambalaya,
    184
  Scalloped Red Potatoes, 251
  Warm German Potato Salad, 105
Open-Faced Asian Chicken
    Sandwiches, 113
orange, 29
  Chilled Cilantro–Soba Noodle
    Salad, 108
  Citrus–Grilled Shrimp Salad, 103
  Orange-Pecan Tea Bread, 262
  Orange-Sesame Chicken, 189
  Sundae Breakfast Smoothie, 86
  Whipped Sweet Potato
    Casseroles, 252

P

pancreas, 9, 10
Papaya-Tomato Bruschetta, 120
Parmesan Chicken Fingers, 191
pasta, 23, 24, 301–2. See also noodles
  Baked Pasta and Vegetables, 231
  Baked Spaghetti with Turkey
    Meat Sauce, 207
  Baked Penne with Turkey, 208
  Broccoli Penne, 230
  Broccoli-Walnut Farfalle Toss, 257

pasta *(continued)*
    Chicken-Mushroom Bake, 181
    Creamy Pasta Salad, 109
    Fettuccine with Basil-Walnut
      Sauce, 259
    Go-To Spaghetti and Meatballs,
      158
    Italian Sausage and Linguine, 175
    Pasta with Summer Vegetables, 228
    Quick, Creamy Chicken Lasagna,
      182
    Roasted Vegetable Mac and
      Cheese, 229
    Salmon Pasta Casserole, 217
    Shrimp Scampi Linguine, 223
    Tex-Mex Pasta and Beans, 260
    Tuna Tetrazzini, 220
    Turkey and Orzo Stuffed
      Peppers, 204
    Vegetable Lo Mein, 232
PB&J Stuffed French Toast, 77
PCOS (polycystic ovary syndrome), 11
Peach-Blueberry Yogurt Parfait, 85
peanuts. *See also* nut butters
    African Stew, 236
    Chicken Pad Thai, 197
    Pork and Broccoli Stir-Fry (SS), 171
pears
    Pear-Ginger Cobbler, 274
    Roast Beef Rolls, 117
    Sweet Turkey Paninis, 114
peas. *See also* chickpeas
    Baked Risotto, 256
    Chicken and Dumplings, 186
    Cornmeal Catfish with Black-
      Eyed Peas, 215
    Pork and Broccoli Stir-Fry, 171
    Salmon-Barley Bake, 219
    Shepherd's Pie, 152
    Sweet Potato and Turkey
      Shepherd's Pie, 200
    Turkey and Orzo Stuffed
      Peppers, 204
    Vegetable Lo Mein, 232
pecans
    Fruit and Nut Clusters, 276
    Orange-Pecan Tea Bread, 262
    Rich Brownies, 278
    Southern Pecan Bread Pudding,
      275
    Stuffed Turkey Tenderloin, 199
    Sunrise Oatmeal, 83
pectin, 11
peppers. *See also* peppers, bell;
    peppers, chile
    Fresh Guacamole with
      Vegetables, 138
    South-of-the-Border Shrimp Soup,
      96
    Tuna Tetrazzini, 220

peppers, bell. *See also* peppers;
    vegetables (mixed)
    Beef Goulash, 159
    Chilled Cilantro–Soba Noodle
      Salad, 108
    Chinese Beef and Vegetables, 150
    Citrus–Grilled Shrimp Salad, 103
    Couscous and Chickpea Salad, 107
    Ground Bison with Spaghetti
      Squash, 162
    Philly Cheese Steaks, 110
    Sausage and Pepper Wraps, 111
    Sizzlin' Beef Fajitas, 147
    Sweet and Sour Shrimp, 223
    Tangy Pork Kabobs, 174
    Tricolor Slaw and Potato Salad, 104
    Turkey and Orzo Stuffed
      Peppers, 204
    Un-Stuffed Peppers, 156
    Vegetable Pizza, 240
peppers, chile. *See also* peppers
    Bacon-Wrapped Chicken, 193
    Chicken and Sausage Jambalaya,
      184
    Fiesta Turkey Soup, 90
    Fire-Roasted Chili, 237
    Grand Slam Nachos, 137
    Grilled Pork Tacos with Mango
      Salsa, 168
    Hawaiian Chicken Skewers, 121
    Kicked-Up Tomato Soup, 97
    Layered Chicken and Bean
      Enchiladas, 194
    Mexican Dip, 139
    Shrimp Tacos, 222
    Tex-Mex Breakfast Pizza, 75
    Turkey and Bean Quesadillas, 205
Philly Cheese Steaks, 110
"Pigs" in a Blanket, 125
pine nuts. *See also* nuts
    Couscous and Chickpea Salad, 107
    Roast Beef Rolls, 117
    Sweet Pork Tagine, 170
pizzas, 75, 240–42
plates, 41, 44, 53, 59
polysaccharides, 11
pork, 306
    Asian Lettuce Cups, 176
    Grilled Pork Tacos with Mango
      Salsa, 168
    Homemade Breakfast Sausage, 76
    Marinated Grilled Boneless Pork
      Ribs, 169
    Pork and Broccoli Stir-Fry, 171
    Pork Chops with Apple Salad, 167
    Rosemary Pork Medallions and
      Mashed Potatoes, 172
    Slow-Cooker Pork Barbecue, 166
    Sweet Pork Tagine, 170
    Tangy Pork Kabobs, 174

potatoes. *See also* vegetables (mixed)
    Apple, Sausage and Potato
      Casserole, 71
    Cheesy Vegetable Chowder, 94
    Chili Cheese Fries, 248
    Country-Style Hash Browns, 73
    Creamy Mashed Potatoes, 250
    Creamy Potato, Lentil and Ham
      Chowder, 93
    Garlic Oven Fries, 247
    Rosemary Pork Medallions and
      Mashed Potatoes, 172
    Salisbury Steak, 155
    Salt-'n'-Vinegar Potato Chips, 136
    Scalloped Red Potatoes, 251
    Shepherd's Pie, 152
    Stuffed Potato Skins, 134
    Tangy Pork Kabobs, 174
    Tricolor Slaw and Potato Salad,
      104
    Warm German Potato Salad, 105
potluck parties, 59, 61
poultry, 305–6. *See also* chicken;
    turkey
prediabetes, 10
protein, 15
    cooking, 41
    lean, 35, 37
    sources, 27, 40
Pumpkin Mousse, Creamy, 283
PureVia, 27

Q
Quick, Creamy Chicken Lasagna,
    182
quinoa
    Good Morning "Grits," 72
    Quinoa Pilaf with Pistachios, 255
    Roast Beef Rolls, 117
    Trout Paella, 216
    Turkey Meat Loaf with Cranberry
      Chutney, 202
    Un-Stuffed Peppers, 156
    Vegetable Sauté with Quinoa, 227

R
raffinose, 11
rice. *See also* wild rice
    Almond Rice Pudding, 282
    Asian Lettuce Cups, 176
    Baked Risotto, 256
    Chicken and Sausage Jambalaya,
      184
    Mexican Fried Rice, 258
    Orange-Sesame Chicken, 189
    Pork and Broccoli Stir-Fry, 171
    Steak Burrito Bowl, 151
    Wild Mushroom and White Bean
      Risotto, 226
Rich Brownies, 278

Rich Chocolate Cream Pie, 272
Rosemary Pork Medallions and
  Mashed Potatoes, 172

S

saccharin, 27
salads, 100–109
Salisbury Steak, 155
salmon, 305
  Apple, Sausage and Potato
    Casserole (SS), 71
  Lox-Cheddar Scones, 82
  Salmon-Barley Bake, 219
  Salmon Breakfast Burrito, 69
  Salmon Pasta Casserole, 217
  Salmon Slider Bites, 128
  Salmon with Avocado Salsa, 218
  Scalloped Red Potatoes (SS), 251
salt, 38–39
Salt-'n'-Vinegar Potato Chips, 136
sandwiches, 110–18, 166, 210, 212
sausage, 307
  Apple, Sausage and Potato
    Casserole, 71
  Baked Penne with Turkey, 208
  Chicken and Sausage Jambalaya,
    184
  Italian Sausage and Linguine, 175
  Minestrone, 91
  Sausage and Pepper Wraps, 111
seafood, 305. See also fish
  Barbecue Shrimp Wraps, 118
  Citrus–Grilled Shrimp Salad, 103
  Crab Cakes with Lemon-Dijon
    Sauce, 130
  Manhattan Clam Chowder, 95
  Scallops with Beans and Arugula,
    224
  Shrimp Scampi Linguine, 223
  Shrimp Tacos, 222
  South-of-the-Border Shrimp
    Soup, 96
  Sweet and Sour Shrimp, 223
  Sweet-'n'-Spicy Grilled Shrimp,
    129
seaweed, 11
seeds, 40, 302–3. See also chia seeds;
    flaxseeds
  Fruit and Nut Clusters, 276
  Hearty Fruit and Nut Granola, 84
  Mexican Fried Rice, 258
  Orange-Sesame Chicken, 189
  Stir-Fried Asparagus with Ginger,
    Sesame, and Soy, 244
  Sundae Breakfast Smoothie, 86
Shepherd's Pie, 152
Shepherd's Pie, Sweet Potato and
    Turkey, 200
Sizzlin' Beef Fajitas, 147
Sloppy Joes, 210

Slow-Cooker Pork Barbecue, 166
Slow-Cooker Pot Roast, Traditional,
    146
snacks, 60, 61, 62, 65
sodium, 38–39
soups, 90–99
Southern Pecan Bread Pudding, 275
South-of-the-Border Shrimp Soup,
    96
Spiced Apple Pancakes, 79
Spiced Sweet Potato Chips, 135
spices, 39, 40
spinach. See also greens, bitter
  Creamed Spinach and Artichokes,
    246
  Fettuccine with Basil-Walnut
    Sauce, 259
  Greek Meatballs, 124
  Grilled Steak and Eggs, 68
  Ground Bison with Spaghetti
    Squash, 162
  Guilt-Free Spinach-Artichoke
    Dip, 140
  Lamb Burgers with Lemon-
    Yogurt Sauce, 165
  Mediterranean Chicken
    Pinwheels, 122
  Pork Chops with Apple Salad, 167
  Quick, Creamy Chicken Lasagna,
    182
  Salmon Breakfast Burrito, 69
  Salmon Pasta Casserole, 217
  Shrimp Scampi Linguine, 223
  Spaghetti and Meatballs, Go-To,
    158
  Spinach-Cranberry Salad, 101
  Vegetable Pizza, 240
  Vegetable Sauté with Quinoa, 227
  Veggie Burger Wraps, 233
  Zesty Italian Cheeseburgers, 157
Splenda, 27, 308
squash. See also zucchini
  Cheese and Vegetable Bake, 249
  Ground Bison with Spaghetti
    Squash, 162
  Mexican Fried Rice, 258
  Pasta with Summer Vegetables,
    228
stachyose, 11
Stages of Change model, 12
starch, 11, 29
START plan, 12–14, 48–63
  Shock stage, 13, 49–51
  Tiptoeing stage, 13, 52–57
  Achieving stage, 13, 58–60
  Repeating stage, 13, 61–62
  Time (maintenance) stage, 13, 63
stevia, 27, 32, 308
Stir-Fried Asparagus with Ginger,
    Sesame, and Soy, 244

Stuffed Potato Skins, 134
Stuffed Turkey Tenderloin, 199
sucralose, 27
sucrose, 16
sugars (dietary), 11, 16, 307–8. See
    also sweeteners
Sugar Twin, 27, 308
Sundae Breakfast Smoothie, 86
Sunrise Oatmeal, 83
sweeteners, 20, 307–8. See also sugars
  fake, 16, 27, 30–32, 308
  and weight gain, 31–32
Sweet'N Low, 27, 308
Sweet-'n'-Spicy Grilled Shrimp, 129
Sweet Pork Tagine, 170
sweet potatoes
  African Stew, 236
  Apple–Sweet Potato Soup, 99
  Fish and Chips, 213
  Spiced Sweet Potato Chips, 135
  Sweet Potato and Turkey
    Shepherd's Pie, 200
  Whipped Sweet Potato
    Casseroles, 252
  Zucchini and Sweet Potato
    Latkes, 74
Sweet Turkey Paninis, 114

T

Tangy Pork Kabobs, 174
Tex-Mex Breakfast Pizza, 75
Tex-Mex Pasta and Beans, 260
Three-Berry Pie, 270
tofu, 301
  Rich Chocolate Cream Pie, 272
  Vegetable-Tofu Wontons, 126
tomatoes and tomato sauce. See also
    vegetables (mixed)
  Baked Spaghetti with Turkey
    Meat Sauce, 207
  Baked Penne with Turkey, 208
  Bean Enchiladas, 238
  Beef Goulash, 159
  Beef Ragù over Polenta, 160
  Broccoli Penne, 230
  Cheesy Scrambled Eggs and
    Ham, 70
  Chicken with Pinto Beans Skillet,
    195
  Corn, Black Bean, and Edamame
    Salad, 106
  Creamy Pasta Salad, 109
  Fire-Roasted Chili, 237
  Grilled Pork Tacos with Mango
    Salsa, 168
  Ground Bison with Spaghetti
    Squash, 162
  Kicked-Up Tomato Soup, 97
  Lemon-Rosemary Lamb Chops,
    164

tomatoes and tomato sauce
(continued)
Manhattan Clam Chowder, 95
Papaya-Tomato Bruschetta, 120
Quick, Creamy Chicken Lasagna, 182
Sausage and Pepper Wraps, 111
Shrimp Scampi Linguine, 223
Sloppy Joes, 210
Spaghetti and Meatballs, Go-To, 158
Turkey and Orzo Stuffed Peppers, 204
Turkey Meatballs and Zucchini Pasta, 206
Un-Stuffed Peppers, 156
Warm Zucchini Salad, 102
tortillas
Barbecue Shrimp Wraps, 118
Bean Enchiladas, 238
Buffalo Chicken Quesadillas, 132
Cobb Salad–Style Buffalo Dogs, 161
Grilled Pork Tacos with Mango Salsa, 168
Kicked-Up Tomato Soup, 97
Layered Chicken and Bean Enchiladas, 194
Salmon Breakfast Burrito, 69
Sausage and Pepper Wraps, 111
Shrimp Tacos, 222
Sizzlin' Beef Fajitas, 147
Sweet Turkey Paninis, 114
Tex-Mex Breakfast Pizza, 75
Tuna Salad Wraps, 117
Turkey and Bean Quesadillas, 205
Veggie Burger Wraps, 233
Traditional Slow-Cooker Pot Roast, 146
Tricolor Slaw and Potato Salad, 104
triglycerides, 33
Trout Paella, 216
Truvia, 27
tuna, 36, 305
Creamy Pasta Salad (SS), 109
Mango-Tuna Spring Rolls, 133
Tuna Salad Wraps, 117
Tuna Steaks on Greens, 221
Tuna Tetrazzini, 220
turkey, 306. See also bacon
Baked Spaghetti with Turkey Meat Sauce, 207
Baked Penne with Turkey, 208
Fiesta Turkey Soup, 90
Greek Meatballs, 124
Homemade Breakfast Sausage, 76
Monte Cristos, 112
Sloppy Joes, 210
Stuffed Turkey Tenderloin, 199

Sweet Potato and Turkey Shepherd's Pie, 200
Sweet Turkey Paninis, 114
Turkey and Bean Quesadillas, 205
Turkey and Orzo Stuffed Peppers, 204
Turkey Cheeseburgers, 203
Turkey Meatballs and Zucchini Pasta, 206
Turkey Meat Loaf with Cranberry Chutney, 202
Turkey Swedish Meatballs, 209

V
vegetables (mixed), 29, 30, 31, 40, 294–97. See also greens; specific vegetables
African Stew, 236
Asian Fish Packets, 214
Baked Pasta and Vegetables, 231
Barley Pilaf with Artichokes and Kale, 254
Beef Barley Soup, 92
Caramelized Onion and Fennel Pizza, 242
Chicken and Dumplings, 186
Chicken Cacciatore, 180
Chicken Pot Pie, 185
Chinese Beef and Vegetables, 150
Fresh Guacamole with Vegetables, 138
Herb-Roasted Chicken Breasts with Vegetables, 188
Lentil–Broccoli Rabe Soup, 98
Manhattan Clam Chowder, 95
Mexican Dip, 139
Minestrone, 91
Pasta with Summer Vegetables, 228
Shepherd's Pie, 152
Slow-Cooker Pot Roast, Traditional, 146
South-of-the-Border Shrimp Soup, 96
Vegetable Lo Mein, 232
Vegetable Pizza, 240
Vegetable Sauté with Quinoa, 227
Vegetable-Tofu Wontons, 126
Veggie Burger Wraps, 233
vitamin D, 38

W
waist circumference, 18, 35
walnuts. See also nuts
Apple and Blue Cheese Salad, 100
Broccoli-Walnut Farfalle Toss, 257
Fettuccine with Basil-Walnut Sauce, 259

Fig Bars, 279
Homemade Breakfast Sausage, 76
Maple-Walnut Cake, 266
Spiced Apple Pancakes, 79
Spinach-Cranberry Salad, 101
Tuna Salad Wraps, 117
Whipped Sweet Potato Casseroles, 252
Wansink, Brian, 41–44
Warm German Potato Salad, 105
Warm Zucchini Salad, 102
water, 32
weight
artificial sweeteners and, 31–32
losing, 10, 17–18, 63
monitoring, 59, 61
Whipped Sweet Potato Casseroles, 252
wieners, 307
Cobb Salad–Style Buffalo Dogs, 161
"Pigs" in a Blanket, 125
wild rice. See also rice
Baked Risotto, 256
Broccoli-Chicken Casserole, 198
Minestrone, 91
wine, 32, 308
Beef Ragù over Polenta, 160
Chicken Cacciatore, 180
Chicken-Mushroom Bake, 181
Shrimp Scampi Linguine, 223
Steak with Mushroom Sauce and Roasted Artichokes, 144

Y
yogurt (Greek), 27, 28
Creamy Pumpkin Mousse, 283
Guilt-Free Spinach-Artichoke Dip, 140
Mexican Dip, 139
Peach-Blueberry Yogurt Parfait, 85
Rich Chocolate Cream Pie, 272
Sundae Breakfast Smoothie, 86

Z
Zesty Italian Cheeseburgers, 157
zucchini
African Stew, 236
Beef Ragù over Polenta, 160
Fiesta Turkey Soup, 90
Mexican Fried Rice, 258
Minestrone, 91
Pasta with Summer Vegetables, 228
Turkey Meatballs and Zucchini Pasta, 206
Warm Zucchini Salad, 102
Zucchini and Sweet Potato Latkes, 74